Principles of Neurotheology

ANDREW B. NEWBERG
University of Pennsylvania, USA

Routledge
Taylor & Francis Group

LONDON AND NEW YORK

First published 2010 by Ashgate Publishing

Published 2016 by Routledge
2 Park Square, Milton Park, Abingdon, Oxon OX14 4RN
711 Third Avenue, New York, NY 10017, USA

Routledge is an imprint of the Taylor & Francis Group, an informa business

British Library Cataloguing in Publication Data
Newberg, Andrew B., 1966-
  Principles of neurotheology. — (Ashgate science and religion series)
  1. Brain—Religious aspects. 2. Psychology, Religious. 3. Theological anthropology.
  I. Title II. Series
  200.1'9—dc22

Library of Congress Cataloging-in-Publication Data
Newberg, Andrew B., 1966-
  Principles of neurotheology / Andrew B. Newberg.
    p. cm. — (Ashgate science and religion series)
  Includes bibliographical references and index.
  ISBN 978-1-4094-0810-9 (hardcover : alk. paper)—ISBN 978-0-7546-6994-4 (pbk. : alk. paper)—ISBN 978-0-7546-9824-1 (ebook)
  1. Psychology, Religious. 2. Experience (Religion) 3. Neurosciences—Religious aspects. 4. Brain—Religious aspects. 5. Religion and science. I. Title.

BL53.N489 2010
201'.66128—dc22

                                                                      2010005817

ISBN 9781409408109 (hbk)
ISBN 9780754669944 (pbk)

Printed and bound in Great Britain by
TJ International Ltd, Padstow, Cornwall

PRINCIPLES OF NEUROTHEOLOGY

"Neurotheology" has garnered substantial attention in the academic and lay communities in recent years. Several books have been written addressing the relationship between the brain and religious experience and numerous scholarly articles have been published on the topic, some in the popular press. The scientific and religious communities have been very interested in obtaining more information regarding neurotheology, how to approach this topic, and how science and religion can be integrated in some manner that preserves both.

If neurotheology is to be considered a viable field going forward, it requires a set of clear principles that can be generally agreed upon and supported by both the theological or religious perspective and the scientific one as well. *Principles of Neurotheology* sets out the necessary principles of neurotheology which can be used as a foundation for future neurotheological discourse. Laying the groundwork for a new synthesis of scientific and theological dialogue, this book proposes that neurotheology, a term fraught with potential problems, is a highly useful and important voice in the greater study of religious and theological ideas and their intersection with science.

Andrew B. Newberg, M.D. is Associate Professor in the Department of Radiology and Psychiatry and holds an adjunct appointment in the Department of Religious Studies at the University of Pennsylvania. He is co-author of the bestselling books, *How God Changes Your Brain* (2009) and *Why God Won't Go Away: Brain Science and the Biology of Belief* (2001) which both explore the relationship between neuroscience and spiritual experience. He has also co-authored *Why We Believe What We Believe* (2008) and *The Mystical Mind: Probing the Biology of Belief* (1999). The latter book received the 2000 award for Outstanding Books in Theology and the Natural Sciences presented by the Center for Theology and the Natural Sciences.

Ashgate Science and Religion Series

Series Editors:

Roger Trigg, *University of Warwick, UK*
J. Wentzel van Huyssteen, *Princeton Theological Seminary, USA*

Science and religion have often been thought to be at loggerheads but much contemporary work in this flourishing interdisciplinary field suggests this is far from the case. The *Ashgate Science and Religion Series* presents exciting new work to advance interdisciplinary study, research and debate across key themes in science and religion, exploring the philosophical relations between the physical and social sciences on the one hand and religious belief on the other. Contemporary issues in philosophy and theology are debated, as are prevailing cultural assumptions arising from the 'post-modernist' distaste for many forms of reasoning. The series enables leading international authors from a range of different disciplinary perspectives to apply the insights of the various sciences, theology and philosophy and look at the relations between the different disciplines and the rational connections that can be made between them. These accessible, stimulating new contributions to key topics across science and religion will appeal particularly to individual academics and researchers, graduates, postgraduates and upper-undergraduate students.

Other titles published in this series:

Science and Religious Anthropology
A Spiritually Evocative Naturalist Interpretation of Human Life
Wesley J. Wildman
9780754665922 (hbk)

Theology, Psychology and the Plural Self
Léon Turner
9780754665199 (hbk)

Creation: Law and Probability
Edited by Fraser Watts
9780754658900 (pbk)

Christology and Science
F. LeRon Shults
9780754652243 (hbk)
9780754652311 (pbk)

Hic liber

spiritui

nos precedentium

atque

mentibus

nos sequentium

datus ac dedicatus.*

*This book is dedicated to the spirit of those who came before

and the minds of those who will follow.

Contents

Preface

I have never been comfortable with the term, "neurotheology." This is, of course, a great problem for someone who is frequently engaged in the field of neurotheology. There are a variety of reasons for my trepidation. However, my greatest concern has always been the lack of clarity about what neurotheology is and what it should try to do as a field. Try as I might to avoid using neurotheology in my articles and books, it seems to be something that simply will not go away—at least any more than God. While my concerns have continued unabated, I have watched the rest of the world continue to use "neurotheology" to describe the field studying the intersection between the brain and religion. This eventually prompted me to begin exploring what neurotheology should be and what principles might guide it. This book is an expanded version of these thought processes. I hope that this will do several things for neurotheology. First, I hope that the Principles of Neurotheology will make a case for the importance of this field in the scholarship of both science and theology. Second, I hope that the principles will help guide myself, as well as future neurotheologians in their own scholarship. And third, I hope that this work will help everyone to be more comfortable with the term, neurotheology.

This work is also the culmination of all of my own research and scholarship in this field to date. And it certainly could not have happened without tremendous support from many wonderful people whom I would like to acknowledge (although the list is actually much longer). Wentzel Van Huyssteen was absolutely essential for making this work come to fruition. It has been very special to have been able to work with someone who shares a similar appreciation and passion for the true interaction between the mind and religion. In terms of the ideas that have led to this work, I need to begin with Dr. Eugene d'Aquili who was a remarkable mentor to me and the person who started me down the formal path of studying neurotheology. Although he passed away over ten years ago, his ideas and fervor for this topic were inspirational to me and continue to be a source of ideas and enthusiasm. While many consider themselves fortunate to find one wonderful and supportive mentor, I have been blessed with two. My other is Dr. Abass Alavi, who opened up the field of brain science and brain imaging to me, and who has similarly been a source of passionate inquiry into science, religion, and the nature of reality. Dr. Solomon Katz has been a steadfast ally, friend, and colleague—a third mentor, and someone who has kept my eyes on neurotheology as a field that has a potentially bright future. Dr. Albert Stunkard, Gene d'Aquili's mentor, has also always been there for me to discuss my interests in spiritual matters and the brain. More recently, I have enjoyed exploring these ideas with my colleague Mark Waldman, who always pushes me in directions I am not sure we should go, only to find that they are sometimes the most important. Nancy Wintering, has single-handedly kept me out of trouble while I continue to explore some of the most troubling questions relating to the brain and religion. I also need to mention my parents who have instilled in me the perpetual desire to explore the world and never to fear tackling the unanswerable, and sometimes the unaskable, questions. My daughter, Amanda, has similarly shown me how always to find the fun in asking questions. And finally, my wife, Stephanie, who has supported me through everything. She was a gem in reviewing every aspect of this manuscript, knowing that her only payment will be that if I ever discover the true meaning of life, the universe, or God, she will be the first to know.

With these acknowledgements, I hope that the reader will appreciate the importance of having so many voices be part of the human quest for knowledge and understanding. Neurotheology, if nothing else, should strive to engage all types of people, cultures, ideas, and beliefs, as a field that will hopefully send humanity in a positive direction. By considering the multidisciplinary issues that might comprise neurotheology, this work will try to establish the foundations and principles of this field with the intent to foster dialogue, scholarship, and perhaps, enlightenment.

Chapter 1

The Case for a Principia Neurotheologica
(Principles of Neurotheology)

"Neurotheology" is a unique field of scholarship and investigation that seeks to understand the relationship specifically between the brain and theology, and more broadly between the mind and religion. As a topic, neurotheology has garnered substantial attention in the academic and lay communities in recent years. Several books have been written addressing the relationship between the brain and religious experience and numerous scholarly articles have been published on the topic. The scientific and religious communities have been very interested in obtaining more information regarding neurotheology, how to approach this topic, and whether science and religion can be integrated in some manner that preserves, and perhaps enhances, both. However, as would be expected, there have been both positive and negative responses to purported neurotheological studies and perspectives.

If neurotheology is to be considered a viable field going forward, it requires a set of clear principles that can be generally agreed upon and supported by both the theological or religious perspective and the scientific one as well. The overall purpose of this book is to set forth the necessary principles of neurotheology which can be used as a foundation for future neurotheological discourse and scholarship. In time, it would be highly valuable to have added input from a wide range of scholars with regard to these principles so that the field of neurotheology remains dynamic in its scope and process. Thus, it is likely that as this field proceeds, the guiding principles will require some welcome modifications. Also, it should be clearly stated that rather than specifically try to answer major theological or scientific questions, this book intends to espouse a program of scholarship and a methodological basis for future inquiry, thereby laying the groundwork for a new synthesis of scientific and theological discourse. In the end, neurotheology, a term fraught with potential problems, might nevertheless, be a highly useful and important voice in the greater study of religious and theological ideas and their intersection with science.

The relationship between the mind and human spirituality has been considered for at least several thousand years. For example, this intersection was described in the ancient Hindu scriptures of the Upanishads in which it was realized that something within us, particularly within the head, enables us to explore and experience the universe via our cognitive and sensory processes and also to discover our own sense of spirituality:

> Between the two palates there hangs the uvula, like a nipple—that is the starting—point of Indra (the lord). Where the root of the hair divides, there he opens the two sides of the head, and saying Bhu, he enters Agni (the fire); saying Bhuvas, he enters Vayu (air); Saying Suvas, he enters Aditya (sun); saying Mahas, he enters Brahman. He there obtains lordship, he reaches the lord of the mind. He becomes lord of speech, lord of sight, lord of hearing, lord of knowledge. Nay, more than this. There is the Brahman whose body is ether, whose nature is true, rejoicing in the senses (prana), delighted in the mind, perfect in peace, and immortal. (Taittiriya Upanishad)

This section from the Upanishads reveals the importance of the body and the brain in achieving spiritual enlightenment. Neurotheology is a more recent attempt at discerning how the study of the human mind and brain (terms we will define later) relates to the pursuit of religions and religious experience. While a growing number of scholars have written a variety of papers and books about this topic, it is still in its nascent stages. One of the greatest shortcomings of neurotheology so far has been the lack of clear principles by which such scholarship should proceed. Thus, in order to establish more thoroughly neurotheology as an academic discipline, it is vital to consider the primary principles necessary for such an endeavor.

It is important to infuse throughout the principles of neurotheology the notion that neurotheology requires an openness to both the scientific as well as the spiritual perspectives. It is also important to preserve the essential elements of both perspectives. The scientific side must progress utilizing adequate definitions, measures, methodology, and interpretations of data. The religious side must maintain a subjective sense of spirituality, a phenomenological assessment of the sense of ultimate reality that may or may not include a divine presence, a notion of the meaning and purpose in life, an adherence to various doctrinal processes, and a careful analysis of religion from the theological perspective.

In short, for neurotheology to be successful, science must be kept rigorous and religion must be kept religious. This book will also have the purpose of facilitating a sharing of ideas and concepts across the boundary between science and religion. Such a dialogue can be considered a constructive approach that informs both perspectives by enriching the understanding of both science and religion.

But it is not an easy task to combine theological and scientific concepts. A primary problem with neurotheology is the need to reach a common starting ground between these two perspectives. This is something that will be attempted in this book. But, by necessity, sometimes one side or the other will have to be oversimplified. After all, there are not many neuroscientists familiar with the most recent theological debates and there are not many theologians who have a detailed understanding of functional neuroanatomy. Thus, another purpose of this book is to provide some starting points for dialogue between neuroscience and religion. Certainly for the theologian or religious scholar, some statements will seem superficial or incomplete. For the neuroscientist, the material may appear "dumbed down," to use a common phrase among scientists. But neurotheology represents a beginning such that from two disparate fields a new multidisciplinary field can emerge. As an example for future scholarship, one might hope that the neuroscientist attempting to study morality will be well versed in the ancient texts and the writings of theologians such as Aquinas and Luther who were important in shaping our understanding of the topics of free will and ethics. Conversely, the theologian studying the writings of Aquinas or Luther might consider what was happening in their frontal lobes and limbic system while pondering their influential ideas. It would also be hoped that any of these approaches would not diminish, defame, debunk, or decry one perspective for another. Rather, the new synthesis would ultimately help human beings to relate better to the world around them and to engage both their biological and spiritual dimensions.

Before proceeding with the principles of neurotheology, it is first necessary to review the foundations upon which neurotheology rests. The foundations of neurotheology include a historical analysis of related concepts, a description of the contributions of theology and science to neurotheology, and an elaboration of the goals that such scholarship should aspire to. Following a description of the foundations of neurotheology, a number of definitions are necessary to review, and from there, the principles of neurotheology can be elaborated.

Historical Foundations of Neurotheology

To evaluate the historical background of neurotheology requires us to delve several thousand years back into history to see how religious traditions have considered the relationship between the mind and the person's attempt to interact with some higher level of reality. It is also of interest to observe how the variety of philosophical and theological concepts regarding the universe and God may be recapitulated in a variety of brain processes. In this way, we can see more directly how various concepts considered throughout history connect to our current understanding of the brain. As will be discussed later in the book, the ability to relate theological concepts to mental and brain processes does not mean in any way to imply that these concepts have been reduced to brain chemistry, but rather may provide at the very least, a new perspective, and at most, an important method for further evaluating the true basis of those concepts.

In Eastern traditions there is significant historical development of the psychological analysis of the human being in relationship to both Buddhist as well as Hindu conceptions of the world and of spirituality.[1] The lines of the Upanishads above certainly indicate a strong interest not only in the functioning of the mind

---

[1]   Austin, J.H. *Zen and the Brain: Toward an Understanding of Meditation and Consciousness.* Cambridge, MA: MIT Press, 1999; Austin, J.H. *Zen-Brain Reflections.* Cambridge, MA: MIT Press, 2006; Kelly, B.D. "Buddhist psychology, psychotherapy and the brain: a critical introduction." *Transcultural Psychiatr.* 2008;45:5-30; Davids, R. *A Buddhist Manual of Psychological Ethics or Buddhist Psychology.* Columbia, MO: South

itself, but in the psychological and possibly biological correlates of mental activity that can be utilized to achieve the highest spiritual state.

Buddhist and Hindu writings have made extensive evaluations of the human mind and psychology focusing on human consciousness of the "self," the emotional attachment human beings have to that "self," and how human consciousness can be altered through various spiritual practices such as meditation. Buddhism elaborates the important elements of human consciousness which it organizes into the "four seals" of belief.[2] The first seal, "dukkha," refers to suffering and is considered a universal aspect of the human condition. The second seal, "anatta," refers to no-self and in particular that there is no separate existing self in the universe, but everything is interconnected. The third seal, "annicca," refers to impermanence such that nothing in this world lasts and thus, personal achievement, success, and happiness should never be associated with transitory phenomena. The fourth seal is that "nirvana," a release from suffering, does exist through the surrendering of attachment to the false sense of self that the mind usually holds.

Each of these seals can also be considered from a neurotheological perspective. For example, one can relate these important ideological concepts to various aspects of the human brain and psyche. Suffering plays a significant role in depression and stress, two topics which are central to current psychiatric research. It is also known that areas of the brain that are involved in the stress response and other negative emotions likely play a role in suffering and ultimately have a long-term effect on the health of the body.[3] Studies have also revealed that emotional suffering may be felt in the brain similarly to physical pain.[4] The second seal of no-self also may have physiological correlates since there are specific areas of the brain and body that contribute to our sense of self.[5] The third seal of impermanence is interesting in the context of the brain since there are specific brain structures that support our sense of change and permanence. Furthermore, the brain itself appears built for change

Asia Books, 1996; McGraw, J.J. *Brain and Belief: An Exploration of the Human Soul.* Del Mar, CA: Aegis Press, 2004.

[2]   Gyatso, T. (Fourteenth Dalai Lama). *The World of Tibetan Buddhism: An Overview of Its Philosophy and Practice.* Translated by Thupten Jinpa. Somerville, MA: Wisdom Publications, 1995.

[3]   Liston., C., McEwen, B.S., and Casey, B.J. "Psychosocial stress reversibly disrupts prefrontal processing and attentional control." *Proc Natl Acad Sci USA.* 2009;106:912-917; Wang, J., Rao, H., Wetmore, G.S., Furlan, P.M., Korczykowski, M., Dinges, D.F., and Detre, J.A. "Perfusion functional MRI reveals cerebral blood flow pattern under psychological stress." *Proc Natl Acad Sci USA.* 2005;102:17804-17809.

[4]   Eisenberger, N.I., Lieberman, M.D., and Williams, K.D. "Does rejection hurt? An FMRI study of social exclusion." *Science.* 2003;302:290-292.

[5]   Newberg, A.B., Alavi, A., Baime, M., Pourdehnad, M., Santanna, J., and d'Aquili, E.G. "The measurement of regional cerebral blood flow during the complex cognitive task of meditation: a preliminary SPECT study." *Psychiatr Res Neuroimaging.* 2001;106:113-122; Newberg, A.B. and Iversen, J. "The neural basis of the complex mental task of meditation: neurotransmitter and neurochemical considerations." *Med Hypothesis.* 2003;61:282-291.

via the process of neuroplasticity which refers to the ability of the brain to change its structure and function.[6] While the neurophysiological correlates of nirvana have yet to be evaluated, various components of letting go and the loss of the sense of self have been associated with specific brain functions.[7] However, understanding the four seals can also help us to understand the human mind. Thus, understanding the relationship between suffering, the self, and change bears directly on how we might strive to understand the workings of the mind and brain.

It is fascinating that without any of the modern methodologies, Buddhist thought captured so well the intricate inner workings of the mind. Buddhist thought also focused substantial attention on consciousness as an energy that is deeply interconnected with the brain, body, and physical world.[8] This has set up, in some sense, a separate biomedical paradigm in Eastern thought which is based on how "energy" moves through the body. While not using the same concept of "energy," current scientific fields such as psychoneuroimmunology and psychoneuroendocrinology have identified many ways in which the interconnection between the brain and body are expressed. These fields might help bridge the gap between Eastern and Western biomedical paradigms, and of course, neurotheology might provide an excellent source for future research.

Another related concept with potential for reconciling differences between Eastern and Western paradigms is that of the *yin* and *yang* that describes the opposing forces that interact within human beings. A corresponding scientific concept of "tone" has been applied to many physiological and neurophysiological systems. Tone refers to the balance between two opposing physiological processes. For example, the autonomic nervous system that governs arousal and calming responses in the body typically rests in a tonal state such that the body is maintained within a certain balance. When one side of the autonomic nervous system is called upon, such as when we need to respond quickly to a threatening situation, the arousal system is activated while the calming system is suppressed. Thus, the notion of opposing forces that govern the mind and body are similar to those found in ancient Buddhist texts.

Similar concepts of the body's "energy" or "Qi" (pronounced Chi) can also be found in Ayurvedic medical practices that developed in India.[9] These practices also consider the human body, health, and psychological well being, from the

---

6   Schwartz, J.M., Begley, S. *The Mind and the Brain: Neuroplasticity and the Power of Mental Force*. New York, NY: Harper Perennial, 2003.

7   Newberg, A.B., Alavi, A., Baime, M., Pourdehnad, M., Santanna, J., and d'Aquili, E.G. "The measurement of regional cerebral blood flow during the complex cognitive task of meditation: a preliminary SPECT study." *Psychiatr Res Neuroimaging*. 2001; Lou, H.C., Nowak, M., and Kjaer, T.W. "The mental self." *Prog Brain Res*. 2005;150:197-204.

8   Scotton, B.W. "Treating Buddhist patients." In Koenig, H.G. (ed.), *Handbook of Religion and Mental Health*. San Diego, CA: Academic Press, 1998.

9   Micozzi, M. *Fundamentals of Complementary and Alternative Medicine*. New York, NY: Churchill Livingstone, 1996.

perspective of the balance of energy flow in the body. By manipulating the energy, the appropriate health—physical, mental, and spiritual—can be restored. Ultimately a balancing of energy can allow the person to strive towards an enlightened state in which the mind has the ability to contact a more fundamental level of reality.

While Eastern traditions approached the notion of the mind and consciousness more directly, Western conceptions of religion typically did not focus specifically on the relationship between the mind and religious phenomena. For example, the Bible itself speaks very little about particular mental or physiological processes. However, the description of human beings, human frailties, and the "evil" actions that are perpetrated by human beings, clearly signifies a deep interest in the human psyche. For example, the story of the creation of human beings in the Book of Genesis appears to relate how God infused humanity with a certain intellect and psychological prowess which differentiates human beings from the rest of the world.[10] From the beginning, "the tree of the knowledge of good and evil"[11] plays a critical role in the development of human beings. We see throughout the biblical stories how human beings have tried to come to grips with the various intra-psychic forces that compel them to various actions both good and evil, "When I looked for good, then evil came unto me: and when I waited for light, there came darkness."[12] The Bible itself provides the rules and guidelines by which human beings should live their lives. The Commandments and covenants with God are based on an understanding of human behavior and human morality. With the advent of Christianity, the focus was shifted somewhat to other aspects of the human psyche including issues pertaining to love, devotion, forgiveness, and redemption. For example, the Bible states in Acts, "Be it known unto you therefore, men and brethren, that through this man is preached unto you the forgiveness of sins"[13] and also in Ephesians I:

> According as he hath chosen us in him before the foundation of the world, that we should be holy and without blame before him in love: Having predestinated us unto the adoption of children by Jesus Christ to himself, according to the good pleasure of his will, To the praise of the glory of his grace, wherein he hath made us accepted in the beloved. In whom we have redemption through his blood, the forgiveness of sins, according to the riches of his grace; Wherein he hath abounded toward us in all wisdom and prudence.[14]

However, the Bible does not usually specify precisely how forgiveness, love, devotion, and redemption come about other than through religion and religious

---

10   Meshberger, F.L. "An interpretation of Michelangelo's *Creation of Adam* based on neuroanatomy." *JAMA*. 1990;264:1837-1841.

11   Genesis 2:9. *King James Bible*.

12   Job 30:26. *King James Bible*.

13   Acts 13:38. *King James Bible*.

14   Ephesians I 4-8. *King James Bible*.

adherence. Nonetheless, there is clearly an important relationship between the mind that allows human beings to be human, and the spirit or soul that allows human beings to connect to a higher, divine realm of existence.

Of course the ancient texts did not have the advantage of more modern scientific analyses of the human psyche and the human central nervous system that can allow for a deeper and richer elaboration of such concepts. Regardless, their rudimentary, and in many ways, highly accurate intuitive analysis of the human being and the human mind clearly demonstrate that psychology and religion were some day going to be integrated in a more profound way.

St. Thomas Aquinas provided an important perspective on the human mind in that he considered all healthy, rational action to proceed from the desire to achieve a good or to pursue an end.[15] Man's end is ultimately for a union with God and thus, a person finds his true perfection in life, only in an everlasting friendship with the God who created him. The evil mind then results from an individual who pursues ends that do not lead toward God. But Aquinas engages the issue of human biology and the mind more directly by distinguishing between the *actus hominis* and the *actus humanus*.[16] The former refers to acts of the body while the latter falls under the domain of reflective, deliberate intelligence. The realization via modern cognitive neuroscience that there is an intricate interrelationship between the body and the mind reveals the difficulty in making the distinction that Aquinas makes and this might lead to a new understanding of how the different aspects of the human being interact.

The Protestant Reformation and the work of Martin Luther (1483-1546) had a significant impact on much of religious as well as philosophical thought over the following several hundred years. The reformation brought about a different perspective on religious thinking and religious doctrine, particularly as it pertains to the individual and the authority of the Christian church. Luther's original conception was intended to restore in each individual the power and authority to hear God's guidance without needing to go through a church authority.[17] In practice, however, he ended up replacing the Pope with a new source of external authority. For Luther would not allow believers to be completely free before God; they could only be guided in ways that were consistent with the Bible. Here again, there are limitations placed on the human mind that constrain how it can help us to be religious.

Luther also had several important interactions with philosophers that resulted in somewhat new perspectives on human psychology. For example, Desiderius Erasmus (ca. 1469-1536) argued that the human being is the center of creation and that the measure of God's goodness is that God created a world in which to

---

[15] Thompson, C.J. "Preliminary remarks toward a constructive encounter between St. Thomas and clinical psychology." *Catholic Soc Sci Rev*. 2005;10:41-52.

[16] Aquinas, T. *Summa Theologica*. Notre Dame, IN: Christian Classics, 1981.

[17] Plass, E.W. *What Luther Says* (3 volumes). St. Louis, MO: Concordia Publishing House, 1959.

unfold the nature of the human being.[18] Erasmus' heated debate with Luther was triggered by Luther's critique of Erasmus' essay *On Free Will*. Erasmus insisted on a role for the human will and personal responsibility, as well as God's grace, in achieving salvation while Luther argued that grace alone provided salvation for human beings.[19] Interestingly, this debate also centers around the functions of the human mind as they pertain to human salvation since the issue of human free will, which would clearly be a mental process, is of crucial importance in determining the basis for salvation. It would be most interesting to consider how Luther and Erasmus might have responded to current cognitive neuroscience research regarding the nature of the moral reasoning and the identification of parts of the brain that appear to function as the "seat of the will."[20]

The relationship between the mind and experience extends beyond simply religious and theological issues. Several philosophical movements in the last 500 years had a profound influence on the integration of spirituality and the human mind. This begins most notably with the work of René Descartes (1596-1650) whose meditations were designed to evaluate the world and that which can be known from a rational, contemplative perspective. His analysis went to great lengths to try to exclude erroneous assumptions and to develop concepts in a logical manner.[21] The result of Descartes' meditations led him to the famous notion that, ironically, lies at the heart of modern cognitive neuroscience—"cogito ergo sum." The fundamental concept of modern cognitive neuroscience is that our thoughts and feelings make us who we are, make up our existence, and can be correlated directly to the functions of the brain.[22] This, of course, was not the ultimate goal or conclusion achieved by Descartes, but clearly his meditations led him to ideas that support the development of modern cognitive neuroscience. The notion that thoughts were occurring and that he could identify these thoughts as being related to existence had a clear import into the relationship between human experience and ultimately human understanding of the world.

Descartes also set up an important dualism between the mind and body that would pervade Western philosophy and science for at least 400 years.

---

[18] Rupp, E.G., Watson, P.S., and Baillie, J. *Luther and Erasmus: Free Will and Salvation* (Library of Christian Classics; Paperback Westminster). Louisville, KY: Westminster John Knox Press, 1995.

[19] Moss, D. "The roots and genealogy of humanistic psychology." In Schneider, K., Bugental, J., and Pierson, J. (ed.), *Handbook of Humanistic Psychology*. Thousand Oaks, CA: Sage, 2001.

[20] Ingvar, D.H. "The will of the brain: cerebral correlates of willful acts." *J Theor Biol.* 1994;171:7-12; Frith, C.D., Friston, K., Liddle, P.F., and Frackowiak, R.S. "Willed action and the prefrontal cortex in man: a study with PET." *Proc R Soc Lond.* 1991;244:241-246.

[21] Descartes, R. *Meditations on First Philosophy: With Selections from the Objections and Replies.* Translated by Michael Moriarty. Oxford: Oxford University Press, 2008.

[22] Gazzaniga, M.S. *The New Cognitive Neurosciences*, 2nd Edition. Cambridge, MA: MIT Press, 2000.

Antonio Damasio, a Professor of Neurology at the University of Iowa School of Medicine, has argued that Descartes erred by assuming that the mind and body were independent of one another and that human emotions and rationality were basically opposed to each other.[23] Descartes argued in favor of reason over emotion, but Damasio contends that our emotions are fundamental to our ability to make decisions and interface with the world, a view that is now widely accepted in the field of cognitive neuroscience. Regardless, the philosophical works of Descartes provided an important impetus for understanding the integration between science and religion, and particularly between religion and the human mind.

Another philosopher whose work should be considered an important contribution to neurotheology was Baruch Spinoza (1632-1677), the Dutch Jew who heavily based his theological and philosophical ideas on mathematics and science. In fact, his conception of God as being attributed to the beauty and clarity of design in mathematics fostered a unique integration of science and religion. While this did not specifically relate to the neurosciences, Spinoza had an understanding that the laws of nature were reflected in the divine presence in the universe, "the universal laws of nature according to which all things happen and are determined are nothing but God's eternal decrees, which always involve eternal truth and necessity."[24] Furthermore, it was believed by Spinoza that through human thought and philosophical and scientific endeavors, human beings could come to know the order of the world and the nature of God. Although Spinoza's work emphasized the physical sciences, it might be argued that his perspective is highly supportive of neurotheology as a way of understanding the human being and the human perspective of the universe via the brain. For example, Spinoza describes the *conatus*: "Each thing, as far as it can by its own power, strives to persevere in its being." Damasio describes the underlying neurobiological correlates of this process by which human beings persevere in relation to the sensory and cognitive systems that aid in adaptability and survival.[25] In this way, Spinoza might have argued that understanding the mind does help understand the divine presence in the universe, or at least in the human being.

In the eighteenth Century, Immanuel Kant (1724-1804) greatly elaborated the rational perspective in human philosophy. His *Critique of Pure Reason* as well as his other works implied that all the universe, both spiritual and non-spiritual, could be understood through a human rational approach separated from sensorial experience.[26] For Kant, there was something inherent in the human mind that

---

[23]   Damasio, A. *Descartes Error: Emotion, Reason, and the Human Brain*. New York, NY: Avon Books, 1994.

[24]   Spinoza, B. *Theological-Political Treatise: Gebhardt Edition*. Translated by Samuel Shirley. Indianapolis, IN: Hackett Publishing Company, 2001.

[25]   Damasio, A. *Looking for Spinoza: Joy, Sorrow, and the Feeling Brain*. New York, NY: Harcourt, 2003.

[26]   Guyer, P. and Wood, A.W. *Critique of Pure Reason by Immanuel Kant*. Cambridge: Cambridge University Press, 1999.

allowed it access to ultimate reality. Thus, "pure reason" was something that could be attainable. However, this rational approach had to be measured and carefully considered. Kant argued that no theoretical argument could prove the existence of God. Kant considered human reason to overreach its powers, and thus in need of self-limitation. The brain itself has its limitations in terms of its cognitive capabilities and capacities. Kant also argued that reason seeks to know what lies beyond the range of "experience"—that is, the apprehension of objects as they are related to one another in a spatio-temporal framework of causal laws.[27] But Kant considered any attempt to claim knowledge outside the limits of human experience to be problematic. This, of course, is commensurate with current neurotheological analysis in that the perceptions of the human brain are considered crucial for knowledge. It is also the tendency of human beings, and human reason, to go beyond the limits of experience and this ultimately results in the representation of ideas of the soul, the world, and God.

In spite of the philosophical consideration of the importance of human experience, until the late eighteenth century, there was practically no attempt at considering religion from the perspective of human experience. Religion until that point was evaluated primarily from the perspective of religion itself. Consequently religions, particularly in the West, were defined by their dogmatic formulations and teachings. It was only with Friedrich Schleiermacher (1768-1834) in the late eighteenth century that an attempt was made to define "religion" as such by switching from a doctrinal emphasis to a more cognitive, visceral, or intuitive one. Schleiermacher, in his book *The Christian Faith*, defined religion as a "feeling of absolute dependence."[28] Since his day, more recent attempts at a general conception of religion have emphasized the intuitive, emotional, or visceral aspects of religion. This shift has important implications for bringing a cognitive neuroscientific approach to the study of religion since feelings and emotions can be shown to be associated with specific brain structures and their function.

Another major step in terms of the understanding of the experience of religion came from the work of William James (1842-1910) at the turn of the last century. In *Varieties of Religious Experience*[29] James considers the different forms that religion takes in terms of how human beings experience the spiritual. This includes aspects of traditional religious practices such as through liturgy and ritual, through deeply personal experiences, and via practices such as those associated with prayer or meditation. James certainly placed an emphasis on subjective experiences and considered the assortment of such experiences ranging from the more traditional to the more exotic and mystical. In this regard, James discussed the phenomenology and the mental processes related to healthy-mindedness, conversion experiences,

---

[27] *Stanford Encyclopedia of Philosophy* on line.

[28] Gerrish, B.A., MacKintosh, H.R., and Stewart, J.S. *The Christian Faith by Friedrich Schleiermacher*. Edinburgh: T. & T. Clark Publishers, 1999.

[29] James, W. *Varieties of Religious Experience*. London: Routledge, 2002.

saintliness, and mystical experiences. In addition, James considered the potentially negative experiences associated with religion and their consequences on the mind.

While James' analysis did not specifically relate religious experience to particular brain functions, this most likely was due to the lack of general knowledge that existed within the scientific community of how the brain actually worked. However, the analysis offered by James can be thought of as providing the initial theoretical bases from which a neuroscientific analysis of religious experiences can proceed. Hence, by observing the particular characteristics and experiences associated with religion and spirituality one might then be able to ascertain the neurobiological correlates of such experiences. This would have to wait until a clearer understanding of overall brain function, particularly as it relates to thoughts, feelings, and experiences was developed. Such development would not occur until the latter part of the twentieth century.

A major step forward in the attempt at formulating a general conception of religion was the rise of anthropological and sociological theory. This approach asserted that religion is always embedded in a cultural matrix and that religious beliefs, customs, and rituals must be understood in a radical relationship to the cultures in which they arise. Emile Durkheim (1858-1917), in his *The Elementary Forms of the Religious Life*,[30] described religion as nothing more than an expression of society and he is attributed the quote, "Religion is society, writ large." On the other hand, many psychologists, beginning with Sigmund Freud (1856-1939), have seen religion as a projection of various intrapsychic dynamics or of hopes and expectations based on previous experience.[31] Thus, religion was nothing more than a creation of the human mind, a mind striving for understanding and purpose in a world that appeared to offer little.

Since the turn of the twentieth century, scholars began to devote themselves to the phenomenology of religion on its own terms. They believed that there were phenomena that needed to be explained which eluded both sociological and psychological determinism. An example of such an approach has been to analyze religion in terms of an awareness of the "sacred" and the "holy." Rudolf Otto, in *The Idea of the Holy*,[32] defined the essence of religious awareness as awe, described as a mixture of fear and fascination before the divine and referred to as a *mysterium tremendum et fascinans*. Such an approach began to get at a dominant form of Western mysticism but was not so applicable to Eastern religions or to primitive ones. A reworking of Otto's concept of the "sacred" as the central core of all religious experience has been espoused by Mircea Eliade.[33] For Eliade, no

---

[30]   Durkheim, E. *The Elementary Forms of Religious Life*. Edited by Mark S. Cladis, Translated by Carol Cosman. New York, NY: Oxford University Press, 2008.

[31]   Freud, S., with Strachey, J. and Gay, P. *The Future of an Illusion*. New York, NY: W.W. Norton & Company, 1989.

[32]   Otto, R. *Idea of the Holy*. Oxford: Oxford University Press, 1958.

[33]   Eliade, M. *The Sacred and the Profane*. New York, NY: Harcourt, Brace, and Jovanovich, 1959.

longer is the sacred to be found almost exclusively in Otto's god-encounter type of experience. Rather, every culture exemplifies the existential sense of the sacred in its rituals and symbols, especially primitive and Asian cultures. However, many anthropologists, linguists, and psychologists question whether the concept of the "sacred" is identifiable in the language, experience, and thought of most primitive societies. Such scholars assert that religious experience is not *sui generis*, but is rather an amalgam of diverse cultural phenomena and experiences.

Paul Tillich should also be considered to have had a substantial impact on neurotheological scholarship. Tillich begins his *Systematic Theology*[34] by discussing the definition of religion as pertaining to "ultimate concerns." He also describes the sources of systematic theology as being ancient texts, church history, and the history of religion and culture. Religious experience is considered a conduit through which the sources of theology are presented to individuals. But this recognition of the experiential aspect as critical to the understanding of theology and the development of the norm of theology[35] underscores the importance of evaluating how religious experience comes about. For Tillich, the cognitive neurosciences were not yet available for incorporation into his analysis of the interrelationship between the sources of theology and the experience of religion. However, neurotheology might be capable of providing not only a subjective assessment of religious experience, but a biological one as well.

As far as the specific development of neurotheology, several scholars are worth mentioning in this regard who developed and helped to advance this emerging field. Some of the earliest scholars to explore these issues were Eugene d'Aquili (1941-1998) and James Ashbrook (1925-1999),[36] whose pioneering work in the 1970s and 1980s ultimately laid the foundation for the work of more recent scholars such as James Austin, Rhawn Joseph, Mario Beauregard, Patrick McNamara, Gregory Peterson, and others.[37] The work of all of these scholars has sought to integrate a neuroscientific analysis with a spiritual perspective without losing too much

---

[34]   Tillich, P. *Systematic Theology* (3 volumes). Chicago, IL: University of Chicago Press, 1951-1963.

[35]   McKelway, A.J. *The Systematic Theology of Paul Tillich: A Review and Analysis.* Richmond, VA: John Knox Press, 1964.

[36]   d'Aquili, E.G. "The neurological basis of myth and concepts of diety." *Zygon.* 1978;13:257-275; d'Aquili, E.G. "Senses of reality in science and religion: a neuroepistemological perspective." *Zygon.* 1982;17:361-384; Ashbrook, J.B. and Albright, C.R. *The Humanizing Brain: Where Religion and Neuroscience Meet.* Cleveland, OH: Pilgrim Press, 1997.

[37]   Joseph, R. (ed.). *Neurotheology: Brain, Science, Spirituality, Religious Experience.* San Jose, CA: University Press, California. 2002; Austin, J.H. *Zen and the Brain: Toward an Understanding of Meditation and Consciousness.* Cambridge, MA: MIT Press, 1999. Beauregard, M. and O'Leary, D. *The Spiritual Brain.* New York, NY: Harper Collins, 2007; Alston, B.C. *What is Neurotheology?* Charleston, SC: BookSurge Publishing, 2007; McNamara, P. *The Neuroscience of Religious Experience.* Cambridge: Cambridge University Press, 2009; McKinney, L. *Neurotheology: Virtual Religion in the 21st Century.*

sight of one or the other. These scholars have worked hard to evaluate current neuroscientific knowledge as well as neuroscientific methods and brought these to bear on a wide variety of religious experiences as well as religious concepts. Initial analyses by Eugene d'Aquili, with his colleagues Charles Laughlin and John McManus, frequently focused on human ritual and its effects on both the mind and body, as well as how ritual was deeply tied to religious experience.[38] Early work also focused on the physiological basis of specific practices such as meditation and prayer. Such analyses were based in part on the existing neuroscientific literature, but also on the growing amount of scientific data obtained by other groups that measured the effects of such practices on various physiological parameters. Researchers such as Gellhorn and Kiely explored the autonomic nervous system effects of meditation.[39] Research conducted at institutions as far ranging as Harvard and the work of Dr. Herbert Benson to the Maharishi Institute and the work of B. Alan Wallace have contributed to the understanding of the relationship between the brain and various religious and spiritual practices. The most recent work has included brain imaging studies of a variety of religious and spiritual practices in addition to studies exploring subjective experiential components of religious and spiritual phenomena.[40]

This brief, and by no means exhaustive, review of the historical foundations of neurotheology was meant to show how and when many philosophical and theological concepts arose that pertain either directly or indirectly to how the mind and brain work. While it clearly was not the intent of many of these early scholars to link philosophical and theological concepts to the brain, now that cognitive neuroscientific techniques exist, we can return to these early developments and review them through a new lens of analysis. Therefore, neurotheology may be capable of creating new avenues for scholarship in the future, but may also allow for a reexamining of prior philosophical and theological ideas from a new perspective.

Cambridge, MA: American Institute for Mindfulness, 1994; Peterson, G.R. *Minding God.* Minneapolis, MN: Augsburg Fortress Press, 2003.

[38] d'Aquili, E.G. and Laughlin, C. "The biopsychological determinants of religious ritual behavior." *Zygon.* 1975; 10:32-58; d'Aquili, E.G., Laughlin, C., and McManus, J. *The Spectrum of Ritual: A Biogenetic Structural Analysis.* New York, NY: Columbia University Press, 1979.

[39] Gellhorn, E., Kiely, W.F. "Mystical states of consciousness: neurophysiological and clinical aspects." *J Nerv Ment Dis.* 1972;154:399-405.

[40] Newberg, A.B., d'Aquili, E.G., and Rause, V.P. *Why God Won't Go Away: Brain Science and the Biology of Belief.* New York, NY: Ballantine Publishing Group, 2001; Newberg, A.B. and Waldman, M.R. *Why We Believe What We Believe: Uncovering Our Biological Need for Meaning, Spirituality, and Truth.* New York, NY: Free Press, 2006; Beauregard, M. and O'Leary, D. *The Spiritual Brain.* New York, NY: Harper Collins, 2007.

Scientific and Theological Foundations of Neurotheology

The approach to neurotheological scholarship requires an understanding of the contemporary state of scientific and theological inquiry as well as acknowledging the current science and religion debate. Historically, particularly in the ancient world, the rudiments of science and religion were frequently viewed in a unified manner. Most people practicing a religion also relied heavily on science or technology in order to help with the expression of that religion. Structures such as the pyramids of Egypt or Stonehenge in England were built with great engineering and technological detail, all for the purpose of facilitating religious beliefs. Much of the field of astronomy also developed as a way of monitoring the heavens and evaluating the times for specific holidays of religious importance. With the development of the Reformation and ultimately the Renaissance, history began to witness a more antagonistic role between science and religion. In many ways this began with the Copernican Revolution which, with Galileo's help, shattered the Catholic church's view of an earth-centered, perfectly designed universe. This set up an antagonism that would last for hundreds of years up to the present day. Of course, Charles Darwin's elaboration of the theory of evolution was, and continues to be, a significant battleground for science and religion. As such, science and religion have typically gone their separate ways over the last hundred years, at times, the intersection being highly contentious. It remains to be seen what will be the ultimate outcome of the science and religion debate, but it may be that neurotheology as a field can offer an alternative to any hostile relationship between science and religion.

Various categories of interaction between science and religion have been expounded with the most elaborate being that of Ian Barbour who identified four types of interactions.[41] The first type of interaction is one of conflict in which it is perceived that only science or religion can present a correct analysis of the world, exclusive of each other. Examples of this conflict include those supporting scientific materialism such as biologists Jacques Monod or Richard Dawkins.[42] In their view, religion became part of human behavior as part of evolutionary forces, or even as an epiphenomenon, and does not represent objective reality as does science. The religious counterpart in this conflict involves those who believe in biblical literalism. Here the Bible is considered to be literally true, and thus it supersedes any scientific data that conflict with the statements of the Bible. This has led to great debate in many scientific and religious arenas. Most notable has been the argument between supporters of the theory of evolution and the adherents of Creationism. In this argument, either science is absolutely accurate or the Bible is absolutely accurate. Because of the vast differences between their descriptions of the origins of life and of the universe, both systems seem to be mutually exclusive.

---

[41]   Barbour, I.G. *Religion in an Age of Science*. New York, NY: Harper & Row, 1990.

[42]   Monod, J. *Chance and Necessity*. New York, NY: Vintage Books, 1972; Dawkins, R. *The God Delusion*. New York, NY: Houghton Mifflin, 2006.

A second interaction between science and theology is a mutual independence from each other. In this way, religion and science function in totally distinct domains. This second approach, which many naturalists have embraced, is that of the type described by Stephen J. Gould as "non-overlapping magisteria."[43] The notion here is that religion and science are in some sense both allowable, only that they refer to domains that are completely distinct. In this view, religion should have nothing to say about the scientific world and science nothing to say about the religious. However, they are not viewed to be mutually exclusive only providing information about two separate "dimensions" of human existence. Thus, science and religion do not conflict because science interprets human understanding of the world while religion interprets God's activity in the world. This notion does preserve both science and religion; however, it does not foster any dialogue between the two, which would at least provide for the possibility of a mutually beneficial interaction. Thus, the domain of each is essentially off-limits to the other.

Barbour defines the final two relationships between science and religion as dialogue and integration. The dialogue consists of boundary questions that exist in both science and religion. Examples include the Big Bang cosmology and quantum mechanics. In these scientific fields, research eventually results in questions that are unanswerable by scientific analysis. Questions such as what existed before the Big Bang, why did the Big Bang occur, and why is the universe here at all, all appear at the edge of present day scientific inquiry. Some of these "why" questions may never be answerable from a scientific perspective, but may be addressed by religion. David Tracy suggested that there are also more subtle examples of boundary questions that occur in everyday human experience.[44] Examples of such experiences include anxiety, joy, basic trust, and death. Science and religion also share certain methodological principles that are not identical, but similar enough to allow for meaningful dialogue. Holmes Rolston suggested that religion interprets and correlates human experience while science does the same with experimental data.[45] Science and religion both function within certain paradigms that form the basis of the accepted practice and can only be changed with great upheavals. Again, while science and religion are certainly not isomorphic, they are similar enough that there can exist a beneficial dialogue between the two.

The final relationship that may exist between science and religion is integration in which the two come together to help explain each other and the world. As noted above, natural theology (such as that described in the work of Thomas Aquinas and other scholastics) attempts to explain the existence of God and religion entirely by human reasoning. A classic approach of natural theology is the design argument which proposes that the inherent order of the universe implies the existence of

---

[43]   Gould, S.J. *Rocks of Ages*. New York, NY: Ballantine, 1999.

[44]   Tracy, D. *Blessed Rage for Order*. New York, NY: Seabury, 1975; Tracy, D. *Plurality and Ambiguity*. San Francisco, CA: Harper & Row, 1987.

[45]   Rolston, H. *Science and Religion: A Critical Survey*. New York, NY: Random House, 1987.

God. The anthropic principle suggests that the conditions of the universe are too perfectly tuned for the development of human life, and that there must have been divine intervention, if only to get things started.[46] Another attempt at integrating science and theology is the development of a "theology of nature." This differs from natural theology in that it begins with a firm religious basis which is then modified in order to accommodate the influx of new scientifically derived information.[47] Science and religion are integrated in "process philosophy" as developed by Alfred North Whitehead.[48] This philosophy was formulated with both scientific and religious concepts in an attempt to create an overarching developmental metaphysics that is applicable to the universe as a whole. More recently, Alan Wallace has suggested that a contemplative science be utilized that incorporates meditation and contemplation as an experimental paradigm to support scientific investigation.[49]

Of course, these four relationships between science and religion—conflict, independence, dialogue, and integration—each has its own advantages and shortcomings. It is also likely that the four possible interactions between science and religion as described by Barbour represent nodal points in the relationship so that there may actually be many variations on these themes and even mixtures to one degree or another. For the purposes of this book, it is important to recognize how each of these possible interactions may eventually be manifested in a neurotheological discourse. It may be the case that sometimes there will be direct conflicts between scientific data on one hand and religious belief on the other. However, there will also be times of dialogue and integration depending on the specific issues being addressed. Either way, it is important to begin the neurotheological pursuit with a framework in which an analysis of theology from the perspective of the mind and brain is considered possible as well as an analysis of science from a religious or theological perspective. This will help clarify and interpret how a synthesis of neuroscience and religion may be useful in the evaluation of epistemological as well as ontological problems.

It is at the neurotheological juncture that the science and religion interaction may be most valuable and help establish a more fundamental link between the spiritual and biological dimensions of the human being. Therefore, neurotheology, which should provide an openness to a number of different perspectives, might also be viewed as a nexus in which those from the religious as well as scientific side can come together to explore deep issues about humanity in a constructive

---

[46]   Carter, B. "Large number coincidences and the anthropic principle in cosmology." *IAU Symposium 63: Confrontation of Cosmological Theories with Observational Data*: 291-298, Dordrecht: Reidel, 1974; Barrow, J.D. and Tipler, F.J. *The Anthropic Cosmological Principle*. Oxford: Oxford University Press, 1986.

[47]   Barbour, I.G. *Religion in an Age of Science*. New York, NY: Harper & Row, 1990.

[48]   Whitehead, A.N. *Process and Reality*. New York, NY: Macmillan, 1929.

[49]   Wallace, B.A. *Contemplative Science*. New York, NY: Columbia University Press, 2007.

and complementary manner. There, no doubt, will be differing viewpoints that will be raised throughout this process, some of which may be more exclusive of one perspective or the other. However, it should be stressed that for neurotheology to grow as a field, it is imperative that one remains open, at least somewhat, to all of the different perspectives including those that are religious or spiritual, cultural, or scientific.

In addition to the complex interrelationship between science and religion over the years, neurotheological research must draw upon the current state of modern scientific methods and existing theological debates. Science has advanced significantly in the past several decades with regard to the study of the human brain. Neurotheology should be prepared to take full advantage of the advances in fields of science such as functional brain imaging, cognitive neuroscience, psychology, and genetics. On the other hand, neurotheological scholarship should also be prepared to engage the full range of theological issues. That theology continues to evolve and change from the more dogmatic perspectives of the past, through natural theology and systematic theology, neurotheology must acknowledge that there are many fascinating theological issues that face each religious tradition. Neurotheology should therefore strive to engage current theological debate to determine where and how this new perspective might provide some additional value. Neurotheological investigations must also clearly acknowledge neurotheology's own limitations as well as the limitations involved with scientific and theological disciplines.

Foundational Goals of Neurotheology

Now that the historical, scientific, and theological foundations have been considered, there is one more aspect of neurotheology that must be reviewed before discussing the principles of neurotheology. The foundational goals of neurotheology should help provide a compelling case for the pursuit of such topics. These goals are critical to establish how we are going to develop neurotheology and provide a defense for its existence as a field of scholarship. There are many important questions that neurotheology may help address that pertain to the nature of subjective experience, consciousness, the mind, and the soul. Neurotheology will hopefully bring new perspectives to the fields of neuroscience and theology. Neurotheology will also likely enhance many of the fields that contribute to its cross-disciplinary nature including, but not limited to, anthropology, sociology, neurobiology, cognitive neuroscience, medicine, genetics, physics, philosophy, religious studies, and theology. These fields will no doubt bring a richness and depth to the study of neurotheology in that each will provide an important perspective on the various issues that arise. Additionally, trying to integrate neuroscientific and religious or theological perspectives will also help to enhance reciprocally our understanding of the other contributing fields. This will hopefully provide an impetus for future studies and investigations not only in the realm of neurotheology but in all of the other contributing fields as well. The methods that are developed as part of neurotheology also may have broader applications with regard to health and possibly global sociopolitical problems.

When considering the *raison d'être* for developing neurotheology as a field, we can consider four foundational goals for scholarship in this area. These are:

1. to improve our understanding of the human mind and brain;
2. to improve our understanding of religion and theology;
3. to improve the human condition, particularly in the context of health and well being;
4. to improve the human condition, particularly in the context of religion and spirituality.

These four goals are reciprocal in that they suggest that both religious and scientific pursuits might benefit from neurotheological research. The first two are meant to be both esoteric as well as pragmatic regarding scientific and theological disciplines. The second two goals refer to the importance of providing practical applications of neurotheological findings towards improving human life both individually and globally.

Let us explore these goals in more detail. The first is one that many critics of neurotheology often forget. Namely, that neurotheological research, especially studies that utilize cognitive neuroscience techniques, actually challenges science to develop strong methodologies. As a field of study, cognitive neuroscience links various aspects of human thoughts, feelings, and perceptions to their underlying biological correlates. Techniques developed through the study of cognitive neuroscience have already advanced tremendously over the past several decades with the advent of many types of brain imaging abilities and other techniques to measure how the brain functions during various mental tasks and perceptions. The development of these techniques, specifically in the study of religious and spiritual phenomena, will undoubtedly be a cornerstone for neurotheology in the future. But neurotheological research will also have a potentially strong impact on the methods of cognitive neuroscience. The reason for this is that religious, spiritual, mystical, and theological phenomena are notoriously difficult to evaluate from any kind of scientific perspective. Determining which subjects to study, what to measure biologically, what to measure phenomenologically or subjectively, when to make measurements, and what type of approach is needed to actually make the measurements, are substantial problems for any empirically-based neurotheological research. To perform such studies in a manner that provides useful results will require an advancement or even reworking of cognitive neuroscience methodology which will hopefully lead to a better overall understanding of the human brain.

In addition to helping improve cognitive neuroscience methods, neurotheological research also provides new perspectives regarding the human mind itself. With so many new studies exploring a range of human mental processes including those relating to morality, love, honesty, and complex behaviors,[50] a thorough study of one of the most important and pervasive dimensions of human beings—the religious and spiritual—should significantly augment our understanding of the human person. Religion and spirituality has had, and will continue to have, a tremendous impact on behavioral, emotional, and cognitive processes within individuals. Religious rituals are highly complex behaviors that affect the brain on multiple sensory, cognitive, and emotional levels. Similarly, theological analysis requires many different elements of human cognition. Causal, teleological, and epistemological arguments challenge the mind at every turn, and understanding that relationship can only help us to understand better how the human brain works.

The second goal, to improve our understanding of religion and theology, is intriguing since the implication is that theology has something to gain through its interaction with cognitive neuroscientific research. This point was partially made above in the description of the historical foundations of neurotheology. Reflecting upon the neurophysiological correlates of theological ideas and their implications, from the Upanishads to Aquinas to Tillich, has the potential to provide an entirely new perspective on theology itself. Of course, the goal of using neurotheological research to improve theology is often met with trepidation from the religious perspective. The concern is not so much that the understanding of religion and theology will be *improved*, but rather that it will be *replaced* by a reductive, impersonal, and unspiritual version using science.[51] Several attempts at providing such an interpretation of the human soul appear to be antithetical to more traditional views of theology and religion. However, while this concern should be maintained during any neurotheological research program, an *a priori* attempt at reducing religion and spirituality to science would be highly biased and flawed and would not result in a fruitful result in the end.

The third goal of neurotheology is to improve the human condition, particularly in the context of health and well being. This goal derives from the first in that improving our understanding of the relationship between religion and the mind should ultimately yield information that will have practical applications. We will explore this in detail later, but here we might at least consider the range of possibilities by which this goal might be achieved. For example, there is a strong and growing literature regarding the relationship between religion and both

---

[50] d'Aquili, E.G. and Newberg, A.B. *The Mystical Mind: Probing the Biology of Religious Experience.* Minneapolis, MN: Fortress Press, 1999; Moll, J. and de Oliveira-Souza, R. "Moral judgments, emotions and the utilitarian brain." *Trends Cogn Sci.* 2007;11:319-321; Gazzaniga, M.S. *The Ethical Brain.* New York, NY: Dana Press, 2005; Talbot, M. "Duped: can brain scans uncover lies?" *New Yorker.* July 2, 2007:52-61; Fisher, H.E., Aron, A., Mashek, D., Li, H., and Brown, L.L. "Defining the brain systems of lust, romantic attraction, and attachment." *Arch Sex Behav.* 2002;31:413-419; Bartels, A. and Zeki, S. "The neural basis of romantic love." *Neuroreport.* 2000;11:3829-3834.

[51] Brown, W.S., Murphy, N., and Malony, H.N. *Whatever Happened to the Soul.* Minneapolis, MN: Fortress Press, 1998.

physical and mental health. Studies revealing how religion might contribute to improved physical health by reducing stress, helping with coping, and improving compliance with medical interventions might improve the overall health of our population. We might also find that specific practices such as meditation or prayer yield improvements in a variety of physical processes including those related to the cardiovascular system, digestive system, and immune system. Neurotheological research might also identify potentially negative consequences of religious and spiritual beliefs.[52] Some of this research might evaluate attitudes of specific traditions regarding the avoidance of medical interventions, while other studies might reveal how individuals develop a negative perspective of religion or God. These negative perspectives can lead to personal strife, anxiety, and depression. However, at the present time, there is not much known about what factors lead to these negative perspectives.

Another area that would lend itself well to neurotheological study is the growing problem with terrorism and the mind of the terrorist. It is not clear how and why some individuals follow extreme religious or spiritual views.[53] Neurotheological research has the opportunity to evaluate thoroughly which type of individual is most likely to follow such a path and perhaps offer methods for appropriately redirecting them. The ability to determine why hatred and exclusivity are fostered and accepted by an individual or group of individuals is information that could have important consequences for global health.

The fourth foundational goal suggests that through neurotheology, it might be possible to improve the religious and spiritual well being of individuals and of humanity in general. Neurotheology might provide a setting in which the improved understanding of religious and theological phenomena lead to practical applications in the ways in which individuals pursue their own spiritual goals. While it is not clear precisely by what mechanism such a goal might be achieved, it could be argued that whenever there is improved knowledge, especially if a new perspective is offered, there is the opportunity to grow. In the context of theology and religion, spiritual growth is always encouraged and neurotheology should be supported as another mechanism by which such growth might occur.

Critics often raise the concern that neurotheology might offer a way of "taking a pill" to become more spiritual. However, human beings have perpetually utilized different techniques from ritual, prayer, and meditation, to starvation, sustained intense physical activity, and pharmacological substances to help induce spiritual or religious states.[54] Thus, the notion of trying to bring about a spiritual or religious experience via some specified mechanism has existed for thousands of years.

---

[52]   Lee, B. and Newberg, A. "Religion and health: a review and critical analysis." *Zygon.* 2005;40:443-468.

[53]   Juergensmeyer, M. *Terror in the Mind of God: The Global Rise of Religious Violence.* Berkeley, CA: University of California Press, 2000.

[54]   Roberts, T.B. (ed.). *Psychoactive Sacramentals: Essays on Entheogens and Religion.* San Francisco, CA: Council on Spiritual Practices, 2001.

It should be no surprise, nor a problem therefore, if neurotheology uncovers better approaches than those that already exist. The important issue will be how to incorporate these approaches appropriately into a specific religious or spiritual paradigm. This, then, is one of the true challenges of neurotheological research.

We might consider one additional, overarching goal of neurotheology which pertains to the nature of reality. In order to address the four foundational goals described above, we must realize that all of them ultimately rest upon one fundamental question: How do we know the true nature of reality? And the corollary question is: Is the reality that we perceive and are conscious of really the real reality? After all, if we are going to try to advance our understanding about ourselves and the world around us, we must try to address better these fundamental epistemological questions.

With these foundational goals in mind, we are close to elaborating the principles of neurotheology. As might be expected, definitions are a crucial step. And this is particularly the case with neurotheology. Neurotheology itself must be defined in addition to many other concepts that can be assessed in this field of research. An exploration of definitions of a variety of religious and scientific concepts will then provide a starting point for delineating the principles of neurotheology.

Before we engage the definitions and, ultimately, the principles of neurotheology, permit me one additional comment regarding an often undervalued, but incredibly important concept in philosophy, theology, and science—humor. Neurotheology must admit the crucial importance of humor in understanding the human mind and its ability to deal with an ever changing and confusing world. In fact, it may be human kind's greatest legacy to be able to look upon an incredibly short life span, often filled with anxiety, fears, loss, suffering, and death and still find some way of laughing at ourselves and at the very world which causes us so much angst. Neurotheology would certainly make sure to include the neurological and theological basis of humor in any final analysis of the human person. And I cannot help but employ a line from the great comedian Groucho Marx with regard to the principles of neurotheology—"These are my principles, and if you don't like them, I have others!" This is a most well taken point since whatever principles we consider in the following pages, we must keep in mind that these principles can and should change as the scholarship, both scientific and theological, that drives neurotheology develops and advances.

Finally, I would like to add that I truly hope that my representation of scholarship in the disparate fields that may contribute to neurotheology is adequate enough to provide a starting point. I certainly look forward to being advised and corrected by other scholars from fields that are different than my own. And this is perhaps the greatest gift of neurotheology, the ability to foster a rich multidisciplinary dialogue in which we help others "get it right" so that we can advance the human person and human thought as it pertains to our mental, biological, and spiritual selves.

Chapter 2
Definitions in Neurotheology

The Principle of Definitions

Of critical importance to the study of neurotheology is the ability to use adequate and appropriate definitions on a number of different levels and topics. We must explore the importance of definitions prior to engaging the principles of neurotheology in order to better understand the various issues and problems that confront neurotheological scholarship. After all, when considering the principles of any field of scholarship, definitions are of the utmost significance since they provide a launching point from which the rest of the scholarship might proceed. For example, we see that in Isaac Newton's *Principia Mathematica* he begins with a lengthy discussion of the definitions of material objects and motion. In Descartes' *Principles of Philosophy*, and Alfred North Whitehead's *Principia Mathematica*, again there is substantial emphasis placed initially on defining concepts and terms before proceeding to the actual principles.

Neurotheology is no exception. In fact, while every field of scholarship requires attention to definitions, neurotheology appears to require this to an even greater degree. This is due in part to the multidisciplinary nature of the field and in part to the complexity of the topic itself. This will provide the first principle for neurotheological investigations. It is a "Principle of Definitions."

Principle I: Neurotheology should strive to provide and seek clear definitions for the topics of its inquiry.

Neurotheology should not only place emphasis on the need to set clear definitions, but also determine the process by which this might happen, and explore the sources of difficulty for establishing specific definitions. A corollary to this principle of definitions is that when a definition cannot be easily described, scholars should strive to be more inclusive than less. For example, in preparing a discussion about the types of experiences people have, it might be more appropriate to utilize the terms "religiosity" and "spirituality" together since some might describe their experiences as one, or the other, or both. Unless a scholar was limiting their focus only to one specific type of experience—for example, a near death experience—should he or she use that specific term.

In the context of neurotheology, there are many different types of definitions and terms that are necessary for consideration. From the neuroscientific perspective, adequate definitions of "mind" and "brain" are necessary in order to define the full scope of the neurosciences as they may be brought to bear on religious and spiritual phenomenon. On the other hand, terms such as "religion," "religiousness," and "spirituality" must also be adequately defined in order to preserve their meaning as well as to allow them to be available, in some regard, to the neurosciences. In addition, there are many other definitions that we may need to consider in some detail. These include, but are not limited to—science, data, research, philosophy, theology, consciousness, morality, and reality. Throughout this chapter, it will be necessary to appear to weave the definitions together from scientific to religious to philosophical, and then back to religious and scientific. The need for this weaving of definitions arises from the multidisciplinary nature of neurotheology as well as how each of these definitions themselves are intertwined.

Throughout this book, we will naturally have to adopt certain definitions which should be elaborated as clearly as possible. It is also recognized that most definitions will likely evolve over time as new research and new scholarship, both on the scientific and on the religious or spiritual side, are pursued. With this in mind, no definition should be accepted without considerable thought and analysis. In this chapter, we will explore several specific definitions and their history. However, in spite of striving to follow the "Principle of Definitions," as will be apparent from the discussion that follows, any definition will necessarily have its advantages and disadvantages as well as its breadth and limitations. Furthermore, as various other topics regarding neurotheology are explored, definitions will become more elaborate, subtle, and specific.

Origins of Definitions

In a cross-disciplinary field such as neurotheology, one fascinating problem is not only how concepts and terms are defined, but where to look for the origins of these definitions. Given the multidisciplinary nature of neurotheology, it is likely that its definitions will likewise come from many different disciplines.

Principle II: The definitions used in neurotheology will necessarily arise from a multitude of disciplines and sources.

If we approach a definition such as that for the term "spirituality," should it be derived from the theological or religious side, or should it be defined with a scientific perspective in mind? Should definitions require a hybrid development in which both scientific and religious perspectives are taken into account? In a similar manner, we might ask, "What are the goals or reasons for making a particular definition?" Are we developing a definition to maintain accuracy with regard to religious traditions, clarity with regard to philosophical investigations, or operationalization so that it can be useful from a scientific or research perspective? Given the multidisciplinary nature of neurotheology, it seems appropriate that definitions must arise from a multitude of contributing disciplines and perspectives.

The field of neurotheology also requires us to explore the origin of definitions from the perspective of the human brain. One might ask why we need definitions at all? Interestingly, from a biblical perspective, naming and defining all the things in the world was one of the first acts of Adam: "And out of the ground the Lord God formed every beast of the field, and every fowl of the air; and brought them unto Adam to see what he would call them: and whatsoever Adam called every living creature, that was the name thereof."[1] The human brain does have a great propensity for trying to understand all aspects of the world that it perceives. One of the major functions of the brain is to name and define various concepts so that it may manipulate them in thought and utilize them for planning future behaviors. In addition to the abstract naming functions of the brain, the brain also attempts to order and categorize various concepts. The brain also attempts to define concepts via their opposites. Thus, as the brain attempts to define "spirituality" it does so in part by comparing this term to other related terms and also by setting it apart from discordant terms such as "atheism." As we now proceed to consider several relevant definitions in the context of neurotheology, we can continue to reflect upon the variations of those definitions and how an assortment of factors, including both theological and biological ones, might affect those very definitions.

Mind and Brain

In starting with the "neuro" side of neurotheology, the initial delineation between mind and brain is of crucial significance. In ancient Greek philosophy, it was not entirely clear where human thought and cognition actually took place. In fact, the derivative of the word "neuron" appears to come from the Greek and Latin words for "sinew" or string, most likely because this is what nerves physically look like. It is well known that the ancient scholar Aristotle believed that human thoughts and feelings actually arose from the heart. The Eastern schools of thought had a more holistic approach to the human body and mind considering there to be an integration of the entire body with the mind. This is reflected in their explanation of the body's energy, which has many different centers and flows throughout the body.[2] While these energies were not necessarily related directly with the mind, they are believed to support the underlying spirit and function of the human being. Consciousness itself is considered a form of energy that permeates the universe. Consciousness is not necessarily created by the brain, but the brain has the ability to "tap into" the vast universal consciousness that underlies all of reality. Thus, the mind, and consciousness, is considered in a more holistic way than in Western thought.

---

[1]   Genesis 2:19. *King James Bible*.

[2]   Micozzi, M. *Fundamentals of Complementary and Alternative Medicine*. New York, NY: Churchill Livingstone, 2006.

The distinction between mind and brain in the West experienced a radical change with the philosophical meditations of Descartes. Descartes proposed a dualistic approach to the mind and brain ultimately concluding that he could doubt whether he had a body, but not doubt whether he had thought. The mind represented for Descartes the more ethereal and the brain the more material.[3] The problem for Descartes was in trying to find a way of reconciling these two dimensions of the human being so that they could be distinct and yet interact. In particular, how could something that has no material basis ultimately have an effect in the material world or even on the material body? This type of analysis ultimately leads to the issue as to whether or not the mind is truly separated from the brain or whether they must be considered linked in some form or another. From an Eastern perspective, a linking of mind and brain is much more acceptable. However, the advent of several schools of thought in Western philosophy, including those associated with the works of Wittgenstein and Husserl, attempted to look past the traditional Cartesian duality to explore the human experiential perspective of the world. In his early years, Ludwig Wittgenstein (1889-1951) wrote the *Tractatus Logico-Philosophicus*[4] in which the basis of philosophy could be derived from logical statements based originally on seven propositions. However, his later work, *Philosophical Investigations*,[5] provided a strong critique of the *Tractatus* and developed a new line of thought based less on logic and more on subjective experience in which language does not have a firm grasp of objects in the world. In the first decade of the twentieth century, Edmund Husserl (1859-1938) considerably refined and modified his method of what he called "transcendental phenomenology."[6] This process required all assumptions regarding the external world to be systematically "bracketed." This enabled the phenomenologist to reconstruct his or her basic views on the world and explore their rational interconnections from a new perspective. Thus, Husserl argued for a phenomenological perspective that required the mind, and brain, to experience the world in a more profound and ultimate manner.

For the purposes of this book, I will try to refer to and define the "mind" as the functions typically attributed to the brain. These functions include the thoughts, feelings, and experiences that a given individual may have. In general, these functions are "less tangible" since they cannot be measured other than by obtaining a first person account of the thoughts, feelings, and experiences.

---

[3]   Descartes, R. "Meditations on first philosophy." Translated by Elizabeth Haldane and G.R.T. Ross in, *The Philosophical Works of Descartes*. Cambridge: Cambridge University Press, 1984.

[4]   Wittgenstein, L. *Tractatus Logico-Philosophicus*. Translated by C.K. Ogden. New York, NY: Cosimo Books, 2007.

[5]   Wittgenstein, L. *Philosophical Investigations*. Translated by G.E.M. Anscombe. New York, NY: Macmillan, 1968.

[6]   Welton, D. *The Essential Husserl: Basic Writings in Transcendental Phenomenology* (Studies in Continental Thought). Bloomington, IN: Indiana University Press, 1999.

In other words, there is no clear way to "take a picture" of a thought. Brain imaging studies and other methods for evaluating brain function can assess the physiological processes associated with thoughts and experiences, but the former can only measure the subjective experiences by comparing to an actual first person narrative of the experiences. Interestingly, this becomes a significant problem for cognitive scientists since they too have experiences that are subjective and their brain has functions that are measurable. Regardless, defining the mind as the "less tangible" functions of the brain does not mean to be an argument to support or refute the possibilities that the mind exists or does not exist outside of the structure and function of the human brain. What is important here is to realize that however one decides to define "mind" and "brain," care must be taken to avoid having the definitions themselves affect the ultimate outcome of any scholarship regarding the nature of the mind and brain. In other words, if we maintain too strongly the notion that the mind is "less tangible," this will clearly bias any research or ideological development towards a distinction between mind and brain. On the other hand, maintaining a definition such that mind and brain are considered completely integrated may not allow any research to find a separation.

For these reasons, I will argue that the mind should be considered the less tangible functions of the brain, even though these functions may be deeply interrelated to the brain itself. The particular issue regarding whether there is in fact a non-material mind that exists will be considered in a later chapter. Here it is important to realize that this issue is of central importance in the study of neurotheology. But, while the philosophical and scientific issues pertaining to the mind/brain problem have important implications for neurotheology, they are not the primary focus of neurotheology.

The brain will be defined as the structures of neurons and support cells that exists within the human head in association with the neurotransmitters, chemicals, and blood vessels that make up and allow the brain to function. Again, however, this differentiation is made for simplification purposes and is not meant to convey bias towards one perspective or the other. When we ultimately discuss characteristics of certain mystical experiences, we will begin to explore whether or not there can be separation between the mind and brain and at that point, we will try to be more explicit with regard to this distinction.

Consciousness

Consciousness is almost as difficult to grasp and consider as the relationship between the mind and brain. In fact, in many ways, consciousness has been a greater problem for scholars because it has no clear tangible basis, but it is something we all feel that we possess. "Anything that we are aware of at a given moment forms part of our consciousness, making conscious experience at once the most familiar and most mysterious aspect of our lives."[7] Furthermore, there is, as far as we know, only one species in the universe that definitively has consciousness—human beings. Scholars such as Daniel Dennett and Owen Flanagan have attempted to explain how consciousness works.[8] The main issue that is often at the core of these discussions is whether consciousness exists in one particular place in the brain or mind, or whether consciousness arises, or emerges, out of the global processes of the brain or mind. There are arguments for and against the nature and origin of consciousness, including those that suggest that consciousness arises outside of the human brain. For example, in the Vedantic texts the development of self-awareness is considered to be primarily a phenomenon of consciousness and not a product of biological processes. And of course, this dualism between the mind or consciousness and the brain was thoroughly considered by Descartes.

Consciousness should be described at least in comparison to "awareness." Thus, I will define awareness as that which refers to the subjective perspective of things in the environment which are actually registered within the individual's sphere of knowledge. Awareness should be distinguished from the mere detection of things in the environment. For example, a video camera can detect light, movement, and objects that it is focused upon. However, the video camera is not aware of these things. Most animals, as well as human beings, have awareness of things in the environment such that they are registered within the animal's or person's view of the world. The human eye for example, in conjunction with the brain does not merely detect an object that is "out there," but acknowledges that object in a statement such as, "I see that object" or "I am aware of that object." Philosophers have argued that awareness requires an object to be aware of and a subject that is in fact aware. Therefore, the requirement for awareness is that there is something or someone who is actually aware. Awareness may be equivalent to subjective experience such that there is a subject or individual who is able to have an experience of something else external to that individual. Of course, a significant problem with all of these definitions is that it is most difficult to avoid circular definitions in which terms such as awareness, experience, and registration end up being used to describe each other.

Consciousness is related to awareness in that consciousness represents an awareness of the self as object. Thus, the individual is both the subjective experiencer as well as that which is experienced. It is this reflexive self-awareness that forms the basis of consciousness and is observed primarily in human beings. However, some investigators have demonstrated rudimentary forms of this reflexive self-awareness in certain animal species such as dolphins and some primates. Unfortunately, due to the language barrier, it is impossible to know whether or not a dolphin truly understands and is aware of its own self or whether they are merely

---

7   Velmans, M. and Schneider, S. (eds.). *The Blackwell Companion to Consciousness*. Malden, MA: Blackwell, 2007.

8   Dennett, D. *Consciousness Explained*. Boston, MA: Little, Brown and Company, 1991; Flanagan, O. *Consciousness Reconsidered*. Cambridge, MA: MIT Press, 1993.

aware of a dolphin that they do not necessarily ascribe as themselves or another. However, the research suggests that they do have a true understanding, responding to an image of themselves in a mirror as representing their self rather than some other dolphin.

There has also been a more spiritual conception of awareness and consciousness such that some traditions and scholars have described a state called "pure awareness" or "pure consciousness."[9] The argument put forth is that such an experience of pure awareness represents awareness without a subject or object. Hence, pure awareness refers only to the act of being aware without there necessarily being something that is aware and something to which that awareness is directed. Such a concept can be found in many meditative approaches in various religious and philosophical traditions including those in both Eastern and Western traditions. The main difference that may distinguish pure awareness from pure consciousness is the notion that there is a sense of self that is associated with the latter experience such that the universe has in many ways a self-reflexive consciousness. In theistic traditions this self-reflexive awareness within the universe, or that pervades the universe, may be described as God. While the nature of consciousness is not a primary topic of neurotheology, it is important to have some knowledge of the various arguments regarding the nature of consciousness, especially when considering the importance of consciousness from a religious or spiritual perspective.

Soul

"Soul" is a fascinating term since it has also come to mean many different things depending on a scholar's perspective. Plato and Aristotle both considered the soul to be the essence of the human being. However, it is not clear whether the soul could exist beyond the body. Ancient Egyptian beliefs certainly indicated a belief that the soul continues into the next realm after death. Other traditions such as Hinduism are based in large part on the notion that the soul returns to subsequent bodies through reincarnation. In Western thought, the soul is similarly considered to be the immortal part of the human person that has influence over the body. Thus, Plato also considered the soul to include reason, emotions, and desires. Augustine described the soul as "a special substance, endowed with reason, adapted to rule the body."[10] The present *Catechism of the Catholic Church* defines the soul as "the innermost aspect of humans, that which is of greatest value in them, that by which they are most especially in God's image: 'soul' signifies the spiritual principle in

---

9   d'Aquili, E.G. and Newberg, A.B. *The Mystical Mind: Probing the Biology of Religious Experience*. Minneapolis, MN: Fortress Press, 1999.

10   *The Works of Saint Augustine: A Translation for the 21st Century*. Translated with notes by, Edmund Hill, edited by John E. Rotelle. Hyde Park, NY: New City Press, 1990.

humans."[11] While these definitions clearly suggest that the soul is not the brain or the mind, the soul appears to have a deep relationship with the brain and mind. If the soul has reason, emotions, and desires, and is the essence of who we are, then it seems apparent that the brain has an intimate relationship to the soul.

A recent reworking of the definition of the soul comes from several scholars including Nancey Murphy and Warren Brown.[12] In their definition, they consider the soul to be related to those attributes that make human beings distinct from other animals. The higher human capacities include language, abstract thought, empathy, future orientation, memory, and modulation of behavior. These are considered to emerge from the processes of the brain, but not reduced to purely brain function. For this reason, they call this conception of the soul, "non-reductive physicalism." This notion of the soul may be quite compatible with neuroscience since we can explore many of these domains of human capacities. However, it will be important to establish how this notion of soul is compatible with religious and theological traditions as well.

In his book *Consilience*, E.O. Wilson indicated that sociology recognized the belief in a soul as one of the universal human cultural elements. Wilson further suggested that biologists investigate how human genes predispose people to believe in a soul.[13] This belies the assumption that the soul is not supernatural, but a consequence of brain function and ultimately genetics. Neurotheology would concur that it would be helpful to understand the neurobiological and genetic underpinnings of the notion of soul, but would also emphasize the importance of ensuring that all concepts of soul, including those that are non-material or spiritual, are considered and evaluated.

Religion and Spirituality

It is difficult to define either religion or spirituality without some reference to the other. Interestingly, their word origins are markedly different. "Spirituality" is derived from the Middle English word "spiritus" which means "breath." In this regard, spirit referred to the basic component of life—the life-giving breath of the individual. The word "religion" is generally thought to derive from both Germanic and English influences from words meaning "to bind." The implication here is that religion is a way to bind people to each other and ultimately to God. Spirituality on the other hand appears to refer to something intrinsic within us that either is our own essence, or the part of us that ultimately helps us find our path back to the God or that which is sacred.

---

[11] *Catechism of the Catholic Church*. New York, NY: Doubleday, 1997. 363.

[12] Brown, W.S., Murphy, N., and Malony, H.N. (eds.). *Whatever Happened to the Soul?* Minneapolis, MN: Augsburg Fortress Press, 1998.

[13] Wilson, E.O. *Consilience: The Unity of Knowledge*. New York, NY: Vintage Books, 1998.

There have been many attempts at defining these concepts in the context of modern science and also in the context of various academic disciplines. Spirituality is usually reserved more for the individual experience and religion more for the doctrinal concepts of an established institution. However, there is obviously extensive overlap. Interestingly, in polls taken of beliefs in the US, the majority of individuals described themselves as both spiritual and religious, but there is also a substantial and growing, percentage that describe themselves as spiritual and not religious, and a smaller, but not insignificant number that consider themselves religious but not spiritual.[14] Finally, there are those who consider themselves to be neither spiritual nor religious. Of course the important point is that we do not know how each person defines religion and spirituality and, thus, the results of such surveys are often difficult to interpret.

Focusing on work since the beginning of the twentieth century, a number of scholars from different fields have attempted to define religion and its characteristics. In Paul Tillich's, *Systematic Theology*,[15] he defines religion as pertaining to "ultimate concern" which he describes as "an abstract translation of the great commandment: 'You shall love the Lord your God with all your heart, and with all your soul and with all your mind, and with all your strength.'"

With the development of a more formal approach to the human mind and brain, scholars tried to define religion in the context of human cognitive, emotional, and perceptual processes. William James defined religion as "the feelings, acts, and experiences of individual men in their solitude, so far as they apprehend themselves to stand in relation to whatever they may consider divine."[16] Schleiermacher described the essential element of religion as experience; a vibrant, deep, and transcendent feeling of the divine which caused him to define religion as a feeling of "absolute dependence."[17] Rudolf Otto defined religion in terms of "the Holy" (*Das Heilige*), that is, the *mysterium tremendum et fascinans*.[18] Jung defined religion as,

> … a peculiar attitude of the mind which could be formulated in accordance with the original use of the word *religio*, which means a careful consideration and observation of certain dynamic factors that are conceived as "powers": spirits, demons, gods, laws, ideas, ideals, or whatever name man has given to such factors in his world as he has found powerful, dangerous, or helpful enough to be taken into careful consideration, or grand, beautiful, and meaningful enough to be devoutly worshiped and loved.

---

[14]   One Nation Under God? Newsweek poll, April 7, 2009.

[15]   Tillich, P. *Systematic Theology* (3 volumes). Chicago, IL: University of Chicago Press, 1963.

[16]   James, W. *Varieties of Religious Experience*. New York, NY: University Books, [1890] 1963.

[17]   Gerrish, B.A., MacKintosh, H.R., and Stewart, J.S. *The Christian Faith by Friedrich Schleiermacher*. Edinburgh: T. & T. Clark Publishers, 1999.

[18]   Otto, R. *Idea of the Holy*. Oxford: Oxford University Press, 1958.

Durkheim defined religion as a unified set of beliefs and practices relative to sacred things, which are set apart and forbidden. This includes sets of beliefs and practices that unite a single moral community among those who adhere to them.[19] Clifford Geertz defined religion as: (1) a system of symbols which acts to (2) establish powerful, pervasive, and long-lasting moods and motivations in men by (3) formulating conceptions of a general order of existence and (4) clothing these conceptions with such an aura of factuality that (5) the moods and motivations seem uniquely realistic.[20] For both Durkheim and Geertz, religion was a construct of human beings specifically related to the establishment of cohesive social groups. More recently, scholars such as Scott Atran, Pascal Boyer, and others have elaborated concepts of religion based upon various evolutionary and neurobiological perspectives.[21] For example, Atran argues that religion is an evolutionary epiphenomenon resulting from the interaction of various cognitive modules.

While many of the above mentioned scholars specialized in either religion, theology, psychology, or sociology, none of the definitions were considered from a purely scientific perspective. One attempt by a group of scientists, brought together in 1997 to discuss the current and future state of the study of spirituality in the healthcare setting, can be provided as an example.[22] This consensus conference provided the following definitions by defining criteria for religiousness and spirituality.

The criteria for spirituality included:

1. the subjective feelings, thoughts, experiences, and behaviors that arise from a search or quest for the sacred;
2. the "Search" refers to attempts to identify, articulate, maintain, or transform; and
3. the "Sacred" refers to what the individual perceives as a divine being, ultimate reality, or ultimate truth.

The criteria for religion/religiousness included:

1. the criteria for spirituality and/or;
2. a search for non-sacred goals (such as identity, belonging, meaning, health, or wellness) in the context of spiritual criteria; and

---

[19] Durkheim, E. cited in Morris, B. *Anthropological Studies of Religion: An Introductory Text*. New York, NY: Cambridge University Press, 1987.

[20] Geertz, C. "Religion as a cultural system." In Bantom, M. (ed.), *Anthropological Approaches to the Study of Religion*. London: Tavistock, 1985.

[21] Atran, S. *In Gods We Trust: The Evolutionary Landscape of Religion*. New York, NY: Oxford University Press, 2002; Boyer, P. *Religion Explained*. New York, NY: Basic Books, 2002; Feierman, J.R. (ed.) *The Biology of Religious Behavior*. Santa Barbara, CA: Praeger, 2009.

[22] Larson, D.B., Swyers, J.P., and McCullough, M.E. (eds.) *Scientific Research on Spirituality and Health: A Consensus Report*. Washington DC: National Institute for Healthcare Research, 1998.

3. the means and methods of the search receive general validation and support from within an identifiable group of people.

One unique characteristic of these definitions is that they provide an operational framework for future investigations and discussions.

Another approach is not necessarily to define religion or spirituality in a specific way, but rather to consider the various dimensions that can be incorporated into religion or spirituality. For example, when evaluating religion from a neurotheological perspective, there are many different elements that can be considered to span both the religious and neuroscientific perspectives. The following dimensions of religiousness are adapted from Koenig, McCullough, and Larson:[23]

1. *Religious belief.* This can refer to the specific beliefs that are held as part of a particular religion that play an important role in defining that religion. However, these beliefs can also be considered from a neuroscientific perspective since the beliefs must be simple enough to be grasped by individuals following the religion, and must make cognitive sense in the context of how the human mind perceives the world. The question can be raised as to whether or not certain beliefs are more likely to be "successful" than others because of how they are capable of drawing on the human mind's functions.

2. *Religious affiliation.* Which religion a particular individual decides to follow is important for understanding how the spiritual and mental dimensions of the person are interrelated. Affiliation itself is not always a useful concept since many individuals follow their religion of origin (that is, the one their parents or family follow) without necessarily believing in it. Furthermore, an individual might have an evolution in their affiliation over time that could be very important for understanding how religion relates to their life. Thus, it is important to understand not only what an individual means when they state the religion they are affiliated with, but how they understand that affiliation.

3. *Organizational religiosity.* This notion of religion relates to how a particular religion develops its doctrines, beliefs, rituals, and system of adherence. Taken together, these elements form the organizational or structural elements of a given religion. However, some religious systems are more amenable to strict, hierarchical design while others have more flexible designs. An important issue is how different structural properties of religions affect the brain differently

4. *Non-organizational religiosity.* Many individuals consider themselves religious without taking part in the more formal organizational apparatus of a given religion. This can take the form of private or family ceremonies, or other activities that involve members of the same religion without necessarily requiring the larger structure. The non-organizational elements

---

[23]   Koenigh, H.G., McCullough, M.E., and Larson, D.B. (eds.) *Handbook of Religion and Health*. New York, NY: Oxford University Press, 2001.

of religion need to be considered in relation to the organizational elements and ultimately to how the brain and mind engages religion.

5. *Subjective religiosity.* This may be more closely related to the spiritual elements of religion since it describes how individuals experience their religion. The subjective experiences that people have can vary widely both within and across traditions. For some, the subjective aspect might be relatively minor and manifested by brief feelings of awe when entering a church. For others, religion might be a calling that they sense and follow throughout their life. Still others may have powerful mystical experiences that form the basis for their religious or spiritual beliefs.

6. *Religious commitment/motivation.* What motivates people to be religious is also an interesting issue to be considered in neurotheology. Motivation is a psychological concept that is also based in brain chemistry. People can be motivated to follow religion out of guilt, anger, fear, love, personal experience, and many other causes. It might be interesting to determine which motivating causes are more compelling than others and which ones have been utilized by some religions and not others.

7. *Religious well-being.* This is an interesting, but important aspect of both religion and psychology. Simply because someone is religious does not necessarily make them happy or satisfied. Perhaps they feel uncomfortable in their religion. Perhaps they are uncomfortable with their own beliefs. Religion can lead individuals to very positive or very negative thoughts and behaviors. Sometimes these negative thoughts can be encouraged by a religion such as in committing violence against opposing religions and sometimes the negativity can be more individualized such as someone who thinks that God is punishing them. Individuals can also have positive experiences that differ from the doctrines of their religion and thus cause substantial anxiety as they try to relate them back to their beliefs. Religions can also support positive self esteem, optimistic beliefs, and a sense of love and compassion.

8. *Religious coping.* Coping is often cited by individuals as crucial for their ability to deal with various issues throughout their life and particularly health issues. Many people turn to religion to help in times of crisis. Individuals can put their suffering in perspective and can deal with that suffering in a more adaptable manner.

9. *Religious knowledge.* Religious knowledge provides insight into many aspects about the world depending on the particular religious doctrine. For some, religious scriptures can provide complete information regarding the physical and metaphysical world. The religion thus provides knowledge regarding the workings and origin of the physical world and also explains our role within that world. Religions can also provide knowledge regarding how human beings are to relate to God. In this way, the religion explains what human beings need to do and think in order to connect to God. Religion can also provide information on how human beings are to interact with one another. For some, this might be antagonistic and for others this might be

compassionate. Religion can also provide a system of ethics which can help us understand how to be a good or bad person.

10. *Religious consequences*. Religion also provides a sense of consequences that are associated with various types of thoughts and behaviors. In this way, religion tells us what happens if we are a good person and what happens if we are a bad person. Studies have suggested how the human conscience forms within the brain as it triggers emotions such as embarrassment or guilt when we do something wrong. Religions also provide some information about what happens to all human beings "in the end." Thus, many religious systems have a judgment day or some other event that will determine the ultimate fate of humanity.

While the above described dimensions are not necessarily exhaustive, they provide an interesting relationship between the thoughts, feelings, experiences, and behaviors that can be addressed through a neurotheological perspective.

While neurotheology may not necessarily define spirituality and religion in any better way than previous approaches, what becomes a crucial realization in neurotheology is that whenever one begins to talk about, discuss, do research, or theorize about religion or spirituality, these terms should be defined at least for that particular dissertation. These working definitions may not necessarily be the best, most accurate, or most encompassing, but they must be provided so that any interpretation can be properly considered. Since neurotheology will examine these concepts from a biological perspective, the definitions are also important for assessing the relationship between these concepts and various thoughts, feelings, behaviors, and experiences.

Belief and Faith

Webster's dictionary defines belief as a "state or habit of mind in which trust or confidence is placed in some person or thing" or "a conviction of the truth of some statement or the reality of some being or phenomenon especially when based on examination of evidence." This is differentiated from "Faith" which is defined as "a belief and trust in and loyalty to God or a firm belief in something for which there is no proof." Clearly there is overlap, but again, it is interesting that belief is primarily distinguished on the basis that a belief has some evidence whereas faith has none. However, this is highly problematic since there is no clear definition for the term "evidence." Evidence can be very different for diverse scholarly pursuits. Evidence in philosophy is different from that in sociology, theology, economics, biology, chemistry, and physics. Thus, the lines between belief and faith are considerably blurred. In accordance with the principle of definitions above, perhaps it is more important that each scholar is clear about what they mean when they refer to belief or faith.

The term "belief" first appeared in English when it was adapted from the gothic word "galaubjan," which meant, literally, "to hold dear." In the fifteenth century, "belief" used to mean "to trust in God" and thus it is not surprising that many people equate "belief" with religious and spiritual views.[24] Thus, to believe in God was to have faith in God's existence, without the need of proof. Faith itself derives from the Latin word "fides" which means trust. Thus, both belief and faith refer to trusting something or accepting something as true without definitive proof. For religion, faith rather than fact, is the key word, for God continues to be a subject that is not immediately susceptible to a scientific notion of proof. On the other hand, the Apostle Paul admonishes us to "prove all things,"[25] which can be interpreted as an instruction to people not to have complete "blind faith," but rather to find some proof of religious beliefs.

However, those who have opposed religion have frequently remarked, as Richard Dawkins puts it, "Faith, being belief that isn't based on evidence, is the principal vice of any religion."[26] Dawkins suggests that since religion is not based on "evidence," it cannot be valid. However, this statement suffers from not following the principle of definitions described above since the term "evidence" is not defined in this statement. The evidence that religions have relied upon throughout the centuries is based on beliefs and truths that are arrived at through personal experience and reflection rather than proofs that are typically accepted by scientific methodology. However, should this invalidate religion because the evidence is of a different type? In the Bible, there is a definition of faith. "Faith is the substance of things hoped for, and the evidence of things not seen."[27] Again, there is the use of the word "evidence," but this time as a way of supporting the importance of belief. Belief itself becomes the evidence. Again, some would argue that this does invalidate religious faith while others would argue that it should not. In further evaluating more specific definitions of belief and faith, many scholars have tried to differentiate these two terms. For example, in Tillich's *Dynamics of Faith*, he defines faith as "a centered act of being ultimately concerned."[28] However, this definition is notably vague and does not clearly establish what "concern" means or what "ultimate" means. Tillich continues by stating that faith is not simply the will to believe, it is a cognitive affirmation of the transcendent nature of ultimate reality. This is achieved, not by a process of intellectual inquiry, but by an act of acceptance and surrender. Tillich also argues that faith may be either dynamic, when uncertainty is recognized and overcome by faith, or non-dynamic, when the possibility of any uncertainty is excluded by faith. Tillich argues that doubt is included in every act of faith.[29] The risk involved in faith is related to the presence of uncertainty. This brings us back to the issue

24   *Online Etymology Dictionary* (http://www.etymonline.com/).

25   Thessalonians 5:21. *King James Bible*.

26   Dawkins, R. "Is science a religion?" *The Humanist*. January/February 1997.

27   Hebrews 11:1. *King James Bible*.

28   Tillich, P. *Dynamics of Faith*. New York, NY: Harper & Row, 1957.

29   Tillich, P. *Systematic Theology* (3 volumes). Chicago, IL: University of Chicago Press, 1963.

of evidence since it is the lack of evidence, the sense of doubt, that allows faith to find its strength.

This problem of evidence is also why science and religion have historically been viewed as opposed to each other. In fact, most beliefs, as far as nonscientists are concerned, are not subjected to the rigors of an organized investigation into their validity or truth. However, if we consider beliefs to be related to ways in which we organize our perceptions of the world into ideas and stories that enable us to interact adaptively to the world, then most of the higher brain functions can be equated with beliefs. Thus, one way of defining beliefs is that they are biologically and psychologically identified as any perception, cognition, emotion, or memory that a person consciously or unconsciously assumes to be true.[30] The value of such a definition is that it is operationalized and can enable an active investigation into the nature and origin of beliefs. This definition also has value since it refers to beliefs that are both conscious and unconscious. Research generally shows that unconscious beliefs can have a tremendous influence over our thoughts and behaviors. One of the important elements of religion is to affect not only conscious beliefs, but also unconscious beliefs so that we act and think in a moral and religiously acceptable way, even if we are not consciously trying to.

Belief and faith are deeply related to each other. Neurotheology might shed light on the meaning of belief and faith especially as people consider these two concepts. Furthermore, it might be most interesting to determine if there are different brain structures associated with things that people claim to believe in and those things that people claim to have faith in.

Theology

Theology is traditionally distinguished academically from religion or spirituality in that theology represents an analysis of a given religious doctrine or belief system. Hence, Christian theology is the deductive and rational analysis of the New Testament and the story of Jesus Christ as the Messiah. Christian theology has also had a very formal development over the ages including the works of Saint Thomas Aquinas and, more recently, the works of Paul Tillich, Pierre Teilard de Chardin, and Alfred North Whitehead. On the other hand, Jewish theology focuses more on the Old Testament, in particular, the Torah, and is elaborated upon in the various texts that have formed the foundation of traditional Jewish religion and life in works such as the Talmud. Other traditions also have their specific theological and ideological development from the original sacred texts or doctrines.

In a very strict sense, theology is the study of a *theos* or God. Both the Jewish and Greek philosophical understanding of God was in personal terms. The Jewish

---

[30]   Newberg, A.B. and Waldman, M.R. *Why We Believe What We Believe: Uncovering Our Biological Need for Meaning, Spirituality, and Truth.* New York, NY: Free Press, 2006.

God was definitely personal, but the philosophical Greek *theos* was considered
to be a "rational hypostasis." The Hellenistic philosophical concept of a "rational
hypostasis" would describe *theos* as an "ultimate center of awareness" who
possessed rationality in a transcendent way, that is, without the sequential states of
reasoning characteristic of the human person.[31] Since both Christianity and Islam
proceeded out of a conflation of the Jewish and Greek concepts of God, they could
not help but see God in personal terms (in some sense at least). Thus, theology can
be seen as the intellectual quest for this ultimate transcendent person. Given this
historical context, the word "theology" should be reserved for theistic religions
only and, even more specifically, from those arising out of the Judeo-Christian
tradition, that is, Judaism, Christianity, and Islam.

However, with the development of comparative theology in the early part of
the twentieth century, it became apparent that the non-personal Eastern traditions
possessed many of the formal characteristics of the classic Western religions. It
became academically fashionable to use the term "theology" for the formal study
of any belief system centered on an Ultimate or Absolute, whether personal or
non-personal, whether understood as God or as an ultimate state. Thus, it is now
more acceptable to speak of a theology of Buddhism, a theology of Hinduism, and
even of a theology of Shamanism.

Within each religious tradition, the word "theology" can be used in two
senses—natural theology and theology proper (or dogmatic theology). Natural
theology is not really theology at all, but rather a branch of philosophy. It attempts
to prove, or at least prove probable, the existence of God, or the Absolute, by
reason alone, without any appeal to Divine Revelation (in the West) or to fairly
rare mystical experiences (in the East). In the nineteenth and twentieth centuries,
this enterprise has attempted to enlist science. In any case, with or without science,
it is a thoroughly rational discipline, theoretically without any axes to grind.

Theology proper represents intellectual deductions from a foundational
doctrine as well as *reasonable* extrapolations upon such a doctrine. The beginning
point of theology proper, at least in the West and in primitive societies, is a belief
in the transcendent truth of the foundational doctrine either at the literal surface
level or at a deeper symbolic level. It is the belief in the truth of the foundational
doctrine which motivates the deductions and extrapolations from that doctrine to
create a body of knowledge that is dependent upon the truth of that doctrine. In
the East, theology proper often develops from a rational attempt to derive meaning
and understanding of reality from the esoteric and mystical experiences of holy
men. In Hinduism, however, there is also a marked admixture of deduction from
ancient foundational concepts.

In the past fifty years, there have been a few attempts at the development of a
"metatheology" utilizing various general scientific or philosophical themes such as
evolution or process theory. A "metatheology" should be an overarching approach

---

[31]   d'Aquili, E.G. and Newberg, A.B. *The Mystical Mind: Probing the Biology of
Religious Experience*. Minneapolis, MN: Fortress Press, 1999.

that can explain the essential features of any theology arising out of any specific religious tradition. "Megatheology" is another term that has been used to describe a theological perspective that theoretically is so broad that it would be acceptable to an individual regardless of their religious or spiritual perspective. Thus, a megatheology could be incorporated into the belief system and dogma of any religious tradition. These concepts, particularly as they pertain to neurotheology will be considered in a later chapter.

It seems that much of religious and theological study today focuses on problems regarding what is the basis of religion, what is the nature of God, and what is the relationship between human beings and God. Again these studies are based primarily on philosophy, epistemology, and ontology, and therefore take place in a more esoteric realm. Furthermore, these studies often use ancient religious texts to help validate their conclusions.

Theology in its more rigorous form has been dominated in the past by Christian thinkers. Thus, Christian theology has developed into an extensive study of the relationship of human beings to God and God incarnate. Of course much of the focus of Christian theology has been on the Bible, including both the Old and New Testaments. As the study of theology developed, various other texts were included as well as the dictums of the papacy. Christian theological thinking slowly evolved from the writings of the Fathers of the Church into medieval concepts of religion and God, through the Renaissance, the Reformation, and eventually to the post-modernism of the present. Today, theological studies have become a formal academic pursuit as well as a religious one. Much of the work in present day theology consists of analysis and understanding of existing texts in a consistently hermeneutical context. But how neurotheology might contribute to these pursuits is part of the goal of setting out the principles of this field.

In comparing philosophy to modern theology, Paul Tillich suggests that philosophy is a "cognitive approach to reality in which reality as such is the object."[32] Philosophy, then, is directed towards the external reality of the universe. Theology, on the other hand, is directed towards the "ultimate concern" of human beings. This "ultimate concern is that which determines our being or not-being." In some sense, theology is directed inward towards an individual's ultimate concerns. While this duality should not be regarded as rigid, it does demonstrate what the fundamental issues of theology are, and how they differ from philosophy. This distinction is similar to the one between theology and science, since science is an empirical philosophy that is directed towards our objective cognitions of the external world. However, the theologian also must start from the state of being in external, material reality, since theology must begin with human experiences if they are to be interpreted. Later in this book, we will discuss some of the theological concepts and questions in more detail, particularly as they relate to neurophysiology and various aspects of brain function.

---

[32] Tillich, P. *Systematic Theology* (3 volumes). Chicago, IL: University of Chicago Press, 1963.

There are a number of theological methods which we also can consider *vis-à-vis* neurotheology. It should also be mentioned that any given approach to theology should not be considered to be competing with, but complementary to other approaches. Biblical theology is the study of the contents of Holy Scripture, systematically arranged, and arrived at through exegesis or interpretation. Historical theology seeks to evaluate the "the progressive development of the doctrines of the Bible, and a survey of the historical development of doctrine in the Church since apostolic times."[33] This provides a longitudinal perspective on how religion evolves over time to maintain its divine message. Systematic theology is based on a strong logical and deductive approach and is currently an important approach to theology. Systematic theology makes more use of philosophy, apologetics, and ethics than do other disciplines. Systematic theology in some ways incorporates both biblical and historical approaches to theology. Practical theology seeks to make religious knowledge applicable to everyday life, and the ministry of the religion, in most cases, Christianity. Process theology was developed by Alfred North Whitehead (1861-1947) and was based on the notion that the world is dynamic and always in motion, always in process. Underlying this dynamic process is a permanent background of order which is mediated by God. Process theology also observes God's causality in the world as influence and persuasion rather than direct causal intervention.

Regardless of the approach one takes toward theological method, it is important to observe the cognitive and emotional elements involved. For example, all theologies are based on a primary faith system. Thus, belief is first and foremost the foundation of any theology. However, the analytical components can have an emphasis on thought, feelings, experiences, practical behaviors, or other elements that can be related eventually back to various functions of the human mind and brain. Thus, any method of theology can theoretically be evaluated from a neurotheological perspective in addition to its more traditional approach.

God

Since much of theology and, consequently, neurotheology entails the examination of the relationship between human beings and God, or at least the perceived relationship, it is also necessary to define precisely what the definition of God represents. The word "God" appears to be derived from the word "gheu" from Middle English from Old English.[34] This derivative means "to call or invoke," but other derivatives of the word, especially those from Germanic languages, refer to being possessed or even insane. Modern conceptions of God or a concept of deity obviously vary dramatically depending on the individual and the individual's

---

[33]   McGrath, A. *Historical Theology: An Introduction to the History of Christian Thought.* Oxford: Blackwell, 1998.

[34]   *Online Etymology Dictionary* (http://www.etymonline.com/).

specific religious tradition. In the Judeo-Christian religions, there is the notion of a single God. God's presence pervades and encompasses the entire universe. However, the specific attributes of God vary dramatically depending on the belief system. From a Christian perspective, God is representative as the Father, Son, and Holy Ghost. In Judaism, there are no similar distinctions. In Buddhism, there is no anthropomorphic notion of God, but there is a conception of ultimate reality that shares many descriptive features. In Hinduism, there may be many different manifestations of God.

One particularly relevant point is that a theistic perspective is not completely necessary to engage in neurotheology. Since there can be overlapping concepts of deity, and also notions of absolute or ultimate reality, each of these can be considered in relation to brain science. However, it is important not to presuppose that one can reduce concepts of God to biology, nor to try to equate all conceptions of God as one. There are clear differences in how various traditions view God and these must be kept separate in any neurotheological analysis. However, it is also important to determine precisely what these differences are and whether there are also similarities. Similarities are often found more in the experiential or phenomenological elements of religion while differences are more often found in religious texts and doctrines. But neurotheology must always carefully consider different belief systems and doctrines as it seeks a deeper understanding of their relationship with the human mind.

In sacred texts, it is interesting how God's actual attributes are construed. In Genesis, God is described as being able to speak, see, create, and rest. Throughout the Bible, God is described as having a number of humanized emotions including anger, vengefulness, love, and forgiveness. In terms of physical attributes, there is very little. Towards the end of Exodus, we read that God will "redeem you with a stretched out arm"[35] suggesting some anatomic-like attribute. But as most religious scholars would likely agree, many of these descriptive terms should not be considered to be related in any way to similar sounding attributes in human beings.

In the Islamic tradition, there are believed to be 99 attributes of God. Some are loving, some are cruel, and others are unique to the Muslim and Sufi traditions:

> Allah is: compassionate, merciful, sovereign, holy, bestower of peace, grantor of security, guardian, mighty, irresistible, majestic, creator, organizer of all, perceiver, illustrious, all inclusive, everlasting, all able, determiner, expeditor, delayer, the first, the last, victorious, hidden, patron, supreme, kind and righteous, relenting, avenger, pardoner, pitying, owner of all, majestic, equitable, unifier, all rich, emancipator, defender, harmful, benefactor, light, guide, incomparable, immutable, inheritor of all, teacher, timeless, fashioner of forms, forgiver, subduer, bestower, provider, victory giver, all knowing, abaser, exalter, giver of honor, giver of dishonor, all hearing, all seeing, arbitrator, just, kind, all aware, indulgent, infinite, all forgiving, grateful, sublime, great, preserver, nourisher,

---

[35] Exodus 6:6. *King James Bible*.

reckoner, majestic, generous, watchful, responsive, vast, wise, loving, glorious, raiser of the dead, the witness, truth, dependable, strong, steadfast, friend and helper, praiseworthy, originator, producer, the restorer, giver of life, bringer of death, ever living, and sustainer.[36]

But again, each of these are words that are understood and defined by the human brain and this is where neurotheology might offer information as to what each of these concepts mean in terms of God.

While deriving the attributes, characteristics, and definition of God from sacred texts, it is also important to know what people actually think about God. This has particular relevance to neurotheology since studying sacred texts to define God can primarily be evaluated from a theological or religious perspective. To some extent, one can question the nature of the passages in sacred texts from a neurobiological perspective by attempting to determine what exactly the authors were thinking and feeling at the time, or perhaps, by determining people's responses to the sacred texts. However, there is also value in assessing more directly how present individuals interpret and define God for themselves.

A recent large survey of religious attitudes conducted at Baylor University showed that the Americans sampled tended to embrace one of four different "personalities" of God: authoritarian, critical, distant, and benevolent.[37] But these four categories could not be easily assigned to any specific denomination or sect. The authoritarian God was generally regarded as angry and willing to punish anyone who was unfaithful or who acted in an ungodly way. They may even believe that God causes earthquakes and human disasters as a wake-up call to sinful people. When individuals view God as critical, they believe in a God that does not intervene in the world, but will cast judgment on people in the afterlife. The second largest group of the Americans sampled considered God as distant and uninvolved. God does not hold opinions about the world or about personal behavior; thus we are left to our own free will to decide what is right and wrong. This God is less of a person and more like a cosmic force that set the laws of the universe into motion and then let it go on its own. The fourth type of God identified by the Baylor study was a benevolent God. God is viewed as gentle, forgiving, and less likely to respond with wrath. Like those who believe in an authoritarian God, believers in a benevolent God think that God is very active in their lives. For such individuals, God generally listens, responds to prayers, and cares deeply about the suffering of others.

It should be emphasized that these four views of God were not distinctly defined, but rather represented nodal points along a wide spectrum of beliefs in God. Thus, there are many variations and hybrids within these beliefs in God.

---

[36] Bawa Muhaiyaddeen, M.R. *Asma'ul-Husna: The 99 Beautiful Names of Allah.* Overbrook, PA: Fellowship Press, 2002.

[37] Stark, R. *What Americans Really Believe: New Findings from the Baylor Surveys of Religion.* Waco, TX: Baylor University Press, 2008.

In addition, there are likely other categories of beliefs in God. Some of the early neurotheological research suggests that there may be another view of God which is a mystical one in which God was not a separate entity, but rather a force that permeates the entire universe. Such a mystical interpretation of God is neither "he" nor "she," nor is it punitive, critical, or distant.

As with the other definitions considered so far, God is a term for something that is essentially impossible to define. However, if we are to reflect on what God is or how people experience God, we must do our best to maintain the principle of using clear definitions so that at least we understand what the scholarly focus is at any particular moment.

Science

Since neurotheology dwells substantially in the scientific domain, it is important to reflect on what science is and how it is defined. Science arose originally from natural philosophy. Natural philosophy referred to the systematic analysis of the natural world. The term, science, derives from the Latin word *scientia* which means "knowledge." Thus, science refers to the methods by which we gain knowledge about the world around us. In ancient times, science and religion were deeply integrated. There are many examples in which science and technology were used to aid in the development of religious concepts. For example, astronomy and engineering were widely employed in the creation of some of the great religious structures such as Stonehenge or the pyramids of Egypt which were associated with elaborate religious beliefs and rituals.

In the past several hundred years, the development of scientific method has taken scientific pursuits in a radically different direction compared to both philosophy and religion. Scientific method refers to a systematic approach of acquiring empirical evidence to support future hypotheses regarding the world. The essential elements of the scientific method are generally considered to be iterations, recursions, interleavings, and orderings of the following:[38]

- characterizations which include observations, definitions, and measurements of the subject of inquiry;
- hypotheses which are theoretical or hypothetical explanations of observations and measurements of the subject;
- predictions which represent reasoning from the hypothesis or theory in an attempt to determine future outcomes;
- experiments which test all of the above to find empirical support.

---

[38] Brody, T.A., with De La Pena, L. and Hodgson, P.E. (eds.). *The Philosophy Behind Physics*. Berlin: Springer Verlag, 1994; Godfrey-Smith, P. *Theory and Reality: An Introduction to the Philosophy of Science*. Chicago, IL: University of Chicago Press, 2003.

These elements provide scientific method a way of evaluating the processes of the natural world. The *a priori* assumption of science is that the world, as we perceive it, is measurable, and that once measured, will continue to be stable such that we might infer future events from previous measurements. One of the elements of any scientific utility function is the refutability of the model. In this way, science is only as good as its last study and last hypothesis that is consistent with that study. As new data come about, scientific knowledge continues to adapt and change. It is interesting that one may question whether the scientific method adapts and changes. In a global way, the answer is "no." The notion of observing and measuring the natural world has not changed. But the ways of going about observing and measuring the natural world clearly have changed over time.

Another aspect related to science is its *a priori* assumption that simplicity tends to be better than complexity. While there are entire fields of study based upon complexity and chaos, much of science still resorts to the notion that a simple description is better than a complex one. This is the Principle of Parsimony also known as Occam's Razor. More recently, the work of Karl Popper and Richard Swinburne similarly argue that, "other things being equal—the simplest hypothesis proposed as an explanation of phenomena is more likely to be the true one than is any other available hypothesis, that its predictions are more likely to be true than those of any other available hypothesis, and that it is an ultimate a priori epistemic principle that simplicity is evidence for truth."[39] Scientists have frequently utilized Occam's Razor and the notion of simplicity as a way of dismissing the argument for the existence of God. Theists, on the other hand, have often argued that problems associated with scientific arguments without God are equally complex compared to arguments that include God. Many scientists, however, reject this argument claiming that information and investigation of the natural world requires the scientific method with its attempts to find the simplest answers to describe the universe.

One additional term to consider is "scientism" which is the belief that science will ultimately be capable of explaining everything about the universe. The essential element of this stance is that the universe is purely material in nature and that scientific method will uncover any and all facts about the universe. In this way, someone believing in scientism will reject any perspectives that appear irrational or supernatural. Further, it is considered that the natural sciences would have authority over all other interpretations of life including those that are sociological, psychological, religious, or spiritual. While this particular stance would likely be too limiting from a neurotheological perspective, as with all belief systems, it must be properly evaluated and accommodated within any overarching theoretical framework regarding the nature of the universe.

---

[39] Swinburne, R. *Simplicity as Evidence for Truth*. Milwaukee, WI: Marquette University Press, 1997.

Defining Neurotheology

Our last definition will be for "neurotheology" itself. In Chapter 1, we considered the variety of topics that fall within the rubric of neurotheology, but let us try to define the term more explicitly. Neurotheology refers to the field of study linking the neurosciences with religion and theology. Neurotheology should not be considered to be specifically limited to the evaluation of theological principles, although this certainly is an important component. However, neurotheology is, in some sense, a misnomer since it should actually refer to the totality of religion and religious experience as well as theology. This ability to consider, in a broad scope, all of the components of religion in association with a neuroscientific perspective would provide neurotheology with an abundant diversity of issues and topics that can ultimately be linked under one heading. As we shall see, the neurosciences also must be considered in a broad scope to include not only what goes on within the human brain, but within the human body as a whole. Furthermore, since the mind and brain are intimately linked, the "neuro" component of neurotheology should be considered to include psychiatry, psychology, cognitive neuroscience, genetics, endocrinology as well as other macro- and micro- perspectives of the neurosciences.

Most importantly, neurotheology should be considered a two-way street with information flowing both from the neurosciences to the religious perspective as well as from a theological perspective to the neurosciences so that ultimately, both perspectives will potentially be augmented by the dialogue. An ardent atheist, who refuses to accept any aspect of religion as possibly being correct or useful, or a devout religious person, who refuses to accept science as providing any value regarding knowledge about the world, would most likely not be considered a neurotheologian. Neurotheology insists on some modicum of acknowledgement of the value, importance, significance, and accuracy of both religion and science. Neurotheology also insists that one be open to the possibility that scholarship some day might show that either science or religion could be devoid of value. But such a determination will likely be difficult if not impossible.

Neurotheological "scholarship" should also be defined. Scholarship in neurotheology should be defined broadly and can include scientific, theological, sociological, anthropological, spiritual, and religious elements. Thus, scholarship might be more scientifically oriented—a brain imaging study of meditation, a study of the health benefits of being religious, or a study of how spiritual practices might improve quality of life and decrease crime in an inner city population—or it might be more theologically oriented—a dissertation on the implications of brain imaging studies for understanding the nature of prayer, a philosophical treatise on morality and rational thought, or a hermeneutical analysis of a sacred text with emphasis on neuropsychological elements. In short, neurotheological scholarship should be inclusive of a diverse array of approaches that might provide insight into the relationship between the mind and religion.

One other way of considering neurotheology is that it, to some degree, represents a hybrid of natural theology and natural philosophy. Natural theology, as mentioned above, refers to the branch of theology based on reason and ordinary experience. Natural philosophy was the study of nature and the physical universe that preceded present day science. Neurotheology asks scholars to evaluate religion and theology from a rational, but also scientific perspective. Neurotheology also recognizes that science might require evaluation from the religious or theological perspective. In this way, neurotheology combines elements of both natural theology and natural philosophy. However, neurotheology is also distinct since, as we have defined it, it is not beholden to either science or religion and hence does not specifically presume, *a priori*, that either the material universe or God should have priority. Rather, neurotheology strives to determine the nature of that relationship and determine priority *a posteriori*.

This overall definition of neurotheology is purposely kept brief, but extremely broad. This demonstrates the multidisciplinary nature of neurotheology and argues for an integrated framework seeking to determine how the various components of religion and spirituality are interrelated with the human mind and brain.

Transforming Definitions

One of the final issues regarding definitions is that whatever definitions might be developed or established, it is imperative to recognize that definitions by their very nature will be transformed over time. This transformation, or perhaps evolution, of definitions will be related to all of the factors we have described above. Thus, some definitions may transform because of changes in philosophical or theological considerations. Some definitions may be altered as a result of various cultural influences. Definitions will also be changed as new neurotheological data are obtained which can include both subjective and objective determinants of current definitions.

This transformational aspect of definitions should be considered another principle of neurotheology:

Principle III: Definitions in neurotheology must be considered to be dynamic, and therefore transformed by many different factors that arise from both theological and scientific inquiry.

This should not be taken to imply that all definitions must necessarily be dynamic and changeable. Rather, all definitions must be continuously evaluated and challenged to ensure their continued validity and relevance to neurotheology scholarship.

Definitions for the Principia

For this work on the principles of neurotheology, based on the above discussion, we will utilize the definitions set out below. The reason for utilizing these definitions is several fold. First, as stated in the principle of definitions, we should attempt to provide clear definitions that can then be used for initial scholarship in neurotheology, and then evolve those definitions as the field progresses. Second, definitions that are based on current ideas and concepts, generally accepted by scholars, are likely to be the most useful initially. Third, there are many ways to define terms, but neurotheology, especially in its early development, should strive to create definitions that are broad rather than narrow. This provides the best means for developing as a field by not excluding certain concepts and ideas too quickly. Finally, as neurotheology is multidisciplinary, the initial definitions will be most useful if they can be accessible by both the religious/theological perspective and the neuroscience/mind perspective. Thus, the definitions below are merely suggestions, but try to satisfy these parameters to enable the general discussion about the principles of neurotheology. However, clearer and more specific definitions over time are the goal related to the principle of definitions.

- *Brain*: This will refer to the structure of cells, molecules, and connections in the organ inside the head. This will include the neocortex, the subcortical structures, limbic system, hypothalamus, cerebellum and brainstem. It will be recognized that the brain has many connections throughout the body that we will refer to specifically when necessary.
- *Mind*: This will refer to the subjectively experienced functions that arise from the brain including our thoughts, feelings, and perceptions. It will be recognized that there is a deep interrelationship between the mind and brain. It will also be understood that while many aspects of the mind might be considered to be specifically *caused* by the brain, there may be (emphasis on "may") mind processes that exist beyond the brain, particularly in the form of consciousness or subjective awareness. However, it will be up to future investigations to determine the precise relationship between mind, brain, and consciousness.
- *Consciousness*: This refers to subjective awareness, and in the context of humans, a reflexive self-awareness. It is recognized that while consciousness might be derived from brain processes, there are also many traditions, particularly Buddhism and Hinduism, that regard consciousness as existing as a primary substantive part of the universe that causes material reality to exist rather than the other way around. This problem will also require substantial investigation to resolve.
- *Soul*: This refers to the aspect of human beings that is a bridge between our physical self and the religious or spiritual realm, particularly God. It might be considered to be the deepest level of being a spiritual person. It remains to be fully determined whether the soul exists, and if so, how it might

interact with both physical and non-physical aspects of reality (presuming the non-physical aspects also exist). It also is not clear whether the soul should refer only to human beings or whether it might also refer to other animals. And finally, it is not clear if the soul survives the body, although many traditions believe this.

- *Religion*: This term refers to a formalized set of practices and beliefs associated with a group of individuals that enable those individuals to interact with God, the Divine, or the Absolute. It is acknowledged that it is not clear at this point how large a group is required, or how acceptable the beliefs and practices are to other people in society, in order for a set of practices and beliefs to be considered a religion as opposed to a cult for example.

- *Religiousness*: This term refers to feelings, practices, and experiences associated with a particular religion.

- *Spirituality*: This term refers to the feelings, thoughts, and experiences associated with something sacred or ultimate, such as God (although God is not required for spirituality). Spirituality also can refer to some aspect of an individual that transcends all feelings, thoughts, and experiences. In fact, this latter connotation may be more accurate when defining spirituality since it is a less tangible or transcendent aspect of human beings. As with the other definitions pertaining to experiential terms, it is not clear as to whether spirituality is derivative from the brain or *vice versa*.

- *Belief*: This refers to any perception, cognition, or emotion that the brain assumes, consciously or unconsciously, to be true. This sometimes assumes a degree of evidence that supports the person's belief.

- *Faith*: This refers to a belief which may have the appearance of being based on relatively less evidence, but which is adhered to with great conviction. Faith usually pertains more particularly to religion. For the religious person, faith is adhered to with a greater degree of intensity than a simple belief since faith is accepted by the person as being grounded in a revelation made by the divine

- *Theology*: This refers to a field of scholarship that evaluates and studies the foundational concepts, doctrines, and texts of a particular religion to determine how to interpret those concepts, doctrines, and texts. A goal of theology is to create a deeper understanding of how the concepts, doctrines, and texts relate to individuals and the world. Theology attempts also to understand not just the meaning of religion, but to look into the nature of God. Augustine's definition is often cited: "Fides quaerens intellectum" (faith trying to understand). Theology more traditionally refers to the traditions of Christianity, Judaism, and Islam, but can potentially be considered a part of other traditions, perhaps even non-theistic traditions, as well.

- *God*: This will refer to a being of transcendent and supernatural power that created the world and can interact personally with the world and with human beings. As with theology, when used in this book we will be more specifically referring to a monotheistic version of God recognizing that there are many variations on this main theme. We will also try to specify when other concepts such as universal consciousness, ultimate reality, or higher power are referred to in a discussion to keep them separated from the concept of God *per se*. However, it is also recognized that the relationship between the different conceptions of universal consciousness, ultimate reality, the divine, and God remain to be fully clarified.

* *Science*: This will refer to the fields in which empirical investigation provides information about the material world (sometimes referred to as the "natural" world). It is recognized that the term "natural world" may require expanding if neurotheological research ultimately determines that science can investigate religious and spiritual phenomena, even those that appear outside of the realm of current scientific methodology.

Conclusion

We have now considered the principles of neurotheology which pertain to the definitions that will potentially be used throughout neurotheology scholarship. We can now consider all of the other principles that pertain to methods and approaches of neurotheological research. However, as we proceed, since we are focusing on general principles of neurotheology, we will try to use the broadest definitions described above, realizing that a scholar interested in pursuing a particular topic will need to narrow the definitions to their purposes.

Chapter 3

The Principles of Interaction Between Neuroscience and Theology

Interactions Between Science and Religion

Ludwig Wittgenstein stated that "philosophy is not a theory but an activity."[1] Neurotheology might be considered similarly in that it is the activity of studying religious and spiritual phenomena in association with a cognitive neuroscientific perspective. But how exactly should this relationship be construed? What are the principles of interaction between neuroscience and theology when considered from the neurotheological context? There are several important issues to consider with regard to these principles of interaction.

To begin with, we should return to Ian Barbour's four possible interactions between science and religion.[2] These interactions lead us to several principles of neurotheology with regard to the interaction between science and religion. The first type of interaction between science and religion is conflict. Neurotheology as a field of study should generally be regarded as antithetical to conflict between science and religion. After all, the very term neurotheology implies an inter-relationship rather than an exclusionary one. On the other hand, neurotheology must acknowledge the possibility for substantial conflict between science and religion. The potential for conflict between science and religion can have its roots in either perspective. For example, religious beliefs virtually always begin with a supernatural foundation. Thus, from any religious perspective, science, which has a natural foundation, is essentially irrelevant to a religion's fundamental beliefs. In this way, at their most fundamental levels, religions perceive science in a somewhat conflicted manner. Of course, religions have great interest in the natural world specifically as it pertains to human beings, human behavior, and human involvement in that world. To this end, religions often perceive science as best relating to God's immanence in the natural world.[3] From the scientific perspective, since religion is based on the supernatural, which is beyond the scope of scientific inquiry, religion is deemed as essentially irrelevant to science's fundamental approach. In this way, at its most fundamental levels, science perceives religions

---

[1]   Wittgenstein, L. *Tractatus Logico-Philosophicus*. Translated by C.K. Ogden. New York, NY: Cosimo Books, 2007.

[2]   Barbour, I.G. *Religion in an Age of Science*. New York, NY: Harper & Row, 1990.

[3]   Peacocke, A. *Theology for a Scientific Age: Being and Becoming—Natural, Divine, and Human*. Minneapolis, MN: Fortress Press, 1993.

in a somewhat conflicted manner. Of course, scientific disciplines can have substantial interests in how religion pertains to human beings, human behavior, and human involvement in the world. This is what is referred to as the science of religion, or the scientific study of religion.

Neurotheology might approach this conflict from a new perspective. In fact, the following should be considered the next principle of neurotheology:

Principle IV: Neurotheology should seek to understand the specific nature of the conflict between science and religion, focusing on the nature of the human mind and/or brain as mediating this conflict.

To this extent, we might begin to understand how the brain establishes binary opposites as categories and proceeds to allow these two opposites to "battle it out" on a perceptual, cognitive, or emotional level. Thus, neurotheology would strive to understand why the brain, and subsequently the mind, would have an interest in supporting an oppositional perspective between scientific and religious ideologies. Neurotheology may even be able to establish if one of these opposites should assume priority over the other. However, short of this possibility, neurotheological research can at best hope to better evaluate and understand the conflict between science and religion.

The second type of interaction between science and religion is that of mutual independence from each other. In some ways, this position is not substantially different from the first, although it is without the antagonistic perspective described above. This notion of "non-overlapping magisteria" implies that science and religion, at their cores, are such fundamentally different approaches that they cannot even address the same topics. Neurotheology would similarly have problems with this type of interaction between science and religion for many of the same reasons mentioned above. Neurotheology would, in fact, argue that while there may be certain topics which meet this non-overlapping criteria, there are, in fact, many potential areas of overlap. This leads us to the next neurotheological principle of interaction between science and religion:

Principle V: Neurotheology should, until such time that it can be definitively shown that non-overlapping magisteria actually exists, strive to evaluate such a relationship while remaining open to the possibility of a fully integrated interaction between science and religion.

Of course, there are those who argue that the notion of non-overlapping magisteria has already been clearly demonstrated. However, since there are also those who do not give credence to the notion of non-overlapping magisteria, it is incumbent upon neurotheology to try to understand both perspectives as fully as possible, especially from a perceptual, cognitive, and emotional standpoint. Neurotheology might be capable of ascertaining the validity of the non-overlapping magisteria concept for both those who accept it as well as those who do not.

Neurotheology has more in common with the third type of interaction between science and religion, namely dialogue. Within the term "neurotheology" there is already a sense of dialogue since it contains elements of both science and religion within one word. In order to create such a combination, it would seem that a dialogue must be implied. And this becomes the next principle of interaction between science and religion:

Principle VI: Neurotheology should strive to foster dialogue between science and religion in order to better understand both perspectives.

As an academic discipline, it is such dialogue that would be crucial to any course, dissertation, program, or department. Anyone engaging in neurotheological scholarship should be fully aware and interested in engaging in extensive dialogue between different perspectives that are under the overarching heading of neurotheology. One would certainly hope that such dialogue would be constructive in nature rather than destructive. Neurotheology should also be willing to explore the actual nature of such dialogue. Questions that could be asked include:

1. Are perceptions, cognitions, or emotions, most important in the dialogue between science and religion?
2. Which religious ideas or beliefs can most easily be brought into a dialogue, and conversely, which religious ideas or beliefs have the most difficulty?
3. If dialogue implies language, which language is most appropriate? Is it philosophy, theology, anthropology, sociology, or science, or some new hybrid?
4. How do sacred texts and scientific research enter into the dialogue?
5. What are the perceptual, cognitive, and emotional barriers that different individuals have that may prevent them from engaging in this dialogue?
6. If there are barriers, what approach should be taken, if any, to try to break through such barriers, or would it be better to leave them intact?

The final type of interaction between science and religion is that of integration. This certainly would represent neurotheology at its core. However, as mentioned above, neurotheology must be fully aware of all of the types of interactions, and even embrace such interactions as part of its overall goals. However, in returning to the integration of science and religion, this appears to lead us toward an important principle.

This principle is based upon the notion that neurotheology as a scholarly field of inquiry, should be considered a "two-way street" with information flowing both from the neurosciences to the theological perspective as well as from the theological perspective to the neurosciences. In other words, neurotheology should not be considered the "neuroscientific study of religious or theological concepts," a procrustean trap that many scholars have fallen into. Theology and religion must also be able to inform us freely about neuroscience and how we interpret the human person from a psychological, social, and spiritual perspective. By enabling a free exchange of ideas, data, and information, neurotheology can achieve a very high level of sophistication. This yields the final neurotheological principle of interaction between science and religion:

Principle VII: Neuroscientific and theological perspectives must be considered to be* comparable contributors *to neurotheological investigations.

By comparable, I mean that both perspectives should have similar, and reciprocal, emphasis in the overall dialogue between neuroscience and theology. However, it must also be clear that there are investigations and arguments that will sometimes be weighted more towards neuroscience or towards theology. For example, an analysis of a specific sacred text might lead to a primarily theological interpretation with minor assistance from the neuroscientific perspective regarding a particular logical argument. On the other hand, a study designed to explore the brain changes during a particular religious practice will more likely require emphasis on neuroscientific methodology. Again, though, any interpretations from such investigations should strive to include both perspectives.

It should be re-emphasized that those scholars and researchers in other fields may not necessarily find this principle applies to their respective areas of work. After all, a biology researcher should not be expected to include any discussion of religion in the context of cloning a mouse genome. Similarly, philosophical and theological arguments might ultimately not require any input from science. Such interactions are more along the lines of the "non-overlapping magisteria." However, neurotheology represents a fundamentally different form of scholarship. Its very name and essence demands a mutual co-interaction between science and religion. Thus, anyone engaging in neurotheology must be, at the minimum, open to both perspectives. It is also reasonable that the individual would feel stronger leanings and biases towards one perspective or the other. But ideally this would not interfere with the individual approaching neurotheology with a healthy respect for both perspectives.

The ability to move between and incorporate science and religion is the great strength of neurotheology as a field, but it is also a very problematic weakness. Many individuals who reside more squarely in the scientific or theological domains might be very opposed to this integrated approach. Scientists might consider the research weak and atypical. Theologians might consider the religious concepts misguided. Such critiques are appropriately directed at inherent shortcomings in neurotheology. After all, it is most difficult to study religious and spiritual phenomena from a scientific perspective. I have previously argued that one of the reasons for doing such research is to strengthen scientific methodology so that it can better observe the complex phenomena associated with religion and spirituality. On the other hand, I have also argued that the scientific pursuits of neurotheology might potentially lead to interesting conceptualizations in the field of theology. Any cross-disciplinary field will naturally have difficulty integrating the disparate systems of study. However, this should not deter neurotheological research, but rather stimulate interest in developing better techniques and measures for improved research.

There is another important issue regarding the principle of interaction between neuroscience and theology. This regards the direction of the causal arrow when considering the results of neurotheological scholarship. While it is very tempting for individuals to want to prove or disprove either a particular theory, or more specifically a particular religious belief or belief system, anyone engaging in neurotheology should be careful when pointing the causal arrow in one direction or another. By this I mean that any analysis or interpretation of data needs to carefully consider where causality has its influence. And to rephrase what we considered in the previous chapter, neurotheological scholarship should not specifically presume, *a priori*, that either the material universe or God should have *causal* priority. Rather, neurotheology should strive to determine the causal nature of that relationship and determine the causal priority *a posteriori*.

As an example, take a hypothetical study in which functional brain imaging is used to measure brain activity in nuns while having the experience of being in God's presence. If we find that there are specific changes in the brain associated with such an experiential state, what causal conclusions can actually be drawn? The most that can be said is: there are certain brain activity levels associated with the experience of being in God's presence. The results do not suggest either that the brain activity *caused* the experience to occur or whether the findings reflected the brain's *response* to the experience of actually being in God's presence. The former interpretation supports the non-religious perspective while the latter interpretation supports the religious perspective. But the brain scan only suggests that there is a link, and does not necessarily help to point the causal arrow one way or the other. On the other hand, it may be possible to conceive of a study in which the causal arrow can be more specifically determined, but that too must be considered carefully.

Similarly, let us grant that a particular study on the effects of intercessory prayer actually yields a positive result such as: cancer patients who are prayed for live longer than those who are not. In this case, the results show that the prayer process improves cancer survival, but does not clearly demonstrate whether the prayer is actually being answered by God who causes the effect. It may be that human conscious thought actually causes the effect, sometimes referred to as distant intentionality. On the other hand, it could be related to some other factor associated with the study. If the study had a negative result (that is, cancer survival was not affected by intercessory prayer), then does that prove that God does not exist? It is imperative that the results only show that this specific study design does not result in a positive effect in cancer patients. It may be that there is no God and no effect. But it might also be that there is a God who simply chose not to "help out."

Importance of Skepticism in Neurotheology

As can be seen from the examples above, neurotheology requires substantial questioning and healthy skepticism. However, because of the multidisciplinary nature of neurotheology, skepticism should be tempered with optimism. Destructive skepticism leads only to a closing of possibilities and neurotheology should strive to maintain possibilities as long as the scholarship and research allows. Constructive skepticism provides the impetus for further research and scholarship. By asking questions of both science and religion, neurotheology can explore the intersection between the two far more thoroughly. This leads us to the next principle:

Principle VIII: Neurotheology must maintain a healthy, but constructive, skepticism about the nature of science and religion as it pertains to humanity.

This principle implies that skepticism should be directed at both scientific and religious concepts and results. In fact, historical evidence has shown that both perspectives can have their limitations and both can change over time. Thus, it is appropriate to question and also to be skeptical of information and data that appears contrary to existing paradigms. But skepticism must also be allowed to give way to new information and new paradigms. Rather than simply rejecting ideas because they do not make sense or do not fit with current paradigms, neurotheology could encourage scholars to evaluate fully all of the possibilities and to continue to be open to new ones as they develop.

For neurotheology to be a viable field of scholarship, it is important to utilize skepticism to help determine which approaches and lines of questioning will be the most fruitful and the least problematic. Neurotheologians should encourage each other in their own work so as to bring as many different perspectives to bear on the complex topics that neurotheology attempts to tackle.

Passion for Inquiry

A crucial element of neurotheology, which really should be true for all academic fields, is a passion or enthusiasm for inquiry. By this I mean that scholars should foster a love of asking questions, especially hard ones, even if they are not sure if the questions can be answered. The reason this is particularly relevant to neurotheology is because many of the questions are quite difficult, if not impossible to answer. However, this should not discourage us from continuing to explore the many issues within neurotheology. Part of the problem with neurotheology is its multidisciplinary nature which makes it complicated to evaluate and answer adequately many of its biggest questions. On the other hand, this problem might also be neurotheology's best asset since we often will not be aware of how specific lines of inquiry might open up answers to other, apparently unrelated questions. For example, a study exploring the effects of meditation on depression may reveal an important relationship between meditation and feelings of compassion. Or perhaps, different brain structures might turn out to be highly involved in a particular religious experience even though they were not believed to be. Regardless, bringing many different lines of inquiry to neurotheological questions will probably provide the approach most likely to help answer them.

Thus, we can consider a "principle of passionate inquiry" to be an important foundation for neurotheological scholarship:

Principle IX: Neurotheology should be pursued with a great passion for inquiry, with an openness and a willingness to explore a broad array of topics and ideas.

The second part of this principle is equally important. It stresses the need not only to have a passion for asking the difficult questions, but to be open to the many possible approaches that might yield and answer. And perhaps, it suggests that scholars look in areas that may not even be expected to be related.

In a similar vein, the passion for inquiry should also encourage scholars to be open to conflicting or divergent ideas. Especially in this early stage of development of neurotheology, becoming too confined by one theory or one point of view might become detrimental for the field as well as for the individual scholar. Furthermore, one would hope that the rest of the academic world would not view neurotheology as being too limited or too related to one line of inquiry. For example, since some of the early research pertaining to neurotheology involved brain imaging studies of specific practices such as prayer and meditation, critics cited that these practices were not religion *per se* and that such studies were irrelevant on that basis. The problem with this criticism is that any neurotheologian should clearly recognize that the brain imaging studies were only one small piece of a much larger puzzle that neurotheology is attempting to evaluate. It is important to evaluate religious practices, but one should be cautious about how much can be extrapolated to other aspects of religion. This is true for both the neurotheologian as well as the critic.

Finally, since the goal of neurotheology should also be to help others explore the fundamental or ultimate questions of human kind, it is essential that the passion for inquiry be extended to those outside of neurotheology. Regardless of a person's field of scholarship, religious beliefs, or spiritual orientation, everyone should be regarded as potentially benefiting from neurotheology. The neurotheologian should reach out to engage others in their own questioning and encourage those others to continue to ask questions and remain open to the vast realm of possible answers. And when another individual has no interest in neurotheology, it might be important at least to explore what the resistance is, in order to determine the factors that prevent that individual's beliefs from accepting a conversation regarding neurotheology.

Neurotheology and Paradigm Shifts

An important element of the interaction between science and religion in the context of neurotheology is whether such scholarship would result in paradigm shifts. It will be important to ensure that a neurotheologian be open to the possibility of paradigm shifts resulting from their scholarship. Of course, the paradigm shift could potentially occur within science or religion. But it is crucial that the scholar be aware that these shifts are possible and be prepared to manage such a shift. In fact, it would be helpful to ensure that all individuals involved in the study of neurotheology be open to these potential shifts in order to facilitate them should they occur.

Let us explore what types of paradigm shifts might occur and how neurotheology might address them. It should be stressed that the following are a few hypothetical examples of scientific and religious shifts. Whether these or other types of shifts occur is something for future neurotheological scholarship.

There are several lines of scholarship that might result in scientific paradigm shifts. A scientific paradigm shift might occur as the result of a better understanding of the effects of consciousness on the world (distant intentionality); the effect of intercessory prayer on health; and the nature of material reality. Perhaps research studying the effects of consciousness on the world might show that concentrating on a random number generator might actually affect the generator's function.[4] If such data would ultimately be strongly supported, it would suggest that the current scientific paradigm in which consciousness exists only within the brain, only affecting the individual's body, might be wrong. The notion of consciousness and its function would have to be radically altered to incorporate some way in which consciousness could actually "reach out" and affect something in the world. But how would such a shift actually occur? Would scientists be open to the new data or try to reject it? Neurotheologians should be ready to deal with the potential results of their work with regard to consciousness.

A variation on the study of distant intentionality, which is also more relevant to neurotheology, is the study of intercessory prayer. If a study confirmed that intercessory prayer for heart surgery patients actually resulted in significantly improved survival, we might have to modify the prevailing theory of biomedicine. The current theory states that the human body is not affected by external supernatural forces that cannot be easily measured by any scientific device. Of course, it would be further interesting to attempt to discern whether such a finding was merely another version of distant intentionality or actually represented yet another mechanism—the actual existence of God. In spite of the obvious interpretation problems, if a study would strongly support the notion that intercessory prayer worked, then how would that change current medical science and practice? Would

---

4   Helfrich, W. "Is the psychokinetic effect as found with binary random number generators suitable to account for mind-brain interaction?" *J Sci Expl.* 2007;21:689-705.

we not have to make these changes and put new emphasis on intercessory prayer as an intervention for improving health?

What if neurotheology discovers a new way of considering the actual nature of reality itself? This can potentially happen as both the neuroscientific perspective and the religious or spiritual perspective combine to evaluate reality. What would such an integration look like? Would such an integration reveal a new perspective on the nature of matter? Perhaps it will be found that matter is the result of spiritual forces, or possibly a universal consciousness. Perhaps the material world will be found to be secondary to some spiritual or absolute realm which science cannot readily address. Alternatively, perhaps the scientific methods must be changed in order to better evaluate what is "apparently beyond" what is currently considered to be material reality. In this way, what is currently considered to be material reality would need to be expanded. This could substantially change what science considers to be data or evidence, and instead replace it with subjective or spiritual experience. The neurotheologian must be aware that such a shift, while perhaps unlikely, is certainly possible. In this way, great care must be taken in order to be as certain as possible before making such a paradigm shift claim. But once it appears certain, then a paradigm shift should be quickly engaged.

Neurotheology should also consider the possibility of religious paradigm shifts. While this is certainly a fear among religious individuals, and appropriately so, it is conceivable that several different paradigm shifts might occur. A potentially major paradigm shift would be to determine that one particular religious tradition is the correct one while all others are false. This would have dire consequences for those who do not adhere to the correct religion. While this is highly unlikely, a neurotheologian should be open, at least to some degree, that such a possibility might exist. But the possibility of establishing one religion as correct over others is a potentially substantial source of fear among those who are religious since no one will want to risk losing their religious beliefs. This could be an impediment to future research since religious individuals might not be interested in participating in research that might potentially prove their religion to be false. However, while this possibility must be considered, it should never be a goal of neurotheology to try to prove or disprove one religious belief or another.

Another possible paradigm shift that would be equally disturbing would be neurotheology scholarship that discovers that *all* religions are wrong. Again, this might be unlikely, and should clearly not be the goal of neurotheology, but it is nonetheless a possibility. Neurotheology must remain open to the possibility that religion is incorrect in its understanding of the world. To some extent, neurotheology must explore the potential impact that such a result would have on religious individuals. How would this be received? Would religious individuals disregard this paradigm shift without truly evaluating the information and data? If so, would that leave them with a hollow faith? Would they have to be forced into the new paradigm shift? Again, a neurotheologian should be open to the possibility of such a paradigm shift and how this might affect others and society.

The point of the above discussion is to elaborate on the most extreme paradigm shifts that might possibly arise from neurotheological scholarship, even though they are probably not likely. However, it is most important that neurotheologians be open to the possibility of these paradigm shifts. They should protect against too rapid a shift to ensure that the data and scholarship truly represent a shift. And then once it is clear that a paradigm shift must occur, the neurotheologian should support such a shift and carefully relate this shift to other scholars, as well as to the world in general.

Reprise of the Four Interactions Between Science and Religion

Now that we have considered several aspects of the interactions between science and religion, we can expand on the ability of neurotheology to address each of the four possible interactions between science and religion. This will help us to understand more precisely how neurotheology might provide a new perspective for dealing with complex issues related to the intersection of science and religion. With regard to the conflict between science and religion, neurotheology can help to better characterize and define the conflict. This might be crucial since it is possible that conflicts may actually represent a misunderstanding rather than a definite rift between science and religion. For example, neurotheology might help in evaluating the abortion issue. In such a case, there is frequently a sharp disagreement between religious and non-religious individuals as to what constitutes life. Both types of individuals might turn to religion or science as a means for bolstering their positions. Clearly the abortion issue is a highly emotionally charged topic with science and religion frequently taking opposing sides.

How might neurotheology approach such a problem? Neurotheology might start by asking about the phenomenology of the beliefs on both sides of the argument. Is the case for the pro-life individual derived from sacred texts, beliefs about the soul, beliefs about what constitutes life, or notions of individual autonomy? Similar questions can be raised regarding the pro-choice side. Is the case for the pro-choice individual derived from sacred texts, beliefs about the soul, beliefs about what constitutes life, or notions of individual autonomy? Neurotheology can delve further to address what are the cognitive and emotional aspects of each of the arguments. In fact, neurotheology might consider research to explore specific brain changes associated with people confronting various aspects of the abortion debate to determine which issues are the most important, most emotional, or most able to change someone's beliefs.

There is another important side to the abortion issue which pertains to ethics and morality. A related topic of neuroethics might be useful, in conjunction with neurotheology, to help evaluate the moral grounds from which the two opposing camps make their arguments. Again, are there certain brain areas involved in the moral thought processes associated with being pro-life or pro-choice? With this line of inquiry, we might ask whether abortion beliefs should relate to society as a whole, or to those who believe in a particular religion. While all of these questions from the neurotheological line of inquiry may not necessarily resolve the conflict, they can certainly provide an important new perspective and might allow for opposing individuals to be able to better consider the arguments from the other side. Optimistically, one can hope that allowing better understanding of the opposing side would at least contribute to more effective dialogue.

In the context of non-overlapping magisteria, one common issue, and certainly primary to religion, is that of God's existence. Many, including Stephen J. Gould, have argued that since God is considered to be supernatural, it is impossible for science to even address the question of God's existence. Thus, the belief in God's existence can reside wholly in religion while science can focus primarily on the natural world. From a neurotheological perspective, the notion of non-overlapping magisteria is comprised of cognitive and possibly emotional elements that have their roots in the brain's function. The primary component of non-overlapping magisteria is the setting up of opposites which cannot be bridged. The ability of the brain to evaluate opposites is crucial to its overall function—letting us know what is good and what is bad, for example. Neurotheology can consider how the brain establishes opposites. Are there certain aspects of opposites that make them impossible to overcome? It is interesting that there are examples of ideologies in which opposites are reconciled on a superordinate level. Hinduism is one approach in which the notion of absolute good actually subsumes both good and evil.[5] However, this ability to provide a holistic compromise between opposites cannot always be realized. Neurotheology might be capable of determining if and how such a compromise might be crafted with respect to God's existence. But such a compromise might not be tenable for a religious individual, or for a scientist for that matter.

Another approach to the issue of God's existence is whether neurotheology can propose a study to evaluate how the brain perceives reality and compare the belief in God's existence to the belief in other elements of reality, or perhaps the belief in God's non-existence? In other words, if the brain reacts to objects in reality such as the United States or a computer, then can we determine if the brain reacts the same way to God? If so, the results would suggest that at least for the brain, God is just as real as the United States. If the results show a difference, then for the brain, God is perceived differently. Of course, this still may not solve the existence question since we might perceive different objects in reality differently. Alternatively, we might experience different states of reality differently (we will consider this later).

Neurotheology also offers one other potentially interesting perspective that has to do with evaluating the phenomenology and biology of mystical experiences. Interestingly, mystical experiences have frequently been described as enabling individuals to perceive ultimate reality, and hence, come to understand the

---

[5]   Eliot, D. and Rohit, D. *The Essential Vedanta: A New Source Book of Advaita Vedanta*. Bloomington, IN: World Wisdom, 2004.

"true nature" of the universe with or without God. It would seem that a thorough evaluation of mystical experiences specifically as they relate to the realization of God's existence is a prime example of what neurotheology can do in the context of the non-overlapping interaction between science and religion. Finally, neurotheology must be able to accept the possibility of a universe both with, and without, God. This would require neurotheology to consider either a neuroscience of theology or a theology of neuroscience. Either approach might provide useful information, even if it can be determined at some point that one view point is commensurate with actual reality.

Even if neuroscience ultimately proves that religion is nothing more than a manifestation of the brain's functions, neurotheology still remains viable in helping to explain to people why this is so and how religion can be modified or even eliminated to accommodate this new information. Conversely, if it is ultimately determined that there unequivocally is a God, then neurotheology may be able to help develop scientific methodologies that accommodate the truthfulness of religion in general, or of a specific religion. But we must be careful that either a neuroscientific or theological approach does not end up proving itself simply because of its own initial *a priori* assumptions and biases. This is a frequent problem especially surrounding the topics associated with neurotheology. For example, if a scholar wanted to disprove religion, they might end up designing the study in such a way that the results support their initial assumptions (for example, using brain imaging to show that religion is nothing more than in the brain). But again, we must be careful and rigorous in how data are interpreted and evaluated so that we do not arrive at false conclusions.

In terms of dialogue between science and religion, neurotheology appears to provide an opportune approach. For example, the nature of consciousness is one topic which can be evaluated from both a scientific or religious perspective. Science can evaluate consciousness from the perspective of the brain structures and functions that underlie the maintenance of consciousness.[6] On the other hand, religious and theological interpretations of consciousness suggest that consciousness itself may be the fundamental "stuff of the universe" as espoused by the panpsychism philosophy.[7] In such a case, the brain derives from consciousness rather than the other way around. Neurotheology can play an important role in fostering a dialogue between scientific and theological perspectives on consciousness. Both perspectives might inform the other without necessarily requiring a full integration of the two approaches. In fact, it has been remarked by several researchers studying highly proficient meditators that these individuals, who have incredible control of their conscious processes, might be ideal subjects

---

[6]   Chalmers, D.J. "How can we construct a science of consciousness?" In Gazzaniga, M. (ed.), *The Cognitive Neurosciences*. Cambridge, MA: MIT Press, 2004.

[7]   David, S. "Panpsychism as an underlying theme in western philosophy: a survey paper." *J Conscious Studies*. 2003;10:4-46.

to study from a scientific perspective.[8] In these ways, science may not assess the reality of their religious or ideological views, but can assess their basis in biology. Either way, such evaluations can enhance the dialogue between science and religion.

Neurotheology has important implications for the potential integrative approach between science and religion. This may be a particularly lofty goal for neurotheology, even though the term itself suggests such an integration. The integrated approach might be applied to health and well being in such a way that we develop a new paradigm of health care that seeks to manage patients by evaluating their social, psychological, biological, and spiritual dimensions.[9] A fully integrated health care approach would consider all of these dimensions as relating to each other and needing to be managed together.

Another integrated approach would be in the context of theology itself, or more specifically a metatheology or megatheology. The notion here is that neurotheology provides an integration of science and religion that might allow for new ways of actually considering the sciences and theology. We must proceed cautiously in this regard. However, we also should not fear whatever possible outcomes we might find through neurotheological scholarship.

Principle X: We must proceed cautiously, but not fear whatever possible outcomes we might find through neurotheological scholarship.

The issue here is that neurotheology may sometimes tread in very problematic areas laced with intense emotions. Research exploring the meaning and nature of religious or spiritual experiences may have profound implications for religion, theology, or science. If we are to be truly open to all perspectives, we must acknowledge a certain *a priori* acceptance of whatever ultimate conclusions we arrive at so that we do not fear results and disregard them incorrectly. In fact, neurotheology should strive to foster greater acceptance and understanding of different and novel concepts as they pertain to science and religion. Perhaps new scientific or theological endeavors can be attempted that truly integrate both perspectives. This obviously will be no simple feat since their methodologies are often incompatible. But neurotheology takes that first step by attempting to merge these two methodologies in one overarching discipline.

---

[8]   Lutz, A. and Thompson, E. "Neurophenomenology integrating subjective experience and brain dynamics in the neuroscience of consciousness." *J Conscious Studies*. 2003;9: 31-52.

[9]   Monti, D.A. and Beitman, B.D. (eds.). *Integrative Psychiatry*. New York, NY: Oxford University Press, 2009; Kligler, B. and Lee, R. (eds.). *Integrative Medicine: Principles and Practice*. New York, NY: McGraw-Hill, 2004.

Neurotheology as a Metatheology

A metatheology can be understood as an attempt to evaluate the overall principles underlying any and all religions or ultimate belief systems and their theologies.[10] A metatheology comprises both the general principles describing, and implicitly the rules for constructing, any concrete theological system. In and of itself, a metatheology would not embrace one particular theology, since it consists of rules and descriptions about how any and all specific theologies are structured. Is it possible that neurotheology, as presented in this book, may be an excellent metatheology? While considering the principles of neurotheology throughout this work, we might find ourselves elaborating a metatheology. After all, the principles of neurotheology can help to establish a field of scholarship that is theoretically applicable to any and all theological systems since all such systems interact with the human brain and mind.

Another principle in particular relates more specifically to the neuroscientific perspective of how the brain affects all of our perceptions, thoughts, and feelings. Thus, "the brain is what processes all external and internal information into a coherent rendition of reality." This notion applies to many different fields of study, but also equally applies to neurotheology:

Principle XI: The brain has universal functions and thus all religious beliefs and all religious systems can be considered from a neurotheological hermeneutic.

This principle also speaks directly to the potential applicability of neurotheology as a metatheology. Let us explore more specifically the requirements of a metatheology to determine if neurotheology might be one. First, a metatheology must help describe how and why foundational, creation, and soteriological doctrines are formed. Second, it must describe how and why such doctrines are elaborated into complex logical systems which we call specific theologies. Third, it must describe how and why the basic doctrines and certain aspects of their theological elaborations are expressed in the behaviors that we call ceremonial rituals.

Neurotheology appears to be poised to address these three constitutive demands of a metatheology and should pursue its potential applicability as a metatheology.

Principle XII: Neurotheological scholarship should pursue its potential applicability as a metatheology.

Neurotheology seeks to explore the nature of foundational doctrines, their origins, and their reciprocal interactions with the human brain. Neurotheology also seeks to understand the complex processes associated with the development of theological

---

[10]   d'Aquili, E.G. and Newberg, A.B. *The Mystical Mind: Probing the Biology of Religious Experience*. Minneapolis, MN: Fortress Press, 1999.

systems, specifically as they have reciprocal interactions with brain processes. Neurotheology also attempts to understand many of the practical elements of religions, such as ritual, in the context of their reciprocal interactions with the human brain. Lastly, any metatheology must account for a broad array of religious and spiritual experiences ranging from the mild to the intense mystical experiences derived from practices such as meditation or prayer.

To summarize this section, therefore, we can see that neurotheology may constitute a great formal apparatus for better understanding foundational doctrines, their theological elaboration, their incarnation and resolution in ceremonial ritual, as well as the otherworldly, transcendent, or mystical experiences that certain practitioners of all religions enjoy.

Neurotheology as a Megatheology

We might consider one additional possibility regarding the nature of neurotheology as a field: whether neurotheology might ultimately constitute a "megatheology." A megatheology should contain content of such a universal nature that it could be adopted by most, if not all, of the world's great religions as a basic element without any serious violation of their essential doctrines.[11] For example, some have argued that Buddhist thought, particularly with regard to meditation practices and the nature of the human mind, is of such a universal content that one could be Buddhist and still adhere to other religious traditions such as Christianity or Judaism. The argument would suggest that one can maintain Christian or Jewish beliefs and still embrace key tenets of Buddhism. Can neurotheology generate content about which there can be meaningful speculation from a universal perspective? To answer such a question, it might be necessary to explore which experiences appear universally in every religious tradition. The most interesting one, which we will consider in detail later, is the absolute unitary experience in which all things are experienced as a total oneness—an experience that appears to be expressed in some form in virtually every religious tradition.

A neurotheological evaluation of such experiences may lead to an understanding of either their true universality across traditions, or perhaps their true distinctiveness across traditions. If the former turns out to be the case, with every religion finding a way to tap into an absolute unitary state, then the added perspective of neurotheology may help establish a universal theological paradigm that incorporates essential elements from all traditions, as well as incorporating science itself. Thus, it is not impossible that neurotheology could lead to a megatheology. What this will look like, and whether a megatheology that derives from neurotheology would be helpful to anyone, only time will tell.

---

[11]   d'Aquili, E.G., Newberg, A.B. *The Mystical Mind: Probing the Biology of Religious Experience*. Minneapolis, MN: Fortress Press, 1999.

However, it seems that such potential may be a highly exciting development from neurotheology.

Principle XIII: Neurotheological scholarship should pursue its potential applicability as a megatheology.

Again, only if the scholarship is careful would there be such a potential for a megatheology. And while there would be appropriate trepidation from religious traditions regarding the possibility of a megatheology arising from neurotheology, it must be remembered that the definition of megatheology implies that it must be acceptable to all religions (and even the non-religious). This is certainly a tall order. One reason for neurotheology's potential in this regard is that its basis rests on two universal elements—religion and the human brain. By attempting to link these elements, any theological concepts that arise might have the capability to apply to all traditions in some form or another.

Neurotheological scholarship might also help determine approaches that can facilitate individuals seeking spiritual or religious paths. Neurotheology may help to show the best pathways for a given individual from a particular tradition. For example, given the theological goal of understanding the nature of God, neurotheology might yield fruitful insights for an individual from any particular tradition. Neurotheology might suggest methods of meditation or prayer that appear to be particularly effective towards attaining the targeted spiritual goals. Or perhaps, neurotheology might stress the importance of waiting for spiritual insights rather than striving for them. Regardless, the point is that neurotheology might provide ideas that are useful regardless of an individual's theological perspective.

While the notion of neurotheology as a megatheology is on one hand grandiose, and on the other, difficult if not impossible to achieve, it should not be completely discounted either. In spite of the emphasis of current theology on the importance of the plurality of religious traditions, attempts have always been made at trying to find a universalizing force in the context of religious and spiritual beliefs. Neurotheology would hopefully be capable of accounting for both the plurality of religious traditions and understanding the significance and distinctiveness of their theologies, while also striving for some of the universalizing concepts that exist across traditions.

Chapter 4

General Principles of
Neurotheological Investigations

We must now explore several principles that will provide a more general or overarching approach to neurotheological investigations. This will be followed later by more specific principles pertaining to a variety of methodological issues that arise in the course of neurotheological scholarship. Some of these principles will arise more from the neuroscientific perspective while others will arise more from the theological one. However, they are all equally important in developing an appropriate neurotheological foundation.

The Principle of Rigor

The first principle with regard to neurotheological investigations might be considered the "principle of rigor." The overarching basis of this principle was previously stated in the introductory chapter:

Principle XIV: For neurotheological investigations, the scientific and theological aspects of these pursuits should be kept as rigorous as possible.

On one hand, this might be an obvious statement. However, in the early development of any nascent field, it is frequently the case that studies are not highly rigorous. This has certainly been one of the criticisms of neurotheological research. There are several reasons for this that derive out of a number of practical limitations that prevent adequate rigor. One of the first limitations is that since the new field of neurotheology is not well established, it is not clear which methods, approaches, or principles are necessary. Usually, it takes many years along with many false starts, in order to slowly mold a new scholarly endeavor into a mature exploration. This is not unlike Thomas Kuhn's concept of a scientific revolution which requires substantial amounts of data and development before the current establishment accepts a new paradigm.[1]

Another limitation is funding. It is well known in the biomedical community that most important research studies require substantial amounts of funding. Typical funding on grants can easily exceed one million dollars over a four to five year period on many grants sponsored by the National Institutes of Health. Larger

---

[1]   Kuhn, T.S. *The Structure of Scientific Revolutions*. Chicago, IL: University of Chicago Press, 1970.

projects such as the Human Genome Project can run into the tens or hundreds of millions of dollars. When a field involving scientific investigations first develops, there are not typically established funding sources. This is particularly problematic for multidisciplinary fields such as neurotheology since they do not fall into any of the existing categories. With a lack of funding comes an inability to perform studies with adequate rigor, power, and detail. Many times, early studies are considered to be pilot studies because they may involve a limited number of subjects, measures, time, and resources. In such a case, rigor is difficult to maintain, but it is hoped that the pilot data or information will be useful for supporting future larger studies, and perhaps, make funding somewhat easier the next time.

Another important limitation is the number of scholars actively involved in such research. For example, there are still only a handful of researchers who have utilized functional brain imaging to study different spiritual states or practices. Larger, more established fields, have a critical mass of scholars who can have mutual communication, annual meetings, and collaborations. All of this helps to push the research forward and enhance its rigor. Early in the development of a field, the limited number of scholars makes it difficult to create a substantial amount of cross collaboration. In part, this is because the scholars may be involved in related, but fairly distinctive areas of research. For example, a theologian trying to understand the psychological correlates of forgiveness may have very little in common with a clinical researcher testing if the rosary decreases anxiety in cancer patients. But both studies can fall under the larger heading of neurotheological studies. Thus, as larger numbers of scholars participate in this research, there will be greater collaboration, more studies, and recognition of the issues required to improve the rigor of studies.

A crucial part of increasing the number of scholars is developing new scholars through education. Again, a nascent field has few established training programs or educational opportunities. But even if several neurotheology programs became established in the near future so that a growing number of students begin to explore the field, it may take a decade or more before these students are established as independent scholars or investigators. Thus, for neurotheology to become fully developed may require many decades.

Assuming a level of overall development that allows for improved scholarship, there is another inherent problem that relates to maintaining a high level of rigor. All too often, studies that pertain to neurotheology may end up appearing to be rigorous in either the scientific or theological domains, but not both. Since most scholars are likely to be proficient in one domain more than the other, a scientist might perform a well thought out research study which ultimately misses an important theological issue and a theologian might have a strong foundation in religion, but not approach science as rigorously as possible. It may be that neurotheology requires scholars with substantial training in both theology and neuroscience. However, both types of training involve substantial time commitments as well as two very different coursework and scholarly projects.

A final obstacle to maintaining rigor in neurotheological research is that the field itself may pose fundamental constraints on the quality of that research. As we will consider later, there are many methodological problems with neurotheological research that are unique compared to other scholarly pursuits. For example, it may not be that problematic to identify study populations or develop appropriate theological arguments independently, but an integrated approach greatly complicates these methodological issues. Thus, the principle of rigor must have an important caveat: rigor should be maintained, but with full acknowledgement that the topics of study may not be able to be studied using the same methods that are more commonly used in either traditional scientific studies or theological studies. Thus, we might have ultimately to redefine "rigor" so that we can appropriately use this term in the context of neurotheology.

The Principle of Assumptions

Assumptions are made in virtually every field of research and scholarship. There are often fundamental *a priori* assumptions that every field requires in order to begin the process of scholarship. For example, science has the *a priori* assumption that the world is as we measure and analyze it. Religions have as their *a priori* assumption the existence of God.

The issue related to making assumptions is particularly relevant to neurotheological investigations. After all, if we take a neurotheological approach, we must realize that the brain is critical to the assumption making process. However, neurotheology, and even more specifically, cognitive neuroscience, leaves us with a very interesting problem with regard to assumptions. Namely, that the brain makes many assumptions on multiple levels based upon our perceptions, cognitions, emotions, and social interactions. These assumptions usually can be considered to be *beliefs* in that they are taken to be true without having definitive "proof" that they are true. As we described in Chapter 2, beliefs are usually considered to be based on some data even though the full data set is not available. This is distinct from faith which is generally regarded as being based on very little, if any, evidence, and strongly adhered to as the basis of a particular belief system. Thus, all beliefs and all we have faith in should be considered to be assumptions. The larger problem is that if we continued to press, we find that both scientifically as well as philosophically, everything that we think about the world is ultimately an assumption because of the fundamental problem that the brain provides for each of us a "pre-processed" view of reality. Whether this view is accurate is most difficult to discern as we shall discuss in depth later. Neurotheology should include as part of its endeavor to seek out the origin of a variety of assumptions, and ultimately try to strip away assumptions to arrive at something more fundamentally true. This is not dissimilar to Descartes' persistence at trying to arrive at some factual element that could not be refuted and is not based on any assumptions. Of course, this is most difficult, if not impossible to do, but we should not forgo engaging this problem simply because of its difficulty.

Thus, all of our thoughts, perceptions, and feelings are assumptions born out of a brain which can, at best, provide us with a "second-hand" rendition of whatever is going on outside of our head in reality. This is a fundamental problem that we will address later when considering epistemological problems associated with neurotheology. Suffice it to state here that we make many assumptions about the world around us. We have to in order to survive, but so often we take these assumptions to be factual. The same is true in science and religion, and neuroscience and theology. Assumptions are made at many levels.

We must be aware of the many assumptions we will make regarding the theories, analyses, and studies that will be used in neurotheological investigations. A prime example has been several brain imaging studies of religious or spiritual individuals performing different practices. To the religious person, the brain changes are assumed to reflect the actual effect of experiencing God or the spirit on the person's brain. To the non-religious person, the brain changes are assumed to represent the brain actually causing the experiences. Both interpretations are clearly assumptions based on the individual's prior belief system. It is precisely these types of assumptions that must be carefully considered. After all, any individual exploring neurotheological questions will necessarily have certain biases and beliefs that affect the assumptions they make in their endeavors. To that end, another principle of neurotheology can be elaborated:

Principle XV: While it is recognized that many assumptions might be made regarding neurotheological investigations, these assumptions should be clearly identified and considered so as to avoid inaccurate interpretations of these investigations.

Of course, it might be difficult for scholars to identify their own biases and beliefs. This is true of every scholarly field including scientific disciplines, but it is important for individuals to try to identify their own assumptions. This was a primary tenet of Michael Polanyi's work regarding the importance of "tacit knowledge," the beliefs and passions that all individuals bring to their respective fields of discovery.[2] It is also important to identify the assumptions in others' work. Given the importance of fostering dialogue between the neurosciences and religion, however, this process should be constructive rather than destructive. In other words, when assumptions are found, a constructive engagement in the discussion should occur so that all scholars evaluating a particular theory or study have a better understanding of its limitations and interpretations. Hopefully, those engaged in neurotheological arguments will maintain a strong respect for other investigators and scholars. In this way, perhaps neurotheology can provide a substantial example of how scholars with different views and backgrounds can foster improved dialogue and healthy debate.

In the principle above, the use of the word "considered" is also relevant. It is purposely broad and vague but speaks to the importance of finding some way to

---

[2]   Polanyi, M. *Personal Knowledge: Towards a Post Critical Philosophy.* London: Routledge, 1998.

address assumptions. Considering such assumptions may range from making a simple statement of the assumptions, to an analysis of how different assumptions might affect the analysis, to frank debate about the problems with different assumptions. It would be hoped that any consideration of assumptions would lead to improved scholarship in the future.

Identification of Assumptions

On a biological and neuropsychological level, assumptions can arise from any perception, cognition, or emotion. Often, such assumptions are taken by the brain, consciously or unconsciously, to be true. Importantly, our assumptions and the belief systems they sustain are influenced by the input we receive from other members of our social community, for if we do not receive adequate *social consensus*, many of our most cherished beliefs and assumptions would never emerge into consciousness.

I have previously argued that these four elements work together within the human brain to enable us to develop our beliefs and assumptions about the world. The relationship between these different elements can be multifactorial. Thus, social influences may affect emotions, which in turn may affect cognitive processes. Alternatively, perhaps cognitive processes affect social influences directly. For these reasons, there is an integrated interaction in the brain between perceptions, emotions, cognitions, and social influence.

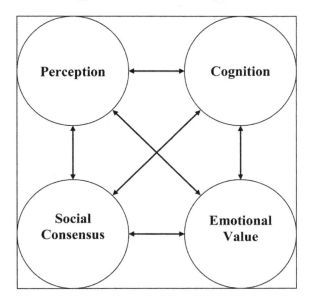

Figure 1   Schematic of the processes that influence beliefs

Together, these four interacting spheres of influence—perception, cognition, emotion, and social consensus—allow us to identify, explore, evaluate, and compare a wide variety of assumptions that we make on a daily basis and throughout our life. Understanding the biological nature of the basis for these assumptions is important as it provides a perspective from which to evaluate such assumptions. Let us briefly review some of the biological mechanisms underlying these factors influencing assumptions. This will also provide a background for further discussion regarding the nature of neurotheological scholarship as well as other principles that relate more specifically to the brain's functions.

Perceptions are generally the first mechanism by which we begin to make assumptions since there is a strong tendency to accept our perceptions at face value as real. The sensory organs of seeing, tasting, hearing, smelling, and touching provide our only window into the external world. They interact with the sensory areas of the brain by sending sensory data which is then processed to provide a smooth and persistent construct of the external world. To some degree, we have no choice but to accept our perceptions. If our perceptions are incorrect, then our brain will have tremendous difficulty helping us to survive. Thus, we make a strong assumption that our perceptions function with a one to one correspondence to the external world. A substantial amount of research has demonstrated that this is often not the case. It is a relatively simple process to "fool" the brain into perceiving things that are not there or not seeing things that are there. Furthermore, there is substantial evidence that the brain can modify and manipulate perceptions about the world. Objects may appear visually larger or closer than they actually are, or perhaps the shape and color can appear modified from the way that they actually are. A larger philosophical problem, however, is in the use of the term "actually are" since there is the implicit assumption that someone, namely the investigator, knows how objects actually are. In fact, even the investigator must be aware that their own perceptions may not always be accurate.

One might argue for the elaboration of a "perceptual theory of relativity" akin to Einstein's theory in that any perception of the external world is dependent in large part on the reference frame from which that perception is made. Thus, an investigator testing a research subject will have one perceptual frame of reference which may be different compared to that of the research subject. When the test is performed, if the research subject perceives something different, that something different is in comparison to the reference frame of the investigator. Arguably, there is some "absolute" reference frame. However, as human beings are always utilizing the perceptual processes of the brain to evaluate the absolute reference frame, our own individual reference frame can never be fully realized.

One final point regarding our perceptions is that the brain goes through multiple processing steps in order to raise a particular perception to consciousness. Thus, our individual perceptual reference frame may actually be altered on a primary level (that is, the brain's initial reception of external data is inaccurate) as well as all the way up to our association areas of the brain that integrate and contextualize our perceptions at the highest levels. If we have a "misperception" compared to somebody else's frame of reference, we may never know whether or not it originates in our primary, secondary, or tertiary processing steps of those perceptions.

There is substantial evidence for specific cognitive processes that are essential for the formulation of everyday assumptions. These cognitive processes include: 1) abstract thought processes, 2) quantitation, 3) identification of causal relationships, 4) establishment of dualistic concepts, 5) reductionism, and 6) holistic contextualization. Each of these functions have been localized to certain areas of the brain with varying degrees of accuracy based upon cognitive neuroscience studies (see Figures 2 and 3). Let us look at how each of these functions works to help us form our everyday assumptions.

Abstract thought, in general, permits the formation of general concepts from the perception of individual facts. The areas of the brain involved in abstract thought include parts of the temporal and parietal lobe. Our abstract thought processes permit a person to place the perceptions of a golden retriever, a poodle, and a Dalmatian into a single conceptual category. This category can then be plugged into the speech center of the brain and can be attributed an auditory, written, and pronounceable name: "dog" in English. Thus, our capability to create, manipulate, and express abstract concepts derives from the perception of various objects, upon which such linguistic naming depends. Thus, all general concepts or ideas underlying much of language are derived from the abstract reasoning processes of the brain.

On a more complex level, abstract thought processes allow us to put ideas together thereby creating a conceptualization that links these ideas. Thus, scientific theories, philosophical assumptions, and religious beliefs can all fall into the realm of abstract functions of the brain and also fall under the category of assumptions. Ideas involving areas such as mathematics, government, justice, culture, and family all are under the influence of the abstract reasoning processes of the brain.

In modern cognitive neuroscience, the term abstract reasoning has given way to more detailed descriptions of various processes that relate to how we maintain our memory, logic, syntax, grammar, and other aspects of rational thought. It should be mentioned that the brain areas involved in many of these higher cognitive processes are capable of performing these functions because they receive input from the association areas of the various sensory modalities. Association areas refer to the highest order of neuronal integration in the brain, the areas that create our clear and coherent version of the external world that is presented within our consciousness.

If one were to describe the regions of the brain involved in many abstract reasoning processes, there are probably multiple areas including the frontal lobes that are involved in executive functions, the temporal lobes which are involved in language and memory, and the parietal lobes, the lower part of which is involved in many higher order cognitive processes.[3] Together, these areas of the brain help to

---

[3]   Luria, A.R. *Higher Cortical Functions in Man*. New York, NY: Basic Books, 1966; Gazzaniga, M. (ed.). *The New Cognitive Neurosciences*. Cambridge, MA: MIT Press, 2004; Goel, V., Gold, B., Kapur, S., and Houle, S. "Neuroanatomical correlates of human reasoning." *J Cogn Neurosci*. 1998;10:293-302.

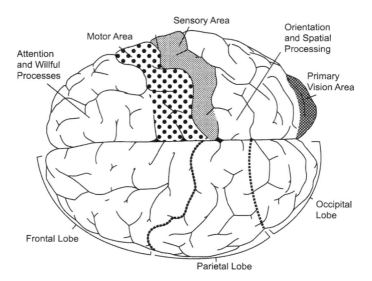

Figure 2   Top view of the brain showing specific lobes—frontal, parietal, and
               occipital. The temporal lobe is below the parietal lobe and is better
               seen from the side. The general location of several functions are
               indicated by specified lines

provide ourselves with the sense of a rational mind and a cohesive understanding
of the world around us.

The brain also allows for substantial quantitative or mathematical processes. In
its basic form, the brain's mathematic capabilities permit the abstraction of quantity
from the perception of various elements. Brain imaging studies suggest that many
subcomponents of quantitative processing occur in the region of the inferior (or
lower) part of the parietal lobe.[4] It seems that from a very young age, we are
capable of counting or quantifying things. In fact, recent studies have indicated
that infants only several months old are able to understand basic mathematical
concepts such as addition and subtraction.[5] We use this quantitative ability to help
us order objects according to some numbering system or else by estimation of
amount. More significantly, this operator is what has allowed human beings to
develop the concepts of mathematics. It is clear that our ability to count things
is critical to our survival. Throughout our life, we must continually be aware of
quantities around us. We need to count time, distance, how much work we have to
do, and how many people are around us. Even in past civilizations, the studies of

---

[4]   Geshwind, N. "Disconnection syndromes in animals and man." *Brain*. 1965;88:
237-294.

[5]   d'Aquili, E.G. "The myth-ritual complex: a biogenetic structural analysis."
In Ashbrook, J.B. (ed.), *Brain, Culture, and the Human Spirit*. New York, NY: Lanham
Press, 1993.

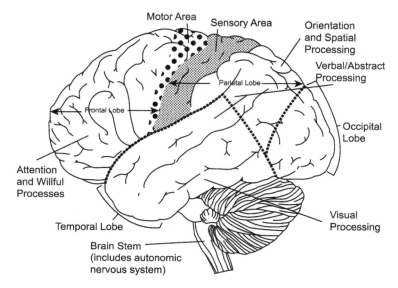

Figure 3   Side view of the brain showing specific lobes—frontal, temporal, parietal, and occipital. The general location of several functions are indicated by specified lines

mathematics, measurement, and time were often focal points of their cultures and religions. Interestingly, mathematics has taken on great importance for the brain so that we tend to assign expanded meaning to numbers and quantitative processes. We tend to believe numbers are more than simple descriptors. For example, we are more likely to believe a poll that shows that 63 percent of the people approve of the president rather than take someone's word that the president is generally popular. We also assign meaning to specific numbers such as "lucky" or "unlucky" numbers. Certain numbers are attributed meaning in sacred texts such as the number "40" in the Bible. This heavy reliance on numbers has a substantial influence on how we make our assumptions about the world.

The brain's ability to perceive and conceive of causal relationships in the world is of crucial importance for planning behaviors and dealing with the environment around us. Our survival is heavily dependent on our ability to perceive causality in the world in order to determine the best ways of dealing with the world. The perception and conception of causal relationships seems to have played a significant role in the development of human thought and this type of processing appears to be associated with activity in the inferior (or lower) part of the parietal lobe and the superior (or upper) part of the temporal lobe.[6] When causality is applied to the physical world, the result is science. When causality is applied to the human

---

[6]   Blakemore, S.J., Fonlupt, P., Pachot-Clouard, M., et al. "How the brain perceives causality: an event-related fMRI study." *Neuroreport*. 2001;12:3741-3746.

world, the result is social science, psychology, and ethics. And when causality is applied to issues of ultimate concern such as existence, the universe, or God, the result is philosophy, theology, or religion. Thus, the causal functions of the brain enable us to question why we are here, why something works the way it does, and what created the universe. In all of these, and in every other instance, we want to know what is the cause that lies behind every event that we experience.

The establishment of oppositional concepts allows us to extract meaning from the external world by ordering abstract elements into dyads. A dyad is a group of two elements which are opposed to each other in their meaning. The brain areas that have been associated with dyadic processing appear to be in the region of the left inferior parietal lobe.[7] Therefore, dyads include—good and evil, right and wrong, justice and injustice, happy and sad, and heaven and hell. It is important to note that each opposite in the dyad, in some ways, derives its meaning from its contrast with the other opposite. In this sense, the opposites do not stand completely on their own, but require each other in order to define themselves individually. This is particularly true since opposites are verbal descriptions of objects. For example, in physics, there are positively and negatively charged particles. However, there is no absolute meaning of "positive" and "negative." They are only defined in relation to the other so that a particle is positive only if it is not negative and *vice versa.* The important point is that these dyads are one of the mind's most important ways of ordering the universe. The ability to create dualistic interpretations of things in the world is particularly important in the generation of workable assumptions.[8] There are examples too numerous to mention in religious and theological concepts in which opposites are set against each other such as good versus evil.

The ability of the brain to create and maintain a reductionist standpoint is another way in which the brain makes assumptions. Reductionist functions in the brain allow us to look at something, and break it down into an analysis of individual parts. Such cognitive processes might yield our scientific, logical, and mathematical approach to studying the universe. It is through these disciplines that we break down the world into small parts that can be controlled and studied.

The brain also appears to have a reciprocal approach which we tend to refer to as a holistic approach. When the brain attempts to contextualize something through a holistic approach, we view that thing as a whole or as a gestalt. This ability allows us to experience a given object, situation, or concept in a more global context. A number of experiments involving animals and human beings have indicated that the parietal lobe in the non-dominant hemisphere is intimately involved in the perception of spatial relations. More specifically, the perceptions generated by this area are of a holistic or gestalt nature. Thus, the holistic processes of the brain

---

[7]   Murphy, G.L., Andrew, J.M. "The conceptual basis of antonymy and synonymy in adjectives." *J Memory Language.* 1993;32:301-319.

[8]   d'Aquili, E.G. "The myth-ritual complex: a biogenetic structural analysis." In Ashbrook, J.B. (ed.), *Brain, Culture, and the Human Spirit.* New York, NY: Lanham Press, 1993.

may reside, in part, in the parietal lobe on the right.[9] It is also interesting to note that this area sits almost directly opposite the area in the dominant hemisphere that is involved in the performance of various logical-grammatical operations. In particular, the parietal lobe on the dominant side is capable of the perception of opposites and the ability to select one object over another. Thus, the right parietal lobe is involved in a holistic approach to things and the left parietal lobe is involved in more reductionist and analytic processes.

Another important element regarding the identification of assumptions is to ascertain the basis of memory. Memory of our assumptions plays a crucial role in how such assumptions might be invoked or utilized. For example, brain imaging studies suggest that the right prefrontal cortex plays a crucial role in integrating current perceptions and ideas with memories via the hippocampus, which is part of the limbic system. Abnormalities within this integrative process can cause strange and unusual beliefs.[10] And if the limbic system is damaged, a patient can lose the ability to suppress fantasies that do not pertain to ongoing reality.[11]

Imaginary memories and reality-based memories are stored in different parts of the brain,[12] and if the neural pathways between these areas are interfered with, a person may lose the ability to determine the accuracy of memories. For example, common anti-anxiety drugs called benzodiazepines also can impair the conscious recollections of memories.[13] The reason for this, presumably, is that accurate memories require a high degree of neural organization, and these can be disrupted by drugs. Other studies have shown that anti-anxiety drugs disrupt

---

[9]   Sperry, R.W., Gazzaniga, M.S., and Bogen, J.E. "Interhemispheric relationships: the neocortical commisures; syndromes of hemisphere disconnection." In Vinken, P.J. and Bruyn, C. (eds.), *Handbook of Clinical Neurology*, Vol. 4. Amsterdam: North Holland Publishing, 1969; Nebes, R.D. and Sperry, R.W. "Hemispheric disconnection syndrome with cerebral birth injury in the dominant arm area." *Neuropsychologia.* 1971;9: 249-259; Gazzaniga, M.S. and Hillyard, S.A. "Language and speech capacity of the right hemisphere." *Neuropsychologia.* 1971;9:273-280; Bogen, J.E. "The other side of the brain. II: An appositional mind." *Bull LA Neurol Soc.* 1969;34:135-162.

[10]   Frith, C. and Dolan, R.J. "The role of memory in the delusions associated with schizophrenia." In Schacter, D. and Scarry, E. (eds.), *Memory, Brain, and Belief.* Cambridge, MA: Harvard University Press, 2000.

[11]   Schnider, A. "Spontaneous confabulation, reality monitoring, and the limbic system: a review." *Brain Res Brain Res Rev.* 2001;36:150-160.

[12]   Conway, M.A., Pleydell-Pearce, C.W., Whitecross, S.E., and Sharpe, H. "Neurophysiological correlates of memory for experienced and imagined events." *Neuropsychologia.* 2003;41:334-340.

[13]   Huron, C., Servais, C., and Danion, J.M. "Lorazepam and diazepam impair true, but not false, recognition in healthy volunteers." *Psychopharmacology* (Berlin). 2001;155: 204-209.

memories by causing us to exaggerate "the personal significance and emotional intensity of past events."[14]

To date, the accumulated research pertaining to the accuracy of our memories and beliefs can be summarized as follows:

1. all memories, beliefs, and assumptions are subject to change and possibly distortion over time;
2. beliefs and assumptions are highly dependent on language, emotion, and social interaction;
3. the older the memory, the more difficult it is to ascertain its accuracy; and
4. neurological disorders and drugs can disrupt the brain's ability to distinguish between true and false memories and beliefs.

In addition to the cognitive and memory aspects of assumptions, emotions play a substantial role in developing and maintaining assumptions. Emotions work on all of our perceptions and thoughts to generate feelings about them. Neuroscientists have demonstrated that the limbic system (Figure 4), which includes the amygdala, the thalamus, and the hippocampus, plays a critical role in the elaboration of our emotions and our emotional drives. It is the limbic system that is associated with our feelings of happiness, sadness, love, and fear. Interestingly, the limbic system is also one of the earliest evolved parts of the mammalian brain. This makes sense since it seems likely that, from an evolutionary view, all animals must be able to respond with some type of emotion to various elements in their environment. Otherwise, there would be nothing that would drive a mother bear to protect her cubs or would cause an animal to run from a predator. While it is difficult to determine with any certainty the emotions of animals, it seems that they must have some type of emotional value response that informs them what to avoid and what to be drawn to. However, whether these responses imply the emotions of fear and love as humans know them is difficult to discern. In both human beings and in other animals, the limbic system is clearly involved in such responses as aggression and sexual behavior.

We have described how the emotions are associated with the limbic system, but we have also indicated that these emotions must be ascribed to all of our higher brain functioning. Studies have suggested that the hippocampus and the amygdala serve to modulate emotions, but they also connect to the higher cortical areas where a variety of cognitive processes occur. Thus, it seems probable that the amygdala and hippocampus function as the mediating structures between the limbic system and the cortex. In fact, there are a vast number of neural connections between the limbic system and the cerebral cortex. In this way, thoughts and experiences are transmitted from the cortex to the limbic system where they are given their

---

[14] Pernot-Marino, E., Danion, J.M., and Hedelin, G. "Relations between emotion and conscious recollection of true and false autobiographical memories: an investigation using lorazepam as a pharmacological tool." *Psychopharmacology* (Berlin). 2004;175:60-67.

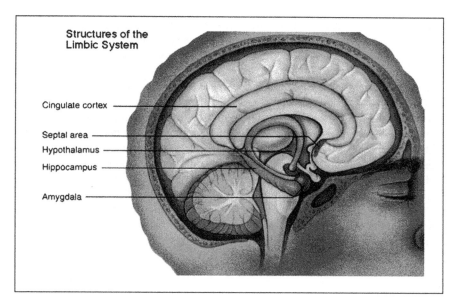

Figure 4   Some of the important limbic structures and how they are located within the brain

emotional value. From here, emotions allow us to interpret our experiences and generate behavioral responses.

Emotions also bind our perceptions to our conscious beliefs, making whatever we are thinking about seem more real at the time. In fact, strong emotions— particularly anger, fear, and passion—can radically change our perceptions of reality. Thus, our emotional responses can modify assumptions. But if a thought or perception does not stimulate an emotional response, it may not even reach consciousness.

The final element associated with our assumptions is the social environment. We typically do not realize how strongly we are influenced by people around us starting from birth through death. Most, if not all, of our initial beliefs and assumptions are given to us by our caregivers, parents, and family. Parents teach us a set of beliefs and assumptions regarding every aspect of the world—politics, culture, morals, and religion. Even mundane assumptions about what to eat, wear, and do on a day-to-day basis are provided by our parents. It is also no accident that many of these early assumptions are the most difficult to break since they are repeated frequently, and are ingrained in the earliest neuronal connections and architecture of the developing brain. Many of these early assumptions become so entrenched that they are below the usual level of consciousness.

As we grow, the social influence moves from parents to teachers, friends, and colleagues. Ultimately, our romantic partners have substantial influence on our beliefs and assumptions. There are strong biases towards believing the same things that people around us believe. The brain appears designed to want to fit in and thereby fosters conformism. One of the mechanisms by which this happens is associated with "mirror" neurons, brain cells that help us to mimic what we perceive. Thus, our brain inherently repeats what is going on around it. The brain also does not want to stay in a social situation of perpetual conflict since this raises the level of anxiety and depression and raises survival concerns.

Given the perceptual, cognitive, emotional, and social elements of our assumptions, a neurotheological approach now allows for a better understanding of the underlying nature and root cause of our assumptions, particularly those regarding religious and spiritual matters. Information regarding the identification and basis of religious and spiritual assumptions might lead to enhanced scholarship in theology and religion by adding the biological dimension. Of course, whether such an analysis of assumptions provides a benefit or not is ultimately an assumption in and of itself. However, at least it is now possible to better identify, and thus, account for that assumption.

Neurotheology's Razor

The principle of assumptions leads us to a variation of a primary notion in science, Occam's Razor which was described earlier. Recall that Occam's Razor originates out of the issue of measurement and attempting to adhere to the limits of what can be measured and how to interpret that measurement. This is particularly relevant in scientific studies associated with neurotheological investigations. In any scientific research, the ability to measure something is the most critical obstacle to studying some phenomenon. The main question to be asked in any circumstance is if the measuring device, whether mechanical, personal, objective, or subjective, actually measures the thing which it is intended to measure. Simplistically, if someone wanted to measure distance, they would choose an odometer rather than a clock, and if somebody wanted to measure time, they would choose the clock over the odometer.

Religious and spiritual phenomena present a complex problem with regard to measurement. On one hand, there is the question of the objective, external reality component of the phenomenon—that is, does the phenomenon truly exist? Trying to measure the existence of God, angels, heaven, or hell would be almost, if not completely impossible from a scientific perspective. To prove the existence of one of these religious phenomena would be tantamount to saying that we could create a device, such as an odometer or a clock, that could actually measure the physical existence of these phenomena. The problem here, aside from the obvious, is that as human beings, we have no clear conception of how an existence of these things would actually appear to a scientific measuring device. How would God or heaven be able to interact with a device in material reality such that they could actually be measured? Especially if God is considered to have attributes such as being infinite and eternal, it would be almost impossible to have any clear notion as to what a measurement of God would actually demonstrate.

Measurements of spirituality and religiousness in human beings is much more achievable, but is also a relatively complex problem because of the subjective nature of these phenomena. There are several important limitations to this problem of measuring human spirituality and religiosity. For example, if someone has had an unusual spiritual experience, the scientific approach would be to ask the individual a number of questions about the experience. Unfortunately, these questions usually pertain to how the person "felt," what they "sensed," or what they "thought." In other words, the researcher would apply concepts grounded in science such as emotion, sensory experience, or cognition. However, part of what is necessary is to get at what is essentially spiritual and separate it from psychology, neurology, and physiology.

There have also been a number of questionnaires and scales that have been developed in order to assess various components of an individual's spiritual or religious perspectives. Many of these scales have provided unique approaches to assessing spirituality and religiosity. Part of the problem up to the last several years has been that many of the assessment tools were not well studied or developed and were even more difficult to find. Researchers interested in studying spirituality or religion in a group of subjects would have great difficulty finding and selecting appropriate measurement tools. An excellent text edited by Hill and Hood (1999) reviewed over 100 types of scales on religiosity including those pertaining to religious belief, religious attitudes, religious orientation, religious development, religious commitment, religious experience, morality, coping, mysticism, concepts of God, fundamentalism, death anxiety, hope, and forgiveness. Each of these scales was developed to ask questions of individuals to somehow "rate" varying degrees of responses that could be compared across individuals and even groups. Many of these have been tested for validity (that they measure what they are intended to measure) and reliability (that they will return similar results when individuals are tested repeatedly). But there is still the fundamental problem of how can we measure religious and spiritual phenomena and how do we interpret or evaluate such a measure? The issue is whether we might be able to infer something about God, heaven, or some other supernatural realm by measuring what we can in the material realm.

This entire issue confronts Occam's Razor, "Pluralitas non est ponenda sine neccesitate" or "plurality should not be posited without necessity." This concept states that scientists should not postulate more than what is necessary in order to describe a phenomena. What this rule was designed to prevent was for people to develop hypotheses or assumptions for which there was no clear way of measuring, and that were not actually necessary in order to explain something. For example, one might consider a study designed to measure the effect of gravity as an object falls to the earth. One might postulate that there is a force that attracts the earth and the object to each other that enables the object to fall toward the earth. Occam's Razor would prevent an additional hypothesis that there are massless, energyless, little green men, that actually push the object towards the earth and then disappear whenever a measuring tool is brought to bear on the event. There would, of course, be no way to prove that the little green men did or did not exist. However, the point is in some sense moot since it is not a necessary requirement in order to explain the phenomenon.

Some scientists, particularly those with a strong materialistic perspective, have utilized the argument of Occam's Razor as a mechanism to disprove or at least disallow the concept of God. Similar to the little green men, a conception of God as being the fundamental cause of the universe, is not "required" from the materialistic perspective in order to explain many aspects of the universe. And, if it is not possible to prove God's existence, then the study of God's existence does not belong as part of science. While it is important to be careful about over using the concept of Occam's Razor with regard to religious and spiritual phenomena, it is necessary to keep in mind its meaning, especially as it pertains to the ability to interpret various results obtained through the study of religious and spiritual phenomena.

Occam's Razor tells us not to assume more than what is needed to explain something. But this of course is an assumption and one that places substantial importance upon the word, "necessity." After all, there is a grand assumption as to what actually constitutes necessity in the context of trying to explain something. This is particularly the case when considering the existence of God. For example, many religious individuals cannot conceive of a universe without God. For them, God is absolutely necessary. A scientist might argue that physical laws explain the phenomena that make up the universe, and, therefore, God is not necessary. For one person, what constitutes necessity is completely different than for another person.

There are even broader problems with the notion of necessity when one considers the "why questions" that may be outside the purview of science. Take the law of gravity mentioned above. Science can explain how gravity works between two objects, but *why* should it be based on the exact equations we find rather than others? In fact, *why* should gravity exist at all? Answering the "why" questions sometimes stretches necessity to its limits. For example, many cosmologists are now entertaining the hypothesis that the universe is actually a multiverse with an infinite number of possible universes, some of which have gravity while others do not. These cosmologists have argued that there is an absolute necessity to have an infinite number of possible universes in order to explain why our universe is the way that it is. They argue that if there is an infinite number of universes, then one of them, by pure chance, would have gravity and all of the other laws of nature exactly as they are. But if we apply Occam's Razor, is it more likely that there is an infinite multitude of universes that we can never measure, or is it more likely that there is a God that we can never measure? Which answer satisfies necessity?

From a neurotheological perspective then, we can argue that in addition to "Pluralitas non est ponenda sine neccesitate" we might also consider "Neccesitas non est ponenda sine Pluralitate" or "necessity should not be posited without plurality." This might be Neurotheology's Razor and perhaps another principle:

Principle XVI: We must not assume what constitutes "necessity" until we have adequately evaluated all of the possible pluralities.

This principle particularly applies when we get to fundamental questions that do not have any foreseeable scientific and/or theological answers.

This notion of evaluating all possibilities seems crucial for addressing a number of fundamental questions that neurotheology might consider. Such questions might pertain to the nature and experience of material reality, the nature and experience of consciousness, and the nature and experience of any potential "supernatural" or immaterial realms of reality. Any attempt at a simplistic answer deriving from a single perspective should be very carefully evaluated for assumptions that might exclude certain possibilities *a priori* without any definitive rationale for such an exclusion. Thus, a materialist argument that God cannot exist because God is not measurable by any current devices that exist in material reality should not be deemed sufficient. There may be many aspects of reality that current science cannot measure at the present moment, but may be able to do so in the future. And, of course, it may be possible that God is totally immeasurable and that the only way to access God is through human consciousness. But is human consciousness not a measuring device in and of itself? Perhaps to explore certain aspects of reality, we must turn away from materialistic measuring devices and utilize the consciousness device that each individual has access to.

It should be stressed that Neurotheology's Razor is not meant to provide a space for the kind of wild speculations and concepts that Occam's Razor was meant to exclude. We should not utilize Neurotheology's Razor to prove God's existence simply because it is a possibility that might help to explain some or all aspects of the world. But Neurotheology's Razor should be kept in mind, in conjunction with Occam's Razor, whenever considering a line of theological argument, the interpretation of a research experiment, or any other assumption we might make regarding reality. At the very least, this should provide a more thoughtful approach to our understanding of reality.

The other issue with regard to Occam's Razor, is that it is designed to apply specifically to scientific methodology and interpretation while the field of neurotheology also incorporates philosophical, ontological, and epistemological issues. In this regard, the use of such a principle is much less clear. It may be appropriate to apply Occam's Razor to the gravitational attraction of two objects, but it might not apply when trying to understand a moral, social, or religious question. What is the best way of ending crime, war, and human suffering? Does Occam's Razor apply to these questions? The use of Occam's Razor is also problematic when one examines how religious and spiritual phenomena are perceived with relation to epistemological questions, something we will address later.

Understanding the Restriction of Brain Processes

We have now explored several broad principles regarding neurotheological investigations. Since neurotheology also includes brain science, we can consider an additional principle that can help guide us through the neurotheological evaluation of a variety of concepts and ideas. When considering general principles related to brain processes, we have already stated that the brain processes all external and internal information into a coherent rendition of reality. We also encountered this above in the discussion regarding beliefs and assumptions. This notion applies to many different fields of study, but also equally applies to neurotheology. Whether one is reading sacred texts, interpreting those texts, using rational and emotional processes to guide theological arguments, or trying to comprehend the meaning of religious ideologies and experiences, it is the brain that helps with processing all of this. This notion can be modified by the religious and theological perspective to lead directly to a crucial neurotheological principle:

Principle XVII: The brain places functional restrictions on all thought processes, and hence how we experience religion, spirituality, and theology.

This principle is so important in theological discourse since it suggests a "neurotheological hermeneutic" which must be considered regarding any sacred text or interpretation of that text. By this I mean that the biological development of the brain, as determined by our genetic heritage and environmental influences, structures the brain and its function along specific lines. In fact, the general functioning of the brain and its structure is amazingly universal on a gross level. For example, virtually every human brain has a cortex containing the frontal, temporal, parietal, and occipital lobes; subcortical structures such as the striatum, thalamus, and hypothalamus; a cerebellum, and a brainstem. When using a variety of functional brain imaging techniques, we can observe numerous functional areas that work for specific tasks. For example, the sensory and the visual areas of the brain integrate our perceptions into a coherent rendition of the world "out there." The structures of the brain that underlie these functions are relatively the same in all people.

Of course, on the microscopic level, each brain is very different since the immense number of neuronal connections in the brain are dependent on each person's development and experiences.[15] Thus, we all have a language area, but the particular language, our accent, and vocabulary, depend on what we listen to and are taught from childhood.[16] In a similar manner, some of the basic brain functions are deeply related to religious experience and theological development. Some of the relevant brain processes described above suggested to be involved in

---

[15] Gazzaniga, M. (ed.). *The New Cognitive Neurosciences*. Cambridge, MA: MIT Press, 2004.

[16] Chomsky, N. *Reflections on Language*. New York, NY: Pantheon Books, 1975.

various aspects of religious phenomena are causal, binary, holistic, reductionist, quantitative, and emotional functions.[17] However, the importance of these functions in the context of theology is related to Principle XVII above, which refers to the restrictions placed on the development of theology by the brain itself. Baruch Spinoza may have put it best when he stated, "I believe that a triangle, if it could speak, would say that God is eminently triangular, and a circle that the divine nature is eminently circular; and thus would every one ascribe his own attributes to God."[18] Thus, our brain shapes the ways in which we can conceive of God and theology. In this regard, we are also referring to the neurotheological hermeneutic in which any theological argument must be considered not only from the perspective of the culture and time, but from the biological restrictions that shaped the argument. We will explore the notion of a neurotheological hermeneutic, and how it might be applied within neurotheology, in the next chapter.

---

[17] d'Aquili, E.G. and Newberg, A.B. *The Mystical Mind: Probing the Biology of Religious Experience*. Minneapolis, MN: Fortress Press, 1999.

[18] Spinoza, B. "Letter to Hugo Boxel." In Wolf, A. (transl.), *Correspondence of Spinoza*. Whitefish, MT: Kessinger Publishing, 2003.

Kensington Central Library

12 Phillimore Walk
London
W8 7RX
020 7361 3010

Borrowed Items 15/10/2016 13:33
XXXXXXXXXX6172

Title	Due Date
inciples of neurotheology	05/11/2016
imate changed : a sonal journey through the nce	05/11/2016
hematics in 10 lessons grand tour	05/11/2016

dicates items borrowed today
e Your Library - Access All Areas
sday 6 September, 10am to 5pm
k on behind the scenes tours, grab a
gain in the book sale and drop in for
lth information and more

ail information services@rbkc.gov.uk

Chapter 5
Towards a Neurotheological Hermeneutic

The Beginnings of a Neurotheological Hermeneutic

In the previous chapter we considered the principle describing how brain function restricts our perceptions, thoughts, and feelings. When applied to theology and philosophy, this can lead to a new hermeneutical approach in which we consider the influence of the brain on a variety of ideological positions. Given the emphasis of this work on theology, it seems appropriate to consider this approach as a neurotheological hermeneutic—how the brain influences theological and/or religious ideas. We will need to initiate an exploration of some of the major ideas and thinkers which have tremendously shaped human theology and philosophy. It should be clear though, that what we are exploring through this neurotheological analysis is how a given individual *experiences* some aspect of neuropsychological function which ultimately is associated with a specific idea or theological conception. In essence then, we are constructing a hermeneutic regarding how neuropsychological experiences affect, alter, and constrain the human ability to think specific theological and philosophical thoughts. We are also developing, in some regard, a new philosophical system which might be called "experientialist" such that all thinking, emotions, and ideas, are tied to human experience. This is akin to the Kantian position that the external world is only known to us through our perceptions and ideas. However, neurotheology has the potential to take this notion further since "experience" in this context does not refer only to sensory experience, but the experience of our own internal cognitive, emotional, and perhaps, spiritual processes. Finally, a neurotheological hermeneutic also offers the potential for obtaining empirical data to support or refute specific ideas.

In addition to empirical data that might be obtained through some scientific method, neurotheology argues for obtaining the equally important data from subjective experience. This might not be too dissimilar from Husserl's phenomenology, but certain distinctions should be identified as we proceed through this neurotheological analysis. The purpose of our experientialist analysis is to determine exactly what parts of the human being allow us to have experiences so that we may understand the subjective nature of the experiences as ascertained through a phenomenological analysis. In this way, neurotheology might actually be a blending of Kantian philosophy and phenomenology. As we will see, such a neuropsychological analysis may have profound implications for theological and philosophical thought, hermeneutics, and phenomenology. This will be particularly the case in the analysis of epistemological issues pertaining to the experience of reality and the identification of the characteristics by which we define reality.

A neurotheological hermeneutic argues that we should strive to understand all of theology, and its associated sacred texts, from the cognitive, emotional, and perceptual processes associated with the brain. But I have argued in the principle of interaction that neurotheology should have a comparable contribution of science and theology. Thus, a neurotheological hermeneutic must also recognize that this approach may prove useful for understanding the basis of the scientific disciplines as well religious ones. Can we not ask why science has developed in the current manner? How much of science is based upon what makes sense to our brain? How much of science is based upon the ways in which religion has shaped how we conceive of the world? A neurotheological hermeneutic can allow us to explore all aspects of human thought and endeavors provided that we maintain neurotheology in its broadest context. Perhaps it would be more appropriate to use the term neurophilosophical hermeneutics if one wanted to approach philosophy, or a neurocultural hermeneutic if one wanted to approach sociology and anthropology. We might even consider a biogenetic hermeneutic since much of how we understand the brain is based upon genetics and biology. However, all of these can still potentially fall under the realm of a neurotheological hermeneutic since there is a great deal of overlap and convergence in the topics that are covered. Since our goal is to establish the principles related to neurotheology, it seems particularly relevant here to focus on the neurotheological hermeneutic more specifically.

How might we begin such an analysis? There are potentially two different ways of approaching this neurotheological hermeneutic. One is to start with various ideas or concepts and attempt to determine the types of brain functions that might be associated. The other is to start with several selected brain functions and try to determine which theological or philosophical concepts might be associated. Both approaches might yield fruitful results. For the purposes of this chapter, we will use the latter approach. This will help streamline the process, but it should also be clearly recognized that the use of a neurotheological hermeneutic could be applicable to a broad range of ideologies. Thus, the use of a neurotheological hermeneutic could eventually be an important tool for examining many theological and philosophical texts, concepts, and movements.

In exploring neurotheological hermeneutics, it would seem that there is the potential for every part and function of the brain to be relevant to the discussion. After all, every part of the brain can affect the ways in which we think and feel about the world around us. And every part of the brain might affect our philosophical and theological pursuits. Whether or not every brain structure is actually involved in our philosophical and theological pursuits is uncertain, but at the outset, it seems appropriate to consider each structure as possibly being involved as part of the principle of neurotheological hermeneutics:

Principle XVIII: Every brain structure and function might be considered to be useful in understanding theological and philosophical concepts.

As we explore the applications of a neurotheological hermeneutic, this principle will be important. We can consider how many different parts of the brain might interact or function in the context of theological and philosophical investigations. In this regard, we will utilize many of the brain functions we considered earlier, such as those pertaining to causality or quantitation. We might consider that among the continuum of possible permutations of functions, the brain might end up using one particular functional domain to a very extreme degree. Theoretically, this could lead to one particular functional domain of the brain as being the sole filter through which all understanding of the world passes, or it could lead to one functional domain as being experienced on its most basic level.

A quick example may help explain these two potential functional states of experience. If we take the quantitative functions of the brain, we might consider what would happen if everything we think and perceive is filtered through these quantitative functions. The result would be that the entire world is experienced through a mathematical analysis. Mathematics could be used to help explain any phenomenon in the world. This is not dissimilar to physics in which mathematical models and equations are frequently used to study and explain phenomena. Thus, everything can be considered, or filtered, through this singular type of brain process. The second functional state mentioned above would be slightly different. In that state, the individual would experience quantitation on its most fundamental level. The result would be the experience of numbers as the essence of all things. The universe is not described through mathematics, it is mathematical at its most fundamental core.

The former approach in which everything appears to be "funneled through" one particular cognitive process might be called the *total* functioning of this cognitive process. The totality of everything that exists is evaluated from the basis of this cognitive function. The latter approach, in which a particular cognitive process appears to provide a "fundamental basis" for everything that exists, might be called the *absolute* functioning of this cognitive process. Thus, everything that exists is considered to be derivative from this concept. It is important to state here that there has been no clear determination of the neurophysiological correlates of such experiences. Several studies have suggested how certain cognitive processes can dominate other processes in the brain. Perhaps more importantly, there are many examples in which one cognitive process comes to the fore and forms the basis of a particular philosophical or theological movement. We will consider several of these movements throughout the history of philosophy, religion, and theology to determine how they might be associated with the total or absolute functioning of various cognitive processes. It is hoped that such an analysis will be a more specific example of how the principles of neurotheology described in this book might have a direct impact on our understanding of science and theology.

It should also be restated here that the experience itself of either the total or absolute functioning of a particular cognitive process does not necessarily alter or affect the actual nature of the universe or God. Wearing a pair of red colored glasses makes everything in the world appear red, but the world itself is still multicolored. It is only our experience that has been affected. Similarly, if a scholar experiences the world through the absolute or total functioning of a particular cognitive process, they are simply seeing the world through that lens, but the world may be completely different.

Given the notion of total and absolute functioning of the various brain processes, we might elaborate a group of principles that can help guide the neurotheological hermeneutic interpretation of various ideas and concepts. It would seem that the brain can function in a multitude of ways. On one hand, the brain may work in such a way that an individual experiences the total or absolute functioning of one particular brain process. Alternatively, the brain processes may work in a variety of lesser ways and may also work either synergistically or antagonistically with each other.

Principle XIX: The following principles of brain functions are likely related to neurotheological hermeneutics: 1. brain functions may be utilized in part or in a total manner; 2. When used in part, brain functions may be used in conjunction with others synergistically or antagonistically; 3. brain functions may be utilized in an absolute manner.

Each of these principles can be considered when interpreting various sacred texts and their associated theological or philosophical commentary. For the purposes of this discussion, we will focus on the absolute and total functioning of different brain processes. But there are many ways of considering brain function as it pertains to hermeneutics.

As we proceed in this neurotheological hermeneutic analysis to understand the total or absolute functions of various processes that underlie specific modalities of thinking, feeling, and experiencing, we do not mean to imply that the full elaboration and complexity of various philosophical ideas are derived solely from such experiences. What we are trying to get at in this analysis are what we might call the "ideological bursts" that are associated with specific theologians or philosophers in their analysis of various problems of ultimate concern. What we are proposing happens in these circumstances, is that a given individual may approach a specific theological, epistemological, or ontological question through the means that they are most familiar with. This may take a scientific person into the realm of mathematics and logical deduction, it may take a spiritual person into the realm of holistic experience, and as we will see, it has taken many different scholars down different paths of causal, existential, or willful thinking. If they proceed long enough down these paths they may develop ever intensifying experiences associated with their own analytical approach. In this regard the paths scholars take might be described, as has been frequently been done, as a form of meditation, or at least contemplation. As such a state deepens in intensity, the result may eventually be the absolute functioning or total functioning of this specific cognitive process. When this occurs, there is also a very intense stimulation of brain structures associated with a sense of realness and oneness, so that it is understood that this approach to reality represents that which is most fundamentally real and pertains to all of reality. These are often very strong emotional and cognitive feelings as well.

I would further propose that while these ideological bursts are crucial to the elaboration of the great concepts in philosophical thinking, what truly makes these experiences so critical in human thought is the person's analysis of the experiences after they have been perceived. Thus, in many ways philosophy may be a description of the experience "after the fact." While someone may have the notion, as we shall see later, of mathematics being the fundamental "stuff" of the universe, they ultimately require a fully integrated analysis using all of the functions of the brain in order to relate and bring to meaning that full understanding. Of course all of the other brain functions will necessarily color and alter what was truly experienced in that ideological burst. Such a fully integrated synthesis is necessary for us as human beings in order to respond to our world and to our own thinking and feeling. Thus, part of the notion being developed here is that while there may be a specific experience which forms the basis of a given philosophical or theological system, how we ultimately make meaning of it and allow that experience to pervade our understanding of the world around us requires the fully integrated functioning of the entire human brain.

Of course, not all theological or philosophical concepts arise from such ideological bursts. But even without such a burst, all theological and philosophical concepts are influenced by the processes of the human brain. Given these limitations, we are going to explore several major theological or philosophical conceptions to determine how they relate to the absolute or total functioning of specific brain processes. This will demonstrate one way in which a neurotheological hermeneutic can be utilized. Thus, with these limitations in mind, let us explore several specific examples of how a neurotheological hermeneutic might be applied to specific theological and philosophical concepts.

Influence of the Frontal Lobes on Concepts of Willfulness and Surrender

Cognitive neuroscience has generally determined that the frontal lobes are particularly important in the establishment of willful behaviors. The frontal lobe tends to be activated when we bring the focus of our attention to a particular task. Research has also shown the frontal lobes to become active during a variety of practices such as prayer and meditation. It is interesting, furthermore, that the frontal lobes, in addition to controlling the initiation of movement and language, are critical for regulating our emotions. Several studies have suggested that the frontal lobes might be the seat of compassion in addition to their function as the seat of the will.

Two particularly important perspectives may be related to willfulness. One is based upon the theological argument that arose between Martin Luther (1483-1546) and Desiderius Erasmus (ca. 1469-1536). Luther's position would not allow believers to be *completely* free before God; they could only be guided in ways that were consistent with the Bible.[1] Thus, there were limitations placed on the human mind's ability to have free will and this constrained how human beings can be religious. Desiderius Erasmus argued that the human being is the center of creation and that the measure of God's goodness is that God created a world in which to unfold the nature of the human being.[2] In *The Free Will*, Erasmus insisted on a role for the human will and personal responsibility, as well as God's grace, in achieving salvation while Luther argued that grace alone provided salvation for human beings.[3] Interestingly, this debate also centers on the functions of the human mind as they pertain to human salvation since the issue of human free will, which would ultimately have a basis in the mental processes of the frontal lobes, is of crucial importance in determining the basis for salvation. It would be most interesting to consider how Luther and Erasmus might have responded to current cognitive neuroscience research regarding the nature of moral reasoning and the identification of parts of the brain that appear to function as the "seat of the will."[4]

Another philosopher, Arthur Schopenhauer, wrote extensively on will, as well as on the importance of the representation of the world in the mind in his four volume work, *The World as Will and Representation*. Schopenhauer begins with the statement, "The world is my idea." But, for Schopenhauer, the human will is the most important thing. Schopenhauer believed that humans were motivated only by their own basic desires, or *Wille zum Leben* (will to live). He argued that this will to live directed all of mankind.[5] Will is a metaphysical existence that controls the actions of individual, intelligent agents, and ultimately all observable phenomena. Will, for Schopenhauer, is what Kant called the "thing-in-itself."

[1]   Plass, E.W. *What Luther Says* (3 volumes). St. Louis, MO: Concordia Publishing House, 1959.

[2]   Rupp, E.G., Watson, P.S., and Baillie, J. *Luther and Erasmus: Free Will and Salvation* (Library of Christian Classics). Louisville, KY: Westminster John Knox Press, 1995.

[3]   Moss, D. "The roots and genealogy of humanistic psychology." In Schneider, K., Bugental, J., and Pierson, J. (eds.), *Handbook of Humanistic Psychology*. Thousand Oaks, CA: Sage, 2001.

[4]   Ingvar, D.H. "The will of the brain: cerebral correlates of willful acts." *J Theor Biol.* 1994;171:7-12; Frith, C.D., Friston, K., Liddle, P.F., et al. "Willed action and the prefrontal cortex in man: a study with PET." *Proc R Soc Lond.* 1991;244:241-246.

[5]   Santayana, G. "Letter to Richard C. Lyon, 1 August 1949." In Holzberger, J. (ed.), *The Letters of George Santayana*. Cambridge, MA: MIT Press, 2003.

This was then applied to life, reproduction, aesthetics, ethics, and politics. Might we consider the notion of the will as having some ultimate control over human beings and the world in general as being related to the absolute functioning of the frontal lobes? Is it possible that Schopenhauer experienced his sense of will as becoming the fundamental thing underlying the universe itself? If so, it seems most reasonable to consider willfulness as the essence of being. Will is the most fundamentally important thing in the universe. It is also interesting to consider how such a notion might relate to God whose will created the universe. Hence, the notion of willfulness appears to have great prominence in these ideologies. It is no surprise given that the frontal lobes in human beings are relatively larger than in any other species. The importance of the frontal lobes in making us human cannot be understated.

Others have considered willfulness in related, but different, ways. Friedrich Nietzsche considered the "will to power" (*der Wille zur Macht*), as the basis for understanding motivation in human behavior. Nietzsche suggests that the will to power is a more important element than the evolutionary pressure for adaptation or survival.[6] Nietzsche's notion of the will to power can be contrasted against Schopenhauer's "will to live" in that Nietzsche argued that people and animals actually want power while life itself appears only as a subsidiary aim in order to gain power. In Nietzsche's conception, the will can be seen as related to both the total and absolute functioning of the frontal lobes. It is the thing by which Nietzsche understands all living things and it is also the essence of those things. However, it would be interesting to know whether Nietzsche's and Schopenhauer's views reflected similar experiences of will, with slightly different interpretations—one based on power and the other based on living. If this were the case, a neurotheological hermeneutic might be interesting to speculate whether their views were different on the basis of fundamentally different experiences of the will or on the basis of the cognitive processes that interpreted their experiences of will.

Will is viewed from a decidedly different perspective in a number of religious traditions in which the will is surrendered to God. Islam makes surrender of the will a particularly prominent part of its ideology. The word Islam is derived from the Arabic verb Aslama, which means "to accept, surrender or submit." Thus, Islam means acceptance of and submission to God. From a neurotheological perspective, this again appears to entail a functioning of the will, but in the completely opposite direction as that described by Schopenhauer or Nietzsche. From a neurotheological perspective, rather than the intense turning on of the will (or the structures subserving willful processes), there is an intense turning off of these processes. While this is clearly a subjective experience that leads to deep spiritual and religious beliefs, it might be possible to observe this effect in the brain itself by demonstrating a reduction of activity in the structures that underlie willful thoughts and behaviors. On the other hand, the will of God is what takes

---

[6] Nietzsche, F. *Beyond Good and Evil*. Edited by R.-P. Horstmann and translated by J. Norman. Cambridge: Cambridge University Press, 2001.

over the will of the individual human being. In fact, there is a humorous Sufi story about Mulla Nasruddin, that shows the importance of God's will and the absence of the human will in the world. One day, Nasruddin was listening as a holy man prayed loudly: "May the will of Allah be done." "It always is, anyway," said Nasruddin. The holy man heard the comment and opened his eyes. "How can you be sure of that, Mulla?" he asked. "Well, if it weren't true, don't you think I would get *my* way just once?" replied Nasruddin.

Wholeness and Fragmentation

Two concepts in many philosophical and religious traditions are those of the importance of wholeness and fragmentation, or perhaps holism and reductionism. A sense of wholeness likely is associated with the holistic processes of the brain and a sense of fragmentation is likely associated with the reductionist processes of the brain. The contrast between wholeness and fragmentation appears in many sacred texts as well as in the field of aesthetics. Let us explore how these concepts are interrelated and how they relate to the brain.

Most approaches to understanding the universe or God take on a holistic approach in which the whole is experienced as fundamental. The Buddhist and Hindu traditions observe the universe as a unified whole, usually with a universal consciousness. Monotheistic traditions view God as a singular whole. Even within Christianity, there is the absolute necessity to understand the trinity as a fundamental wholeness. The ability to perceive and experience wholeness clearly resides within the human brain as one of its cognitive processes. Total function of this holistic process might lead to a notion in which everything should be considered to be related to the larger whole. Absolute functioning of this cognitive process would lead to the notion that wholeness is fundamental to the universe or to God. This would be the sense that oneness of God or the universe is the ultimate basis for reality itself.

An interesting example of the relationship between reductionism and holism can be found in the Atomists view of the world in a highly reductionist manner. The Atomists conception of the universe and of all objects as being comprised of fundamental particles (not unlike current modern scientific thought) was in some senses a total functioning of the cognitive process involved in reductionism. The Atomist observed that everything in the universe, including all discrete objects, could ultimately be broken down into their constituent parts. In the case of the Atomists, this was experienced as a total functioning of reductionism such that all objects could be reduced to fundamental component parts which could then be identified. Hence, any given structure in the universe was the sum of the parts from which it was comprised. In spite of this reductionism, it was also realized that, in some senses, all things were connected to each other because all things were made of similar atomic elements. The Atomists believed that by understanding these fundamental particles and their relationship to each other, all objects in the world and, subsequently, the macro connections between objects in the world could be understood and, perhaps, even predicted. One side benefit of such an approach included the possibility of empirical research, which could then be utilized to explore whether or not certain fundamental concepts derived from an understanding of atomic components could be accurate and predict future functions and structures.

Of course, it is natural for all of us to be able to analyze our world in a way that reduces objects to more fundamental components. We understand the human body to be comprised of individual organs which are comprised of individual cells which are comprised of individual atoms. However, during the more usual function of the reductionist operator, we can allow ourselves to have this understanding without then concluding that the human body is nothing more than the sum of its most fundamental components. In this way, we have a notion that there are emergent or superordinate properties that arise out of the combined functioning of more basic parts. We can have an understanding of more holistic conceptions of the human being such as we are not just a mass of chemistry and physics, but that we have in many ways a more holistic psychological, social, and perhaps spiritual dimension as well.

The superior parietal lobe has an important function with regard to self orientation. Brain imaging research and stroke studies have shown that this part of the brain integrates information from many sensory systems to provide a sense of our self and a spatial relationship of that self to the world. This is probably not the only part of the brain involved in self orientation, but it is likely to be an important part of the network that performs this function. There are also several studies that have suggested that this region is involved in orientation changes during religious and spiritual practices. Evidence has suggested that a decrease of activity in this region may be associated with the sense of a loss of orientation and a blurring of the boundary between the self and the rest of the world. The blurring of this boundary might contribute to the experience of wholeness since the separation of the self from the rest of the world evaporates and the person has the subjective experience of being completely connected, or perhaps more accurately, absorbed into the universe or God. Thus, all things might be considered unified, and the self become part of this wholeness.

In the Christian context, this is eventually experienced as the *unio mystica* or the mystical union with God, although care is taken by Christian theologians who reflect on this state to preserve the ontological independence of the soul. They would agree that in this state the union of God and the individual soul is so perfect and so complete that an observer, if such were possible, could not perceive where one ended and the other began. Nevertheless, for theological reasons, Christian mystical theologians maintain the ontological integrity of the individual although they would concede that the individual has, as it were, expanded to a perfect and a complete union with God. In the psychiatric literature, a similar type of experience was most carefully described by Richard M. Bucke in his book *Cosmic*

Consciousness.[7] The experience consists of an elated sense of well being and joy, in which the universe is perceived to be fundamentally good and all its parts are sensed to be related in a unified whole. Bucke apparently had this experience himself, and in his magnum opus, he presented evidence of similar experiences in the lives of many people including the Buddha, Socrates, St. Paul, Francis Bacon, Blaise Pascal, Baruch Spinoza, and William Blake as well as many of his own contemporaries.

From a neurotheological hermeneutic, a potentially fascinating question may find interesting evidence in the exploration of a neurological substrate of such experiences. It seems that many individuals have described such unitary experiences throughout history and throughout traditions. However, their descriptions, while often similar, also have certain distinctions, especially when one attempts to interpret these experiences from a particular religious framework. The question then is, "Are these experiences fundamentally the same and simply interpreted differently or are these experiences fundamentally different?" Put more specifically, is the *unio mystica* of the Christian the same as the nirvana of the Buddhist, but simply described differently because of the different ideological position that the experiencing individual may have? Or did the Christian and Buddhist have two fundamentally distinct experiences? Theoretically, if these experiences have the same neurological signature, then this lends support to the notion that they are really one and the same experience. If on the other hand the experiences are associated with completely different neurological signatures, then perhaps they are, in fact, separate and distinct experiences. It is in this context that a neurotheological hermeneutic might be able to contribute to our knowledge regarding such experiences and perhaps inform us about an important theological question.

The opposing experience, that of fragmentation, is also important in theology. Many religions begin with the idea of human beings being fragmented or separated from God. This is certainly the case in the Bible when Adam and Eve are cast out from the Garden of Eden. Whenever one is separate or cast out from God's wholeness and goodness, there is the fundamental problem of trying to reestablish that wholeness. It is interesting to note that many rituals appear to activate brain structures that enable people to come together. In the context of religion, prayers and ceremonies certainly are designed in part to reintegrate the participants with God. And there is some evidence that the actual act of these rituals may affect brain structures in such a way as to foster this reintegration experience.

One other element of wholeness and fragmentation that is related to religion and theology is aesthetics. Friedrich Nietzsche, following the ancient Greek model, divided aesthetics into a kind of positive aesthetics which he called Apollonian and a negative aesthetics which he called Dionysian.[8] Apollonian aesthetics represent what is usually considered the aesthetics of beauty and light.

---

[7]   Bucke, R.M. *Cosmic Consciousness*. Secaucus, NJ: Citadel Press, 1961.

[8]   Nietzsche, F. *The Birth of Tragedy: Out of the Spirit of Music*. Edited by M. Tanner. London: Penguin Classics, 1994.

It is comprised of a sense of wholeness and harmony, and is affectively marked by a sense of pleasantness, at the very least, and often a sense of joy or elation. Dionysian aesthetics, on the other hand, named after the myth of Dionysus being torn apart alive by the Bachae, is marked by a sense of fragmentation, disharmony, death or dying, and is affectively marked by sadness and melancholy, at least, and often by a sense of fundamental hopelessness, futility, and even terror.

Based on ancient philosophers, the medieval scholastics defined the essential characteristics of positive aesthetics as

1. *Integritas* or wholeness
2. *Consonantia Partium* or harmony of parts
3. *Claritas Formae* or a radiance of form[9]

Thus for a work of art to have a positive aesthetic the medievals required that it generate an overall sense of wholeness and a sense of harmony of its composite parts. The radiance or clarity of form seems to have referred to the emotional effect on human beings which should be at the very least pleasant, and hopefully edifying and joyful.

The medieval scholastics were hesitant to deal with negative aesthetics, since, in their view, negative aesthetics were diabolical, while positive aesthetics were from God. Nevertheless, since they followed the ancients, they did summarily treat negative aesthetics as well. To a great extent, although not completely, the defining characteristics of negative aesthetics were considered to be the opposites of those defining positive aesthetics. They were

1. *Integritas in Fragmentatione* or wholeness in fragmentation
2. *Dissonantia Partium* or disharmony of parts
3. *Tenebra Formae* or darkness of form

It is interesting that if the defining characteristics of negative aesthetics were simply the opposite of the defining characteristics of positive aesthetics, then the first characteristic of negative aesthetics should be *Fragmentatio* or fragmentation, pure and simple. But the medievals insisted that, for a work of art to be a work of art, however diabolical, and not simply a rendering of the horror of human life, there had to be some sense of wholeness or integrity even if the subject matter itself was fragmented. Thus, for a medieval aesthetician, and probably for an ancient one as well, "Guernica" or "Waiting for Godot" are works of art at least because they are defined spatially and temporally, by a frame in the case of "Guernica" and by the production time and temporal sequencing in the case of "Waiting for Godot." The medievals would probably maintain that the use of words, and possibly of sentences, and the delimitation of formal elements within a painting contribute

---

[9]   Eco, U. *The Aesthetics of Thomas Aquinas*. Cambridge, MA: Harvard University Press, 1988.

to the formal wholeness in spite of the fragmentation of overall subject matter. One can ask a neurotheological question, "Why is wholeness deemed aesthetically positive while fragmentation is considered negative?" Is it possible that there is an underlying neurological substrate that constrains our perception of beauty? Perhaps wholeness activates structures that subserve our positive emotions and reward centers of the brain. Perhaps fragmentation may activate the fear centers of the brain. These possibilities can lead to a neurotheological hermeneutic investigation of aesthetics.

Rationalism, Logic, and Abstract Thought

Abstract thought processes are also critical to theology and philosophy. There are a number of cognitive functions that appear to make up what we would refer to philosophically as abstract thought. Abstract thought processes include inquiry, categorization of objects, rationality, logic, and language. These processes allow us to consider different ideas related to religion, theology, ethics, ontology, and epistemology. Furthermore, these processes enable us to hold different ideas in our mind while we manipulate them into various ideological systems.

The works of Plato span a tremendous diversity of ideas covering philosophical thought. Certain details of these ideas will be worth considering from a neurotheological hermeneutic. However, it makes sense to begin by evaluating the overall methodology that is pervasive in Plato's writings. In Plato's work, specific concepts are thought of and defined through a logical/deductive analysis. In the works on Socrates this analysis takes the form of the well known "Socratic method." The Socratic method involves persistent questioning of a particular philosophical idea which must then prove itself by standing up to a detailed analysis. If various *a priori* statements are made, then they must have some degree of either internal consistency or consistency with regard to what is typically observed in the real world. The basis of such an approach is that there may be inherent contradictions within a particular philosophical ideal or philosophical system which would therefore negate that idea or system.

His discussions about God suggest that several key functions of the verbal and abstract thought processes of the brain are at work. In particular, the ability to hold abstract categorizations of things and to think in a binary mode allow human beings to consider a variety of opposing concepts and attempt to either reconcile or ultimately dismiss one on the basis of logical argument. Thus, issues about good versus evil, justice versus injustice, and man versus God, could all be contemplated with a strong sense of how the abstract conceptualization of these opposites could be compared and whether such a comparison would ultimately result in inconsistencies which would subsequently deny one or the other as being valid.

We can see such analyses in Plato's works such as the *Phaedo*, *Euthyphro*, and even in his larger work *The Republic*. In each of these philosophical discussions, we see Socrates, via Plato's writings, addressing various abstract concepts and defining their characteristics and their boundaries with other members of the discussion, determining which of the opposites has a truer validity with regards to what is "known," and what is arrived at through rational deduction.

For example, in the *Phaedo*[10] we begin with Socrates asking the question:

> So you think that we should assume two classes of things, one visible and the other invisible?

> Yes, we should.

> The invisible being invariable, and the visible never being the same?

> Yes, we should assume that, too.

> Well, now, said Socrates, are we not part body, part soul?

> Certainly.

> Then to which class do we say that the body would have the closer resemblance and relation?

> Quite obviously the visible.

> And the soul, is it visible or invisible?

> Invisible to men, at any rate, Socrates, he said.

Later the dialogue continues with Socrates stating:

> Look at it in this way too. When soul and body are both in the same place, nature teaches the one to serve and be subject, the other to rule and govern. In this relation which do you think resembles the divine and which the mortal part? Don't you think that it is the nature of the divine to rule and direct, and that of the mortal to be subject and serve?

> I do.

> Then which does the soul resemble?

> Obviously, Socrates, soul resembles the divine, and body the mortal.

---

[10]   Hamilton, E. and Cairns, H. *Plato: The Collected Dialogues*. Princeton, NJ: Princeton University Press, 1961.

Here we see an excellent example of binary thinking—there is the visible and invisible, the variable and invariable, and the body and the soul. From these concepts, arguments are made so that the soul is considered invisible and unchangeable. While it is clear that the concepts of soul and the divine are different than what is believed in current monotheistic traditions, the point here is that a neurotheological hermeneutic might show why this type of argument holds value for us. These rational arguments make sense, but do they inherently make sense on some fundamental level, or do they make sense because the human brain perceives them as making sense?

A neurotheological hermeneutic might argue that much of the work of Plato and the elaboration of the Socratic method is based upon a rigorous analysis of all things as evaluated through the rational and reductive processes. The Socratic method appears predicated on abstract and rational thought processes of the brain that enable us to ask questions and to analyze the world that we perceive so that we can make meaning and make sense of the various things that are observed in the external world.

Let us now consider the work of St. Anselm of Canterbury, who wrote: "Neque enim quaero intelligere ut credam, sed credo ut intelligam. Nam et hoc credo, quia, nisi credidero, non intelligam." ("Nor do I seek to understand that I may believe, but I believe that I may understand. For this, too, I believe, that, unless I first believe, I shall not understand.") In his view, faith preceded reason, but reason could be derived from and expand upon faith.[11] But consider this statement from a neurotheological perspective. There are a number of elements that have cognitive components—understanding, faith, and reason. Anselm argued that belief was necessary first so that reason and understanding could follow. Given current knowledge of brain function, this is a very reasonable position since the brain makes many assumptions and beliefs which it then attempts to integrate into a clear understanding of the world. Is it possible that this statement presages the need of a neurotheological hermeneutic to provide the full understanding required in order to explore faith?

In the eighteenth century, Immanuel Kant greatly elaborated the rational perspective in human philosophy. His *Critique of Pure Reason* as well as his other works implied that all the universe, both spiritual and non-spiritual, could be understood through a human rational approach separated from sensorial experience.[12] For Kant, there was something inherent in the human mind that allowed it access to ultimate reality. Thus, "pure reason" was something that could be attainable. However, this rational approach had to be measured and carefully considered. Kant argued that no theoretical argument, could prove the existence of God. Kant considered human reason to overreach its powers, and thus was in need

---

[11]   Warren, H.C. *Medieval Europe: A Short History*. New York, NY: John Wiley & Sons, 1982.

[12]   Kant, I. *Critique of Pure Reason*. Edited by P. Guyer and A.W. Wood. Cambridge: Cambridge University Press, 1999.

of self-limitation. Kant also argued that reason seeks to know what lies beyond the range of "experience" so that we can apprehend objects as they are related to one another in some type of spatio-temporal framework with causal laws. But, Kant considered any attempt to claim knowledge outside the limits of human experience to be problematic. This, of course, is commensurate with current neurotheological analysis in that the perceptions of the human brain are considered crucial for knowledge. But it is also the tendency of human beings, and human reason, to go beyond the limits of experience and this ultimately results in the representation of ideas of the soul, the spirit, and God. The problem is that as representations in the brain or mind, concepts such as soul, spirit, or God, may be very problematic and be restrained by the very functions that help us understand them.

Causality in the Brain and in Theology

Causality has been a central issue for theology, philosophy, and science for thousands of years. Human beings have been fascinated by causal sequences in the world and have long sought to understand them as fully as possible. The fact that we can perceive cause and effect indicates that we have a brain capable of perceiving cause and effect. In fact, the brain also appears capable of attributing cause and effect, even though it sometimes is inaccurate. On a practical side, it seems most crucial to be able to determine causality since this allows the brain to prepare for future events. If we walk down a certain street and we are mugged, we will avoid that street in the future since we observed a cause and effect. On the other hand, if something good happens to us when we engage in a particular practice, then we will want to keep doing that practice. This is imminently practical, but there are many interesting issues, and mistakes, that arise with the brain's view of causality.

One problem that the brain has is how it attributes causality to sequences of things. We have a tendency to believe that if something comes after something else in a temporal sequence, the latter was caused by the former. This mistake, referred to as "post hoc ergo propter hoc," results in many circumstances, sometimes amusing, in which causality is improperly attributed on these grounds:

> A woman in a suburb of New York City steps out of her house on to her front stoop each morning and exclaims, "Let this house be safe from tigers!" Then she goes back inside. Finally, she was asked by one of her neighbors, "What is that all about. There isn't a tiger within a thousand miles of here." And she said, "See? It works."[13]

This problem is always a challenge from a theological perspective when certain acts are observed to follow from each other and divine intervention is implicated

---

[13]   Cathcart, T. and Klein, D. *Plato and a Platypus Walk into a Bar*. New York, NY: Penguin Books, 2007.

because there is either no clear preceding causal event or because the causal link is not evident. One can ponder whether the problem is with the data or with the human brain trying to interpret the data.

The brain would generally prefer clear causal relationships, but what happens when causal relationships are not well established? One possibility is to invoke a material cause that can be measured by some type of scientific experiment. This leads to science as a way of trying to establish cause and effect. While this may work well for many events, especially those that apply to non-living objects, it is far more problematic when trying to use experimentation to address causality in the context of interpersonal relationships. After all, it is most difficult to experiment with emotions, social conventions, and intuitive responses. Another possibility, when causal relationships are not clear is to invoke something that is beyond "normal" or "material" causality—perhaps a supernatural or divine cause. This is commensurate with religious beliefs about the world, but scientists typically argue that since this would lead towards unmeasurable processes, it is more likely that the causal mechanism is simply beyond the current methodology available. This is not an inappropriate interpretation, but not necessarily correct either. In fact, as we shall consider later, several major breakthroughs in science and logic in the twentieth century put causality on rather tenuous grounds. Perhaps it might be more accurate to state that the brain seeks causality in the material world through scientific exploration. But there remain many issues pertaining to human behavior, culture, consciousness, subjective awareness, spirituality, and religion which are difficult if not impossible to address via experimentation and therefore frequently dismissed by the scientific community.

More formally, the classic elaboration of causality began with that of Aristotle's four fundamental causes—Material, Essential, Formal, and Final causality. One might imagine his brain function at the time of conceiving the four fundamental causes of the universe. This might have been associated with both the total and absolute functioning of his brain's causal process since he argued that all things can be understood via these causes. Furthermore, causality is a fundamental construct of the universe. Of course, the notion of final cause, or *telos*, is the purpose, or end, that something is supposed to serve, and this leads to teleology, a principle argument for the proof of God's existence. It is interesting that the brain has a tendency to assume a creator of something else which has a certain degree of complexity. Aristotle described the Prime Mover in his *Metaphysics*. Again this relates to the need to explain purpose and causality in the universe. In *de Natura Deorum (On the Nature of the Gods)* Cicero states, "The divine power is to be found in a principle of reason that pervades the whole of nature." He goes on to state the classical "watchmaker" argument regarding the creation of a clock:

When you see a sundial or a water-clock, you see that it tells the time by design and not by chance. How then can you imagine that the universe as a whole is devoid of purpose and intelligence, when it embraces everything, including these artifacts themselves and their artificers?[14]

Over the years, many thinkers have rejected this concept since it is difficult for us to understand fully the basis for creation and how things are actually caused in the universe. The brain has difficulty accepting things as "just happening" because the brain seeks meaning and purpose in the world. Thus, a neurotheological perspective might provide a framework from which we can better understand the allure of the teleological argument and encourage careful use of such an argument given the limitations of how the brain perceives causality.

Quantitative Processes and the Nature of the Universe

Another of the ancient Greek thinkers was Pythagoras, whose fundamental construction of universal concepts was primarily based on mathematics. To this end, Pythagoras' teachings included evaluating various structures and functions in the world from a mathematical perspective. Mathematics was used in the evaluation of various physical structures to determine their relationship to each other as well as the various dimensions of their specific structures. There was also a notion that this extended to the functionality of given structures in the universe including human beings and human thought. Thus, to Pythagoras, all things could ultimately be broken down into a mathematical construction that could then be expressed in geometric or other forms of mathematical expression. But Pythagoras went further by considering mathematics to be the fundamental substance of the universe. As Aristotle described in his *Metaphysics*:

The so-called Pythagoreans, who were the first to take up mathematics, not only advanced this subject, but saturated with it, they fancied that the principles of mathematics were the principles of all things.[15]

When correlating such ideas to neuropsychological function, we can envision that Pythagoras experienced a total functioning of his quantitative processes that essentially allowed all objects in the world to pass through for analysis. Brain imaging studies have implicated the inferior part of the parietal lobe to be involved in mathematical and quantitative processes. So perhaps, it is this area that contributes to experiences of either the total or absolute functioning of quantitative processes.

---

[14] Cicero. *De Natura Deorum*. Quoted in Gjersen, D. *Science and Philosophy: Past and Present*. London: Penguin, 1989.

[15] *Aristotle's Metaphysics*. Translated by J. Sachs. 2nd Edition. Santa Fe, NM: Green Lion Press, 2002.

Since it appears that Pythagoras also experienced the absolute functioning of the quantitative processes, for him mathematics became the fundamental substance of the universe that described not only objects within the universe, but God as well.

Another philosopher whose work should be considered an important contribution to neurotheology was Baruch Spinoza (1632-1677), the Dutch Jew who heavily based his theological and philosophical ideas on mathematics and science. In fact, his conception of God as being attributed to the beauty and clarity of design in mathematics fostered a unique integration of science and religion. Spinoza describes, "From the infinite nature of God all things ... follow by the same necessity, and in the same way, as it follows from the nature of a triangle, from eternity to eternity, that its three angles are equal to two right angles."[16] Mathematics forms the basis of how we understand God, eternity, and the universe. While this does not specifically relate to the neurosciences, Spinoza had an understanding that the laws of nature were reflected in the divine presence in the universe, "the universal laws of nature according to which all things happen and are determined are nothing but God's eternal decrees, which always involve eternal truth and necessity."[17] Furthermore, it was believed by Spinoza that through human thought and philosophical and scientific endeavors, human beings could come to know the order of the world and the nature of God. Although Spinoza's work emphasized the physical sciences, it might be argued that his perspective is highly supportive of neurotheology as a way of understanding the human being and the human perspective of the universe via the brain. For example, Spinoza describes the *conatus*: "Each thing, as far as it can by its own power, strives to persevere in its being." Damasio describes the underlying neurobiological correlates of this process by which human beings persevere in relation to the sensory and cognitive systems that aid in adaptability and survival.[18] In this way, Spinoza might have argued that understanding the mind does help understand the divine presence in the universe, or at least in the human being.

It should also be stated that this type of functioning of the quantitative processes also underlies the more general field of mathematics in which researchers and scholars will explore mathematical concepts and break things down according to quantitative analysis. However, there is a fundamental distinction between those scholars who pursue mathematics and explore the world through mathematics compared to the more ontological notion that mathematics represents the true nature of the universe. However, because of the intense scrutiny that a given scholar may apply even in the mathematical arena, it is likely that there is at least

[16]   Spinoza, B. "Ethics." In Ariew, R. and Watkins, E. (eds.), *Readings in Modern Philosophy: Descartes, Spinoza, Leibniz and Associated Texts*. Indianapolis, IN: Hackett Publishing Company, 2000. Ethics I:17.

[17]   Spinoza, B. *Theological-Political Treatise: Gebhardt Edition*. Edited by Samuel Shirley and Seymour Feldman. Indianapolis, IN: Hackett Publishing Company, 2001.

[18]   Damasio, A. *Looking for Spinoza: Joy, Sorrow, and the Feeling Brain*. New York, NY: Harcourt, 2003.

some sense in mathematicians that quantitation does in fact represent some more fundamental level of reality, whether or not they ultimately believe that all of reality including ontological and epistemological questions can be answered on the basis of mathematics.

Binary Opposition and Theology

The ability of the brain to set apart opposites and work with them to either maintain their separateness or integrate them plays a large role in many philosophical and theological systems. Many theological arguments and issues appear to arise from an apparent multiplicity of dyadic relationships:

- inside–outside
- above–below
- left–right
- in front–behind
- all–nothing
- before–after
- simultaneous–sequential[19]

These relatively few basic spatio-temporal relationships can be enriched by combining them with emotional tone and elaborated by adding other cognitive and experiential information. Thus, "within" is usually identified with good and "without" with bad, "above" with good and "below" with bad, "right" with good and "left" with bad, "in front" with good and "behind" with bad, "all" with good and "nothing" with bad, and so on. These emotional responses certainly are not absolute and the reverse of any of them may also occur. It is also important to note that certain brain structures appear to be associated not only with these spatio-temporal relationships, but also for helping establish the notion of opposites or binary thinking.

It is interesting, however, to reflect on how common, if not universal, are the relationships just mentioned. In other words, the same relationships are found in many religious traditions throughout the world. There may be a readily apparent reason for this common association which involves issues of simple preservation and hence evolutionary significance. For example, "above" is usually safer than "below" because one can look out for predators more easily when one is situated high up rather than when the predator is situated higher. The result is that "above" is considered good while "below," which may be more dangerous, is considered bad. Of course, it is interesting to point out that heaven is above and hell is below.

---

[19]   d'Aquili, E.G. "The myth-ritual complex: a biogenetic structural analysis." In Ashbrook, J.B. (ed.), *Brain, Culture, and the Human Spirit*. New York, NY: Lanham Press, 1993.

But as we have considered all along, we can ask: is the relationship between heaven and hell responsible for the brain's perception of up being good and down being bad or is the brain responsible for the ways in which we perceive of heaven and hell?

In religion and theology, the most important oppositional dyad is the relationship between God and human beings. This is a fundamental problem in religious and theological thought since we must establish some way in which the imperfect, mortal, and limited human can have any kind of relationship with God who is perfect, eternal, and infinite. On one hand, religion establishes what this difference is, and on the other, religion helps to reconcile the opposites. Religion provides a means by which human beings can have a relationship with God. Through practices, behaviors, and covenants, human beings establish and fulfill their relationship with God. But to some extent, this can only happen if our brain understands the dyad as well as the way towards integration. Other theological problems that are presented as dyads include those related to life–death, good–evil, moral–immoral, right–wrong, existence–nonexistence, or heaven–hell.[20] Often, religion finds a resolution to these dyadic problems via some form of integration or wholeness. This wholeness might even recognize both elements of the dyad as requiring the other.

This notion of dyadic relationships is taken a step further in some of the Eastern traditions. One example is the notion of the *yin* and *yang* that describes the opposing forces that interact within human beings. These two forces push and pull on human beings to establish their various behaviors. In Hindu thought, there is the notion of an Absolute Good which actually integrates both good and evil. In this manner, good and evil are fully integrated to the state in which they are essentially one and the same. While this seems problematic from a Western perspective, the holistic functions of the brain apparently can allow such a wholeness in the minds of those who believe in this concept.

Even science has many dyadic concepts. Positively and negatively charged particles show how important a dyadic interaction actually is since the different charged particles interact in specific ways based upon their oppositional nature. A corresponding biological concept of "tone" has been applied to many physiological and neurophysiological systems. Tone refers to the balance between two opposing physiological processes. For example, the autonomic nervous system that governs arousal and calming responses in the body typically rests in a tonal state such that the body is maintained within a certain balance. When one side of the autonomic nervous system is called upon such as when we need to respond quickly to a threatening situation, the arousal system is activated while the calming system is suppressed. Thus, the notion of opposing forces that govern the mind and body are similar to those found in ancient Buddhist texts.

---

    [20]   Jung, C.G. *Psyche and Symbol*. New York, NY: Doubleday Anchor Books, 1958; Levi-Strauss, C. *Structural Anthropology*. New York, NY: Anchor Books, 1963.

A neurotheological hermeneutic asks us to explore these dyadic elements in many different theological and philosophical systems. Does the knowledge of the dyadic processing by the human brain help to understand the importance of these dyads in religious belief systems? How can we see scholars and theologians struggling to understand dyadic elements and how do they try to integrate them, if at all?

Emotions and Feelings in Theology

While cognition and rational thought processes are a cornerstone of theology, another crucial aspect relates to emotions and feelings. Emotions have been at the heart of many schools of thought, both philosophical and theological. For example, Stoic philosophy of ancient Greece incorporated a highly rational approach to human behaviors and thoughts, with an essential shutting off of human emotions. It was believed that emotions merely got in the way of rational thinking and that the best way to think successfully about the world and to understand the world would be to clear the mind of interfering, and perhaps unwanted emotions. Epictetus stated, "Freedom is secured not by the fulfilling of one's desires, but by the removal of desire."[21] Thus the Stoic's philosophy centered on rational thought as the primary means of understanding the world and of processing information. From the neuropsychological perspective one can clearly see an attempt to shut down the various parts of the brain involved in emotional processing. Thus, limbic system functions, including that of the amygdala, hippocampus and hypothalamus, should be markedly reduced. Concomitantly, there should be an increase in activity in the more logical deductive parts of the brain. This might be attributable to what we have referred to in the past as the verbal and conceptual areas of the brain. In fact, what we might anticipate happening in the brain of a Stoic would be their experience of all information being processed in a total way through the verbal conceptual area resulting in a highly rational and ruled-based approach to the world. If this occurs in the absence of significant limbic system activity, the result would be a very Stoic, rational analysis of cognitive and sensory information.

Stoic philosophy was the antithesis of a strong emotional perspective on philosophy or theology. It is also similar in many respects to the goals of Buddhist thought to end human suffering by releasing oneself from attachments in the world. But Judeo-Christian traditions take a very different perspective with substantial influence of emotions both from humans and from God. Many different emotions are emphasized throughout the Bible. God demonstrates feelings of anger, love, and jealousy. In Exodus, "for I the LORD thy God am a jealous God, visiting the iniquity of the fathers upon the children unto the third and fourth generation of them that hate me; And shewing mercy unto thousands of them that love me, and

---

[21]   Dobbin, R. (trans.). *Epictetus: Discourses and Selected Writings*. London: Penguin Classics, 2008.

keep my commandments."[22] Human beings experience great sadness and great joy. In Psalm 16 we read, "Thou wilt shew me the path of life: in thy presence is fulness of joy; at thy right hand there are pleasures for evermore."[23]

It is also interesting to observe how emotions have been utilized by different religious leaders and scholars throughout history. Martin Luther said, "I never work better than when I am inspired by anger; when I am angry, I can write, pray, and preach well, for then my whole temperament is quickened, my understanding sharpened, and all mundane vexations and temptations depart."[24] The American theologian, Jonathan Edwards expanded on the importance of emotions in religion in his work *A Treatise on Religious Affections*. He argued that both emotions and reason play a role in the true conversion to Christianity.[25] Since the turn of the twentieth century, scholars began to devote themselves to the phenomenology of religion on its own terms. They believed that there were phenomena that needed to be explained which eluded both sociological and psychological determinism. An example of such an approach has been to analyze religion in terms of an awareness of the "sacred" and the "holy." Rudolf Otto, in *The Idea of the Holy*,[26] defined the essence of religious awareness as awe, described as a mixture of fear and fascination before the divine and referred to as a *mysterium tremendum et fascinans*. Robert Roberts, a Presbyterian theologian, emphasized the need for discipline in Christian emotional life. Roberts begins his book *Spirituality and Human Emotion* by stating:

> Whatever else Christianity may be, it is a set of emotions. It is love of God and neighbor, grief about one's own waywardness, joy in the merciful salvation of our God, gratitude, hope and peace. So if I don't love God and my neighbor, abhor my sins, and rejoice in my redemption, if I am not grateful, hopeful and at peace with God and myself, then it follows that I am alienated from Christianity, though I was born and bred in the bosom of the Presbyterian church, am baptized and confirmed and willing in good conscience to affirm the articles of the Creed.[27]

But where and how do these emotions arise? How do we know which ones to hold on to and which ones to eschew? How do we balance the positive and negative elements of emotions. While the theological ideas above provide one answer to these questions, a neurotheological hermeneutic may help to better understand

---

[22]   Exodus 20:5-6. *King James Bible*.

[23]   Psalms 16:11. *King James Bible*.

[24]   Plass, E.W. *What Luther Says* (3 volumes). St. Louis, MO: Concordia Publishing House, 1959.

[25]   Edwards, J. *A Treatise Concerning Religious Affections*. New York, NY: Cosimo Classics, 2007.

[26]   Otto, R. *Idea of the Holy*. Oxford: Oxford University Press, 1958.

[27]   Roberts, R.C. *Spirituality and Human Emotion*. New York, NY: Eerdmans, 1982.

the nature of emotions in theology. Perhaps we can develop a more systematic approach to the nature of religious affections so that we might better describe them and better evaluate how to manage such affections properly.

Permanence, Change, and Spiritual Transformation

One of the most fundamental processes of the brain is its ability to change over time. This occurs in almost every part of the brain since every part is capable of reacting to some change brought about either by internal or external stimuli. The brain is designed to be able to respond so that it changes its connections between nerve cells, the concentration of neurotransmitters, or the amount of receptors. These changes can occur on a moment to moment basis, although some changes require more time than others.

Another important aspect of change is neuroplasticity, which refers to the brain's ability to grow new nerve cells and new neural connections. It is the ability to change that enables the brain to learn and adapt throughout the life span. A 70 year old is still the same person as he was at 40 and at four years of age, but the brain has created new connections and adopted new behaviors that enable the person to grow and develop throughout their life span.

Consciously, the brain experiences change in different ways. For many, the brain does not allow them to consciously see the change even though it is occurring. The brain convinces us that our beliefs and ideas are firm and generally unchanging. However, much research suggests that just the opposite is true.

This battle between permanence and change is critical to the human mind, but also to theology, philosophy, and science. For example, a religion needs to have sufficient permanence in order to maintain its own structure and belief system. Thus, religions must clearly determine their primary tenets so that these become unwavering. Religions must also allow for some degree of adaptability so that they can maintain their relevance in a changing world. If a religion never changes, it may become stagnant or outdated. On the other hand, if it changes too much, it might lose its own identity. Heraclitus considered change the one permanent aspect of the universe with his famous statement: "We both step and do not step in the same rivers." This is the notion that the river is constantly changing and we can never step into the same river twice. For Heraclitus, then, change or flow was the essence of the universe. This would represent the absolute functioning of the brain processes that enable us to perceive change in the world. On the other hand, we can observe that other philosophers, such as Plato, who disagreed with Heraclitus, were not accessing that same part of the brain. For Plato, permanence was the only way in which objects could come into existence:

> How can that be a real thing which is never in the same state? ... for at the
> moment that the observer approaches, then they become other ... so that you

cannot get any further in knowing their nature or state ... but if that which knows
and that which is known exist ever ... then I do not think they can resemble a
process or flux ...[28]

We can ponder how different brain structures and functions contributed to these
disparate belief systems. And of course, these concepts have had substantial
influence on theology, especially in terms of dealing with change and permanence.
For the theologian, the issue confronting his brain would be to account for God's
permanence in a universe that is ever changing. Does this imply that God also
changes? This is certainly a battle between opposing processes in the brain as well
as whatever might be the case in actuality.

Thomas Kuhn, in his *The Structure of Scientific Revolutions*, addresses this
topic in terms of the nature of paradigm shifts. Kuhn argued that science does
not progress in a linear manner, but undergoes periodic revolutions in new
ideas.[29] The prevailing paradigm represents the current state of science and
the perspective by which current thinkers and researchers approach the world.
However, as increasing data accumulate, there eventually is an entire shift from
one paradigm to the next. Excellent examples in the twentieth century include
the shift from Newtonian physics to Einstein's relativity and the prevailing static
model of the atom and subatomic particles to the field of quantum mechanics. It
is interesting that this larger reflection on the nature of science parallels what the
brain appears to do as well. The brain typically must rely on a prevailing world
view paradigm which it uses to interact with the world. This paradigm might
include moral, religious, political, and interpersonal notions about the world
and how to enact such ideas via specific behaviors. It is most difficult to change
one's mind about basic elements of that prevailing belief system. When initially
confronted with contrary information, the typical reaction is for the individual to
reject that information. This is similar to what is observed in science and religion.
But if the evidence becomes overwhelming, there reaches some threshold at which
time there is a relatively sudden realization that a shift must occur to maintain an
accurate account of the world. Kuhn argued that there were five elements that were
associated with prevailing scientific paradigms: accuracy, consistency, broadness
in scope, simplicity, and the ability to provide fruitful future investigations.
The neurotheological hermeneutic can potentially evaluate the merits of these
criteria and determine how and why the brain might consider these elements so
valuable. Would science be completely different if the human brain had different
characteristics?

Kuhn's ideas of paradigm shifts might be applicable to spiritual shifts as well.
Spiritual shifts might occur in individuals as well as in groups. While it is possible
to offer several ideas about how such spiritual shifts might come about from a

---

[29]   Kuhn, T.S. *The Structure of Scientific Revolutions*. Chicago, IL: University of
Chicago Press, 1970.

neurobiological perspective, this would not necessarily explain the basis for the transformation itself. It is known that the brain has a characteristic called plasticity in which various connections can be rewired in order to learn or acquire some new memory, piece of information, or behavior. With spiritually transformative experiences, there is a fundamental problem with the more established notion of plasticity. The ability of neural connections to change does take some time and usually some degree of repetition. How then can we explain a momentary experience that results in a lifetime of change based on what we currently understand about neurobiology? The nerve cells could not break old connections and make new ones in such a short period of time. One possibility is that there are existing connections that are either inactivated, suppressed, or are excluded from the primary modes of consciousness, that suddenly become activated and in some sense overpower the existing neural connections. If this is the case, then one might argue that we all harbor within us the potential for transformative experiences. At this time, there is no research that has shown that this is the case, but at the moment it is difficult to find an alternative explanation.

Much work still needs to be done to better elucidate the intricate mechanisms underlying spiritual transformation. Most available studies have explored specific spiritual practices such as meditation or prayer which may or may not be extrapolated to intense mystical experiences which can also be transformative. Regardless, the neurophysiological effects that have been observed during meditative states seem to outline a consistent pattern of changes involving certain key cerebral structures in conjunction with autonomic and hormonal changes. These changes are also reflected in neurochemical changes involving the endogenous opioid, GABA, norepinephrine, and serotonergic receptor systems. It should also be restated that whatever neurophysiological bases of spiritual transformation are eventually discovered, they do not necessarily reduce such experiences to mere biology. The subjective state and the phenomenology of such experiences cannot be ignored or dismissed especially considering that such experiences carry with them not only transformative properties, but a very strong sense they represent a more fundamental reality compared to that observed by science. Furthermore, the physiological means of entering into a spiritual state may simply reflect the brain's response to that experience rather than establish a true causal relationship. Regardless of the ultimate basis of such experiences, elucidating their physiological and psychological basis can only help in our overall understanding of how spiritual transformation comes about.

Final Reflections on Neurotheological Hermeneutics

Given the above relatively limited examples of how neurotheology might be applied to a hermeneutical approach to theology and philosophy, we can consider a few expanded concepts pertaining to hermeneutics in general. It is important to note that the various theological positions considered below are specifically presented for the purpose of understanding how a neurotheological hermeneutic might be useful. Neurotheology is not meant in any way or form specifically to make judgments regarding the validity of these theological approaches. Whether neurotheology might be able to provide information that could lead to additional arguments of validity is something that would need to be explored later, after the groundwork for neurotheology itself is more fully explicated.

If we begin by exploring biblical hermeneutics as the study of the principles of interpretation concerning the books of the Bible, we can see that neurotheology might offer an interesting perspective. Since the work of Schleiermacher, mentioned in the first chapter, biblical hermeneutics is typically considered to be expanded from not only an understanding and interpretation of scripture as assumed to be the theological principles of exegesis, but also from a broader philosophical or linguistic hermeneutic. From either perspective, neurotheology may offer some useful applications. For example, biblical exegesis already assumes that the Bible is a whole work from God rather than a text to be interpreted as being written and edited over time in pieces. However, there are many ways of interpreting the meaning of the text and this ultimately requires a variety of cognitive processes.

One hermeneutical approach referred to as the historical-grammatical method attempts to determine the original meaning of the biblical text through examination of the grammatical and syntactical aspects as well as from the historical background.[30] The historical-grammatical method distinguishes between the one original meaning of the text and its significance. One might apply neurotheology in this context since there is a substantial database on cognitive processes related to grammar and syntax. There are many interesting issues that can be evaluated in terms of how the brain actually determines meaning through grammar and syntax. Several interesting studies have evaluated the parts of the brain that activate when there are deviations from normal syntax. If the goal of the historical-grammatical method is to evaluate such meaning, adding a neurotheological perspective may aid in the fuller interpretation of this meaning. A related approach, the lexical-grammatical approach,[31] should also find interesting information arising from a neurotheological analysis of language, syntax, and lexicons. Further, since there is emphasis on how individuals' readings of biblical passages may have changed over time, it could be quite valuable to observe how these passages actually affect people today and determine if there may be correlations with the effects at other periods.

Conversely, the hermeneutical approach to theology that examines grammar and syntax might also provide important information for the study of language from a cognitive neuroscience perspective. In fact, regardless of whether one believes in God or not, understanding that these specific grammatical and lexical sequences have had the most dramatic influence on human history might provide

---

[30]   Johnson, E. *Expository Hermeneutics: An Introduction*. Grand Rapids, MI: Academie Books, 1990.

[31]   Virkler, H.A. and Ayayo, K.G. *Hermeneutics: Principles and Processes of Biblical Interpretation*. Grand Rapids, MI: Baker House Book Company, 1981.

a target for research that explores whether there is something inherently powerful about such sequences. Thus, the way in which the Bible provides knowledge (for example, via the Psalms) obviously has a profound impact on the brain's functions. Could we better understand the brain by understanding how the Psalms have such a strong influence on our brain, our thoughts, and our feelings?

Covenant theology views the history of God's dealings with mankind under the framework of three overarching theological covenants—the covenants of redemption, of works, and of grace. What might be interesting from a neurotheological perspective would be to determine how such covenants are understood by the brain and how easy or difficult they are to follow based on the limitations of the brain. For example, the covenant of grace, which promises eternal blessing for all people who trust in the successive promises of God, requires that the human brain is, in fact, capable of understanding God accurately and of being able to believe appropriately in God's promises. Obviously there are many individuals who do not believe in God and it would be potentially fascinating to explore the differences in the brain that exist between those who do and those who do not believe. Is it possible that the same brain functions and structures that result in non-belief are actually in all people, but only turned on in some? Alternatively, is it possible that believers are built completely differently? It would seem that there would be significant theological implications depending on the answers to these questions as they relate to the ability of human beings to follow the covenants of God. In addition, covenant theology should tell us something about how we as human beings work. What is going on in the brain when we read and understand a covenant? Obviously, this is a powerful way to influence us and perhaps we can learn more about how the brain works when we are asked or told to enter into a covenant.

Contextual approaches to theology explore the context of a verse in its chapter, book, and even the entire Bible in order to ascertain its meaning. It is interesting to consider how the mind contextualizes things. We ask children to try to define a word based upon its context so the brain clearly has a way of doing this. However, we can also test how well contextual analyses work for us. It may also be important to determine how much influence the context should have in helping establish the meaning of a particular passage. After all, some passages ultimately may stand on their own while others require substantial context. How and why does this happen and how does our brain comprehend this? Again, we could potentially utilize contextual theology to help cognitive neuroscience by demonstrating the ways in which the brain does contextualize things. We could then study this application to determine how the brain actually does this.

Two interesting principles of theology are the First Mention Principle and the Progressive Mention Principle. The First Mention Principle refers to how God indicates in the first mention of a subject the truth with which that subject stands. Through this first mention, the subject also remains connected in the mind of God. The Progressive Mention Principle states that "God makes the revelation of any given truth increasingly clear as the word proceeds to its consummation."[32] Both of these concepts have a potentially interesting relationship with brain function since the brain can also do either of these. It can accept as truth the first thing it hears, and it also can figure out truths over time, even those that seem contradictory to first impressions. Much has been made over the years of the importance of first impressions. Once a connection forms in the brain, added effort is required in order to break it. So there is a neurobiological mechanism by which people utilize a version of the first mention principle. On the other hand, the human brain can develop ideas and clarify concepts over time. Whether the ability of the human brain to process information in these two ways has any relationship to the understanding of how God makes meaning is unclear. However, it may be important in understanding how we as human beings decide which things to take as true at first mention and which things to take as true over time.

Neurotheological hermeneutics can potentially play an important role in understanding why some believe in the inerrancy of God and the Bible. From this perspective, God is the principal author of the Bible, and thus it can contain no error, no self-contradiction, and nothing contrary to scientific or historical truth. Catholic theologians generally believe that the Bible is God's message put in words by men, with the imperfections this very fact necessarily implies. According to Pope John Paul II,

> Addressing men and women, from the beginnings of the Old Testament onward, God made use of all the possibilities of human language, while at the same time accepting that his word be subject to the constraints caused by the limitations of this language. Proper respect for inspired Scripture requires undertaking all the labors necessary to gain a thorough grasp of its meaning.[33]

However, even if one assumes that the written word is perfect, it still must be read and understood by the human brain. Understanding the limitations of the brain regarding language, comprehension, emotion, and biases could be crucial for developing a more thorough hermeneutic that takes into account these biological influences.

Thus, there are many opportunities to expand a neurotheological hermeneutic as a way of evaluating a variety of theological and philosophical concepts. While it is unlikely that neurotheology will replace other hermeneutical approaches, it has the potential to offer an alternative perspective that might best be combined with other, more traditional, approaches.

---

[32] Hartill, J.E. *Principles of Biblical Hermeneutics*. Grand Rapids, MI: Zondervan Publishing House, 1960.

[33] "The interpretation of the Bible in the Church." Presented by the Pontifical Biblical Commission to Pope John Paul II on April 23, 1993 (http://catholic-resources. org/ChurchDocs/PBC_Interp5.htm).

Chapter 6

Principles Relating to the Methods of Neurotheological Research

Origins and Goals of Neurotheological Methods

With the rapidly expanding field of research exploring religious and spiritual phenomena, there have been many perspectives on the validity, importance, relevance, and need for such research. There is also the ultimate issue of how such research should be interpreted with regard to epistemological questions. The best way to evaluate the field of neurotheology is to determine the methodological issues that currently affect the field and explore how best to address such issues so that future investigations can be as robust as possible and make this body of research more mainstream. Thus, this chapter will focus on more specific principles regarding the methods by which neurotheological research and scholarship should proceed. Interestingly, within the Bible itself, we find the first notion of how a research study might actually be designed. In the Book of Daniel (verses 12-15) we read:

> Please test your servants for ten days, and let us be given some vegetables to eat and water to drink. Then let our appearance be observed in your presence and the appearance of the youths who are eating the king's choice food; and deal with your servants according to what you see. So he listened to them in this matter and tested them for ten days. At the end of ten days their appearance seemed better and they were fatter than all the youths who had been eating the king's choice food.[1]

Thus, even in the earliest religious texts, there was a notion that there could be some way of evaluating the effects of religiousness on the human person. This example may well be one of the first descriptions of a controlled trial since there are two groups to be compared, those receiving the king's choice food and those who simply are the more religious. It was realized even then, that an adequate evaluation of religiosity required some type of comparison group. Otherwise, one might not be able to determine fully the effects of religiosity on an individual. Biomedical research has obviously advanced significantly since biblical times even though the study of religious phenomena is often difficult.

---

[1]   Daniel 10-15. *New King James Bible.*

We will explore four dimensions of this area of research with a critical perspective on methodology and statistical analysis. The four dimensions as they relate to the neuroscientific study of religious and spiritual phenomena are:

1. appropriate measures and definitions
2. subject selection and comparison groups
3. study design and biostatistics
4. theological and epistemological implications

Regarding the process of neurotheological research, it is important to keep the following principles in mind when beginning a study utilizing both the neuroscientific and theological perspectives. These principles should ideally propel such research in a beneficial direction for both science and religion and also open up new avenues of thought. One principle, in particular, has to do with the general goals of such research:

Principle XX: Neurotheology must strive to support both practical and esoteric goals of scholarship and research.

This principle refers to the importance of focusing neurotheology on both practical as well as theoretical problems. This principle also recognizes the interrelatedness of both types of problems. Thus, neurotheology research may involve a study of religiosity in schizophrenia, but ultimately yield information regarding the meaning of religious experiences. On the other hand, neurotheology may explore the significance of a specific sacred text, and find valuable information regarding the basis of good mental health. Each issue may require its own distinct paradigm in order to arrive at some conclusion, but the results may ultimately have implications for the other.

It is important to continue to advance the scientific evaluation of various aspects of religious experience and practice. Studies relating religiosity to health and well-being as well as neurological studies of specific types of religious phenomena help to provide a foundation of data from which neurotheology can address many different questions. An additional benefit is the ability for neurotheology research to advance scientific methodology in evaluating subjective experience and complex neurocognitive processes. Neurotheology also helps to advance our overall understanding of the human person and human health from both a biological as well as a spiritual perspective.

Esoteric goals of research may include both philosophical and theological analyses of various types of rational, emotional, and perceptual concepts in the theological arguments. These goals would help to address traditional theological issues relating to the nature of God, the interpretation of sacred texts, and the ability to relate such ideas to human life and behavior. In many circumstances, such an analysis may rely very little on actual neuroscientific data, but rather focus on theoretical aspects pertaining to the human psyche and mind.

Esoteric goals may also relate to questions regarding the possible dual nature of the human body and the human spirit. Questions regarding the soul, consciousness, spirit, mind, and brain should all be accessible to the field of neurotheology. The esoteric goals of neurotheology may also relate to models of ethical behavior and thus lead toward concepts associated with neuroethics.

There is another principle that stresses the need to recognize the complexity of the field of neurotheology in the context of how this field should proceed from a methodological perspective:

Principle XXI: Theology and neuroscience must allow for new methods, concepts, and conclusions to arise from neurotheological scholarship.

The implication here is that the questions involved in neurotheology are so multidisciplinary and complex that existing methods in both science and theology may ultimately be limited in their capabilities. This does not mean that the existing methods should be circumvented. Quite the contrary, existing methods should be the initial approaches for neurotheological scholarship. However, should various issues and problems arise that go beyond the ability of current methods, it is critical to be open to the possibility of developing new methods and new paradigms for understanding neuroscience and theology. As an example, it has been frequently discussed among scholars engaged in neurotheology research that the traditional randomized double-blind controlled trial associated with Western biomedical research may not be able to capture important issues related to the subjective experience of religious and spiritual phenomena as well as the inter-individual differences that might arise from such phenomena.[2] Similarly, theology often proceeds through a variety of rational arguments originating from a complex foundational doctrine often grounded in historical events. But now, theology may also have to find ways of incorporating information obtained through scientific methods. For neurotheology research to proceed in earnest, scholars should also be open to the possibility that *a priori* assumptions and *a posteriori* conclusions may not always hold up in a multidisciplinary dialogue. However, great care must be taken in drawing quick conclusions that might dismiss either theology or science before unequivocal results are obtained.

It should also be mentioned that a new approach that fully integrates theological and scientific perspectives might be necessary. Such an approach may represent a "contemplative science" in which scholars engage in both contemplative practices such as meditation as well as empirical research found in the neurosciences. Several scholars have suggested this path may be necessary for a deeper understanding of the universe.[3] Recognizing inherent limitations in both science and religion,

---

[2]   Newberg, A. and Lee, B. "The neuroscientific study of religious and spiritual phenomena: or why God doesn't use biostatistics." *Zygon.* 2005;40:469-489.

[3]   Wallace, B.A. *Contemplative Science.* New York, NY: Columbia University Press, 2007.

a combined approach, if performed carefully, may provide a methodology for bypassing such limitations. Let us now explore in more detail some of the specific methodological issues affecting the process of neurotheological research. These methodological issues are likely only scratching the surface of the many possible issues that arise in neurotheological research. However, this discussion should provide an initial foundation from which future methodologies can be developed and refined.

Measurement and Definition of Spirituality and Religiousness

One of the most important issues related to the measurement of religious and spiritual phenomena has to do with correlating subjective and objective measures. For example, if a particular type of meditation reduces blood pressure or is associated with changes in cerebral metabolism, it is critical to know what was actually experienced by the individual and what type of meditation was actually performed.

Subjective Measures

In many ways, the most important measures of religious and spiritual phenomena are those that pertain to the subjective nature of the experience. When any person has a religious or spiritual experience, they can usually try to describe it in terms of various cognitive, behavioral, and emotional parameters. Furthermore, a person will usually define the experience as "spiritual" which distinguishes that experience from others which are regarded as "non-spiritual." Some will further distinguish "spiritual" from "religious" experiences. The issue of measuring the subjective nature of these phenomena is akin to opening the mysterious "black box" in which something is happening, but it is not immediately observable to an outside investigator. The problem becomes more difficult when trying to compare experiences across individuals and across cultures. A spiritual experience for a Jew may be vastly different than a spiritual experience for a Hindu. Furthermore, there is likely to be a continuum of experiences ranging from barely perceptible to absolutely mystical.[4] The question for any researcher is how to grasp the subjective component of these experiences. Is there a way to quantify and compare these subjective feelings and thoughts that individuals have regarding their spiritual experiences? If it is difficult to develop adequate scales to measure spirituality and religiousness, it is often even more difficult to find them in the research literature.

---

[4]   d'Aquili, E.G. and Newberg, A.B. "Religious and mystical states: a neuropsychological model." *Zygon*. 1993;28: 177-200.

Many scales are difficult to find, especially when they are reported in non-scientific journals that are not typically cited or referenced in literature reviews.[5]

A number of attempts have been described in the literature to develop a self-reporting scale that measures the subjective nature of a particular religious or spiritual phenomenon. The book *Measures of Religiosity*[6] provides various scales and questionnaires that assess everything from a person's feeling of religious commitment to awe, to hope, to the direct apprehension of God. Some scales have been assessed for validity and reliability, which is critical if these scales are to have any use in future research studies. Testing the validity implies that the results return information about what the scale is supposed to measure.[7] For example, a valid scale of a feeling of hopefulness would ask questions regarding the amount of hope a person has. If this scale did not address hope, but rather happy emotional responses, it would not be a valid measure of hope. Reliability assesses whether the scale, when given to the same person at different time points, yields roughly the same results (assuming that the person has not changed).[8] While it is important to assess the reliability and validity of scales, this is particularly problematic with regard to religious and spiritual phenomena. The reason for this difficulty is the problem with defining these terms in the first place, as previously discussed. If someone defines spirituality as a feeling of "awe" and another defines it as a feeling of "oneness," what types of questions should be used to assess spirituality? A questionnaire that asks about feelings of awe might not truly be measuring spirituality and therefore, until clear and operational definitions of spirituality and religiousness can be determined, there will always be the potential problem of developing valid scales. Reliability is also a problem since individuals might feel different over the course of their life, and, therefore, the reliability of any scale, with the intention to measure spirituality, is always problematic.

Another problem with individual scales is whether they are useful across traditions and cultures. For example, many of the scales that are referenced in *Measures of Religiosity* are Christian-based, and, therefore, may not be useful for evaluating Jewish or Buddhist perspectives for example. Fortunately, there are other scales which either have a more universal quality or at least can be modified to accommodate other perspectives. However, this might bring into question the validity and reliability of such scales in different contexts.

---

[5]   Larson, D.B., Swyers, J.P., and McCullough, M.E. (eds.). *Scientific Research on Spirituality and Health: A Consensus Report.* Washington, DC: National Institute for Healthcare Research, 1998.

[6]   Hill, P.C. and Hood, R.W. *Measures of Religiosity.* Birmingham, AL: Religious Education Press, 1999.

[7]   Patten, M.D. *Understanding Research Methods*, 2nd Edition. Los Angeles, CA: Pyrczak Publishing, 2000.

[8]   Patten, M.D. *Understanding Research Methods*, 2nd Edition. Los Angeles, CA: Pyrczak Publishing, 2000.

There is another interesting problem with scales that attempt to measure the subjective nature of spiritual or religious phenomena. This arises from the fact that most scales of spirituality and religiousness require the individual to respond in terms of psychological, affective, or cognitive processes. Thus, questions are phrased: How did it make you feel? What sensory experiences did you have? What did you think about your experience? On one hand, such measures are very valuable to individuals interested in exploring the neural correlates of religious and spiritual experiences because psychological, affective, and cognitive elements can usually be related to specific brain structures or function. But the problem with phrasing questions in this way is that one never actually escapes the neurocognitive perspective to get at something that might be "truly" spiritual. It might be suggested that the only way in which an investigator can scientifically measure something which is truly spiritual would be through a process of elimination in which all other factors—cognitive, emotional, sensory—are eliminated through the analysis, leaving only the spiritual components of the experience. In other words, the most interesting result from a brain scan of someone in prayer would be to find no significant change in the brain during the time that the individual has the most profound spiritual experience. Only then might the investigator have captured something inherently spiritual, without any biological correlate. The only problem is that the spiritual would not have actually been measured.

As described above, part of the problem with developing adequate measures is ensuring that they measure what they claim to measure. A subjective scale designed to measure the degree of an individual's religiosity needs to focus on the things which make someone religious. However, this first requires a clear definition of religiousness and spirituality. We considered the problem of definitions in Chapter 2, but the practical problem of measurement brings the definitional issue to the fore. We cannot measure something accurately if there is an inadequate or vague definition. Furthermore, these definitions must be operationalized[9] so that any measure or study can have a firm enough grasp to actually measure something.

To that end, it is important to avoid narrow definitions that might impede research and also to avoid broad definitions that cannot be measured. For example, definitions of religion that pertain to a single God would eliminate almost two billion Hindu and Buddhist individuals from analysis. On the other hand, a definition of religiousness that is too broad might end up including many bizarre experiences and practices such as cults or devil worship.

One final issue, which is related to problems with definitions, is that there are so many approaches to religious and spiritual phenomena that it is often difficult to generalize from one study to another. Some scholars have pointed out that one type of meditation practice may be very different from other types, or one type

---

[9]   Koenig, H.G., McCullough, M.E., and Larson, D.B. (eds.). *Handbook of Religion and Health.* New York, NY: Oxford University Press, 2001; Koenig, H.G. (ed.). *Handbook of Religion and Mental Health.* San Diego, CA: Academic Press, 1998.

of experience might be substantially different from other types.[10] It is certainly critical to ensure that any study clearly states the specific practices, sub-practices, and traditions involved. Furthermore, changes in the brain associated with one type of meditative practice may not be specifically related to a different type of practice. Of course, the dynamic nature of this body of research may also provide new ways of categorizing certain practices or experiences so that one can address the question regarding whether different types of meditation truly are different, or are only experienced to be different.

Objective Measures of Spirituality

Objective measures of religious and spiritual phenomena that pertain to the neurosciences include a variety of physiological and neurophysiological measures. Currently, there are a number of different approaches for studying the brain. Some approaches directly image different physiological processes such as metabolism, blood flow, or neurotransmitter activity. Other approaches might use indirect methods by measuring changes in the blood stream or body. Recent advances in fields such as psychoneuroendocrinology and psychoneuroimmunology address the important interrelationship between the brain and body. Any thoughts or feelings perceived in the brain ultimately have effects on the functions throughout the body. While this can complicate measures as well as introduce confounding factors, this integrated approach allows for a more thorough analysis of religious and spiritual phenomena.[11]

One group of physiological measures which has already been reported in the literature are measures of autonomic nervous system activity. Use of these has been a common approach to measure the effects of religious and spiritual practices such as meditation or prayer. For example, a number of studies have revealed changes in blood pressure and heart rate associated with such practices.[12] It is interesting that the actual changes may be quite complex involving either a relaxation response, an arousal response, or both of these responses simultaneously. In fact, a

---

[10]   Andresen, J. and Forman, R.K.C. "Methodological pluralism in the study of religion: how the study of consciousness and mapping spiritual experiences can reshape religious methodology." *J Cons Studies.* 2000;7:7-14; Andresen, J. "Meditation meets behavioural medicine: the story of experimental research on meditation." *J Cons Studies.* 2000;7:17-73.

[11]   Newberg, A.B. and Iversen, J. "The neural basis of the complex mental task of meditation: neurotransmitter and neurochemical considerations." *Med Hypothesis.* 2003;61:282-291.

[12]   Sudsuang, R., Chentanez, V., and Veluvan, K. "Effects of Buddhist meditation on serum cortisol and total protein levels, blood pressure, pulse rate, lung volume and reaction time." *Physiol Behav.* 1991;50:543-548; Jevning, R., Wallace, R.K., and Beidebach, M. "The physiology of meditation: a review. A wakeful hypometabolic integrated response." *Neurosci Biobehav Rev.* 1992;16:415-424; Koenig, H.G., McCullough, M.E., and Larson, D.B. (eds.). *Handbook of Religion and Health.* New York, NY: Oxford University Press, 2001.

recent study of two separate meditative techniques suggested a mutual activation of parasympathetic and sympathetic systems by demonstrating an increase in the variability of heart rate during meditation.[13] The increased variation in heart rate was hypothesized to reflect activation of both arms of the autonomic nervous system—the sympathetic (or arousal) and the parasympathetic (or quiescent). This notion also fits the characteristic description of meditative states in which there is a sense of overwhelming calmness as well as intense alertness.

Measures of hormone and immune function have more recently been explored, especially as an adjunct measure to various clinical outcomes.[14] Thus, if a hypothetical study showed that the practice of meditation resulted in reductions in breast cancer rates, then it might be valuable to measure the immunological and/or hormonal status of the individuals to determine the physiological basis of the effect. Certain cancers are related to abnormalities in the immune system (for example, leukemia or lymphoma) or hormonal system (for example, breast and prostate cancer). It is also important to note that alterations in various hormones and immune activity may be related to more specific changes in brain function. For example, activation of higher cortical brain structures such as the frontal lobe can eventually result in alterations in the activity in the limbic system with subsequent changes in the autonomic nervous system and hormonal systems. This interaction can be bidirectional. Thus, certain brain states may enhance hormonal status, but these hormonal states may in turn affect brain function. This can particularly be observed in women with premenstrual syndrome, but there are other circumstances in which various neurohormones can alter emotional, cognitive, and behavioral states.

In terms of the brain itself, there are many ways of measuring functional changes. Early studies of meditation practices made substantial use of electroencephalography (EEG) that measures electrical activity in the brain.[15]

---

[13]   Peng, C.K., Mietus, J.E., Liu, Y., et al. "Exaggerated heart rate oscillations during two meditation techniques." *Intern J Cardiol.* 1999;70:101-107.

[14]   O'Halloran, J.P., Jevning, R., Wilson, A.F., Skowsky, R., Walsh, R.N., and Alexander, C. "Hormonal control in a state of decreased activation: potentiation of arginine vasopressin secretion." *Physiol Behav.* 1985;35:591-595; Walton, K.G., Pugh, N.D., Gelderloos, P., and Macrae, P. "Stress reduction and preventing hypertension: preliminary support for a psychoneuroendocrine mechanism." *J Altern Complement Med.* 1995;1:263-283; Tooley, G.A., Armstrong, S.M., Norman, T.R., and Sali, A. "Acute increases in night-time plasma melatonin levels following a period of meditation." *Biol Psychol.* 2000;53:69-78; Infante, J.R., Torres-Avisbal, M., Pinel, P., Vallejo, J.A., Peran, F., Gonzalez, F., Contreras, P., Pacheco, C., Roldan, A., and Latre, J.M. "Catecholamine levels in practitioners of the transcendental meditation technique." *Physiol Behav.* 2001;72:141-146.

[15]   Banquet, J.P. "Spectral analysis of the EEG in meditation." *Electroencephalogr Clin Neurophysiol.* 1973;35:143-151; Hirai, T. *Psychophysiology of Zen.* Tokyo: Igaku Shoin, 1974; Hebert, R. and Lehmann, D. "Theta bursts: an EEG pattern in normal subjects practising the transcendental meditation technique." *Electroencephalogr Clin Neurophysiol.* 1977;42:397-405; Corby, J.C., Roth, W.T., Zarcone, V.P. Jr., and Kopell,

EEG is valuable because it is relatively non-invasive and has very good temporal resolution. The instant that an individual achieves a certain state, the EEG should change accordingly. For this reason, it has continued to be useful in the evaluation of specific meditation states.[16] The major problem with EEG is that spatial resolution is very low so that any change can only be localized over very broad areas of the brain. Another problem is that EEG analysis can be difficult because of the extensive amount of recordings that are made during any session. However, EEG may be particularly valuable to include in studies employing functional brain imaging techniques since the EEG may help to signal certain states, or at the very least, ensure that the individual being studied has not fallen asleep.

Functional Brain Imaging Studies

Functional neuroimaging studies of religious and spiritual phenomena have utilized positron emission tomography (PET), single photon emission computed tomography (SPECT), and functional magnetic resonance imaging (fMRI). In general, such techniques can measure functional changes in the brain in pathological conditions, in response to pharmacological interventions, and during various activation states. Activation states have included sensory stimulation (visual, auditory, and so on), motor function and coordination, language, and higher cognitive functions (for example, concentration).[17] The changes that can be measured include more general physiological processes such as cerebral blood flow and metabolism, in addition to many aspects of the neurotransmitter systems. For example, the serotonin, dopamine, opiate, benzodiazepine, glutamate, and acetylcholine systems have all been evaluated in a number of brain states.[18]

B.S. "Psychophysiological correlates of the practice of tantric yoga meditation." *Arch Gen Psych.* 1978;35:571-577.

[16] Lehmann, D., Faber, P.L., Achermann, P., Jeanmonod, D., Gianotti, L.R., and Pizzagalli, D. "Brain sources of EEG gamma frequency during volitionally meditation-induced, altered states of consciousness, and experience of the self." *Psychiatry Res.* 2001;108:111-121; Aftanas, L.I. and Golocheikine, S.A. "Non-linear dynamic complexity of the human EEG during meditation." *Neurosci Lett.* 2002;330:143-146; Travis, F. and Arenander, A. "EEG asymmetry and mindfulness meditation." *Psychosom Med.* 2004;66(1):147-148.

[17] Newberg, A.B. and Alavi, A. "The study of the neurological disorders using positron emission tomography and single photon emission computed tomography." *J Neurol Sci.* 1996;135:91-108.

[18] Newberg, A.B. and Alavi, A. "Role of positron emission tomography in the investigation of neuropsychiatric disorders." In Sandler, M.P., Coleman, R.E., Patton, J.A., Wackers, F.J.T., Gottschalk, A., and Hoffer, P.B. (eds.), *Diagnostic Nuclear Medicine*, 4th Edition. Philadelphia, PA: Lippincott Williams & Wilkins, 2003; Warwick, J.M. "Imaging of brain function using SPECT." *Metab Brain Dis.* 2004;19:113-123; Kennedy, S.E. and Zubieta, J.K. "Neuroreceptor imaging of stress and mood disorders." *CNS Spectr.* 2004;9:292-301.

While functional neuroimaging studies have contributed greatly to our understanding of the human brain, the techniques each have their own advantages and limitations with respect to evaluating religious and spiritual phenomena. Functional MRI primarily measures changes in cerebral blood flow. In general, this is a valid method for measuring brain activity since a brain region that is activated during a specific task will experience a concomitant increase in blood flow. This coupling of blood flow and activity provides a method for observing which parts of the brain have increased activity (increased blood flow) and decreased activity (decreased blood flow). Functional MRI has several advantages. It has very good spatial resolution and can be coregistered with an anatomical MRI scan that can be obtained in the same imaging session. This allows for a very accurate determination of the specific areas of the brain that are involved. It also has very good temporal resolution so that many images can be obtained over short periods of time, as short as a second. Thus, if a subject was asked to perform 10 different prayers sequentially while in the MRI, the differences in blood flow could be detected in each of those 10 prayer states. Finally, fMRI does not involve any radioactive exposure. The disadvantages are that images must be obtained while the subject is in the scanner and the scanner can make up to 100 decibels of noise. This can be very distracting when individuals are performing spiritual practices such as meditation or prayer. However, several investigators have successfully utilized fMRI for the evaluation of different spiritual states.[19] The MRI noise can also affect brain activity, particularly in the auditory cortex. FMRI also relies on a tight coupling between cerebral blood flow and actual brain activity, which while a reasonable assumption, is not true in all cases. Well known examples in which brain activity and blood flow are not coupled include stroke, head injury, and pharmacological interventions.[20] However, a detailed evaluation of this coupling in all brain states has not been performed. One final disadvantage is that at present, fMRI cannot be used to evaluate individual neurotransmitter systems such as dopamine or serotonin which may be important mediators of spiritual practices and experiences.

PET and SPECT imaging also have advantages and disadvantages. The advantages include relatively good spatial resolution for PET (comparable to fMRI) and slightly worse for SPECT imaging. PET and SPECT images can also be coregistered with anatomical MRI, but the MRI must be obtained during a separate session and, therefore, matching the scans is more difficult. PET and SPECT both require the

---

[19]   Lazar, S.W., Bush, G., Gollub, R.L., Fricchione, G.L., Khalsa, G., and Benson, H. "Functional brain mapping of the relaxation response and meditation." *Neuroreport*. 2000;11:1581-1585; Beauregard, M. and O'Leary, D. *The Spiritual Brain*. New York, NY: Harper Collins, 2007.

[20]   Newberg, A.B. and Alavi, A. "Role of positron emission tomography in the investigation of neuropsychiatric disorders." In Sandler, M.P., Coleman, R.E., Patton, J.A., Wackers, F.J.T., Gottschalk, A., and Hoffer, P.B. (eds.), *Diagnostic Nuclear Medicine*, 4th Edition. Philadelphia, PA: Lippincott Williams & Wilkins, 2003.

injection of a radioactive tracer so radioactivity is involved, although usually this is in fairly low amounts. Depending on the radioactive tracer used, a variety of functional parameters can be measured including blood flow, metabolism (which more accurately depicts cerebral activity), and many different neurotransmitter components. The ability to measure these neurotransmitter systems is unique to PET and SPECT imaging. Such tracers can measure either state or trait responses (that is, long term or short term effects). It should also be mentioned that some of the more common radioactive materials such as the PET tracer, fluorodeoxyglucose (that measures glucose metabolism), or the SPECT tracer ethylene cysteinate dimer (that measures blood flow) can be injected through an existing intravenous catheter when the subject is not in the scanner. This allows for a more conducive environment for performing practices such as meditation and prayer. These tracers become "locked" in the brain during the injection period and the person can then be scanned after the person has completed their practice to measure changes associated with the performance of the practice.[21] A major drawback to PET and SPECT imaging, in addition to the radioactive exposure, is that these techniques have reduced temporal resolution because the uptake of the tracer takes from several minutes to several hours. PET or SPECT would be difficult to use to study 10 different prayer states in the same session. However, two or three states might be measured in the same imaging session if the appropriate radiopharmaceutical is used.[22] The conclusion of this discussion is that depending on the goals of the study, various neuroimaging techniques might be better or worse.

There are other more global problems that affect the ability to interpret the results of all functional brain imaging studies. The most important of which is how to be certain what is actually being measured physiologically and how it compares to various subjective experiences. These problems lead to the inability to determine definitively the causal relationship between brain processes and the subjective experiences. These problems also lead to the next principle of neurotheology which relates to the ability to ascribe causality based upon various brain imaging studies.

---

[21]   Herzog, H., Lele, V.R., Kuwert, T., Langen, K.J., Rota Kops, E., and Feinendegen, L.E. "Changed pattern of regional glucose metabolism during yoga meditative relaxation." *Neuropsychobiol.* 1990-1991;23:182-187; Newberg, A.B., Alavi, A., Baime, M., Pourdehnad, M., Santanna, J., and d'Aquili, E.G. "The measurement of regional cerebral blood flow during the complex cognitive task of meditation: a preliminary SPECT study." *Psych Res Neuroimaging.* 2001;106:113-122.

[22]   Lou, H.C., Kjaer, T.W., Friberg, L., Wildschiodtz, G., Holm, S., and Nowak, M. "A 15O-H2O PET study of meditation and the resting state of normal consciousness." *Hum Brain Mapp.* 1999;7:98-105.

Principle XXII: Care must be taken when assigning causal relationships or eliminating spiritual explanations when interpreting brain studies of religious and spiritual phenomena.

At issue here is that a brain scan may not be able to distinguish the brain creating an experience or responding to one. If we perceive an image of a table in front of us, how do we know if the brain created the image of the table or was merely responding to the table actually being there? The brain scan might help to differentiate hallucinatory from non-hallucinatory experiences to some degree, but ultimately, as we have considered, everything is a manifestation of the brain's processes and it becomes more and more difficult to differentiate an external object from its internal representation in the brain.

There are other potential problems that address what a particular scan finding means in terms of the actual activity state of the brain. For example, it is not clear what will be observed if there is increased activity in a group of inhibitory neurons. Would that result in increased or decreased cerebral activity as measured by PET or fMRI? The bigger problem is trying to compare the observed physiological changes to the subjective state. With regard to religious and spiritual experience, it is not possible to intervene at some "peak" experience to ask the person what they are feeling. Therefore, if a person undergoes fMRI during a meditation session and they have a peak experience, how will the researcher know which scan findings it relates to? In addition, there are typically a number of changes in the brain with varying degrees of strength. It is not clear what degree of change should be considered a relevant change (10 or 20 percent, and so on). From a statistical perspective, analyzing images has a number of problems including how to compare images across subjects and conditions and how to take into account the problems of multiple comparisons both in terms of activation states and also in terms of individual brain regions. Multiple comparisons refers to the problem that occurs if many analyses are run because usually a few will end up being statistically significant by random chance. This can be corrected for, but then sometimes findings that are actually present can be missed.

In spite of these limitations, functional neuroimaging studies have been successfully utilized to evaluate specific spiritual and meditative practices. Thus, the level of complexity of our understanding continues to improve as more studies are performed. Future studies will certainly be necessary to evaluate more thoroughly the neurophysiological changes that occur in the brain during various religious and spiritual phenomena.

Inducing or Altering Spiritual Phenomena

Another approach to studying religious and spiritual phenomena uses pharmacological agents or other interventions in an attempt to induce or alter spiritual phenomena. Using this paradigm, a study might be designed simply to determine if a certain pharmacological agent, when given, results in some type of spiritual experience. Alternatively, a previously measured spiritual practice or experience will be compared to the same intervention with the addition of some other intervention. For example, studies might use a drug that blocks the brain's opiate receptors to see if it affects the subjective experience of meditation or prayer. Preliminary studies (on one or a few subjects) of this type have shown no effect on EEG patterns during meditation when subjects were given either an opiate or benzodiazepine blocker.[23] The effects of transcranial magnetic stimulation (a new technique that sends strong magnetic fields into the brain), other pharmacological agents, or even surgical procedures (performed for other purposes) can be evaluated. However, it is clear that more extensive studies measuring a number of neurophysiological parameters are required. Other agonist and antagonist drugs may be utilized to determine their ability to augment or diminish spiritual experiences. A recent study from Johns Hopkins showed that psilocybin administration results in powerful experiences that are frequently described in spiritual terms.[24] In addition, the exploration of various drugs on spiritual interventions may help to delineate the role of different neurotransmitter systems. Such studies also offer the possibility of measuring dose responses in terms of spiritual interventions. In other words, how much of a substance might be needed to either induce or block an experience.

A related paradigm that might be employed utilizes those people whose use of hallucinogenic agents has already resulted in intense spiritual experiences. Since it has long been observed that drugs such as opiates, lysergic acid diethylamide (LSD), and stimulants can sometimes induce spiritual experiences, careful studies of the types and characteristics of drug-induced spiritual experiences, perhaps utilizing modern imaging techniques, may help elucidate which neurobiological mechanisms are involved in more "naturally derived" spiritual experiences.

Some studies related to the use of such hallucinogenic agents have already been performed.[25] In many of these studies, the experiences that people have as the result of taking some type of psychotropic substance have been extremely

---

[23] Sim, M.K., Tsoi, W.F. "The effects of centrally acting drugs on the EEG correlates of meditation." *Biofeed Self-Reg.* 1992;17:215-220.

[24] Griffiths, R., Richards, W., Johnson, M., McCann, U., and Jesse, R. "Mystical-type experiences occasioned by psilocybin mediate the attribution of personal meaning and spiritual significance 14 months later." *J Psychopharmacol.* 2008;22:621-632.

[25] Vollenweider, F.X., Leenders, K.L., Scharfetter, C., Maguire, P., Stadelmann, O., and Angst, J. "Positron emission tomography and fluorodeoxyglucose studies of metabolic hyperfrontality and psychopathology in the psilocybin model of psychosis." *Neuropsychopharmacol.* 1997;16:357-372; Vollenweider, F.X., Vontobel, P., Hell, D., and Leenders, K.L. "5-HT modulation of dopamine release in basal ganglia in psilocybin-induced psychosis in man: a PET study with [11C]raclopride." *Neuropsychopharmacol.* 1999;20:424-433; Vollenweider, F.X., Vontobel, P., Oye, I., Hell, D., and Leenders, K.L. "Effects of (S)-ketamine on striatal dopamine: a [11C]raclopride PET study of a model psychosis in humans." *J Psychiatr Res.* 2000;34:35-43.

powerful. Such drug induced experiences are considered to be spiritual by some, but not by others. These distinctions could provide additional information regarding the nature of religious and spiritual experiences. However, a more extensive study of such agents, particularly in relation to religious and spiritual experiences is required.

One very important point is that the induction or alteration of a spiritual experience by a substance does not necessarily imply that the experience is purely biological with no spiritual aspects:

Principle XXIII: It should be realized that the use of psychotropic substances to induce or alter religious and spiritual experiences does not necessarily demonstrate a causal relationship or eliminate a spiritual explanation.

Many shamanic cultures and native American Indian groups have used psychotropic compounds for thousands of years to induce spiritual states. But rather than conceive of such experiences as biological or artificial, these cultures see the drugs as opening the mind up to the spiritual realm. For them, it is not unlike putting on a pair of glasses to make the world appear clearer. The drugs merely take the brain to another level where it can perceive and experience the world in a clearer, or perhaps higher way. From this viewpoint, the brain would be considered to be designed to enable spiritual and religious phenomena rather than to actually cause them to occur. Thus, for the Shaman, brain function is affected by the spiritual realm rather than the other way around.

There are obvious ethical and legal considerations with studies such as these (although studies outside of the United States may be more possible). However, subjects who have already had pharmacologically induced spiritual experiences can be studied using radioactive analogues of such agents as a means of determining the concentration of receptors and their agonists. Another related approach would be to study the effects of drug withdrawal on spiritual experience, but there are no reports in the literature of such findings.

Neuropathologic and Psychopathologic Spiritual Experiences

Spiritual experiences can also be studied from the perspective of known neuropathologic and psychopathologic conditions. Neurological conditions including seizure disorders, particularly in the temporal lobes, brain tumors, and stroke, have been associated with spiritual experiences or alterations in religious beliefs. For example, temporal lobe epilepsy has been associated with hyperreligiosity and religious conversions.[26] Psychiatric disorders such as schizophrenia and mania also have been associated with spiritual experiences

---

[26]   Bear, D.M. and Fedio, P. "Quantitative analysis of interictal behavior in temporal lobe epilepsy." *Arch Neurol.* 1977;34:454-467; Bear, D.M. "Temporal lobe epilepsy: a syndrome of sensory-limbic hyperconnection." *Cortex.* 1979;15:357-384.

and religious conversions. Delineating the type of pathology and the location of that pathology will aid in determining the neurobiological substrate of spiritual experience. Thus, neuropsychiatric disorders can be an effective tool for the neuroscience of spiritual experience.

Research on pathological conditions has classically been used to elucidate the normal functions of biological systems. Spiritual experiences in psychiatric and neurological disorders may be central to the identification of largely nascent neurobiological systems that subserve "normal" spiritual experience. This presents a crucial distinction to the historic psychiatric implication that religious and spiritual experience is an expression of psycho- or neuro- pathology.

Principle XXIV: Care must be taken to define and differentiate "normal" and "abnormal" religious and spiritual experiences and not to over-pathologize such experiences inappropriately.

This provides a framework in which normal spiritual experience can occur in pathological and normal conditions and pathologic spiritual episodes might occur in individuals with or without psychopathological disorders. However, care must be taken to avoid referring to spiritual experience only in pathological terms or associated with pathological conditions, as well as not reducing spiritual experiences only to neurophysiological mechanisms.

Spiritual Experiential Development

There is fairly extensive literature regarding the developmental aspects of religion and spiritual experience.[27] These reports consider the overall development of spiritual experience from infancy through adolescence and into adulthood. This is important for understanding the overall impact of religion and spirituality in a person's life and growth. There is also consideration of the necessary neurocognitive developments for spiritual experience to arise. In other words, an individual may require substantial maturity and change over many years prior to eliciting a powerful spiritual experience. Thus, it is important to evaluate the current state, and the overall development of the individual, if one is to truly understand the nature of religious and spiritual experiences:

---

[27]   Fowler, J.W. *Stages of Faith*. San Francisco, CA: Harper Collins, 1981; Tamminen, K. "Religious experiences in childhood and adolescence: a viewpoint of religious development between the ages of 7 and 20." *Int J Psychol Relig*. 1994;4:61-85; Oser, F.K. "The development of religious judgement." *New Dir Child Dev*. 1991;52:5-25.

***Principle XXV: It is important not only to understand the current state of
spiritual development for an individual, but to try to understand the different
stages of their development when evaluating them with subjective or objective
measures.***

For example, a more primitive form of undifferentiated faith may occur in infancy
while the more complex aspects of spiritual experience which include cognitive,
cultural, and affective components usually requires growth into adulthood.[28] Most
of these analyses of spiritual experiential development are grounded in psychology.
However, neuroscience may be able to utilize these findings and compare them to
the development of various brain structures and neurocognitive processes. This
may help elucidate which brain structures and functions are required for various
components of spiritual experience. The developmental approach can also be
viewed from the end of life perspective. For example, alterations in spirituality
or religiousness may be associated with diffuse neuropathological conditions
(for example, dementia). Furthermore, it may be useful to study alterations in
spiritual functions that are associated with decrements in neurocognitive functions
as well as decrements in physical health.

Global Study Design Issues

There are many different types of studies that could be utilized to address religious
and spiritual phenomena. Each of these study types has its strengths and weaknesses
with regard to evaluating religious and spiritual phenomena. Determining whether
a study type is appropriate for addressing a particular hypothesis is critical as an
initial step in either developing a new study or evaluating the results of a study
reported in the literature. It is also helpful to consider other types of studies that
may help answer the question better or address potential problems that might be
overcome the next time.

Case Studies and Descriptive Analyses

Case studies and descriptive analyses, in some ways, may be the most appropriate
study types for evaluating individual religious and spiritual experiences that
people may have. A case study, for example, focuses on one or a limited group
of subjects who have some kind of experience or problem. For example, in a case
study of mystical experiences, clear descriptions should be made of the person's
background, medical history, psychiatric history, socioeconomic history, and
religious history. A particular religious or spiritual experience or feeling can be
described in great detail and possibly contribute to various factors in the person's
background. If several similar types of experiences are described, this would

---

28   Fowler, J.W. *Stages of Faith*. San Francisco, CA: Harper Collins, 1981.

lend support to being able to understand some of the factors associated with such experiences. The advantage with such a study is that the individual characteristics of both the person and the experience can be elaborated upon and presented in a way that provides information for other investigators who may have people or patients who have had similar types of experiences or similar types of backgrounds that may be prone to such experiences. In medical science, case studies are very helpful for describing new types of disorders, new diagnostic problems, or unusual variations of existing disorders. With regard to religious and spiritual experiences, case studies may be very helpful for describing unusual experiences or experiences associated with people with unusual characteristics.

The negative side of case studies is that they provide little scientific support for understanding a given phenomenon and usually cannot be generalized to other people. These studies also provide very limited information about the cause and nature of such experiences and how they relate to other types of religious and spiritual experiences. This type of information requires larger studies that involve a greater number of subjects with similar types of experiences. For example, when the first patients with temporal lobe epilepsy, a seizure disorder that affects the temporal lobes, reported unusual religious experiences or a feeling of hyper-religiousness, these were described as part of a case study. Several cases of such patients and their experiences were described to document that temporal lobe seizures may actually have an association with such experiences. These case studies would not be able to address how frequently such experiences occur, whether certain types of temporal lobe epilepsy are more commonly associated with such experiences, whether these experiences are truly distinct from other types of religious experiences, and how to understand these experiences in the greater context of scientific and spiritual knowledge. In fact, while much has been made of patients with temporal lobe epilepsy and religious experience, subsequent studies of large numbers of such patients have shown that only a limited number actually express unusual religious feelings or hyper-religious feelings (the data have varied from 10-70 percent, but most larger studies suggest that it is the lower number). While a relationship between temporal lobe epilepsy and spiritual experiences appears to exist, its full development and understanding must await other types of studies.

Descriptive analysis studies have certain similarities as well as some distinctions from case reports. On one hand, descriptive analyses can provide a much more detailed perspective of subjective experiences that people may have. The approach that most of these studies take is to evaluate either a written description by an individual or record a personal interview obtained with an individual who related extensive details about a given experience. Such an approach would have obvious benefits in the study of religious and spiritual phenomena due to their highly subjective nature and the diversity both within cultures and across cultures. The primary advantage of descriptive studies is that the focus is on individual experiences that can then be compared through various methods of analysis. The descriptions themselves do not try to generalize various experiences of an entire group. On the other hand, analysis of descriptive material will frequently search for certain phrases or words which are universally applied.

An example of such a descriptive analysis study may be in the case of evaluating mystical experiences in individuals from four different traditions such as Catholicism, Judaism, Buddhism, and Islam. A simplistic description of the mystical experience of four individuals, one from each tradition, may appear along the lines of the following:

1. The Catholic may describe the experience as "a sense of connection to Jesus Christ."
2. The Jewish person may describe the experience as "a perceived connection to the God of all things."
3. The Buddhist might describe the experience as "a felt connection to the Ultimate Reality of the Universe."
4. The Islamic person might describe the experience as "a sense of surrender to Allah."

These four descriptions might then be compared for similarities and differences. The first three of these samples all use the phrase "connection to." What the individual felt connected to was different depending on their individual perspective or tradition. However, there clearly was a sense of a connection between the self and something religious or sacred. The use of the phrase surrender in the fourth example presents an interesting problem for descriptive analysis since the term itself would need to be compared to the phrase "connection to." If one wants to consider a sense of surrender to be similar to a sense of connection, then one might conclude that all four experiences are identical in terms of how the self is perceived with regard to a divine or sacred object. However, one might explore further the distinctions between "surrender" and "connection" to determine whether the fundamental aspect of the experience itself was different or similar across all four experiences.

One of the similarities between descriptive analysis and case studies is that they frequently rely on a small number of subjects. Part of this is due to the detailed analysis that is obtained from each individual subject. Therefore, it would be difficult to compare descriptions of mystical experiences when there are 500 subjects involved as compared to when there are 10 to 15 subjects involved. On the other hand, having a small number of subjects does limit the overall ability to generalize the interpretations from such a study.

Longitudinal and Cross-sectional Studies

Sometimes it is important to conduct a study to observe changes that occur over time in a given population. Two ways of performing this type of study are to do a cross-sectional study or a longitudinal study. There are advantages and disadvantages to both types of approaches. The primary purpose of both of these types of studies is to assess the effects of change over time. For example, a reason to do a longitudinal study would be to determine how a person's sense of spirituality changes over the course of their life span. Of course, longitudinal studies may be of shorter duration such that someone might be interested in investigating how spirituality changes near the end of life, how spirituality is associated with specific diseases such as dementia, or how spiritual practices change during childhood. Either way, one of the most difficult problems with longitudinal studies is that they take a long time to complete and that makes it difficult to retain subjects. For example, if one wanted to determine the change in spirituality over an individual's lifetime, then a number of subjects would be assessed when they were 20, 30, 40, 50, 60, 70, and 80. This would take 60 years to complete such a study. The advantage of cross-sectional studies is that they require a much shorter period because they sample various individuals who are at different ages but all at the same time. Thus, to evaluate how spirituality changes with aging, one might study different individuals who are ages 20, 30, 40, 50, 60, 70, and 80. In this way, the degree of spirituality at the different ages can be assessed all at the same time even though the purpose will be to attempt to determine how spirituality changes over a period of time. Cross-sectional studies potentially provide similar data to longitudinal studies by assessing members of a population who are already at the different stages. On the other hand, they will frequently miss the transitions and important aspects that change with time. This can frequently lead to a misinterpretation of the findings. A perfect example as to how a cross-sectional study may ultimately go awry is the traditional statistics joke about doing a cross-sectional study of different age groups in the state of Florida. By looking across the different age groups, one might conclude that people are born Hispanic and die Jewish since many of the young are Hispanic and many elderly are Jewish individuals who have retired there. Obviously, the cross-sectional analysis does not allow for an interpretation of how people come to be where they are and how various age groups are actually populated in that particular area. On the other hand, doing a longitudinal study to follow populations of various ethnic groups across time in the state of Florida might require 40 or 50 years in order to develop adequate data.

To apply this concept more specifically to spiritual and religious phenomena, we might consider a study to evaluate the effects of Alzheimer's disease, which results in a progressive cognitive decline and loss of memory, with a person's sense of religiousness or spirituality. A cross-sectional study might choose to evaluate patients with Alzheimer's Disease of varying degrees of severity, or who have been battling the disease for various periods of time. They might ask questions about a person's sense of spirituality or commitment to the Church and see how those feelings are different depending on what the person's cognitive status is or how long they have had the illness. While such a cross-sectional study may give some indication of the effects of Alzheimer's disease over time, such conclusions would have to be weighed very carefully and would be better confirmed through a longitudinal study in which individuals are followed over time to determine how their sense of spirituality and religion is affected. A reason for this may be that as people with Alzheimer's disease enter the latter stages of cognitive impairment, they may no longer understand the questions presented to them regarding their spirituality. Therefore, it may not be that they lose their sense of spirituality so much as they can no longer describe how they feel about spirituality. Or perhaps as individuals become progressively disabled, they can no longer participate in church so they may appear less religious even though they would be were it not for the disease state. A cross-sectional study may miss this progressive change in which the person appears to lose their sense of spirituality even though their progressive cognitive impairment cannot be taken into consideration on an individual basis. Again, though, to do a longitudinal study of people with Alzheimer's disease may require up to 10 years or more before significant progression of the disease occurs in enough subjects to be able to provide data that can be used to draw specific conclusions. Another advantage of longitudinal studies is that one can better track other parameters that may also have an effect. For example, if subjects are treated with medications in the early phase of Alzheimer's disease, but are not treated in the later phases, then the effects of the medications themselves may be lost in a cross-sectional study while standardizing the overall treatment and management of patients over time may provide more reliable data.

Subject Selection and Number

Once it has been determined what type of study is necessary for evaluating a particular aspect of religious or spiritual phenomena, usually the next question has to do with the kind of subjects and the number of subjects that would be involved with that study. This implies having the ability both to select appropriate subjects as well as to determine how many subjects are necessary in order to prove or disprove a particular hypothesis. In religious and spiritual studies, selecting appropriate subjects is obviously of crucial significance. Depending on whether one is looking at a particular type of practice, experience, or idea will heavily affect the types of individuals that will be chosen to participate. For example, if a particular type of practice such as the rosary were going to be studied, then the appropriate subject group would involve people who know how to do the rosary. While this seems obvious in this particular example, other types of practices or other types of experiences may have more universal applications. For example, a study designed to observe the effects of spiritual beliefs on mental health might look at the question more broadly and include subjects from many different spiritual and religious traditions. The question in this case would be whether or not people from divergent groups should be considered together or analyzed separately. This might also depend on specific characteristics of an experience to be evaluated so that a relaxation experience may be a more universal trait whereas a sense of forgiveness may be more specific to Christian groups.

Other more practical factors may also weigh in on subject selection including the age of the subjects, the gender, medical and psychological problems, medications, education, and socioeconomic status. Each of these factors may contribute to the response observed in a particular individual and, therefore, many of these factors need to be considered when selecting subjects. For example, age may be very relevant depending on whether the effects of religion are considered in the short-term or long-term, especially in some traditions in which the path toward spirituality can take a life time. When looking at specific practices, it might be important to consider people of varying degrees of expertise or proficiency. A study of Tibetan Buddhist meditators, for example, may choose to observe people in the first several months of their training, after several years of training, or after many years of training. Each of these groups would provide, theoretically, a different result depending on the measures which are being studied. However, one might need to consider age as a factor since it is most likely that those with less experience will be younger than those with more experience. The researcher undertaking such a study would want to ensure that the changes observed are related to the duration of practice rather than age.

It is important to realize that the more groups that become involved in a study the more complex is the data analysis. A comparison of two groups and a particular effect is much simpler to perform than a comparison across seven or eight groups. Also, the number of subjects that would have to be involved in a study would increase dramatically. This would likely increase complexity as well as cost. Therefore, conducting studies with a limited number of groups is most likely to provide a focused analysis in the most efficient manner.

The number of subjects that should be studied in a given experiment is also a very important issue. Typically, statistics deals with this in a very straightforward way, through what is called a "power calculation." A power calculation assumes a specific effect size that is to be measured. Usually the effect size is determined from preliminary studies or similar kinds of studies. For example, a study that is undertaken to observe the effects of a specific prayer practice on heart rate may turn to prior studies that showed the heart rate dropping an average of 10 percent in association with prayer. This would suggest that a 10 percent drop in heart rate is a reasonable effect size to try to measure. The power calculation takes into consideration this effect size as well as the standard deviation that is typically observed. The standard deviation is a measure of the variability of the values. This variability is important since measures that yield results within a narrow range more easily demonstrate a difference than values spread over a large range. The power calculation then determines the minimum number of subjects that would be necessary to demonstrate a statistically significant effect. The primary reason for such a power analysis and consideration of the number of subjects is to avoid what is known as a Type 2 error. A Type 2 error is one in which there are not enough subjects to prove a particular hypothesis. This is considered an error since a negative result may only be related to the fact that there were too few subjects studied. In our example, if the power calculation suggests that 20 subjects are necessary to prove a 10 percent change and the investigators recruit only five subjects and show no change, then it is possible that the effect was simply missed even though it was actually there. If, on the other hand, the investigators recruited the full 20 subjects and the result was still negative, then the researcher appropriately concludes that there is no effect of prayer on heart rate. Thus, when evaluating various studies of religious and spiritual phenomena, especially those that report a negative result, careful attention must be paid to the number of subjects and the type of subjects that are involved so that it seems reasonable that, if the effect was actually there, it would be measured appropriately by the study.

Randomized, Blinded, Controlled Studies

The current standard type of study in the biomedical literature is the randomized, double blind, controlled study. These studies are primarily used to help in the evaluation of various therapeutic interventions as well as diagnostic or measurement related techniques that can be applied in specific circumstances. Randomization, first described in the early 1900s, applies to the selection of interventions or tests that the study subjects will undergo. As an example, if an investigator wished to test three different types of interventions to determine if they lower a person's level of depression, then the researcher might choose to randomize subjects into one of three groups—a prayer group, an educational group, and a drug group. Typically, through the use of computers or other mathematical techniques, the subjects are placed into each group in a completely arbitrary way, which should be outside the ability of the investigator to control. This is what is referred to as randomization— placing subjects into groups in an arbitrary, investigator-independent manner. The purpose of this is to ensure an equal distribution of subjects into each category with the hope of matching various levels of disease, age, education, and in this case, spiritual perspective.

More importantly, randomization prevents the investigator from knowingly or unknowingly affecting the study by putting certain subjects into certain groups. In the example given, if the investigator would place the most religious into the prayer group, then prayer might demonstrate a much greater effect than the education or drug group on the basis of the characteristics of the individuals of that group and not because of the intervention itself. Conversely, if the researcher put the patients with the most severe forms of depression into the education and drug groups, it would be less likely that those groups would demonstrate an effect because of the overall severity of the depressive symptoms. The results would show that prayer had a much better effect even if it had nothing to do with the intervention and everything to do with the severity of the disease in the different groups. Thus, randomization tries to eliminate bias by distributing subjects into various categories without any clear basis. In terms of religion and spirituality, randomization may be possible under certain circumstances and impractical in others. In the example given, it would not make sense to put people in a prayer group who do not believe in religion or prayer. These people would not likely even understand prayer or know how to pray, and hence such a prayer group would be ineffective. However, this study could be randomized by selecting all people who are interested and believe in religion and prayer, and then randomizing them into the various groups. On the other hand, if all of the subjects are religious, then they might all pray even if they are not specifically in the prayer group. This might confound the ability of the researchers to test specific interventions.

"Blinding" in a study is also critical from a scientific perspective but raises certain potential problems in terms of the study of religion and religious experience. Double blinding refers to the notion that neither the subject nor the investigator is aware of what category subjects have been placed into. The advantage of such an approach is obvious in that it prevents patient knowledge or researcher knowledge of the specific groups that might affect the outcome of the study. For example, if the investigator wanted to try to demonstrate that prayer was more effective than the educational or drug group, their knowledge of which subjects were in each group may affect the way they administer psychological tests and evaluate data. This could push the results of the study towards a positive end point for prayer. The analysis and the collection of data should proceed from a perspective in which the investigator is unaware of which subjects are in which categories.

While it is certainly important for the investigators to be blinded to the various groups involved in the study, it is also very helpful when the subjects themselves have no specific understanding of what the study is about or which group they have been placed in. When people are studying the effects of various medications, they simply give a similar looking pill to all the groups involved—this pill is called the placebo (see below). Neither the patients nor the researchers know which pill had actually been given until the end of the study when all of the data is evaluated. In the example we have been considering here, comparing prayer to education, it would be impossible to blind the patients to the study groups because they clearly would know if they were in the prayer group or education group. However, what could be achieved is to insure that the subjects do not understand the underlying purpose of the study so that they are not aware of what kind of effects are being evaluated through the various interventional groups. To emphasize the point, when subjects are participating in various spiritual practices or interventions, it is impossible for the subjects to be completely blinded since they will be aware of what type of practice they are performing. On the other hand, researchers can still be blinded as to which subjects are in which groups so that the data cannot be manipulated or affected by the researcher's knowledge of the different subject groups.

Control groups are also critical for most types of biomedical research since there typically has to be a comparison between the investigational group, the group for which the intervention is being measured, and some other group not subject to that intervention—the control group. The issue of control groups in research on religious and spiritual phenomena is a very intriguing and complex topic. In the world of medicine, the ideal control is one in which the subject in the control group receives the exact same material or intervention as the investigational group with the exception of the active ingredient. In medical research, if a researcher was attempting to test the effects of a new blood pressure medicine, they would give the blood pressure medicine to the investigational group, and they would give a pill that appears to look exactly like the investigational drug, but has no effect on the body, to the control group (for example, a sugar pill). This type of control, called a placebo, attempts to eliminate the fact that the human mind can frequently affect the human body. Sir William Gull and Henry Sutton in 1865 first described an experiment with a placebo group as a comparison to the treatment group in the evaluation of rheumatic fever. It is interesting to note that the word placebo derives from the middle English word meaning "I shall please," which makes sense since the purpose of the placebo is to give subjects the expectation that something is going to happen to them even though nothing actually should. In this regard, the very fact that someone is aware that they have received a pill that may lower their blood pressure sometimes has just that effect regardless of whether the pill actually has any pharmacological effect.

The "placebo effect" has garnered significant attention in the scientific community over the past several decades.[29] It is fascinating to point out that in most studies, the placebo group frequently demonstrates an effect in as many as 30 percent of individuals.[30] This is particularly true in the study of the treatment of psychological disorders such as depression or anxiety. However, even in studies of physical parameters such as blood pressure, heart rate, or cancer, the placebo still may have some beneficial effect in spite of the fact that no active benefit should really be derived. Conversely, individuals in the placebo group frequently report a number of side effects which are not completely dissimilar to the active drug group.

In studies of religious and spiritual phenomena, the appropriate control group can be a very complex issue. For example, in the study aiming to determine the effects of prayer on depression, one could ask the question, what is the appropriate placebo control group for prayer? One could argue that the control group should be a group that does nothing, a group that repeats stories with no religious significance, a group that learns about depression and its causes, or a person who does prayer from a different tradition. There are probably many other possible control groups that could be imagined with regard to prayer in order to have an adequate comparison. Constructing the adequate control is crucial in being able to interpret a study's findings because the investigator would want to be certain that they have truly measured the specific effects of prayer and have not detected simply the effects of talking, participating in a group, or learning about something spiritual. Other factors may be involved in religious and spiritual phenomena that affect many different aspects of the human brain or body. For example, a study of a musical prayer or ritual may need to be compared not only to the baseline state of the person doing nothing, but also to the person when they are engaged in other musical activity that does not have a specifically spiritual perspective. Some,

[29]   Harrington, A. (ed.). *The Placebo Effect*. Cambridge, MA: Harvard University Press, 1997.

[30]   Newberg, A.B., Waldman, M.R. *Why We Believe What We Believe: Uncovering Our Biological Need for Meaning, Spirituality, and Truth*. New York, NY: Free Press, 2006.

however, might argue that all music has some spiritual quality. In the evaluation of various religious perspectives, a researcher might compare people who are devoutly religious to other people who are devoutly religious but who have not been participating in the religion for the same length (that is, novices), to people who may be believers in the religion but to a much lesser extent, to people who believe in a different religion, or to people who do not believe in religion at all. The most important point with regard to selecting a control group for a given study is to determine precisely what is being evaluated and what are its phenomenological characteristics. Once this is determined, the adequate control group or groups can be determined more accurately.

Religion's View of Science

We have now considered how, in general, science may be utilized in the study of various religious and spiritual phenomena. Equally important as the principles regarding the scientific process of neurotheology is the religious perspective of science. Religious beliefs have particular perspectives on how science should be performed and interpreted. Neurotheology must be aware of these views in order to help shape its scientific elements appropriately. By this I do not necessarily imply that neurotheology should allow science to be manipulated by religion. Rather, scholars must be aware of how religion views scientific methods in order to make sure that any study they design does not miss some important characteristic of religion on the basis of not understanding religion in the first place. This issue may have an impact on study design itself, or possibly on the ways in which the study results are ultimately interpreted:

Principle XXVI: It is necessary to understand how religions view science since any pursuit of neurotheology will have to understand various religious views of science.

On one hand, religion has had a long-standing positive relationship with science and scientific methodology. Science and religion were at one time deeply integrated and only became separated with the Reformation and more recent approaches to scientific reductionism. However, since science provides critical information about the natural world, and religion must clearly take into account the natural world, religions in general should take a fairly positive stance towards science, and hence neurotheology as well. This typically is the case provided that science does not "overstep its bounds" from the perspective of religion by trying to prove or disprove the veracity of religion or the existence of God. Historically, the classic example is the Catholic Church's treatment of Galileo, who forcibly argued in his 1632 work, *Dialogue Concerning the Two Chief World Systems*, that the earth was not the center of the universe as described in the Bible. Suffice it to say that his work was not well tolerated by the Catholic Church at that time and it was not until 2008 that the Vatican sought to complete its rehabilitation of Galileo. More recently, strong fundamentalist beliefs will sometimes reject various scientific studies or theories such as evolution or even medical science. However, many religions have also come to understand the benefit and value of scientific method and the information that science brings about the world.

Ultimately, classic religious doctrine itself tends not to weigh in much on the benefits or detriments of science, especially since the majority of scientific discovery has happened substantially after the original sacred texts of religions were written down. It is the practitioners of a particular religion that attempt to make interpretations of religious writings and teachings to help guide their ability to evaluate scientific studies and ideas. Adherents of religions have had a great deal of difficulty with certain scientific-related topics such as evolution, cloning, and abortion, while other fields of study such as those related to medicine (for example, surgical techniques or pharmaceutical development) or quantum mechanics have typically not received as much attention or are even supported. Of course, this is not the case for every religion since there are specific religions, such as the Jehovah's Witnesses, who refuse to have human blood products administered to them.

Thus, the main concern that religions would have in general about science would be where science intends to tread upon more spiritual matters. Scientific approaches that actually attempt to *explain away* religion and religious beliefs are clearly the most problematic issues facing science and religion. The following discussion of five of the world's major religions is designed to give a very brief perspective of specific religions and their views on science. This discussion in no way implies that every adherent of those particular religious traditions feels the same way or has the same perspective on science. Furthermore, care must be taken not to lump many different sects of a given religion into one overall religious doctrine since there are clear differences. For example, within Christianity, Catholicism, Protestantism, and Lutheranism all may have different perspectives on science. Regardless, it is still worthwhile to get a general sense of how religions view science, since any pursuit of neurotheology will necessarily have to understand how these religions, and particularly in regard to their associated practices, behaviors, and thoughts, view scientific studies.

Christianity

Christianity in general has developed an extensive theological analysis of its primary tenets. This, ultimately, has been elaborated into various forms including Catholicism, Protestantism, Lutheranism, Episcopalianism, and a number of others. Taken as a whole, the basic notion of salvation through the works and teachings of Jesus Christ would likely suggest that as long as science was in line with this goal, there should be very little in conflict with religious doctrine.[31]

---

[31]   *Catechism of the Catholic Church.* New York, NY: Doubleday, 1997.

Hence, primary issues associated with the religion such as divine creation of the world in contrast to evolution, and the sacredness of the human soul in contrast to technologies involved in human reproduction (for example, abortion techniques, artificial insemination, and human cloning), are typically the areas in which there is significant conflict. In these specific cases, either science or scientists espousing such ideas are considered to be entering territory they should not, or the scientific evidence in and of itself is in error. For example, proponents of creationism—the notion that the universe was created by God in six days—have frequently tried to disprove various supportive evidence for the theory of evolution including a critique of the fossil records and dating techniques that establish various ages of specific archeological and paleontological finds.[32] However, since scientists typically build their theories from a large amount of data, it is frequently difficult to discount all aspects of a scientific theory.

Neurotheology itself may potentially find Christianity in a conflicted stance in cases where the findings of scientific investigation suggest that religious experiences and ideas are nothing more than the creation of the human brain. While this is not the explicit goal of neurotheological investigations, if such a conclusion were proven to be true, then clearly a person with a religious perspective would find that position untenable. On the other hand, when such epistemological and ontological questions arise in the context of scientific pursuits, the issues are frequently more complex than either simple materialism or simple spiritualism. This hopefully provides room for neurotheology to help in the evaluation of epistemological questions by looking towards an integration of both science and religion. Furthermore, neurotheology has the opportunity to provide a source of scientific data that theoretically could help enhance a person's ability to comprehend and experience their own spirituality. In this way, neurotheology may actually prove to contribute towards the original goal of Christian thought. Neurotheology may also help in the further understanding of theological development and analysis which is a crucial aspect of Christian thought and methodology.

Judaism

The Jewish emphasis on practical living and education typically has allowed science to flourish within Jewish societies. Furthermore, science has historically been a field in which religious affiliation has been less relevant, hence allowing Jews, who frequently were oppressed, to function and succeed in society. The more orthodox perspectives of Judaism may ultimately find similar problems as their Christian counterparts with certain scientific results or ideas. This was certainly the case with the excommunication of Baruch Spinoza by the Synagogue

---

[32] Ham, K. *Creation Evangelism for the New Millennium*. Green Forest, AR: Master Books, 1999; Brown, W. *In the Beginning: Compelling Evidence for Creation and the Flood*. Phoenix, AZ: Center for Scientific Creation, 2008; Scott, E.C. *Evolution vs. Creationism: An Introduction*. Berkeley, CA: University of California Press, 2004.

in a similar manner to the handling of Galileo. In more recent history, Jewish thought has tended to be somewhat more accepting of science. Jewish emphasis on analysis of biblical scripture as a major role in Jewish thinking also provides an ideological framework for scientific pursuits and methodology. Such extensive analysis based on logical and rational approaches has been extensively written in the Talmud, Midrash, and the Haftorah. So the notion of performing extensive analysis on the natural world through research is commensurate with such an ideology. Jewish thinkers are probably more likely to be accepting of science, or neurotheology, if its goal is to strive to enhance the overall human condition. Conversely, Jewish thought would be considerably more opposed to technologies that might potentially stifle religious freedom and pursuits.

Islam

The Islamic perspective has changed dramatically over the centuries. In the early history of Islam, many scholars viewed science in a very positive light, with many Arab centers providing the highest developments of science at the time.[33] Of course, some of this is in contrast to the medieval period that left Europe generally lacking in scientific development. The Islamic world, therefore, provided substantial scientific underpinnings that in many ways would form the basis of future science that arose in Europe during the Renaissance and into the modern era. On the other hand, several outspoken groups in the Islamic world have tended to approach modern science and its associated technologies in a more negative perspective over the past century.[34] This has particularly been the case from a sociopolitical perspective since much of current scientific advancement occurs in Western countries, particularly the United States, which are viewed poorly by both governments and frequently the populations of Arab nations. With this in mind, a number of Islamic societies have tried to diminish or even outright eliminate some scientific concepts. On the other hand, many of the intellectual elite of Islamic society still hold science in high regard recognizing its importance in helping human beings understand the world around them. Furthermore, since much of Islamic writing is directed toward the human relationship with God and the notion of surrendering oneself to God, most scientific disciplines do not readily interfere with such a concept. As with other religious traditions, unless science comes into direct conflict with Islamic doctrine, from a purely theological perspective, Islam should have little problem with science and its approach to the natural world. With regard to neurotheology, Islamic traditions could consider the perspective of trying to understand brain function as it relates to an individual's pursuit of God in a positive light. Thus, as long as neurotheology does not try to eliminate the concept of God, the Islamic religion could be fairly accepting of such an endeavor.

---

[33] Masood, E. *Science and Islam: A History*. London: Icon Books, 2009.
[34] Iqbal, M. *Science and Islam*. Westport, CT: Greenwood Press, 2007.

Buddhism

The Buddhist doctrines typically have viewed science as constructive since science does allow for a thorough description and analysis of the natural world. As long as science aids humanity towards a higher awareness and consciousness, possibly even towards enlightenment, science would be considered quite positively. However, there are also historical differences between how the cultures in which Buddhism flourishes perform science compared to Western societies.[35] This distinction makes it somewhat more difficult to evaluate the Buddhist perspective on science since science itself is a variable in the equation. The result is that while Buddhism itself has espoused significant scientific concepts, particularly pertaining to the human mind and consciousness, it has typically not pursued such analyses utilizing the more materialistic Western approach. However, most Buddhist intellectuals would endeavor for integration between different approaches to science in order to find ways of linking the different world perspectives. In more recent times, this has already begun to emerge as Western science has become more holistic and more interested in subtle types of phenomena, while Eastern science has evolved to resemble more closely Western science. The Buddhist perspective on neurotheology would also be expected to be relatively positive since understanding the human mind and consciousness is particularly relevant. In fact, much Buddhist writing pertains to psychology and consciousness. To further that understanding by implicating neuroscientific concepts as a fundamental part of human experience, Buddhism would likely embrace such a notion.

Hinduism

Hinduism, with regard to science, has a similar perspective to that of Buddhism in that so long as science aids in the understanding of the natural world and does not specifically interfere with the human endeavor towards an enlightened state, science should be highly regarded. In fact, since science may actually assist in both the individual as well as societal movement towards a greater understanding of human beings and the world, science should be well embraced by Hindu doctrines. Hinduism has certain primary tenets which in many ways transcend the information obtainable through modern science. With this in mind, science could be viewed as an adjunct to supporting a clear understanding about the world even though it would in no definite way conflict with the realm of absolute reality espoused by both Hinduism and Buddhism. On the other hand, those who are deeply engaged in both Hindu and Buddhist practices of meditation may potentially view science as superfluous since the information they provide is only on the natural world and does not typically pertain to or allow one to get at the "absolute reality."

---

[35]   Wallace, B.A. (ed.). *Buddhism and Science: Breaking New Ground.* New York, NY: Columbia University Press, 2003; Lopez, Jr., D.S. *Buddhism and Science: A Guide for the Perplexed.* Chicago, IL: University of Chicago Press, 2008.

The only way in which an individual would discover this realm, is through inward contemplation allowing the human mind to somehow touch this most fundamental level of the universe. While neurotheology may shed empirical evidence on the nature of such experiences from a biological perspective, Hindu thought would argue that it is still up to each individual to pursue an enlightened mind. Should such an endeavor include science, there is no problem, but the goals of science are intellectual enlightenment rather than enlightenment of each soul.

Science from the Religious Perspective

The brief analysis above describing the perspectives of individual religions on science is meant to provide a sense of how neurotheology might be considered from these different traditions. What is particularly relevant is that each religion appears to provide a foundational ideology that is then brought to bear on science. If science appears to enhance the basic tenets of a religion or helps individuals towards accomplishing what is required as part of the doctrine of that religion, then science will be viewed positively. If science is in direct conflict with one or more fundamental principles of a religion, then science will be viewed negatively. For any particular religion or sect, what is important is to obtain a thorough understanding of the specific ideological stand point and then determine how science may enhance or diminish that perspective. Rather than an all or none approach, most likely, some scientific pursuits will be viewed positively while others viewed negatively by any given religion.

Neurotheology will most likely be considered in a similar framework since it can provide beneficial information regarding spirituality and religion or it might provide results that run counter to religious doctrine. Most importantly, for an individual pursuing neurotheological studies, it is necessary to recognize the religious perspectives on science. This is also crucial for the adequate interpretation of neurotheological findings.

Religious Implications of Scientific Studies

One of the most important issues that might arise out of the process of neurotheology is how science can ultimately affect religion. The implication here is that through scientific study, it is entirely conceivable that results may arise that alter or affect a person's individual sense of spirituality or perhaps effect an overall doctrinal change to an entire religion. Certainly this is not without precedent since there are many examples throughout history where a scientific study or approach dramatically altered how a religion perceived the world or even how individuals perceived their own sense of spirituality. Historical examples include the works of Copernicus and Galileo who together established that the sun was the center of the solar system, dramatically altering the Catholic Church's prevailing world view of the earth being the center of the universe; Darwin's theory of evolution that poses significant problems for a creationist perspective; cosmology and the study of the "Big Bang" that likewise poses important questions regarding the origins of the universe; and quantum mechanics that led Einstein to comment that "God does not play dice with the universe." Each of these scientific advances demonstrated a new understanding of some aspect of the universe that altered religious perspectives and existing doctrine on that aspect of the universe.

Neuroscientific studies of religious experience also have the potential to affect general religious doctrine as well as a given individual's perspectives or beliefs. This of course is not necessarily the goal of neurotheological investigations, but such a result is a possibility. It must be made clear as well, that the end result of neurotheology could theoretically be either an enhancement or diminishment of a given person's specific conception of spirituality. It is entirely possible that someone may interpret scientific studies of the neurological underpinnings of religious and spiritual experience to find support for their own beliefs and their own religious doctrine. On the other hand, it may also be possible for such studies to yield a conclusion in which religion and spirituality is completely reducible to neuronal firings and brain function. Therefore, while it may be possible for an individual to come away from any given study or set of studies with a specific conclusion about their own sense of religion and spirituality, hopefully through a careful development of neurotheology, these changes will be made appropriately and with well supported interpretations of the data as well as the spiritual phenomena which may be the subject of the investigation.

Final Considerations

The description of the principles of the process of neurotheology concludes with the notion that neurotheology does not carry the purpose to ultimately attempt to change a given person's perspective, but to provide people the necessary tools in order to evaluate their perspectives on spirituality and religion. Whether they are fervent believers or steadfast atheists, they will need to be able to assess their particular perspective in order to learn and evaluate the complexities of various questions and issues raised by religious and scientific considerations. Therefore, we might consider the following principle:

Principle XXVII: Neurotheology must be a path or approach to a deeper understanding of the human brain and its associated capacity for responding to religious beliefs and having spiritual experiences.

It must be cautioned, however, that such a path, at times, may prove difficult and even perilous for a given individual since the appropriate merging of science, religion, and spirituality does require significant questioning and analysis of any given viewpoint. Any attempt at neurotheology which is too heavily biased by initial perspectives, either religious or nonreligious, can invalidate any findings or interpretations of those findings. On the other hand, asking an ardent believer to forego their specific belief system, even temporarily, has the potential to produce internal conflicts within the given individual which might also invalidate the investigation. Neurotheology hopefully provides a framework in which a person can hold onto their beliefs and biases, at least to some degree, while still being open enough to be able to explore legitimately, through appropriate scientific and theological means, the issues regarding the neurobiological correlates of spiritual experiences and beliefs.

Chapter 7

Physiological and Phenomenological Correlates of Spiritual Practices

Understanding Spiritual Experiences and Practices

When considering the physiological and phenomenological correlates of religious and spiritual practices and experiences, there are several important principles required to guide the investigation. To begin, it is important to recognize the mutual requirement of understanding both the phenomenological and physiological correlates. Without understanding both aspects of any particular experience or practice, the information that one obtains is far less useful. This leads us to the first principle in this regard:

Principle XXVIII: Both phenomenological and physiological information are required for the full understanding of any religious experience or practice.

As a principle, this stands in stark contrast to those who might espouse either the purely religious or scientific views of the world. The religious individual might argue that only the phenomenological elements are necessary, while the biological correlates are essentially meaningless. The religious beliefs, doctrines, and experiences of an individual or group are all that is needed to understand these phenomena. Biology, they would argue, is not relevant. The scientist might counter that since everything ultimately derives from our biology, the phenomenology is not relevant for ascertaining the truth.

Neurotheology again walks a line somewhere between these two perspectives. The neurotheological perspective would argue that both biology and phenomenology are relevant. It is the biology that helps to interpret and make use of religious experiences, but it is the religious experience that might lead to a deeper understanding of the human person. In fact, neurotheology would argue that whether we are searching for actual answers to truth claims of different religions or whether we are simply trying to understand the practical implications of religion in the human world, both the phenomenological and biological elements are necessary. Understanding one without the other will simply not provide the total information that is necessary to understand fully who we are as human beings. Clearly the biology and the phenomenology weave an intricate braid that results in making us human.

Thus, in this chapter, we will consider a variety of religious experiences and attempt to ascertain their phenomenological and physiological elements. Important, in the context of neurotheology, will be the attempt to compare these elements to each other so as to enhance our understanding of each element and the experience as a whole.

The systematic evaluation of religious or spiritual experiences actually dates back thousands of years. The oral, and later, written traditions describe many different types of spiritual experiences resulting from a wide variety of conditions. Biblical accounts of religious experiences range from those of Moses having experienced God's presence on Mount Sinai to the experiences of the apostles such as Paul's on the Road to Damascus. The descriptions of these experiences also have a range from being highly elaborate to fairly vague. However, when descriptions include emotional and cognitive responses, physical behaviors, and life altering consequences, this begins a phenomenological "database" of religious and spiritual experiences. It also offers us an opportunity to consider the physiological aspects of such experiences to determine if this information provides additional value for interpreting and understanding the nature of those experiences. For the purposes of this chapter, I will use the term "spiritual experience" to include experiences that the individual might consider either spiritual (that is, separate from a specific religious tradition) or religious (that is, related specifically to a religious tradition). I will use the term "religious experience" to include only those experiences that the individual considers to be related to a specific religious tradition. While this is an oversimplification, especially since many experiences have elements of both, it will be easier to use the singular term "spiritual experience" when referring to all types of experiences.

Ultimately, it becomes vital to understand the rich diversity of religious experiences as well as the biological complexities of the brain and body. In this chapter, it will be impossible to consider all types of experiences, however, we will consider several important types of experiences and attempt to understand them from both the phenomenological and physiological perspectives.

What is a Spiritual Experience?

We considered earlier the definitions of spirituality and religiousness, but in the context of spiritual experiences, it is important not only to try to define them, but to explore their phenomenological elements. As mentioned in the principle above, in order for neurotheology to be able to address spiritual experiences, it is necessary to consider the phenomenological as well as the physiological elements of such experiences. Both elements can potentially be studied and even measured, although the methodology required is markedly different.

Many factors need to be considered in such an analysis of the subjective nature of spiritual experiences. These factors include the present and past state of the individual having the experience including their emotional, cognitive, behavioral, physical, and social status. It is also important to consider the person's religious, cultural, political, and socioeconomic background. The biological, neuropsychological, and even genetic factors must also be considered. All of these factors may potentially affect not only the experience itself, but how that experience is understood and interpreted in the person's life.

However, the phenomenological nature of spiritual experiences should be addressed initially in order to determine the full scope and variety of categories of experiences as well as the individual components of any given experience. Thus, understanding an experience requires a review of the subjective descriptions of individuals who have had such experiences. This is important since each individual usually uses different descriptors and language. It might be argued that there are as many different types of experiences as there are experiencers who have had them. We can, however, select a few specific examples and reflect on how neurotheology might treat each of them by evaluating the phenomenological elements as well as the other elements that also affect these experiences.

One interesting example is of a fourteenth-century German nun named Margareta Ebner who spent several days absorbed in reverent silence and constant, contemplative prayer. One night, as she prayed alone in her convent's chapel, she perceived in the choir loft a wondrous presence which she later described in her journal:

> And then it happened on Shrove Tuesday that I was alone in the choir after matins and knelt before the altar, and a great fear came upon me, and there in the fear I was surrounded by a grace beyond measure. I call the pure truth of Jesus Christ to witness for my words. I felt myself grasped by an inner divine power of God, so that my human heart was taken from me, and I speak in the truth— who is my Lord Jesus Christ—that I never again felt the like. An immeasurable sweetness was given to me, so that I felt as if my soul was separated from my body. And the sweetest of all names, the name of Jesus Christ, was given to me then with such a great fervor of his love, that I could pray nothing but a continuous saying that was instilled in me by the divine power of God and that I could not resist and of which I can write nothing, except to say that the name Jesus Christ was in it continually.[1]

It is interesting to reflect upon what she actually perceived. She experienced several emotional responses, including fear and grace. She felt her soul separated from her physical body. And she understood the name Jesus Christ was an inherent part of the experience. Thus, there were a number of emotional and cognitive elements that coincided with what was ultimately a profound mystical experience. In addition, the intense prayer state likely helped contribute towards her experience.

---

[1]   Quoted in: Cooper, D.A. *Silence, Simplicity, and Solitude*. New York, NY: Bell Tower, 1992.

In her book *Mysticism*, a preeminent study of mystical spirituality, Evelyn Underhill states that mysticism,

> ... is not an opinion: it is not a philosophy. It has nothing in common with the pursuit of occult knowledge ... It is the name of that organic process which involves the perfect consummation of the Love of God: the achievement here and now of the immortal heritage of man. Or, if you like it better—for this means exactly the same thing—it is the art of establishing his conscious relation with the Absolute.[2]

Other historical scholars have arrived at a similar description of mysticism. The fourteenth-century German mystic John Tauler described how the mystic's soul becomes

> ... sunk and lost in the Abyss of the Deity, and loses the consciousness of all creature distinctions. All things are gathered together in one with the divine sweetness, and the man's being is so penetrated with the divine substance that he loses himself therein, as a drop of water is lost in a cask of strong wine.[3]

In 1997, neurological researchers Jeffrey Saver and John Rabin, presented a paper which drew upon these accounts to elaborate specific core elements of the mystical experience.[4] They argued that mystical states are often characterized by strong, contradictory emotions—for example, terrifying fear might co-exist with overpowering joy as in the nun's account above. In mystical experience, time and space are perceived as altered or non-existent, and normal rational thought processes give way to more intuitive ways of understanding the world.

Another important element of many mystical experiences is the sense of a presence of the sacred or the holy. This is frequently considered to be attributed to God, Jesus, or some other spiritual being, as in the case of the nun's experience above. Dr. Michael Persinger, a neuroscientist from Laurentian University, has argued that the temporal lobes are important in perceiving a "sensed presence."[5] However, the larger question is whether a sensed presence is ascribed to God or other supernatural source depending on the cultural and religious context of the individual having that experience. Another interesting phenomenon, studied

---

[2]   Underhill, E. *Mysticism*. New York, NY: Doubleday, 1990.

[3]   Quoted in: Underhill, E. *Mysticism*. New York, NY: Doubleday, 1990.

[4]   Saver, J.L. and Rabin, J. "The neural substrates of religious experience." *J Neuropsychiatry Clin Neurosci*. 1997;9(3):498-510.

[5]   Persinger, M.A. and Healey, F. "Experimental facilitation of the sensed presence: possible intercalation between the hemispheres induced by complex magnetic fields." *J Nerv Ment Dis*. Aug 2002;190(8):533-541; Persinger, M.A. "The sensed presence within experimental settings: implications for the male and female concept of self." *J Psychol*. Jan 2003;137(1):5-16.

extensively by Dr. David Hufford from the University of Pennsylvania, is that of sleep paralysis.[6] In this state, an individual awakens but is paralyzed, has intense feelings of fear, and senses a presence that typically feels as if it is sitting on their chest. In this state, the presence is often perceived to be evil, perhaps due to the negative emotional content. Regardless, it speaks to the notion that there may be many different types of experiences that include a sensed presence.

At the heart of virtually all the mystic's descriptions, however, is the compelling sense that they have risen above the material existence of their body, and have spiritually united with the divine or absolute. This connection with something greater than the self appears to be a prominent element in most mystical experiences. In addition to this sense of oneness with the divine, comes the frequent description of a oneness of all things. In this way, the person is not just connected to God or ultimate reality, but God and ultimate reality are perceived to be an absolute oneness. Let us explore several additional descriptions of such experiences.

The Sufi master Husain Ibn Mansur, a resident of medieval Iraq, described his experience:

> I am He Whom I love, and He whom I love is I:
> We are two spirits dwelling in one body.
> If thou seest me, thou seest Him,
> And if thou seest Him, thou seest us both.[7]

This describes of the unity of two opposites in a singular concept—Him and me. This appears to draw from both the binary, as well as the holistic processes, of the brain. By contrasting God and the individual at one moment, and then intensely integrating them in the next, we see how this sense of connection is critical to the experience.

The medieval Catholic scholar Meister Eckhart wrote:

> How then am I to love the Godhead? Thou shalt not love him as he is: not as a God, not as a spirit, not as a Person, not as an image, but as sheer, pure One. And into this One we are to sink from nothing to nothing, so help us God.[8]

Eckhart also observed God as a unity into which the human soul or spirit can be absorbed or connected. In fact, the holistic properties of the brain appear to

---

[6]   Hufford, D.J. *The Terror That Comes in the Night: An Experience-Centered Study of Supernatural Assault Traditions*. Philadelphia, PA: University of Pennsylvania Press, 1989.

[7]   Quoted in: Nicholson, R.A. *The Mystics of Islam*. London: Routledge and Kegan Paul, 1963.

[8]   Quoted in: Underhill, E. *The Essentials of Mysticism*. Boston, MA: Oneworld Publications, 1999.

be particularly strong in this notion of God. God cannot be approached as anything other than a powerful sense of oneness.

Black Elk, the Oglala mystic and shaman stated:

> Peace comes within the souls of men
> When they realize their oneness with the universe.[9]

One additional interesting element here is the emotion of peacefulness which is intimately associated with the feeling of oneness with the universe. Mystical experiences are frequently described in such positive emotional terms— peacefulness, joy, love, and compassion.

A part of this sense of oneness is the dissolution of the ego, or individual, self. The self becomes part of the greater oneness of God or the absolute. For example, Dr. Patrick McNamara utilizes this component of spirituality as a focal discussion point regarding the relationship between neurobiology and religion.[10] He argues that religion aids in the development of the higher sense of self and also provides a mechanism for "decentering" the self which improves our overall relationship with both others and the universe as a whole. The sense of self includes several brain structures and functions which have been shown to be affected during practices such as meditation and prayer.

The frontal lobes are involved in our willful behaviors. The frontal lobes are also important for what is referred to as the executive self that mediates our social behaviors, plans future events, and provides a sense of conscience and compassion. The limbic system attaches emotions to our sense of self. The temporal lobes provide a memory stream for our self and also enables us to think in abstract ways about that self. Finally, the parietal lobe helps to provide a sense of space and orientation of the self. Data supports that each of these structures appears to play a role in religious and spiritual practices and experiences. But the full relationship is not known.

"The separate self dissolves in the sea of pure consciousness, infinite and immortal," says Hindu scripture.[11] "Separateness arises from identifying the Self with the body, which is made up of the elements; when this physical identification dissolves, there can be no more separate self. This is what I want to tell you, beloved."

Thus, there does seem to be an interrelationship between the brain structures that underlie the sense of self and the loss of the sense of self that is associated with many religious and spiritual experiences. The spiritual need to transcend the

---

[9]   Quoted in: Kabat-Zinn, J. *Wherever You Go There You Are*. New York, NY: Hyperion, 1994.

[10]   McNamara, P. *The Neuroscience of Religious Experience*. Cambridge: Cambridge University Press, 2009.

[11]   Quoted in: Teasdale, W. *The Mystic Heart: Discovering a Universal Spirituality in the World's Religions*. Novato, CA: New World Library, 1999.

self is a central theme of Eastern traditions, including Taoism, as is made clear in this excerpt from an ancient Chinese text:

> The Taoist first transcends worldly affairs, then material things, and finally even his own existence. Through this step-by-step non attachment he achieves enlightenment and is able to see all things as One.[12]

The same ideas, however, also lie at the heart of Western schools of mysticism as revealed by the following quote from Rabbi Eleazar:

> Think of yourself as nothing and totally forget yourself as you pray. Only remember that you are praying for the Divine Presence. You may then enter the Universe of Thought, a state of consciousness which is beyond time. Everything in this realm is the same—life and death, land, and sea ... but in order to enter this realm you must relinquish your ego and forget all your troubles.[13]

Both the Taoist and the Jewish mystic might find the sense of oneness a powerful core of their mystical experiences. In similar fashion, Greek Orthodox mystics in the fifth century came to believe that God could only be known by a mind that has been cleansed of all distracting thoughts and images. The Orthodox mystics called this stillness of mind "hesychia," or an "inner silence," and taught that it was the way to open the door to a mystical union with God.

In her book *A History of God*, religion scholar Karen Armstrong describes that the goal of Greek mysticism was to gain

> a freedom from distraction and multiplicity, and the loss of ego—an experience that is clearly akin to that produced by contemplatives in nontheistic religions like Buddhism. By systematically weaning their minds away from their "passions"—such as pride, greed, sadness or anger which tied them to the ego— hesychiasts would transcend themselves and become deified like Jesus on Mt Tabor, transfigured by the divine "energies."[14]

Armstrong finds similar ideas among the Sufi mystics who developed the concept of "*fana*," or "annihilation," brought about by a combination of fasting, sleepless vigils, chanting, and contemplation. All of these practices together were intended to induce mystical states. It is interesting that these behaviors often resulted in actions that seemed bizarre and uncontrolled, which, according to Armstrong, earned those mystics who practiced such techniques the nickname of the

---

[12]   Quoted in: Epstein, P. *Kabbalah: The Way of the Jewish Mystic*. Boston, MA: Shambhala Publications, 1988.

[13]   Quoted in: Epstein, P. *Kabbalah: The Way of the Jewish Mystic*. Boston, MA: Shambhala Publications, 1988.

[14]   Armstrong, K. *A History of God*. New York, NY: Ballantine, 1993.

"drunken" Sufis. The first drunken Sufi was Abu Yizad Bistami[15] who lived in the ninth century, and whose introspective disciplines carried him beyond the more traditional personalized conceptions of God:

> I gazed upon [al-Lah] with the eye of truth and said to Him: "Who is this?" He said, "This is neither I nor other than I. There is no God but I." Then he changed me out of my identity into His Selfhood ... Then I communed with him with the tongue of his Face saying: "How fares it with me with Thee?" He said, "I am through Thee, there is no god but Thou."

Bistami had united with God, Armstrong says, had become a part of God, and appears to have experienced going beyond his self, much like the experiences described by the other mystics considered thus far. But what does it mean from a brain perspective to go beyond the self? Does the individual activate a different set of brain structures from those that typically help maintain the usual sense of self? Does the original sense of self go away, or is it replaced by a new sense of self? One can also consider whether these different possibilities can have any concordance with known biological functions of the brain. Perhaps there is a biological, as well as spiritual, reason that mystical states seem to share so many similar characteristics.

In his *Varieties of Religious Experience*, William James states, "The overcoming of all the usual barriers between the individual and the Absolute is the great mystic achievement." Thus, in mystical states the individual both becomes one with the Absolute and becomes aware of a powerful sense of oneness. James continues,

> This is the everlasting and triumphant mystical tradition, hardly altered by differences of clime or creed. In Hinduism, in Neoplatonism, in Sufism, in Christian mysticism ... we find the same recurring note, so that there is about mystical utterance an eternal unanimity which ought to make a critic stop and think, and which brings it about that the mystical classics have, as has been said, neither birthday nor native land. Perpetually telling of the unity of man with God, their speech antedates languages, and they do not grow old.[16]

These various descriptions of intense mystical states display a certain type of phenomenological characteristic. A neurotheologian might do an evaluation of other similar types of religious or spiritual experiences. By evaluating a number of types of experiences, especially across traditions, one can begin to get at underlying neurophysiological correlates. Just to reiterate, this does not imply a causal arrow from brain function to spiritual experience. But it does provide a new perspective for evaluating such experiences. Perhaps such an analysis will help

---

[15]   See Hodgson, M.G.S. *The Venture of Islam, Conscience and History in a World Civilization.* Chicago, IL: Chicago University Press, 1974.

[16]   James, W. *Varieties of Religious Experience.* London: Routledge, 2002.

better link biology and spirituality. Perhaps we will better understand the nature of spiritual experiences. And perhaps, we will find either a tremendous plurality of experiences, or a merging of experiences. Either way, once we have begun to establish some of the phenomenological elements, we can begin to explore other aspects of these experiences.

General Methods of Attaining Spiritual Experiences

In addition to the phenomenological elements of spiritual experiences themselves, it is also necessary to evaluate how spiritual experiences are actually attained. These methods can also be evaluated from a neurotheological perspective. Methods such as prayer or meditation appear to have very specific attributes that likely affect specific brain functions. It may also be possible to tie more clearly the various methods to particular types of experiences. Such an understanding could have profound implications for individuals in search of specific spiritual or religious paths since the information might be useful for guiding individuals down the proper pathways.

There are several broad categories of methods used to attain spiritual experiences. To begin, spiritual experiences can occur in either a group or individual setting. Group practices such as religious rituals and ceremonies, services, and pilgrimages can have profound effects on people. The brain has specific neurons called "mirror neurons" that are excited when we see other people doing something. These neurons are believed actually to mimic what we see others doing. Ritual may tap into such a mechanism by getting many individuals to do the same thing, in large part, by having them observe the behavior and activities of the people around them. Individual practices such as meditation and prayer also elicit powerful experiences, but typically only for the participant. However, as is the case in monasteries around the world, sometimes meditation works best when performed with other people, even though there is no formal interaction.

There are also a number of examples of spontaneous experiences which can include sudden mystical experiences or near death experiences. However, when one looks closer at spiritual experiences, they are, to some extent, all spontaneous. Even for the meditator purposely practicing for 40 years, the actual moment of enlightenment is never pre-planned. With few exceptions, no one has ever been able to state, "Today I will have a spiritual experience," and then go out and actually have one. It is even more difficult to know precisely *when* a spiritual or mystical experience might happen. We might differentiate mystical experiences from spiritual experiences. Mystical experiences are usually regarded as spiritual, but include elements such as an altered sense of self or consciousness that goes beyond many types of spiritual experiences. Some scholars have argued that there is a continuum of spiritual states that may lead up to a specifically mystical experience. Whether mystical experiences are a fundamentally different type of experience or exist along a continuum, any comprehensive neurotheological approach must be able to account for a wide variety of different experiences ranging from the very mild religious or spiritual to the deeply mystical. In fact, an integrated approach such as neurotheology may be able to help better delineate the nature and effects of a wide range of experiences.

Individual Practices and Approaches to their Study

Neurotheological study might find it easier to begin with the evaluation of individual practices and experiences since they are likely to be easier to measure and evaluate compared to group practices. There are thousands of specific approaches for attaining spiritual experiences on an individual basis. The most common forms are various types of meditation or prayer which include the Eastern traditions as well as a number of specific Western approaches. Prayer, when pursued with great repetition and vigor, is also regarded as a form of meditation and thus there can be significant overlap in these terms, at least as they are practiced. All of these meditation-like approaches involve the purposeful pursuit of some type of practice (for example, focusing on a prayer, word, sacred object) with the goal of attaining some spiritual result. The spiritual result may include feeling a sense of oneness with something sacred, feeling a sense of cleansing or forgiveness, feeling closer to God, surrendering oneself to God, or feeling a sense of ultimate reality. Some practices might strive for specific sensory or cognitive experiences pertaining to the spiritual tradition. Even creative activities related to music, art, and poetry may have relevance in terms of religiousness and spirituality. Regardless, all of these approaches appear to include the use of cognitive processes in order to attain a spiritual experience through some type of spiritual or mental exercise. The use of terms such as "feel" or "surrender" have an experiential element that involves certain brain processes.

In spite of the tremendous variety of practices, there appear to be certain fundamental similarities among spiritual experiences, and thus it may be reasonable to simplify greatly such approaches into two basic categories, at least for the purpose of initial neurotheological investigation. However, once this division is discussed, it is important to revisit specific types of practices to determine to what extent they fall into one or a combination of these categories and then analyze them respectively. The first category might be called "passive meditation" in which the subject simply attempts to clear all thought from their sphere of attention.[17] This form of meditation is an attempt to reach a subjective state characterized by a sense of no space, no time, and no thought. Further, this state is cognitively experienced as fully integrated and unified such that there is no sense of a self and other. A variant of this meditation is referred to as open monitoring or mindfulness in which the individual simply pays attention without judgment to whatever

---

[17]   d'Aquili, E.G. and Newberg, A.B. *The Mystical Mind: Probing the Biology of Religious Experience*. Minneapolis, MN: Fortress Press, 1999.

thoughts, feelings, or experiences arise in the mind of the meditator.[18] There is a second category which might be called "active" meditation, where the subject focuses their attention on a particular object, image, phrase, or word. Active meditation techniques are probably more widely used especially since it is this technique that is employed in prayer practices. But there are many other practices such as transcendental meditation and various forms of Tibetan Buddhism that would constitute an active meditation. Active meditation is designed to lead to a subjective experience of absorption with the object of focus.

While the overall network of brain structures that might be involved is likely quite complex, we can consider several areas and functions that may be particularly relevant for discussing neurobiological correlates of these practices and their associated experiences. One other differentiation among spiritual practices might be related to whether the practice is guided or done volitionally. Guided practices are those in which an individual follows a person or a recording that tells the person what to do. Volitional practices are those in which the individual uses their own will to initiate and maintain a practice. They decide what to do and when to do it. The brain likely responds in a different fashion depending on whether it is following along or actively doing the practice. The frontal lobes appear to be particularly involved in this regard since studies have shown them to be active when purposely and willfully focusing on a task while they usually have decreased activity when simply following or repeating something.

It should be clear though that the specific characteristics of a given meditation practice, including how the practice is performed (verbal vs. visual vs. movement) and what is experienced during different states of the practice, will likely have a profound effect on brain function. This leads to another principle which asks scholars to fully utilize the phenomenological elements of a particular practice to provide necessary information for helping to bring in the neuroscientific perspective.

Principle XXIX: It is necessary to ensure that the phenomenological characteristics of any given practice inform the neuroscientific perspective of the types of changes that might be expected.

Utilizing phenomenology in this way should greatly enhance the quality and impact of any neuroscientific information that might be obtained through various studies. Otherwise, brain changes associated with a particular practice might appear "disconnected" since they cannot be related to individual elements of that practice.

Non-contemplative approaches such as dance or music also can be performed individually or as a group. These approaches may or may not have cognitive components in a manner similar to meditation practices. Even though there is not a specific cognitive approach within these practices, they too might be divided into an active and passive category. An example of an active category might be

---

[18]   Lutz, A., Slagter, H.A., Dunne, J.D., Davidson, R.J. "Attention regulation and monitoring in meditation." *Trends in Cognitive Science.* 2008;12(4):163-169.

spiritual dancing since the individual must purposely maintain the practice in order to attain the spiritual state. Music itself might be either passive or active depending on whether the practitioner performs the music or listens to the music allowing it to take him or her to some spiritual experience. As with contemplative approaches, there should be some specific neurobiological differences between those practices that are actively performed and those in which the individual is passive. However, many of the experiences associated with non-contemplative approaches should be considered from a similar phenomenological manner as contemplative practices in order to help facilitate a neurotheological analysis. This will allow for theories designed to develop overall models of physiological states associated with such practices and their associated experiences. From here, more specific and detailed analyses of specific practices can be considered.

Types of Group Ceremonial Rituals

Historically, some scholars have emphasized the supposed inverse relationship between ritual (usually performed by a group) and meditation (usually performed privately by an individual).[19] By this it is meant that people who practice a great deal of ritualistic group behaviors tend not to practice much individual meditation and those people who hold individual meditation as a highly important practice tend not to participate in group rituals. Whether a rigidly inverse relationship between religious ritual behavior and private devotion and/or meditation can be strictly maintained is an open question, even within the Western tradition. But certainly, when one looks across cultures the argument becomes considerably more tenuous. In the Eastern traditions of Hinduism and Buddhism, there is usually a comfortable complementary relationship between ceremonial ritual and meditative practices which seems to render the supposed inverse relationship between ritual and meditation anything but a cultural universal. Indeed an argument could be made that the inverse relationship between ritual and meditation is an unusual condition arising from the particular cultural circumstances of modern European history.

Human ceremonial ritual should probably be considered a "morally neutral technology" which, depending on the belief system in which it is imbedded, can either promote or minimize particular aspects of a society and promote or minimize overall aggressive behavior.[20] In particular, rituals appear to create an experience of group unity and cohesiveness around a specific set of beliefs or doctrines. If a doctrine which achieves its incarnation in a ritual defines the experiences generated as applying only to the specific group, then what one ends up with is

---

[19]   Barnes, A.E. "Ces sortes de penitence imaginaires: the counter-reformation assault on communitas." In Barnes, A.E. and Stearnes, P.N.S. (eds.), *Social History and Issues in Human Consciousness*. New York, NY: University Press, 1989.

[20]   d'Aquili, E.G. and Newberg, A.B. *The Mystical Mind: Probing the Biology of Religious Experience*. Minneapolis, MN: Fortress Press, 1999.

only the unification of the group. It is probably true that aggression within the group will be minimized or eliminated by the unifying experience generated by the ritual. However, this may only serve to emphasize the special cohesiveness of the group *vis-à-vis* other groups. The result may be an increase in overall aggression (specifically inter-group rather than intra-group). The doctrine and its embodying ritual may, of course, apply to all members of a religion, a nation state, an ideology, all of humanity, or all of reality. Obviously, as one increases the scope of what is included in the unifying experience, the amount of overall aggressive behavior decreases and the sense of cohesiveness and connectedness increases.

The states which can be produced during ceremonial and religious ritual seem to overlap with some of the unitary states generated by various meditative practices. It is probably not too strong a statement that human ceremonial ritual provides the "common man" access to spiritual or mystical experience. This by no means implies that the mystic is impervious to the effects of ceremonial ritual. Indeed, precisely because of their intense unitary experiences arising from meditation, mystics are probably more affected by group ceremonial ritual than the average person. Viewed dispassionately one must conclude that ceremonial ritual, at its most effective, is an incredibly powerful technology whether for good or ill. Further, because of its essentially social nature, it tends to have much greater social significance than meditation or contemplation. Although meditation and contemplation may produce more intense and more extended unitary states compared to the relatively brief flashes generated by ritual, the former nevertheless are solitary experiences. They may be of immense significance to the individual. Indeed, the significance of meditative states may be of a genuinely transcendent nature, but they are not essentially social experiences although they may have social consequences.

Many scholars have struggled with the definition of ritual. From a neurotheological perspective, rituals, either individual or group, appear to have several common elements:

1. Rituals are structured or patterned.
2. Rituals are rhythmic and repetitive (to some degree at least), that is, they tend to recur in the same or nearly the same form with some regularity.
3. Rituals act to synchronize affective, perceptual-cognitive, and motor processes within the central nervous system of individual participants.
4. Rituals synchronize these processes among the various individual participants.

The last component necessarily refers only to rituals performed in groups and not to individual rituals such as that often associated with meditation. Individual rituals appear to help synchronize the participant with some higher form of being whether it is the rest of the world, the universe, or God.

Focusing on the components of group ritual and the synchronization that occurs between individuals involved in group ritual, a number of animal studies have shown that there is something about the repetitive or rhythmic emanation of signals from a participant (member of the same species) which generates a high degree of arousal in the limbic, or emotional, system of the brain.[21] With respect to this rhythmic quality of ritual, K. Lorenz notes:

> The display of animals during threat and courtship furnishes an abundance of examples, and so does the culturally developed ceremonial of humans. The deans of the university walked into the hall with a "measured step"; pitch, rhythm and loudness of the Catholic priests chanting during mass are all strictly regulated by liturgical prescription. The unambiguity of the communication is also increased by its frequent repetition. Rhythmical repetition of the same movement is so characteristic of very many rituals, both instinctive and cultural, that it is hardly necessary to describe examples.[22]

Other researchers have shown that such repetitive auditory and visual stimuli can drive neuronal rhythms in the brain and eventually produce an intensely pleasurable, ineffable experience in humans.[23] Furthermore, such repetitive stimuli can bring about simultaneous intense discharge from both the human sympathetic (arousal) and parasympathetic (quiescent) nervous systems.[24] It is interesting to consider how stimulating the arousal or quiescent centers of the nervous system might be associated with intense feelings of alertness and energy or perhaps blissfulness and calmness. In fact, it might even be possible to consider the simultaneous action of calming and arousal mechanisms that could be associated with an "active bliss" or ecstasy amidst great tranquility. Such opposing emotional responses have certainly been reported in association with various rituals and spiritual practices.

It may be that the various ecstatic states, which can occur in human beings after exposure to rhythmic auditory, visual, or tactile stimuli produce a feeling of union with other participants in that ritual. In fact, oneness of all participants is a theme that runs through the elements of most human rituals. It is probably also the sense of oneness and the vagueness of boundaries between self and other, which are experienced at certain "nodal points" in ritual to allow for a given symbol (that is, a religious symbol) to be experienced as that for which it stands. This fusion of symbols and their referents at various points in human religious ritual

---

[21]   Schein, M.W. and Hale, E.B. "Stimuli eliciting sexual behavior." In Beach, F.A. (ed.), *Sex and Behavior*. New York, NY: John Wiley & Sons, 1965; Tinbergen, N. *The Study of Instinct*. London: Oxford University Press, 1951; Rosenblatt, J.S. "Effects of experience on sexual behavior in male cats." In Beach, F.A. (ed.), Sex *and Behavior*. New York, NY: John Wiley & Sons, 1965.

[22]   Lorenz, K. *On Aggression*. New York, NY: Bantam Books, 1966.

[23]   Walter, V.J. and Walter, W.G. "The central effects on rhythmic sensory stimulation." *Electroencephalogr Clin Neurophysiol*. 1949;1:57-85.

[24]   Gellhorn, E. and Kiely, W.F. "Mystical states of consciousness: neurophysiological and clinical aspects." *J Nerv Ment Dis*. 1972;154:399-405; Gellhorn, E. and Kiely, W.F. "Autonomic nervous system in psychiatric disorder." In Mendels, J. (ed.), *Biological Psychiatry*. New York, NY: John Wiley & Sons, 1973.

is undoubtedly accomplished by the underlying feeling of oneness which occurs when a particular ritual triggers the holistic processes of the brain. Although it is very difficult to extrapolate from humans to animals, it is probable that some sort of analogous affective state is produced by rhythmic, repeated ritual behavior in other species. This state may vary in intensity, but it always has the effect at least of unifying participants.

Thus, it seems that rhythmic or repetitive behavior synchronizes the limbic system's emotional responses of a group of participants. It can generate a level of arousal which is both pleasurable and reasonably uniform among the individuals so that necessary group action is facilitated. Rhythmic activity likely causes these effects, in part, via its ability to function as a form of communication. The position of many ethnologists is that rhythmicity evolved in lower animal species as a primary form of communication. However, rhythmicity also evolved an autonomous effect of its own, separate from its communication function. Lorenz states:

> Both instinctive and cultural rituals become independent motivations of behavior by creating new ends or goals toward which the organisms strive for their own sake. It is in their character of independent motivating factors that rituals transcend their original function of communication and become able to perform their equally important secondary tasks of controlling aggression and of forming a bond among certain individuals.[25]

Given these considerations of the effects of ritual, we can attempt to evaluate ritual more fully from a neurotheological perspective, especially because of the importance of ritual in religious and spiritual traditions. For example, there is some evidence that simultaneous stimulation of the sympathetic and parasympathetic systems may ultimately cause both hemispheres of the brain to function in a simultaneous fashion. However, this specific functional relationship is far from clear since simply stimulating the autonomic nervous system through drugs does not typically result in cognitive or affective functioning. On the other hand, neuroscientists such as Antonio Damasio, who wrote *The Feeling of What Happens*,[26] have suggested that many thoughts and feelings are interpretations of bodily and physiological processes in more of a "bottom-up" phenomenon rather than "top-down." In ritual, this may be manifested by the presentation of a particular dyadic concept (for example, good vs. evil or human beings vs. God), by the binary processes in the brain and the simultaneous experience of their union via the activation of the holistic function. This could explain the often reported experience of the resolution of unexplainable paradoxes by individuals during certain meditation states on the one hand or during states induced by ritual behavior on the other. In fact, there may be significant similarities from a neuropsychological perspective between meditation and ritual

---

[25]   Lorenz, K. *On Aggression*. New York, NY: Bantam Books, 1966.

[26]   Damasio, A. *The Feeling of What Happens: Body and Emotion in the Making of Consciousness*. San Diego, CA: A Harvest Book, Harcourt, 1999.

in terms of the resolution of opposites. The neuropsychological similarity may rest in the common activation of the holistic processes associated with a unitary experience which reconciles the opposites. It should be obvious that the overall neuropsychological mechanisms underlying meditation on the one hand and ritual on the other are actually quite different except, perhaps, in the latter stages. Meditation may be considered to be a top-down process while ritual is a bottom-up process. However, such a clear distinction is likely too simplistic and would not account for many of the complexities of both meditation and ritual practices. For now, suffice it to say that meditation, as well as effective ritual, can, and usually does, produce the powerful subjective experience of the integration of opposites. Thus, during certain meditation and/or ritual states, logical paradoxes or the awareness of polar opposites may appear simultaneously, both as antinomies and as unified wholes. This experience is coupled with an intensely emotional, oceanic or blissful experience. During intense meditative experiences, the experience of the union of opposites is expanded to the experience of the total union of self and other. In the *unio mystica* of the Christian tradition, the experience of the union of opposites, or *conjunctio oppositorum*, is expanded to the experience of the union of the self with God.

Once a basic model of ritual behaviors from a neurotheological perspective is developed, different aspects of ritual can be considered in more detail. For example, ritual might now be considered in terms of rapid and slow rituals in terms of their different phenomenological characteristics as well as their different associated neuropsychological processes. There is likely an initial parasympathetic, or calming, drive associated with "slow" rhythmic rituals like Christian or Shinto liturgy. This can be contrasted with the mechanism associated with "rapid" rituals such as Sufi dancing, the Umbanda of Brazil, or Voodoo frenzy. However, there is obviously more to ritual than autonomic nervous system-related processes. The cognitive and emotional processes associated with ritual practices are also crucial. But the autonomic nervous system activity is an important mediator of such experiences and also aids in the transmission of the neuronal activity to the rest of the body. The ability of the autonomic nervous system to connect the brain and body provides the means by which ritual can result in very visceral feelings.

In addition to the direct effect of rhythmicity, there are other neuropsychological components of ceremonial ritual that might be evaluated to determine if they augment the effect of rhythmicity, and help cause changes in the autonomic activity during rituals. First of all, human ceremonial ritual incorporates "marked" actions. Thus, any action such as a prostration, a slow bow, a slow and deliberately excursive movement of the arms and hands, or any other action which by its form or meaning draws attention to itself as different from ordinary baseline actions should produce an orienting response by the brain, usually in a structure called the amygdala. The amygdala acts to perform environmental surveillance and can direct attention towards something of interest in the environment. In animals, electrical stimulation of the amygdala initially produces sustained attention and orienting reactions. If the stimulation continues, fear and/or anger reactions are elicited.

When some degree of fear follows the attention response, the pupils dilate and the animal will cringe or withdraw, which are all functions of the sympathetic system. Thus, during human ceremonial ritual, the amygdale, which helps fix attention, should be more than normally responsive to specifically "marked" ritual actions. This tends to produce sustained attention and orienting reactions accompanied by a mild fear response which, in this context, humans call "religious awe."

In addition to the amygdalar response to ritually marked actions, it should be noted that the sense of smell can function as a driver of the nervous system. The middle part of the amygdala receives fibers from the olfactory tract which are the neurons for the sense of smell or olfaction. During times when we experience a strong smell, there is concomitant activation of the amygdala.[27] It would seem, then, that the use of incense or other fragrances might cause direct stimulation of the amygdala subsequently augmenting the general sympathetic drive via "marked" ritual actions.

The importance of this consideration of rituals again demonstrates the capability of neurotheology to explore a particular aspect of religious or spiritual activity from a new perspective. By evaluating the possible underlying brain processes associated with ritual, we might be able to better understand ritual, relate ritual to various religious and spiritual doctrines or phenomena, and possibly help to improve the effectiveness of ritual.

Phenomenological Aspects of Religious Experience

We have now considered the relationships and neuronal mechanisms associated with different types of religious and spiritual practices in broad terms and this has enabled us to explore how neurotheology might provide a new perspective on such practices. Of course, these practices eventually result in a variety of experiences which can also be evaluated from a neurotheological perspective. Let us explore how neurotheology might reflect on the nature of religious and spiritual experiences.

Similar Elements of Spiritual Experiences Across Practices

One neurotheological approach to spiritual experiences is to determine what are the similarities across different traditions and practices. This is an important principle of neurotheology since it helps to relate such experiences to scientific methods which tend to rely more on group effects:

---

[27]   Winston, J.S., Gottfried, J.A., Kilner, J.M., and Dolan, R.J. "Integrated neural representations of odor intensity and affective valence in human amygdala." *J Neurosci.* 2005;25:8903-8907.

Principle XXX: Neurotheology should investigate the similarities of religious and spiritual experiences across individuals, traditions, and practices.

In such an analysis, one feature that appears common among many different types of spiritual experiences is a sense of unity or connectedness between the individual and the group, community, society, nation, world, and God or Ultimate Reality. These unitary experiences can range from very mild to a sense of complete oneness. One approach to evaluating these experiences would be to consider them to lie along a unitary continuum. On one end of the spectrum are experiences such as those attained through a church liturgy or watching a sunset. These experiences carry with them a mild sense of being connected with something greater than the self. On the other end of the spectrum are the types of experiences usually described as mystical or transcendent. This unitary element of spiritual experiences should not be thought of as limiting the specific aspects and experiences associated with them. It simply appears to be the case that unitary feelings are a crucial part of spiritual experiences. In fact, many scholars have focused on the more intense experiences because of ease of study and analysis—the most intense experiences provide the most robust responses that can be qualitatively and perhaps even quantitatively measured. For example, Frederick Streng described the most intense types of spiritual experiences as relating to a variety of phenomena including occult experience, trance, a vague sense of unaccountable uneasiness, sudden extraordinary visions and words of divine beings, or aesthetic sensitivity.[28] Ninian Smart has distinguished mysticism in this sense from an experience of a "dynamic external presence."[29] Smart argued that certain sects of Hinduism, Buddhism, and Taoism differ markedly from prophetic religions such as Judaism and Islam and from religions related to the prophetic-like Christianity, in that the religious experience most characteristic of the former group is "mystical" whereas that most characteristic of the latter is "numinous."

Somewhat similar to Smart's distinction between mystical and numinous experiences is that of Walter T. Stace who distinguishes between what he calls extrovertive mystical experiences and introvertive mystical experiences.[30] Stace characterizes these respectively as follows:

Extrovertive mystical experiences:
1. the Unifying Vision—all things are one
2. the more concrete apprehension of the One as an inner subjectivity, or life, in all things
3. sense of objectivity or reality
4. blessedness, peace, etc.

---

[28] Streng, F. "Language and mystical awareness." In Katz, S. (ed.), *Mysticism and Philosophical Analysis*. New York, NY: Oxford University Press, 1978.

[29] Smart, N. *The Religious Experience of Mankind*. London: Macmillan, 1969.

[30] Stace, W.T. *Mysticism and Philosophy*. London: Macmillan, 1961.

5. feeling of the holy, sacred, divine
6. paradoxicality
7. alleged by mystics to be ineffable

Introvertive mystical experiences:
1. the Unitary Consciousness; the One, the Void; pure consciousness
2. nonspatial, nontemporal
3. sense of objectivity or reality
4. blessedness, peace, etc.
5. feeling of the holy, sacred, or divine
6. paradoxicality
7. alleged by mystics to be ineffable

Stace then concludes that characteristics 3 through 7 are identical in the two lists and are therefore universal common characteristics of mystical experiences in all cultures, ages, religions, and civilizations of the world. However, it is characteristics 1 and 2 in which the distinction is made between extrovertive and introvertive mystical experiences in his typology. There is a clear similarity between Stace's extrovertive mystical experience and Smart's numinous experience and between Stace's introvertive mystical experiences and Smart's mystical experience proper.

As shown in the above example of criteria for mystical experiences, the unitary state is an important element, but there are other elements that can also potentially be evaluated such as paradoxicality or ineffability. A neurotheological analysis of spiritual experiences might clarify some of the issues regarding mystical and spiritual experiences by allowing for a better understanding and typology based on the underlying brain structures and their related cognitive functions. It would be fascinating to determine which parts of the brain are involved when an individual focuses on paradoxicality rather than ineffability. Paradoxicality might invoke the dyadic function of the brain while ineffability might be associated with a loss of activity in the language and abstract functions of the brain.

The ability to find commonality within and across different traditions and experiences could have powerful cultural and theological implications. After all, if a variety of traditions ultimately are found to have great commonality in their experiences, then they may prove to be more related than expressed in the doctrinal elements.

Disparate Elements of Spiritual Experiences Across Practices

If there are similarities between spiritual experiences, it has also been observed that there are many individual differences between spiritual experiences both in terms of what any given individual experiences even within a specific tradition as well as in terms of expected differences across practices and traditions. Exploring the interindividual differences is crucial since this implies that even for subjects performing the exact same ritual or practice, the subjective experience may be quite different:

Principle XXXI: *Neurotheology should investigate the differences between various religious and spiritual experiences across individuals and practices.*

It is also important to relate the differences to the similarities mentioned above. Together, by exploring the similarities and differences from a neurotheological perspective, we might best understand the true nature of these experiences. Furthermore, differences in experiences may relate to what specifically is experienced, how the experience is interpreted after the fact, and how the experience is reflected in cognitive, emotional, and behavior changes within the individual. For example, of a group of 100 Catholics at a mass, each person might be affected differently by the service. Some might feel energized, some loved, and some forgiven. Certain songs or phrases may have greater meaning to one individual than to another. It might be that each person has a "favorite" prayer or song. This, in part, explains why practices and rituals have such a variety of elements since it makes sense that the more a practice can accommodate a large number of individuals, the more successful it will be at inducing various spiritual experiences. Out of the 100 participants perhaps one or two will have a deeper experience in which they undergo a new "realization" about their belief system. Occasionally, someone will have a mystical experience which may have life changing consequences for the individual. In comparing these deeper experiences, how does a researcher avoid similar issues with regard to interindividual differences? If a researcher wanted to determine whether the rosary or Zen meditation produced the stronger spiritual experience, how would the researcher measure the "strength" of any individual experience. A number of scales and measures have been developed, but these too are subjective. Even if a scale or scoring system could be developed (for example, a scale from 1 to 10 with 10 being the most spiritual feeling), how could a researcher differentiate one person's high score to another person's low score. A highly religious or spiritual person may require a much deeper or more profound experience than a relative novice in order to register highly on any subjective scoring measure.

Interindividual differences may also play out in terms of the interpretation of spiritual experiences after the fact. For example, if two individuals have a spiritual experience, an optimistic individual may have a very different interpretation of that experience compared to a pessimist. While this is an overly simplistic example, the point is that individuals may interpret such experiences very differently depending on their inherent personality and disposition, their current life state, their upbringing, their socioeconomic status, and any other number of factors. Gender may also be a very important mediator of religious and spiritual phenomena and has been studied in only a limited manner. Thus, even if people have essentially the same experience, in and of itself, by the time they describe it to someone, it might appear to be very different.

Intertraditional Differences in Spiritual Experiences

The differences across traditions is also a considerable challenge for any scholarly analysis, and particularly a neurotheological one.

Principle XXXII: Neurotheology should investigate the differences between various religious and spiritual experiences across religions and traditions.

Depending on the cultural, doctrinal, and behavioral differences that arise in distinct traditions, there are many possible outcomes to spiritual practices and experiences. For example, does a Christian's God encounter correlate to a Buddhist's nirvana experience? Are there any similarities or are they completely different? And if they have similarities and differences, how do these relate to different brain changes? It is not possible to elaborate to any great extent on all of the potential differences since selecting one or two examples will leave out thousands of others. However, what is important to emphasize is that whatever practice or experience is being considered, the phenomenological characteristics must be described as clearly as possible. While difficult, it is important to attempt to correlate ideas, concepts, and experiences across traditions. Such an analysis might allow for a deeper understanding of the relationship between theistic and non-theistic traditions, contemplative and ceremonial based approaches, energizing versus relaxing practices, and many others.

A related element in the differences across traditions is the incorporation of various doctrinal elements. Thus a meditation practice based in Buddhism might yield different results than a meditation practice based in Christianity. The doctrinal differences may dictate how the practice is performed, what types of experiences are perceived, how those experiences are incorporated into the person's behaviors, and how the religious or spiritual beliefs are affected. Some traditions may be more open to unusual types of experiences while others might be closed. The important point from a neurotheological perspective is that all of these differences can potentially be evaluated in the context of brain function. However, a neurotheological approach might also provide a unique vantage point for comparing different traditions since one could attempt to observe if the described differences correlate with different neurophysiological patterns. This might be a crucial strong point for neurotheology since it can address the issue as to whether differences perceived across traditions are truly distinct or are merely different interpretations of the same phenomena.

Cognitive Neuroscience Assessment of Spiritual Experiences

Now that we have considered many phenomenological aspects of religious and spiritual experiences, we can begin to evaluate in more detail potential neurophysiological correlates of such experiences. This section will be one of the few sections of this book that will focus more on the neuroscience of spiritual experiences rather than the two-way street mentioned as a crucial principle in the first chapter. However, it is sometimes necessary to explore unidirectional approaches since these too have value, although this is only if such an analysis is maintained within a larger bidirectional approach. Thus, any neurophysiological correlates of spiritual experiences *must* be considered just that—correlates—rather than causal mechanisms by which such experiences occur. With this in mind, we can explore methodological issues and scientific aspects that might be helpful for the neurotheological scholarship.

Overview of Specific Measurement Techniques

Clearly, one of the most important aspects for attempting to utilize neuroscience in the evaluation of spiritual experiences is to find careful, rigorous methods for empirically testing hypotheses. One such example of empirical evidence comes from the studies that have measured neurophysiological activity during religious and spiritual practices or states. Meditative and prayer states comprise perhaps the most fertile testing ground from a scientific perspective because of the predictable, reproducible, and well described nature of such practices; although, theoretically, any type of religious or spiritual phenomenon might be assessed with neuroscientific methods. Studies of religious and spiritual phenomena have evolved over the years to utilize the most advanced technologies for studying neurophysiology. Given the complex and dynamic nature of such phenomena, it may be necessary to consider using a wide array of possible neuroscientific methods.

Principle XXXIII: All possible methods—scientific, religious, and phenomenological—should be considered potentially useful in the evaluation of spiritual experiences.

Originally, studies analyzed the relationship between electrical changes in the brain (measured by electroencephalography, EEG) and meditative states. Proficient meditation practitioners have been shown to have significant changes in the electrical activity in the brain, particularly in the frontal lobes that are typically regarded as the part of the brain involved in attentional focus. Furthermore, the EEG patterns of meditation practices indicate that they represent a unique state of consciousness that is different from normal waking and from sleep. Although EEG is limited in its ability to distinguish particular regions of the brain that may have increased or decreased activity, newer quantitative and spectroscopic methods have substantially improved the spatial capabilities of EEG.

More recent studies of religious and spiritual practices have utilized brain imaging techniques such as single photon emission computed tomography (SPECT), positron emission tomography (PET), and functional magnetic resonance imaging (fMRI). In the past decade, brain activation studies have utilized neuroimaging techniques to explore cerebral function during various behavioral, motor, and cognitive tasks. These studies have helped to determine which parts of the brain are responsible for a variety of neurocognitive processes. These imaging techniques have also allowed for the uncovering of complex neural networks and cognitive modules that have become a basis for cognitive neuroscience research. Activation studies with the functional neuroimaging techniques have been employed to determine the areas in the brain that are involved in the production and understanding of language, visual processing, and pain reception and sensation. In a typical activation study, the subject is asked to perform some kind of task (for example, motor, reading, problem solving) while being scanned and the activation state (that is, the state during the task) is then compared to some control state (that is, resting).

Since most spiritual practices and their concomitant experiences might be considered from the perspective of an activation paradigm, functional brain imaging techniques may be extremely useful in detecting neurophysiological changes associated with those states. PET and SPECT can also be utilized to explore a wide variety of neurotransmitter systems within the brain such as dopamine, serotonin, or endorphins.

There are limitations to each type of technique for the study of religion and spirituality. It is important to ensure that the imaging technique is sensitive enough to measure the expected changes. Also, each of these techniques may interfere with the normal environment in which spiritual practices take place. Placing a subject in a scanner with noise or in uncomfortable positions might adversely affect the ability to study accurately a particular practice. In spite of the potential limitations, early data of meditative practices has generally shown activity changes in a number of brain structures. However, more studies with improved methods will be necessary to further elucidate the neurocognitive aspects of meditation and spiritual experiences. That the underlying neurophysiology of intense meditative states can be considered at all allows for the conceptualization of many other experiences that lie along the religious/spiritual continuum.

What should be kept in mind in interpreting the results of imaging studies of religious and spiritual phenomena is that they each demonstrate certain similarities and certain differences depending on the type of practice and experience. It has long been a hope to develop a comprehensive model of a few basic types of religious/spiritual practice that could then be extrapolated to explore other types of practices.

Neuropsychological Models of Spiritual Experiences

Several scholars have attempted to construct neuropsychological models of spiritual experiences. Such models have involved the temporal lobes, the autonomic nervous system, or some integrated function of a number of brain structures. Given the tremendous diversity and richness of religious and spiritual experiences, it seems that it would be almost impossible to find one part of the brain to be the spiritual part. Most likely there are many parts of the brain that become involved and thus, all parts of the brain should be explored and considered possible contributors to such experiences.

Principle XXXIV: Because religious and spiritual experiences likely involve many brain areas and functions, all brain processes should be considered to have the potential to contribute.

Several possible models that involve different brain regions and functions are described below in an attempt to demonstrate how such models might be constructed. The models presented are not meant to be exhaustive or complete and most likely will require significant empirical evidence for validation. Furthermore, it is likely that any model will go through a progressive development with new additions and subtractions made continually. What is important is to observe how different models might be able to address a variety of phenomenological characteristics of spiritual experiences. Where possible, critiques of such models will also be given.

Models with a Focus on the Temporal Lobes

Several scholars have placed significant emphasis on the temporal lobes with regard to the "seat" of spiritual experiences, also sometimes called, "the God module." There are a number of important reasons that support such a notion. The temporal lobes house the limbic system structures such as the amygdala and hippocampus, that are the seat of emotional responses and also play a key role in memory. Since spiritual experiences are typically very strong emotionally and also elicit a number of intense sensory experiences, the temporal lobe could certainly be associated with many of these phenomena. The temporal lobe is also heavily involved in cognition and language so this could also be somewhat supportive of religious experiences, especially in terms of how they are expressed through language.

There are also specific examples in which the temporal lobes are related to spiritual experiences. The ground-breaking work of neurosurgeon Wilder Penfield, involving electrical stimulation of various parts of the brain, indicated that the temporal lobes are involved in eliciting vivid memories, complex hallucinations, dream-like states, and unusual attribution of emotional significance to otherwise neutral thoughts and external experiences.[31] This research was performed on subjects undergoing brain surgery. This is possible since the brain itself has no pain sensation and, therefore, an individual can be awake during the surgery and can relate various experiences. During surgery, when certain parts of the temporal lobe were stimulated with a mild electrical current, a number of unusual

---

[31]   Jasper, H. and Penfield, W. *Epilepsy and the Functional Anatomy of the Human Brain*, 2nd Edition. London: Little, Brown and Co., 1954.

experiences could be elicited. In particular, patients would relate strong visual or auditory experiences. These experiences were described in terms that frequently were similar to the kinds of vivid experiences associated with religious/spiritual experiences. However, this research has become controversial since these intense experiences occurred in a limited number of patients and have been difficult to replicate.

One also finds that hallucinations become increasingly complex as stimulation is applied to areas that have more complex functions. Thus, stimulation of the association areas will elicit more complex hallucinations than will stimulation of the primary sensory areas.[32] It has frequently been reported that the most complex forms of hallucinations involve activation of both the hippocampus and amygdala in conjunction with other parts of the temporal lobe.[33] It appears that limbic activation is necessary to bring elements that are being processed in the temporal lobes to the realm of conscious understanding. It is further interesting that the hallucinatory effect of psychedelic drugs such as LSD, which often produce archetypal elements, appears to be generated in the temporal lobes.[34]

Researcher Michael Persinger in Canada has written a number of articles on the topic and has tried to demonstrate a certain pattern of temporal lobe findings associated with individuals who have strong or unusual religious experiences. Dr. Persinger has also built upon some of the neurosurgery research of stimulation of certain parts of the temporal lobes such as the amygdala or hippocampus during open brain surgery. Dr. Persinger's work has attempted to stimulate religious experiences through the use of electromagnetic fields on the temporal lobes. His reports suggest that such stimulation can result in certain elements of spiritual experiences such as a sensed presence.[35]

While this evidence supports the importance of the temporal lobes in religious experience, there may be several problems focusing only on the temporal lobes and excluding other parts of the brain as alluded to in the principle elaborated at

---

[32] Penfield, W. and Perot, P. "The brain's record of auditory and visual experience." *Brain.* 1963;86:595-695; Braun, C.M.J., Dumont, M., Duval, J., Hamel-Hébert, I., and Godbout, L. "Brain modules of hallucination: an analysis of multiple patients with brain lesions." *J Psychiatry Neurosci.* 2003;28:432-449; Diederich, N.J., Alesch, F., and Goetz, C.G. "Visual hallucinations induced by deep brain stimulation in Parkinson's disease." *Clin Neuropharmacol.* 2000;23:287-289.

[33] Elliott, B., Joyce, E., and Shorvon, S. "Delusions, illusions and hallucinations in epilepsy: 2. Complex phenomena and psychosis." *Epilepsy Res.* 2009;85:172-186; Devinsky, O. and Lai, G. "Spirituality and religion in epilepsy." *Epilepsy Behav.* 2008;12(4):636-643.

[34] Serafetinides, E.A. "The EEG effects of LSD-25 in epileptic patients before and after temporal lobectomy." *Psychopharmacologia.* 1965;7:453-460.

[35] Persinger, M.A. and Healey, F. "Experimental facilitation of the sensed presence: possible intercalation between the hemispheres induced by complex magnetic fields." *J Nerv Ment Dis.* Aug 2002;190(8):533-541; Persinger, M.A. "The sensed presence within experimental settings: implications for the male and female concept of self." *J Psychol.* Jan 2003;137(1):5-16.

the beginning of this section. There are so many elements to religious/spiritual experiences, that it seems unlikely that a single brain structure could result in the tremendous diversity of experiences. With regard to the temporal lobe in particular, it should additionally be noted that of patients with temporal lobe seizures, it turns out that only a small subset of patients actually describe unusual religious experiences. Also, few individuals who have had their temporal lobes stimulated in one way or another have specifically labeled that experience as spiritual or even felt that it was identical to "actual" religious experiences. Thus, the temporal lobes may be important, but are also likely to only be part of the neurobiological substrate of spiritual experiences.

Models with a Focus on the Frontal Lobes

A number of studies have focused on the frontal lobes as being an important mediator in religious and spiritual practices. Early studies of meditation techniques frequently reported changes in electrical activity in the frontal lobes. The frontal lobes are also important in the elaboration of ritual since the frontal lobes are well known to be involved in the initiation and coordination of movement. The frontal lobes are also crucial to the expression of language. Thus, rituals that involve body movement (for example, bowing or dancing) as well as verbal activity (for example, singing or praying) likely involve the frontal lobe. More recent work has implicated the frontal lobes in the modulation of emotion such that the frontal lobes might be particularly important in the development of empathy and compassion. If these concepts are to be important in religion, then the frontal lobes might be necessary in enabling these processes to arise within each of us.

Patrick McNamara has recently described his model of religion as pertaining to the sense of self and how that self is integrated into God or the absolute. He argues that decentering the self is crucial for religion and religious experience and cites the frontal lobes as the primary neurological correlate of such an experience.[36] Thus, much like the temporal lobes, the frontal lobes also appear to offer a substantial contribution to the brain's ability to practice and experience religion. However, also as described in the context of the temporal lobes, it is unlikely that the frontal lobe functions can be used to correlate with all aspects of religious and spiritual phenomena. The frontal lobes should therefore be an important focus of future studies of religious practices and experiences.

Models with a Focus on the Autonomic Nervous System

Some of the earliest work on religious experiences and practices focused on the autonomic nervous system. It has long been observed that spiritual practices such as meditation can cause significant changes in blood pressure, heart rate,

---

[36]   McNamara, P. *The Neuroscience of Religious Experience*. Cambridge: Cambridge University Press, 2009.

and body metabolism. Since these processes are modulated by the autonomic nervous system, several early scholars sought to develop a model based upon autonomic function. In the early 1970s, Gellhorn and Kiely developed a model of the physiological processes involved in meditation based almost exclusively on autonomic nervous system (ANS) activity.[37] The idea is that the two arms of the autonomic nervous system—the sympathetic which mediates arousal and excitation and the parasympathetic with mediates calmness and quiescence—can each contribute to different experiences. Intense ecstatic religious states might be associated with sympathetic activity while intense quiescent and blissful religious states might be associated with parasympathetic activity. Another important part of the brain is the hypothalamus that regulates the autonomic nervous system, but is also associated with changes in a variety of hormone levels. The hypothalamus is also extensively interconnected with the limbic system. This creates a circuit such that the emotions generated by the limbic system result in hypothalamic changes and subsequent changes in the autonomic nervous system.[38]

Gellhorn and Kiely implicate the importance of the ANS during religious and spiritual experiences.[39] These authors suggested that intense stimulation of either the sympathetic or parasympathetic system, if continued, could ultimately result in simultaneous discharge of both systems (what might be considered a "breakthrough" of the other system). Several studies have demonstrated predominant parasympathetic activity during meditation associated with decreased heart rate and blood pressure, decreased respiratory rate, and decreased oxygen metabolism.[40] However, a recent study of two separate meditative techniques suggested a mutual activation of parasympathetic and sympathetic systems by demonstrating an increase in the variability of heart rate during meditation.[41] The increased variation in heart rate was hypothesized to reflect activation of both arms of the autonomic nervous system. This notion also fits the characteristic description of meditative states in which there is a sense of overwhelming calmness as well as significant alertness. Furthermore, the notion of mutual activation of both arms of the ANS is consistent with recent developments in the study of autonomic

---

[37]   Gellhorn, E. and Kiely, W.F. "Mystical states of consciousness: neurophysiological and clinical aspects." *J Nerv Mental Dis.* 1972;154:399-405.

[38]   Davis, M. "The role of the amygdala in fear and anxiety." *Ann Rev Neurosci.* 1992;15:353-375.

[39]   Gellhorn, E. and Kiely, W.F. "Mystical states of consciousness: neurophysiological and clinical aspects." *J Nerv Mental Dis.* 1972;154:399-405.

[40]   Travis, F. "Autonomic and EEG patterns distinguish transcending from other experiences during transcendental meditation practice." *Int J Psychophysiol.* 2001;42:1-9.

[41]   Peng, C.K., Mietus, J.E., Liu, Y., Khalsa, G., Douglas, P.S., Benson, H., and Goldberger, A.L. "Exaggerated heart rate oscillations during two meditation techniques." *Int J Cardiol.* 1999;70:101-107.

interactions.[42] As with other models, an autonomic nervous system model is limited due to the inability to extrapolate to the rich diversity of religious and spiritual experiences. However, it seems reasonable that the autonomic nervous system should be included in future studies of spiritual experiences since it is likely affected during such practices and experiences.

Integrated Models of Spiritual Experiences

To date, several investigators have developed relatively comprehensive models of religious experiences. An integrated model would be most consistent with the principle above and would suggest that a number of brain structures and functions work together during spiritual practices and experiences. The implication is that there is not a single spiritual structure in the brain, but that such experiences require many different parts of the brain. The strength of integrated models is that they provide for a wide variety of different types of experiences and different elements of experiences. The potential problem with such a model is that while it predicts a number of neurophysiological correlates for such experiences, it may be very difficult to verify since so many different functional components are hypothesized to occur. Furthermore, since there is an implied interaction between the different brain structures, it is much easier to demonstrate empirically changes in specific brain structures rather than assess how different structures interact with each other. As with most scientific models, it is likely that there will be substantial changes made in this model over time and as more empirical data become available.

Integrated models usually include changes in the temporal and frontal lobes similar to those described above. It is also recognized that the autonomic nervous system plays a role. There are also a number of other brain structures that are involved as well as a variety of neurotransmitter systems. Furthermore, integrated models frequently consider how the different functional parts of the brain work together. For example, it is known that frontal lobe activity modulates activity in the thalamus and limbic system. These areas in turn can affect other changes in the brain. It has also been argued that there may be a network of structures that are involved in religious and spiritual experiences but that the structures are affected differently depending on the type and phenomenological nature of those experiences.

Let us explore several additional areas and consider how they may be associated with various practices and experiences. The thalamus works in conjunction with the frontal lobes, particularly as part of a more global attentional network.[43] The thalamus itself governs the flow of sensory information to cortical processing

---

[42]   Hugdahl, K. "Cognitive influences on human autonomic nervous system function." *Curr Opin Neurobiol.* 1996;6:252-258.

[43]   Portas, C.M., Rees, G., Howseman, A.M., Josephs, O., Turner, R., and Frith, C.D. "A specific role for the thalamus in mediating the interaction attention and arousal in humans." *J Neurosci.* 1998;18:8979-8989.

areas. Thus, the thalamus is involved in helping with our sensory perception of the world. Hence, one might expect changes in the thalamus to be associated with alterations in our perceptions of reality. The thalamus also utilizes inhibitory neurons to block sensory information into different areas. It can do this utilizing a molecule called gamma-amino butyric acid (GABA) which is the primary inhibitory neurotransmitter in the brain. In fact, one study suggested that there was a release of GABA during meditation.[44] Thus, one hypothesis has suggested that a blocking (deafferentation) of sensory input into the parietal lobes during meditation and prayer practices might be associated with alterations in the perception of the sense of self and the elaboration of an experience of oneness.[45] The parietal lobe is heavily involved in the analysis and integration of higher-order visual, auditory, and somaesthetic information.[46] It is also involved in a complex attentional network that includes the frontal lobe and thalamus.[47] Through the reception of auditory and visual input from the thalamus, the parietal lobe is able to help generate a three-dimensional image of the body in space and provide a sense of spatial coordinates in which the body is oriented. Recent studies have focused on the junction between the parietal lobe and temporal lobe in relation to out-of-body experiences.[48] For these reasons, the parietal lobe, and its junction with the temporal lobe, can also be a target for future studies as a mediator of the sense of self during spiritual experiences.

Other structures and neurotransmitters to consider would include the basal ganglia which are involved in the dopaminergic system and functionally with movement and emotions. Thus, since religious and spiritual experiences frequently involve movement, and definitely involve strong emotional states, it is likely that the basal ganglia play a role. For example, a recent PET study utilizing 11C-Raclopride to measure the dopaminergic tone during Yoga Nidra meditation demonstrated a significant increase in dopamine levels during the meditation

---

[44] Streeter, C.C., Jensen, J.E., Perlmutter, R.M., Cabral, H.J., Tian, H., Terhune, D.B., Ciraulo, D.A., and Renshaw, P.F. "Yoga asana sessions increase brain GABA levels: a pilot study." *J Altern Complement Med.* 2007;13:419-426.

[45] d'Aquili, E.G., Newberg, A.B., and Rause, V. *Why God Won't Go Away: Brain Science and the Biology of Belief.* New York, NY: Ballantine, 2001.

[46] Adair, J.C., Gilmore, R.L., Fennell, E.B., Gold, M., and Heilman, K.M. "Anosognosia during intracarotid barbiturate anaesthesia: unawareness or amnesia for weakness." *Neurology.* 1995;45:241-243.

[47] Fernandez-Duque, D., Posner, M.I. "Brain imaging of attentional networks in normal and pathological states." *J Clin Exper Neuropsychol.* 2001;23:74-93.

[48] De Ridder, D., Van Laere, K., Dupont, P., Menovsky, T., and Van de Heyning, P. "Visualizing out-of-body experience in the brain." *N Engl J Med.* 2007;357:1829-1833. Lynch, J.C. "The functional organization of posterior parietal association cortex." *Behavior Brain Sci.* 1980;3:485-499; Lenggenhager, B., Smith, S.T., and Blanke, O. "Functional and neural mechanisms of embodiment: importance of the vestibular system and the temporal parietal junction." *Rev Neurosci.* 2006;17:643-657.

practice.[49] The authors hypothesized that this increase may be associated with the regulation of brain interactions that leads to an overall decrease in readiness for action that is associated with this particular type of meditation. It should also be noted that the dopamine system, via the basal ganglia, is believed to participate in regulating the glutamate system which is the primary excitatory neurotransmitter in the brain. Glutamate can stimulate activity in many other areas of the brain and facilitates interactions between the frontal lobes and a variety of other brain structures. Future studies will be necessary to elaborate on the role of dopamine during meditative practices as well as the interactions between dopamine and other neurotransmitter systems.

Increased glutamate can stimulate the hypothalamus to release beta-endorphin.[50] Beta-endorphin (BE) is an opioid which is known to depress respiration, reduce fear, reduce pain, and produce sensations of joy and euphoria.[51] That such effects have been described during spiritual practices and experiences may implicate some degree of BE release related to the increased prefrontal cortex activity. However, it is likely that BE is not the sole mediator in such experiences because simply taking morphine-related substances does not produce experiences equivalent to those in spiritual practices. Furthermore, one very limited study demonstrated that blocking the opiate receptors with the drug naloxone did not affect the experience or EEG associated with meditation.[52]

In the brain, glutamate activates another type of receptor called the N-methyl d-Aspartate (NMDA) receptors. Interestingly, drugs that block these NMDA receptors have been found to produce a variety of states that may be characterized as either schizophrenomimetic or mystical, such as out-of-body and near-death experiences.[53]

Serotonin is another molecule, related to dopamine, that is involved in emotional states. This molecule is most widely known in relation to antidepressant medications such as Zoloft and Prozac which affect the serotonin system. Moderately

---

[49]   Kjaer, T.W., Bertelsen, C., Piccini, P., Brooks, D., Alving, J., and Lou, H.C. "Increased dopamine tone during meditation-induced change of consciousness." *Brain Res Cogn Brain Res*. 2002;13:255-259.

[50]   Kiss, J., Kocsis, K., Csaki, A., Gorcs, T.J., and Halasz, B. "Metabotropic glutamate receptor in GHRH and beta-endorphin neurons of the hypothalamic arcuate nucleus." *Neuroreport*. 1997;8:3703-3707.

[51]   Janal, M.N., Colt, E.W., Clark, W.C., and Glusman, M. "Pain sensitivity, mood and plasma endocrine levels in man following long-distance running: effects of naxalone." *Pain*. 1984;19:13-25.

[52]   Sim, M.K. and Tsoi, W.F. "The effects of centrally acting drugs on the EEG correlates of meditation." *Biofeedback Self Regul*. 1992;17:215-220.

[53]   Vollenweider, F.X., Leenders, K.L., Scharfetter, C., Antonini, A., Maguire, P., Missimer, J., and Angst, J. "Metabolic hyperfrontality and psychopathology in the ketamine model of psychosis using positron emission tomography (PET) and [18F]fluorodeoxyglucose (FDG)." *Eur Neuropsychopharmacol*. 1997;7:9-24.

increased levels of serotonin appear to correlate with positive emotional effects, while low serotonin often signifies depression.[54] This relationship has clearly been demonstrated with regards to the effects of the selective serotonin reuptake inhibitor medications which are widely used for the treatment of depression. When cortical serotonin receptors (especially in the temporal lobes) are activated, however, the stimulation can result in a hallucinogenic effect. Tryptamine psychedelics such as psilocybin and LSD seem to take advantage of this mechanism to produce their extraordinary hallucinations.[55] Increased serotonin levels can affect several other neurochemical systems. An increase in serotonin has a modulatory effect on dopamine, suggesting a link between the serotonergic and dopaminergic system that may enhance feelings of euphoria,[56] which is frequently described during religious and spiritual states. Serotonin, in conjunction with increased glutamate, has been shown to stimulate the release of yet another neurotransmitter, acetylcholine, which has important influences throughout the brain.[57] Increased acetylcholine in the frontal lobes has been shown to augment the attentional system and in the parietal lobes to enhance orienting without altering sensory input.[58] While no studies have evaluated the role of acetylcholine in religious and spiritual phenomena, it appears that this neurotransmitter may enhance the attentional component as well as the orienting response associated with different spiritual practices. Another part of the brain, the pineal gland, was originally made famous by Descartes' claim that it was the seat of the soul since it rested at the very base of the brain. The pineal gland produces several compounds that might also be important targets for future studies. Melatonin, produced by the pineal gland, has been shown to depress the central nervous system and reduce pain sensitivity[59] and in one study of meditation, blood levels of melatonin were found to increase sharply.[60] Could

---

[54]   Van Praag, H., De Haan, S. "Depression vulnerability and 5-Hydroxytryptophan prophylaxis." *Psychiatr Res.* 1980;3:75-83.

[55]   Aghajanian, G.K. and Marek, G.J. "Serotonin and hallucinogens." *Neuropsychopharmacol.* 1999;21:16S-23S.

[56]   Vollenweider, F.X., Vontobel, P., Hell, D., and Leenders, K.L. "5-HT modulation of dopamine release in basal ganglia in psilocybin-induced psychosis in man: a PET study with [11C]raclopride." *Neuropsychopharmacol.* 1999;20:424-433.

[57]   Manfridi, A., Brambilla, D., and Mancia, M. "Stimulation of NMDA and AMPA receptors in the rat nucleus basalis of Meynert affects sleep." *Amer J Physiol.* 1999;277: R1488-1492; Zhelyazkova-Savova, M.G., Giovannini, G., and Pepeu, G. "Increase of cortical acetylcholine release after systemic administration of chlorophenylpiperazine in the rat: an in vivo microdialysis study." *Neurosci Let.* 1997;236:151-154.

[58]   Fernandez-Duque, D., Posner, M.I. "Brain imaging of attentional networks in normal and pathological states." *J Clin Exper Neuropsychol.* 2001;23:74-93.

[59]   Shaji, A.V. and Kulkarni, S.K. "Central nervous system depressant activities of melatonin in rats and mice." *Indian J Exp Biol.* 1998;36:257-263.

[60]   Tooley, G.A., Armstrong, S.M., Norman, T.R., and Sali A. "Acute increases in night-time plasma melatonin levels following a period of meditation." *Biol Psychol.* 2000;53: 69-78.

this possibly contribute to the feelings of calmness and decreased awareness of pain[61] during such practices? Under circumstances of heightened activation, pineal enzymes can also endogenously synthesize the powerful hallucinogen 5-methoxy-dimethyltryptamine (DMT).[62] Several studies have linked DMT to a variety of mystical states, including out-of-body experiences, distortion of time and space, and interaction with supernatural entities.[63] This suggests that DMT may also be important for future studies.

Based upon the above description of many of the brain structures and neurotransmitters, it would seem that there are many possible approaches that can be taken in future neurotheological investigations. It is also important to recognize that none of the structures and functions mentioned operate completely independently from the rest of the brain. For these reasons, a balance must be maintained between focusing on specific structures and functions while keeping in mind the more global integrated functional nature of the brain. And of course, we also must maintain the notion that simply because a neurophysiological change is observed in connection with some type of religious or spiritual phenomenon, this does not necessarily explain the causal basis of the phenomenon. Furthermore, it is crucial to understand the subjective and ideological elements of any phenomenon. Without this, any neurotheological pursuit will ultimately be significantly limited.

Studying Specific Types of Spiritual Experiences

We can now turn to the issue of studying specific types of experiences. This issue comes to the fore when we consider the practical approach neurotheological investigations must take in order to evaluate religious and spiritual experiences in general. On one hand, careful study would likely require focusing on a specific type of experience. On the other hand, any comprehensive approach to religious experience must somehow be able to contend with the tremendous variety of different experiences not only in kind, but in intensity. One issue would be whether different religious experiences represent points along a continuum of experiences. If it is assumed that there is a continuum of experiences, then in conjunction with the above discussion of models of spiritual experiences, it

---

[61] Dollins, A.B., Lynch, H.J., Wurtman, R.J., Deng, M.H., Kischka, K.U., Gleason, R.E., and Lieberman, H.R. "Effect of pharmacological daytime doses of melatonin on human mood and performance." *Psychopharmacol.* 1993;112:490-496.

[62] Monti, J.A. and Christian, S.T. "N-N-Dimethyltryptamine: an endogenous hallucinogen." *Intern Rev Neurobiol.* 1981;22:83-110.

[63] Strassman, R.J., Clifford, R., Qualls, R., and Berg, L. "Differential tolerance to biological and subjective effects of four closely spaced doses of N,N-Dimethyltrypamine in humans." *Biological Psychiatr.* 1996;39:784-795; Strassman, R.J. and Clifford, R. "Dose-response study of N,N-Dimethyltrypamine in humans. I: Neuroendocrine, autonomic, and cardiovascular effects." *Arch Gen Psychiatr.* 1994;51:85-97.

might be possible to gain preliminary insight into how different mystical states and religious experiences relate to each other. For example the experience which Carl Jung and others referred to as numinosity can be described as a combination of the experience of both fear and exaltation usually described as "religious awe," and almost always associated with religious symbols, sacred images, or "archetypal" symbols. Otto's *mysterium tremendum et fascinans* is the sense of the mighty and wholly other "Cause of All" filling the world, and it is experienced as a mysterious and awesome presence to the subject. Are these one and the same experiences? Perhaps neurotheological investigations might shed light on the nature of these two experiences and help determine the similarities and differences.

Another problematic issue for neurotheological research is that many individuals have what might be called "spontaneous" spiritual experiences. Spontaneous experiences refer to those that are not actually intended or sought after by the individual via some type of spiritual practice. Even in those who practice meditation over a lifetime with the intent to try to attain some spiritual state, the moment of attainment may be spontaneous even though the individual has trained and practiced for many years in order to achieve such as state. There may also those highly proficient practitioners who may be able to literally will such an experience to happen on command. However, such individuals are probably quite rare.

With regard to the actual phenomenology of spontaneous spiritual experiences, there appears to be close similarities to those which are purposely attained. Thus many spiritual experiences including the sense of the *mysterium tremendum* and the sense of numinosity can also occur spontaneously, without meditation or other types of practices. Any model of spiritual experiences should also be able to account for the spontaneous types in addition to those which are purposely obtained.

Several of the different models currently entertained could account for spontaneous experiences. Certainly spiritual experiences triggered by temporal lobe seizures would be of a spontaneous origin. Such experiences could be fairly elaborate depending on the specific areas of the temporal lobe involved and the duration of the seizure. One potential drawback of this model is that most individuals with seizures tend to have repeated seizures with relatively similar types of symptoms. Since most strong spiritual experiences occur only once or a few times in an individual's life, the possibility that they are somehow related to spontaneous seizure activity seems less likely. The autonomic model of spiritual experiences could also account for spontaneous experiences and would be particularly relevant to states in which there is already unusual autonomic activity such as in highly fearful situations, near death experiences, or deep relaxation, possibly secondary to sleep deprivation. As the autonomic nervous system becomes highly active, it is possible that the areas of the brain associated with autonomic activity, including the hypothalamus and limbic system would similarly be activated resulting in a range of spontaneous experiences. This model would not be as successful in trying to explain spiritual experiences that arise when there is no particular type of autonomic functioning.

One unique example of a spontaneous spiritual experience is the near death experience (NDE) which is one of the most compelling experiences that human beings can encounter. Since there has been a great deal of study devoted to these experiences, and because they also provide unique information about the human brain and spiritual experiences, it is useful to explore such experiences in more detail. As mentioned, NDEs have already been widely reported and studied and there are several scholarly journals dedicated to their study. Research has included phenomenological analysis as well as some approaches to the neuropsychological correlates of these experiences. Because of the richness of the information regarding such experiences, this subsection will be slightly larger than others. However, the information regarding these experiences can potentially provide important perspectives on the study and analysis of spiritual experiences. In the *Tibetan Book of the Dead*, during the Middle Ages, and to present day, NDEs have been experienced, written about, and argued about. There is little doubt that many people perceive themselves to have had NDEs. However, precisely how and why the NDE occurs has yet to be fully determined. In fact, there has been much controversy regarding the true nature and origin of the NDE.

A number of explanations have been postulated to describe the mechanism responsible for creating the NDE. The problem with developing a satisfactory explanation is that the NDEs have many different components and occur under a wide variety of circumstances. Thus, any explanation must be capable of explaining the many aspects of the NDE. The proposed mechanisms include the realization of a psychological expectation of an afterlife, a psychological defense mechanism against personal death, hallucinations, involvement of psychotropic substances (endogenous or exogenous), decreased oxygen and blood to the brain, a depersonalization syndrome, temporal lobe seizure-like activity, hyperactivity in the limbic system, or that there actually is an after-life. The problem with most of these explanations is that they fail to explain every aspect of the NDE including positive and negative NDEs, the remarkable similarity among NDEs, decreased NDEs with drugs, NDEs in people in life threatening situations, out-of-body experiences (OBEs), and even some of the "paranormal-type" occurrences.

There is a rich literature both in terms of phenomenology and in terms of neurobiology that relates to the use of certain pharmacological substances inducing various spiritual experiences. Since it has long been observed that psychoactive substances such as opiates, peyote, lysergic acid (LSD), and various stimulants (for example, amphetamines) can be used to induce spiritual experiences, careful studies of the types and characteristics of drug-induced spiritual experiences, perhaps utilizing modern imaging techniques, may help elucidate which neurobiological mechanisms are involved in more "naturally derived" spiritual experiences. It is also important to stress that this "artificial" approach to spirituality is not viewed as such by these cultures. According to the specific traditions, psychopharmacological substances merely provide *access* to the spiritual world and thus the spiritual elements are still perceived as very real. This reveals an important Western bias that spiritual states induced by psychoactive substances are less real or artificial. Neurotheology suggests that there may be specific neurological correlates, but that at this point, it is not certain whether the reality experienced under the influence of such substances truly represents a superior or inferior spiritual state to those attained by other means. Neurotheological investigations might be useful in approaching such issues and questions.

There have also been a number of scientific studies related to the use of hallucinogenic agents. These studies have demonstrated significant changes in a number of brain structures and systems. For example, it is well known that LSD causes increased activity in the serotonin system and that this mechanism is probably responsible for the unusual sensory experiences. Drugs that block another receptor called N-methyl d-Aspartate (NMDA) produce a variety of states that may be characterized as either schizophrenomimetic or mystical, such as out-of-body and near-death experiences.[64] Other intrinsic neurotransmitters in the brain have been found to functionally similarly to disassociative hallucinogens such as ketamine, phencyclidine, and nitrous oxide.[65] However, more extensive studies of such agents, particularly in relation to religious and spiritual experiences is required. Comparing this paradigm to naturally occurring spiritual phenomena may allow for a better distinction of pathologic and non-pathologic spiritual experiences.

There are obvious ethical, legal, and medical considerations with studies such as these (although studies outside of the United States may be more possible). However, subjects who have had pharmacologically induced spiritual experiences can be studied using radioactive analogues of such agents as a means of determining the concentration of receptors and their agonists. Another related approach would be to study the effects of drug withdrawal on spiritual experience. However, there are no reports in the literature of such findings.

Another related approach to investigating spiritual experiences from a neuroscientific approach utilizes pharmacological agents or other interventions in an attempt to alter spiritual practices or experiences. Thus, using this paradigm, a previously measured spiritual practice would be compared to the same practice with the addition of some intervention. For example, studies might attempt to show the effects of an opiate antagonist on the strength of the subjective experience of meditation or prayer. Preliminary studies (on one or a few subjects) of this type have shown no effect on EEG patterns during meditation when subjects were given

---

[64] Vollenweider, F.X., Leenders, K.L., Scharfetter, C., Antonini, A., Maguire, P., Missimer, J., and Angst, J. "Metabolic hyperfrontality and psychopathology in the ketamine model of psychosis using positron emission tomography (PET) and [18F]fluorodeoxyglucose (FDG)." *Eur Neuropsychopharmacol.* 1997;7:9-24.

[65] Jevtovic-Todorovic, V., Wozniak, D.F., Benshoff, N.D., and Olney, J.W. "A comparative evaluation of the neurotoxic properties of ketamine and nitrous oxide." *Brain Res.* 2001;895:264-267.

either an opiate or benzodiazepine antagonist.[66] The effects of a method called transcranial magnetic stimulation which sends strong magnetic waves into the brain, other pharmacological agents, or even surgical procedures (performed for other purposes) could be evaluated. However, it is clear that more extensive studies measuring a number of neurophysiological parameters are required. In addition, the exploration of various pharmacological agents on spiritual interventions may help to delineate the role of different neurotransmitter systems. Such studies also offer the possibility of measuring dose responses in terms of spiritual interventions.

In spite of the potential for such studies using pharmacological substances (sometimes referred to as "entheogens"), the current legal and ethical issues involved with performing such studies limit the new data that can be incorporated from this area into the topic of neurotheology. However, there are still many potential opportunities that involve subjective accounts, studies performed abroad, and neurotransmitter studies, that can all have important implications for the neurochemical correlates of religious and spiritual states.

Isolating the Spiritual from the Neuropsychological

One issue that has frequently arisen in the neuropsychological analysis of spiritual experience is that its major flaw is that everything becomes described in neurophysiological or psychological terminology. Thus, a spiritual experience is related to how the individual "feels," what is their "emotional" state, and what "sensory" experiences they have. However, if the soul or spirit is truly something distinct from the human brain and psyche and something that is immaterial, then one might expect that after thorough neuropsychological analysis, there might be an additional "something" that is unaccounted for. That something would theoretically be the soul or spirit. For example, if an individual was placed in an MRI machine to record changes in their brain while they had a mystical experience, the most interesting result would be that there were no changes in the brain's function. If the person had an unusual experience, but no change in the brain, then something spiritual, or non-biological, may have actually been observed. At the present time, there are no known instruments that could actually detect the soul. However, part of the reason for this is that there is no good scientific description of what exactly a soul would be and how it would manifest in the material world.

A neurotheological approach might provide some hypotheses along these lines by studying religious and spiritual literature, studying the phenomenology of spiritual experiences, and trying to construct models that will help to explain not only the physiological correlates of such experiences, but other potential ways of evaluating and understanding spirituality. What form such models and their associated hypotheses may take is uncertain, but if this field is permitted to move

---

[66] Sim, M.K. and Tsoi, W.F. "The effects of centrally acting drugs on the EEG correlates of meditation." *Biofeedback Self Regul.* 1992;17:215-220.

forward carefully from both a scientific and spiritual perspective, preserving the rigorousness of science and the subjective (and spiritual) part of spirituality, this may provide the best opportunity to better understand human spirituality and the human person.

Conclusion

In returning to the bidirectional approach of neurotheology, it must be strongly reiterated that the ability to identify neurophysiological correlates of religious and spiritual phenomena sheds light on these phenomena, but does not necessarily dismiss them as purely biological. Of course neurotheology would argue that all possibilities must be maintained, especially until there is sufficient data to warrant any definitive conclusions. Until the time when sufficient research either proves or disproves the actual relationship between neurophysiology and spiritual phenomena, neurotheologians must remain open to both possible outcomes. However, the purpose of this chapter was to consider how neurophysiological correlates of spiritual phenomena might be ascertained and what mechanisms and principles might be involved.

Chapter 8
Reflections on Major Topics of Neuroscience

Neurotheology and Neuroscience

Neurotheological investigations have as their goal a number of scientific and religious implications. From a scientific perspective, neurotheology has the potential to offer a plethora of useful results and ideas. That neurotheology can advance science is something that can be easily overlooked, but, nonetheless, is critical to neurotheology as a field. Major topics of neuroscience that can be advanced by neurotheology include a deeper understanding of subjective experience and human consciousness; of brain processes and functions; of the mechanisms of interaction between religion and health; of the implications of pastoral care in the health care setting; of the neurological basis of ethics, and of the inherent uncertainty in our brain's ability to perceive reality. We can consider a number of these topics in some substantial detail since several of these areas have been among the most widely studied in the domain of neurotheology. Taken all together, these topics might be considered to be associated with the "principle of cognitive applicability"—how neurotheology can help us evaluate and improve our cognitive processes and health:

Principle XXXV: Neurotheology should be applied to a wide range of cognitive processes and health related issues.

In this section, several of the major concepts associated with neuroscience will be considered from the neurotheological perspective. These are issues that challenge neuroscience itself as well as the methodology used in order to acquire neuroscientific information. The ability to advance human understanding of a variety of important topics related to neuroscience should be an important goal of neurotheology. Whether this refers to the nature of subjective experience or consciousness, health and well being, ethics, or the experience of reality itself, neurotheology may prove to be highly useful in providing a unique perspective with regard to these issues. This is the challenge of neurotheological research, and thus neurotheologians should consider their purview to be wide ranging. Of course, any individual study may not take on such lofty goals, but overall the field should always consider its potential contribution to neuroscience and *vice versa*.

Subjective Experience, Consciousness, and Neurotheology

The neuroscientific study of religious and spiritual practices and experiences is also a study of complex mental processes. It might be argued that such studies may also be one of the most important areas of research that can be pursued by science in the next decade. This may not be an understatement since such experiences offer a fascinating window into human consciousness and psychology; the relationship between mental states and body physiology; emotional and cognitive processing; and the biological correlates of religious and spiritual experiences.

There is a tremendous richness and diversity in religious and spiritual phenomena. There are many religious and spiritual states that involve an alteration in mental processes, particularly consciousness. Many of the most profound states including ritual states, unitary states, mystical states, and other intense experiences possess a quality of altered consciousness. As I have suggested, it is critical to compare the subjective elements of such states with physiological elements. In many ways, the subjective experience is the key to religious and spiritual phenomena. But it is the ability to evaluate these states neuroscientifically that is a key strength of neurotheology. It is what people perceive, think, and feel that makes these experiences significant and potentially transformative. But if these experiences are associated with the perception of an altered sense of consciousness, then neurotheology might help us to understand better the nature of human consciousness by evaluating what happens to it during religious and spiritual phenomena.

Consciousness has been a particularly knotty problem for philosophy, theology, and cognitive neuroscience. Many scholars have either studied, or hypothesized about, with varying success, the nature of consciousness. Some have suggested that there are certain brain structures and functions that are necessary for consciousness. Others have debated about whether there is a single observer consciousness within the brain or whether it is related to the sum total of all brain processes. In Buddhist thought, particularly the Yogacara tradition, it is argued that consciousness is not specific to the human brain, but rather is present in the universe as its most fundamental level of existence. In this approach, the brain can access this universal consciousness.[1]

Thus, the problem of consciousness and its ability to arise in the brain is of primary concern in the neurosciences. Consciousness of anything, and particularly self-reflexive consciousness in human beings, is something that has not been adequately elucidated on the basis of current empirical research.[2] As mentioned, spiritual and religious states often involve altered states of consciousness. And in many circumstances, these states are purposefully manipulated. Those individuals

---

[1] Zim, R. *Basic Ideas of Yogacara Buddhism.* San Francisco, CA: San Francisco State University, 1995.

[2] d'Aquili, E.G. and Newberg, A.B. "Consciousness and the machine." *Zygon.* 1996;31:235-252.

who are most capable of altering their consciousness and enable that consciousness to affect other parts of their body, might be particularly useful in furthering our understanding of human consciousness. This would be akin to studying the brain of Mozart and Beethoven in order to understand how music is associated with brain function.

Let us explore briefly how neurotheology might approach and advance the field of consciousness studies. If material reality is accepted as primary for the moment (and we will discuss the potential problems with this later), the question which we must answer is: how is consciousness generated by the brain and nervous system? A corollary question is to determine how consciousness entered into the human brain in the first place—God, evolution, or some epiphenomenal process? From the neuroscientific context, the causal arrow is generally regarded as flowing from the brain to consciousness.

We must realize that neuropsychology up to the present, and parallel to Franz Brentano's philosophy, has always understood consciousness to refer to a consciousness of something. That some type of "pure consciousness," devoid of content, might exist has generally not even been entertained as a problem in the field of cognitive neuroscience. Therefore, obviously, there has been little attempt at understanding its physical basis. We will return to the issue of pure consciousness later. First, let us consider the basic and classical neuropsychological problem of how consciousness of anything is possible. In this regard, we are considering consciousness in its very simplest sense of awareness. This is not consciousness of the self, or how the self comes to be conscious. In this context, we are simply referring to consciousness as subjective awareness, whether in lower animals or in human beings.

To this point, we have been using the words consciousness and awareness interchangeably. But if we refer back to the definitions discussed in Chapter 2, we might consider a more detailed definition for both subjective awareness and consciousness which might be useful for further considering the nature of these two phenomena.

- Subjective awareness could be defined as any and all mental content that inheres in a subject, excepting only a reified sense of self.
- Consciousness could be defined as any and all mental content that inheres in a subject, one element of which is a reified sense of self.

By these definitions, consciousness involves the generation of a self as an element in subjective awareness. Thus, subjective awareness would be more fundamental than consciousness since, presumably, awareness is possible without consciousness, but not the other way around. Others might equate the term consciousness with awareness and thus use them interchangeably as we have above. Regardless, the important point is that there is a sense of subjective awareness that we can have with regard to our experiences. It would seem that the brain becomes aware of a certain set of sensory input which ultimately arises from the body or from the body's interaction with the external world—what we are calling awareness. If the brain perceives its multiple activities and organizes them into a reified category then we call it the self—what we are calling consciousness. Considered evolutionarily, the processes of awareness and consciousness only became possible with the evolution of structures such as the inferior parietal region and its interconnections with various sensory association areas. These structures are known to underlie the reification of classes of objects generating abstract categories and the ability to recognize the self.[3] If this is so, then the neuroanatomical requirements of "selfhood" must restrict the clear sense of self to human beings and possibly some primates and dolphins. There is, in fact, good evidence that this is so. For example, only higher primates respond to their image in a mirror as if it were a representation of themselves. All other animals apparently perceive another animal.

Finally, the inferior parietal lobe and its interconnected sensory association areas can operate on, and reify, the self perceiving the self, which has been called reflexive consciousness.[4] It is generally thought that clear reflexive consciousness is only a property of *Homo sapiens*. However, this is still an open question, and some anthropoid apes may possess it. However, these issues also pertain to theology in which the notion of human beings as set aside from other animals is frequently a crucial element. The expanded study of consciousness in human beings as well as that in animals might provide some important information regarding the nature of human uniqueness.

But there is another aspect of awareness which is related to the notion of "pure awareness" or awareness devoid of content, sometimes described as a clear and vivid awareness of nothing, or perhaps of everything at the same time. Again, it should be noted that some people refer to this as pure consciousness as well, although, in this context, it does not refer to a sense of self since that would then be an object within awareness. Most descriptions of such an experience relate it as an intense unitary state which also feels incredibly real to the individual. For example, Erwin Schrödinger, the father of quantum theory, reflected on the significance of his encounter what seems to be such an experience with these words:

> The only possible alternative (to the plurality of souls hypothesis) is simply to keep to the immediate experience that consciousness (i.e., Mind) is a singular of which the plural is unknown; that there is only one thing and that what seems to be a plurality is merely a series of different aspects of this one thing, produced by a deception; the same illusion is produced in a gallery of mirrors, and in the

---

3   Kaplan, J.T., Aziz-Zadeh, L., Uddin, L.Q., and Iacoboni, M. "The self across the senses: an fMRI study of self-face and self-voice recognition." *Soc Cogn Affect Neurosci.* 2008;3:218-223.

4   d'Aquili, E.G. and Newberg, A.B. *The Mystical Mind: Probing the Biology of Religious Experience*. Minneapolis, MN: Fortress Press, 1999.

same way Gaurisankar and Mount Everest turned out to be the same peak seen from different valleys.[5]

Of the modern secular mystics, in addition to Schrödinger, we can add Julius Oppenheimer, Neils Bohr, and a number of other theoretical physicists. Dag Hammarskjöld, the famous diplomat and Secretary-General of the United Nations was another among the modern Western secular mystics who have described the experience of a profound unitary experience. Furthermore, this state has been described by mystics of all the world's religions. Here we will let one example suffice. Zen Master Huang Po wrote:

> All the Buddha's [sic] and all sentient beings are nothing but One Mind, beside which nothing exists. This Mind, which is without beginning is unborn and indestructible. It is not green or yellow, and has neither form nor appearance, it does not belong to the categories of things which exist or do not exist, nor can it be thought of in terms of new or old. It is neither long nor short, big nor small, for it transcends all limits, measures, names, traces, and comparisons. Only awake to the One Mind.[6]

In a profound unitary state, there are no boundaries of discrete beings, there is no sense of the passage of time, no sense of the extension of space, and the self–other dichotomy is totally obliterated. In other words, the state consists of an absolute sense of unity without thought, without words, without sensation, and not even being sensed to inhere in a subject. Is there a neurophysiological correlate of such an experience and if so, will a neurotheological perspective provide additional insight into the meaning of this experience?

While a neurophysiological mechanism might be correlated with awareness and may even be the cause of awareness, at the present moment, neurophysiology does not explain the stuff of awareness itself. In this regard, Roger Penrose notes:

> If it were not for the puzzling aspects of consciousness that relate to the presence of "awareness", which as yet seem[s] to elude physical description, we should not need to feel tempted to look beyond the standard methods of science for explanation of minds as a feature of the physical behavior of brains. It may well be that in order to accommodate the mystery of the mind, we shall need a broadening of what we presently mean by "science", but I see no reason to make any clean break with those methods that have served us so extraordinarily well.[7]

---

5   Schrodinger, E. *What is Life? The Physical Aspect of the Living Cell and Mind and Matter.* Cambridge: Cambridge University Press, 1967.

6   Quoted in: Blofied, S.J. *The Zen Teaching of Huang Po.* New York, NY: Grove, 1970.

7   Penrose, R. *Shadows of the Mind.* Oxford: Oxford University Press, 1994.

A neurotheological perspective would agree with Penrose that a clean break with traditional science is neither required nor desirable. But a broadening of what is meant by science, perhaps a realignment towards combining cognitive science with the systematic study of consciousness or awareness may be required.

If one looks at the traditional Aristotelian four types of causality which were considered necessary to explain a phenomenon fully—that is, efficient causality, material causality, formal causality, and final causality—we find that our scientific explanation of awareness satisfies only one of the four requirements, efficient causality. Efficient causality is knowledge of a phenomenon in terms of anterior sequential causes. It is what we ordinarily mean by causality in modern parlance. Material causality is knowledge of the constitutive substance of the phenomenon. We do not have a clear idea of what the biological stuff of awareness actually is. This is not to say that we have no idea what some of the brain structures involved in awareness are, but we do not fully understand the direct mechanism by which consciousness or awareness might arise. Formal causality is knowledge of a phenomenon in the organization of its constituent parts. Awareness itself has no constituent parts. The contents of awareness are its objects and not part of what it is itself. It would seem that awareness itself is simple and hence may not have a formal cause. Final causality is a knowledge of things in their purpose, or, in modern terminology, in terms of their adaptive function. Although final causality as originally formulated is subject to the critique of teleology, its reformulation as teleonomy has an important function in the philosophy of science. Nonetheless, it is not clear what is the purpose of consciousness or awareness and whether such a purpose might be related to evolutionary or spiritual causes, or perhaps something else altogether.

Neurotheology may be able to provide an additional perspective on the issues related to awareness and consciousness. Neurotheology would argue that there are two possible poles in the discussion of consciousness and that each must be fully evaluated. One is that the material world is primary and that consciousness derives from a material cause. Simply stated, consciousness somehow arises from and is caused by the functions of the brain. This is typically the neuroscientific view of consciousness. The other pole in this debate is that consciousness is primary such that it exists outside of material mechanisms. In fact, if consciousness itself is primary, then somehow the material world would be derived from or caused by consciousness. This is more often the spiritual or religious account of consciousness. This is clearly the case in Eastern traditions such as Buddhism and Hinduism. But it is also the case in Western traditions. The only difference is that in Western traditions the material world does not arise from a universal consciousness, but rather God's consciousness. With these issues in mind, neurotheology can engage the topic of the nature of reality from the perspective of consciousness and material reality:

Principle XXXVI: Neurotheology must encourage the exploration of whether matter or consciousness is the primary substance of the universe and the implications of this issue for both science and theology.

We can see arguments ranging from one of these poles to another in the work of a number of scholars and theories. One approach would be to propose a "psychoneural identity" which maintains that the neural events themselves are conscious. This position does not state that the neural events cause awareness, or are correlated with conscious phenomena, but that they are the very thing itself. This is tantamount to saying that the machinery of an automobile is the movement of the automobile itself, or that the structure of a computer is the solution it generates to a problem. Some scholars, like Turing, suggest that "there is no mind separate from matter."[8] Kurt Gödel maintained that although the physical brain must itself behave computationally, the mind is something beyond the brain. In his view, the mind is not constrained to behave according to the computational laws that he believed must control the brain's behavior.[9] In this way, Gödel's view is as extreme as the view of those who maintain psychoneural identity in the opposite direction.

This brings us to the biggest problem of all which is why should subjective awareness or consciousness exist at all? If we start from the perspective that the material world is primary, then if every change in awareness, every change in the contents of awareness, and even if the generation of pure consciousness itself, are all caused by physical (that is, neural) events, why should awareness exist? Is there any reason why the entire social universe that we know, with every product of our individual endeavors, every product of our social interactions, and, in short, every psychological or cultural product, from science through art and religion, should not be produced by biologically evolved robots that do not possess consciousness. In other words, an objective observer (for example, from another galaxy) could view everything as it is on Earth today, including the appearance of subjective awareness without there ever having to be any actual subjectivity. For all intents and purposes, the brain is an electrical input/output system of immense complexity. However, it is no more than that, or so it would appear, from the material perspective. No matter what degree of complexity the brain has attained or will attain in the future, this complexity does not appear to imply in itself the existence of subjective awareness or consciousness. It might produce the appearance of subjective awareness to an external observer, but at the moment, there is no clear reason why subjective awareness or consciousness should, in fact, exist if we begin the philosophical analysis of reality with the primacy of material reality.

---

8   Turing, A.M. "Computing machinery and intelligence." *Mind*, 1950;59:433-460.

9   Gödel, K. *Kurt Gödel: Collected Works*. Edited by S. Feferman, J.W. Dawson Jr., and S.C. Kleene, Vol. 2 (Publications 1938-1974). New York, NY: Oxford University Press, 1990.

This problem should certainly be explored by neurotheology to determine if there are any possible causes of consciousness from a material account of the world.

To this point, we have been considering consciousness and awareness as if it derives specifically from a material cause. However, a careful phenomenological analysis might strongly challenge this basic premise. Indeed, as Husserl implied, from the point of view of any careful conscious examiner of the world, the only thing that is certain is that all of material reality, including the laws of science and the brain itself, exists within subjective awareness. Whether it has any other substantive reality is an open question in neurotheological discourse, but what is certain is that it all exists within awareness. Furthermore, what also exists within subjective awareness is the vivid sense that the external world is substantively real and that matter is something other than consciousness. But this vivid sense of reality, which has been called *phantasia catalyptica* by the Stoics, intentionality by some phenomenologists, and *anwesenheit* by certain modern German philosophers, likewise exists within awareness or is an aspect of awareness. Thus, it would appear that all the vividness of the reality of the material world is at least a subset of awareness, whatever else that vividness may or may not imply. But if all of science and the material world is considered within our awareness, then we need at least to consider what happens to our analysis of reality when we give awareness ontological priority.

What are the advantages and disadvantages of starting our analysis of the relationship of subjective awareness to external material reality by granting the primacy to subjective awareness? The greatest advantage is that the problem of explaining the development of subjective awareness evaporates since subjective awareness is the fundamental stuff of the universe which permeates everything. In this case, the problem now becomes explaining how material reality comes into being. Thus, it is not a question of subjective awareness arising out of material reality but of material reality, in some sense, arising out of subjective awareness. From this perspective, all of physical reality exists in present subjective awareness, including the knowing brain, all the laws of science, the compelling sense of the otherness of an external material reality, the compelling sense of a past of completed events, and of a future of possible ones. But how is this possible? This might be answered if one considers the material world to be part of that universal awareness. Thus, the Big Bang itself becomes an aspect of subjective awareness, a conclusion tending to support the strong anthropic principle, although for reasons somewhat different from those usually put forward in support of it. And with the priority of subjective awareness, there is no question of subjective awareness *per se* evolving from a material system since material externality is itself an aspect of subjective awareness. From a theological perspective, such a conclusion may be similar to that of God creating the universe out of God's own will. Creation is derived from God's conscious awareness and is a manifestation of that awareness. The material world is simply God's awareness expressed in a physical way. Such a conclusion is also consistent with Eastern traditions with the difference being a non-personal consciousness pervading the universe rather than the personal one of Western religions. Science does not usually take this perspective since there is no definite evidence that the universe was created from awareness. In fact, it is difficult to determine how such a possibility could be evaluated by current science.

Neurotheology might provide important information that would be useful for distinguishing whether the material world or subjective awareness has priority. By combining scientific investigation with phenomenological analysis, neurotheology might approach these two perspectives to determine which is consistent with existing data and which might satisfy the scientific as well as the religious perspectives. One might also conceive of a third possible approach that might attempt to integrate the material world with awareness. Analogously to the wave-particle nature of light, perhaps awareness and matter merely represent two different views of the same thing. Perhaps if we look for awareness through subjective and phenomenological analyses, that is precisely what we find. On the other hand, if we look for the biological basis of awareness, that is what we find. A new integrated approach might be a potential outcome of neurotheological scholarship in the context of awareness and the material world. Regardless of the outcome of such analyses, neurotheology should, at the minimum, provide an important approach to the question of awareness and consciousness.

Neurotheology and Understanding the Human Brain

One element of neurotheology that is frequently overlooked is the potential impact such research might have for understanding the human brain. The field of cognitive neuroscience has rapidly developed over the past two decades and has explored topics ranging from basic motor and sensory function to the highest level of cognitive processes. The latter have included an extensive analysis of language, abstract thought, and a variety of human emotions.[10] Religious and spiritual phenomena are among the most complex that human beings experience. And it would be expected that such phenomena are associated with equally complex neurobiological substrates.

The methodological challenges associated with neurotheological research might also be applied to the broader field of cognitive neuroscience. Practices such as prayer or meditation, that involve concentration, sensory elements, and emotional elements, are likely associated with a coordinated set of functions and processes within the human brain. This being the case, studies of such practices and related experiences may shed light on the complex interaction of different brain structures and their functions. For example, studying a meditation practice that evokes strong emotions of love in conjunction with an altered perception

---

[10]   Gazzaniga, M.S. *The New Cognitive Neurosciences*, 2nd Edition. Cambridge, MA: MIT Press, 2000.

of space could yield information regarding the interrelationship between brain structures that subserve emotions and spatial perception. Since religious and spiritual phenomena are highly subjective experiences, advancing studies to explore the nature of these experiences may prove useful for the study of other types of subjective experiences such as love, aesthetics, or morality. Since these methodological advances may be useful in the broader study of emotions and complex cognitive processes, neurotheology could be considered a branch of cognitive neuroscience. However, this is only true in as much as neurotheological investigations provide empirical data on the specific relationship between the brain and religious experience. Neurotheology also requires a thorough investigation of non-empirical data such as individual mystical experiences, and epistemological and ontological issues.

Another facet of neurotheology is the ability to study individuals highly adept at performing certain tasks. For example, it has been suggested that an attempt to explore specific cognitive processes such as attention might best be performed by studying individuals that demonstrate the highest levels of attentional focus. Turning to those individuals who are highly proficient meditators, who can maintain focused attention for many hours, may help us to understand better the nature of attention and its neurobiological substrate. This could yield important information not only about attention, but also about disorders of attention. Perhaps study of meditators who are able to maintain sustained attention for long periods of time could reveal areas of activity in the brain that are particularly affected by disorders such as attention deficit disorder. This might even lead to new treatment modalities by targeting interventions toward those structures that are specifically involved.

Human creativity is another important process of the human brain. Creativity enables the elaboration of music, art, and poetry which are essential elements of virtually all religious and spiritual traditions, and are also an essential part of humanity as a whole. Understanding creativity from the neurotheological perspective may be useful for advancing our understanding not only of religion and spirituality, but also of the creative aspects of the human mind in general. Creativity is not well understood from the neuroscientific perspective. The complexity and spontaneity of creative acts makes them difficult to study in the first place. But creativity is so pervasive in human activities that the larger study of creativity should be highly beneficial. Neurotheology may provide specific insights into the creative processes.

Thus, the result of these studies ultimately can have practical applications for human physical and mental health. Studying how the brain works in individuals with highly trained minds that can regulate attention and emotion might provide a new perspective on a variety of disorders such as depression, dementia, and aggression. The impact on health may be even more broad-based than this, especially when one considers the intimate link between the brain and body functions.

An important future area of research of the brain, and also for neurotheology involves the study of the various neurotransmitters in the brain. Understanding the function of, and the relationship between, different neurotransmitters is critical for understanding the brain. Neurotransmitter abnormalities lie at the heart of virtually all neurological and psychiatric disorders. For example, Parkinson's disease is associated with the loss of dopaminergic function, depression is associated with alterations in serotonin function, and different addictive states are associated with the brain's opiate system. There is also increasing evidence that different religious states and practices might be associated with changes in these neurotransmitter systems.[11] Furthermore, understanding how religion and spirituality is affected by disorders associated with derangements in neurotransmitters might provide important clinical and physiological information. Thus, future neurotheological research should focus on the neurotransmitters as much as possible.

Neurotheology and Human Health

Another area in which neurotheology could provide important information is in understanding the link between spirituality and health. A growing number of studies have shown positive, and sometimes negative, effects of religion on various components of mental and physical health.[12] Such effects have included an improvement in depression and anxiety, enhanced immune system, and reduced overall mortality associated with individuals who are more religious. On the other hand, research has also shown that those individuals engaged in religious struggle or who have a negative view of God or religion, can experience increased stress, anxiety, and health problems. But overall, the research is still in its nascent stages, with significant controversy in a number of areas.[13] Research into the brain's responses to positive and negative influences of religion might be of great value in furthering our understanding of the relationship between spirituality and health.

Principle XXXVII: Neurotheological research should seek information regarding the relationship between spirituality and health.

Again, though, it is important to be aware that there may not be any relationship, or that the relationship might be negative as well as positive. However, the ability

---

[11] Kjaer, T.W., Bertelsen, C., Piccini, P., Brooks, D., Alving, J., and Lou, H.C. "Increased dopamine tone during meditation-induced change of consciousness." *Brain Res Cogn Brain Res*. 2002;13:255-259; Newberg, A.B. and Iversen, J. "The neural basis of the complex mental task of meditation: neurotransmitter and neurochemical considerations." *Med Hypotheses*. 2003;61:282-291.

[12] Koenig, H.G. (ed.). *Handbook of Religion and Mental Health*. San Diego, CA: Academic Press, 1998; Koenig, H.G., McCullough, M.E., and Larson, D.B. (eds.). *Handbook of Religion and Health*. New York, NY: Oxford University Press, 2001.

[13] Sloan, R.P. *Blind Faith: The Unholy Alliance of Religion and Medicine*. New York, NY: St Martin's Griffin, 2006.

of neurotheology to contribute information on the brain might provide a better mechanistic hypothesis from which to base future studies on health.

The Importance of Religion and Spirituality to Patients and Physicians

Religion and spirituality play significant roles in many people's lives. A neurotheological approach would support population studies and phenomenological assessments to evaluate the impact. For example, surveys have generally reported that over 90 percent of Americans believe in God or a higher power, 90 percent pray, 67-75 percent pray on a daily basis, 69 percent are members of a church or synagogue, 40 percent attend a church or synagogue regularly, 60 percent consider religion to be very important in their lives, and 82 percent acknowledge a personal need for spiritual growth.[14] Additionally, many patients seem interested in integrating religion with their health care. Over 75 percent of surveyed patients want physicians to include spiritual issues in their medical care, approximately 40 percent want physicians to discuss their religious faith with them, and nearly 50 percent would like physicians to pray with them.[15] Although many physicians seem to agree that spiritual well-being is an important component of health that should be addressed with patients, only a minority (less than 20 percent) do so with any regularity.[16] According to surveyed physicians, lack of time, inadequate training, discomfort in addressing the topics, and difficulty in identifying patients who want to discuss spiritual issues are responsible for this discrepancy.[17]

---

[14]   Bezilla, R. (ed.). *Religion in America, 1992-1993*. Princeton, NJ: Princeton Religious Center (Gallup Organization), 1993; Poloma, M. and Pendleton, B. "The effects of prayer and prayer experience on measures of general well being." *J Psych Theol.* 1991;10:71-83; Shuler, P.A., Gelberg, L., and Brown, M. "The effects of spiritual/religious practices on psychological well-being among inner city homeless women." *Nurse Pract Forum.* 1994;5:106-113; *The Gallup Report: Religion in America:1993-1994*. Princeton, NJ: Gallup Poll, 1994; Miller, W.R. and Thoresen, C.E. "Spirituality, religion, and health: an emerging research field." *Am Psychol.* 2003;58:24-35.

[15]   Daaleman, T.P. and Nease, D.E., Jr. "Patient attitudes regarding physician inquiry into spiritual and religious issues." *J Fam Pract.* 1994;39:564-568; King, D.E. and Bushwick, B. "Beliefs and attitudes of hospital inpatients about faith healing and prayer." *J Fam Pract.* 1994;39:349-352; King, D.E., Hueston, W., and Rudy, M. "Religious affiliation and obstetric outcome." *South Med J.* 1994;87:1125-1128; Matthews, D.A., McCullough, M.E., Larson, D.B., Koenig, H.G., Swyers, J.P., and Milano, M.G. "Religious commitment and health status: a review of the research and implications for family medicine." *Arch Fam Med.* 1998;7:118-124.

[16]   Monroe, M.H., Bynum, D., Susi, B., et al. "Primary care physician preferences regarding spiritual behavior in medical practice." *Arch Intern Med.* 2003;163:2751-2756; MacLean, C.D., Susi, B., Phifer, N., et al. "Patient preference for physician discussion and practice of spirituality." *J Gen Intern Med.* 2003;18:38-43.

[17]   Ellis, M.R., Vinson, D.C., and Ewigman, B. "Addressing spiritual concerns of patients: family physicians' attitudes and practices." *J Fam Pract.* 1999;48:105-109;

On the other hand, some question the relevance and appropriateness of discussing religion and spirituality in the health care setting, fearing that health care workers may impose personal religious beliefs on others and replace necessary medical interventions with religious interventions. Critics have also been worried that patients may be forced to believe that their illnesses are due solely to poor faith rather than poor health.[18] Moreover, there is considerable debate over how religion should be integrated within health care and who should be responsible, especially when health care providers are agnostic or atheist.[19] A neurotheological approach would seek to better understand the psychology associated with patients and doctors both for and against the integration of religion into healthcare. Understanding the emotions associated with these different positions could be beneficial. Neurotheology may be able to evaluate the feelings and mechanisms associated with health related issues.

Some have recommended that physicians and other health care providers routinely take religious and spiritual histories of their patients to better understand the patients' religious background, determine how he or she may be using religion to cope with illness, open the door for future discussions about any spiritual or religious issues, and help detect potentially deleterious side effects from religious and spiritual activities.[20] It may also be a way of detecting spiritual distress.[21] There also has been greater emphasis in integrating various religious resources and professionals into patient care, especially when the patient is near the end of their life.[22] Again, neurotheology may be able to contribute to many of these lines of investigation. Perhaps understanding the brain processes involved with those who want religion and those who do not want religion better integrated into health care might be useful for guiding future research.

Armbruster, C.A., Chibnall, J.T., and Legett, S. "Pediatrician beliefs about spirituality and religion in medicine: associations with clinical practice." *Pediatrics.* 2003;111:e227-235; Chibnall, J.T. and Brooks, C.A. "Religion in the clinic: the role of physician beliefs." *South Med J.* 2001;94:374-379.

[18] Sloan, R.P. and Bagiella, E. "Claims about religious involvement and health outcomes." *Ann Behav Med.* 2002;24:14-21; Sloan, R.P., Bagiella, E., and Powell, T. "Religion, spirituality, and medicine." *Lancet.* 1999;353:664-667.

[19] Levin, J.S., Larson, D.B., and Puchalski, C.M. "Religion and spirituality in medicine: research and education." *Jama.* 1997;278:792-793.

[20] Matthews, D.A. and Clark, C. *The Faith Factor: Proof of the Healing Power of Prayer.* New York, NY: Viking (Penguin-Putnam), 1998; Kuhn, C.C. "A spiritual inventory of the medically ill patient." *Psychiatr Med.* 1988;6:87-100; Lo, B., Quill, T., and Tulsky, J. "Discussing palliative care with patients." ACP-ASIM End-of-Life Care Consensus Panel. American College of Physicians-American Society of Internal Medicine. *Ann Intern Med.* 1999;130:744-749.

[21] Abrahm, J. "Pain management for dying patients: how to assess needs and provide pharmacologic relief." *Postgrad Med.* 2001;110:99-100.

[22] Lo, B., Ruston, D., Kates, L.W., et al. "Discussing religious and spiritual issues at the end of life: a practical guide for physicians." *Jama.* 2002;287:749-754.

Methodological Issues with Studies of Health and Religion

Like most nascent research areas, the study of religion and health has had to contend with a lack of adequate funding, institutional support, and training for investigators. These challenges have helped limit the number of well-designed studies in the medical literature. Rather than true scientific studies, many "studies" actually have been anecdotes and editorials, which can galvanize discussions, germinate ideas, and fuel future studies, but cannot establish causality or scientifically justify the use of specific interventions. But as the study of religion and health progresses, the number and sophistication of scientific studies should continue to grow. Neurotheology offers a potentially important interface with regard to studies of health and religion by providing the basis for an integrated foundation which establishes both scientific rigor and religious understanding.

The study of religion in the context of health has some unique challenges as well. Understanding these inherent challenges is crucial when either designing or interpreting studies. Otherwise, researchers may conduct significantly flawed studies, draw inappropriate conclusions, pursue the wrong research questions, or neglect to pursue further necessary research. These challenges and questions include:

1. *Defining the differences between religion and spirituality.* As we have considered in the chapter on definitions, an important element of neurotheological research studies is that whenever a study is evaluated, it is critical to know how the researchers actually defined their terms and then what measures they used to support their definitions.
2. *Recruiting and retaining study subjects.* Finding appropriate and compliant subjects is not easy especially when beliefs and practices may be incompatible with the study design or environment.
3. *Monitoring and measuring subject compliance.* Many religious and spiritual activities such as prayer and meditation are private, silent, subtle, or integrated with or indistinguishable from social interactions. How does one verify if and how often a subject prays or meditates, how intensely, or for what purpose? How does one ensure that a subject performs a religious or spiritual activity in a "proper" manner?
4. *Measuring religiousness or spirituality.* Many possible categories of measures of religiousness and spirituality exist. Someone who scores high in one dimension of religiousness may not necessarily score high in others. Some measures are more valuable for one religion compared to another. Spirituality and religiousness are not always commensurate with some individuals considering themselves spiritual and not religious or religious and not spiritual. How valid are tests and measures of religiosity or spirituality? What are the correct units of measure? Is the duration or intensity of an activity more important than the frequency? Is reading scriptures everyday for one hour equivalent to reading scriptures three days

a week for four hours? What if someone reads the scriptures as a rote ritual instead of truly feeling connected with what is being read?

5. *The positive externalities of religion may confound results.* Participating in religious activities can alter a person's life in many ways. Church groups often provide a social support network. Many church activities also function as social and recreational activities. They may offer opportunities for people to exercise and stay away from unhealthy environments. Religion can provide structure and discipline to a person's life. These favorable secondary effects of religious activities (that is, "positive externalities" of religion) may be responsible for some health benefits. So when a study shows a positive effect of religion, differentiating what is truly responsible for the effect can be difficult.

6. *A patient's religious activity can cause the observed effects on his or her health or the patient's health status can affect his or her religious activity.* Establishing the direction of causality can be challenging. A person's health status may influence whether he or she participates in a religious activity. Physical disabilities may prevent a person from traveling to or engaging in certain religious activities. Someone depressed or anxious may feel unmotivated or embarrassed to see others. Conversely, serious health problems may motivate patients to attend religious activities to seek solace or healing.

7. *Practices and doctrines vary significantly among and within different religious affiliations and denominations.* People practice religion in many different ways. What constitutes devoted religious behavior in one sect or denomination may be inadequate or irreverent in other sects or denominations. For example, proper dress in one denomination may be sacrilegious in more orthodox denominations.

8. *Religions are affected by the local environment.* Each religion may hold a variable social status in different countries during different times. Practically all religions have faced persecution, discrimination, and isolation at some time and place during their history. Belonging to the dominant religion in a society can confer greater social acceptance, a stronger and more extensive social network, and more access to resources, all of which can have psychological and physical consequences. Minority religious sects may endure psychological or physical stress or in some severe cases, physical punishment. Moreover, minority or fringe religious sects which are unable to convince mainstream individuals to join their cause may have to recruit among societal outcasts, many of whom could have psychological or physical illness to begin with. Therefore, any study of a specific religious group should account for the location of that group and its relationship with the ambient society.

9. *Proper timing of studies is complicated.* How long should you follow and observe individuals or populations before seeing effects? Some spiritual activities such as prayer, yoga, and meditation may have both immediate

and delayed effects on physical parameters such as heart rate and blood pressure and psychological parameters such as stress and anxiety. Some of the delayed effects of religious and spiritual activities may take years or even an entire lifetime to manifest. Therefore, observing subjects over only a short period of time may miss important findings. However, the longer the follow-up, the more difficult the study is to perform, and the greater chance that more confounding variables will emerge.

10. *Multidisciplinary research is challenging.* The study of religion and health, as with neurotheology, involves scholars from different disciplines and professions. Ultimately, interdisciplinary research can be more productive than research confined to a single discipline. People from different fields and professions bring different interests, experiences, perspectives, and abilities to the table. However, every discipline and profession has its own language, culture, structure, and motivations. Health researchers and religion researchers often are not familiar with important publications in each others' specialty. Separate meetings, separate departments, different methodologies, and different lexicons can hinder collaboration. However, neurotheology might provide a foundation for beginning such a multidisciplinary approach.

The Positive Effects of Religion on Health

In spite of the limitations mentioned above, there are a variety of studies that have explored the positive and negative effects of religion on health. In developing neurotheology as a field, a brief overview is warranted. However, it must be kept in mind that each of the results described below may suffer from a variety of methodological issues. Hopefully, by considering these methodological issues and initial results, we will have an opportunity to pursue further these areas of research. This will help to advance our understanding of the relationship between spirituality and health. And hopefully neurotheology can be an important contributor.

Various systematic reviews and meta-analyses have demonstrated that religious involvement correlates with decreased morbidity and mortality and high levels of religious involvement may be associated with up to an additional seven years of life expectancy.[23] For example, in an analysis of 91,000 people in a Maryland

---

[23]   Oman, D., Kurata, J.H., Strawbridge, W.J., and Cohen, R.D. "Religious attendance and cause of death over 31 years." *Int J Psychiatry Med.* 2002;32:69-89; McCullough, M.E. and Larson, D.B. "Religion and depression: a review of the literature." *Twin Res.* 1999;2:126-136; Kark, J.D., Shemi, G., Friedlander, Y., Martin, O., Manor, O., and Blondheim, S.H. "Does religious observance promote health? Mortality in secular vs religious kibbutzim in Israel." *Am J Public Health.* 1996;86:341-346; McCullough, M.E., Hoyt, W.T., Larson, D.B., Koenig, H.G., and Thoresen, C. "Religious involvement and mortality: a meta-analytic review." *Health Psychol.* 2000;19:211-222; Strawbridge, W.J., Cohen, R.D., Shema, S.J., and Kaplan, G.A. "Frequent attendance at religious services and

county, those who regularly attended church had a lower prevalence of cirrhosis, emphysema, suicide, and death from ischemic heart disease.[24]

Some studies have suggested that members of different religions may have different mortality and morbidity, even when adjusting for major biological, behavioral, and socioeconomic differences.[25] However, as mentioned previously, the experience of individuals within a given religion can depend significantly on the local environment, the person's status within the religious group, and the religious group's status within the surroundings. Greater morbidity and mortality have been reported among Irish Catholics in Britain, which may reflect their disadvantaged socio-economic status in that country.[26] A study in Holland suggested that smaller religious groups may be less susceptible to infectious disease because of social isolation.[27] In general, there have not been enough studies looking at how mortality and morbidity for different religions vary over time and place. Moreover, many religions and religious sects have received little attention from investigators. Consequently, the body of literature comparing morbidity and mortality rates among religions is not large enough to draw any definitive conclusions.

Studies also have suggested that people with high religiousness may have better outcomes after major illnesses and medical procedures. In an analysis of patients following elective open heart surgery, lack of participation in social or community groups and absence of strength and comfort from religion were consistent predictors of mortality.[28] On the other hand, another study did not find that the level of spirituality as measured by the INSPIRIT questionnaire (a frequently used measure that evaluates a variety of parameters associated

---

mortality over 28 years." *Am J Public Health.* 1997;87:957-961; Hummer, R.A., Rogers, R.G., Nam, C.B., and Ellison, C.G. "Religious involvement and U.S. adult mortality." *Demography.* 1999;36:273-285.

[24] Koenig, H.G., Hays, J.C., Larson, D.B., et al. "Does religious attendance prolong survival? A six-year follow-up study of 3,968 older adults." *J Gerontol A Biol Sci Med Sci.* 1999;54:M370-376.

[25] Rasanen, J., Kauhanen, J., Lakka, T.A., Kaplan, G.A., and Salonen, J.T. "Religious affiliation and all-cause mortality: a prospective population study in middle-aged men in eastern Finland." *Int J Epidemiol.* 1996;25:1244-1249.

[26] Abbotts, J., Williams, R., and Ford, G. "Morbidity and Irish Catholic descent in Britain: relating health disadvantage to socio-economic position." *Soc Sci Med.* 2001;52:999-1005; Abbotts, J., Williams, R., Ford, G., Hunt, K., and West, P. "Morbidity and Irish Catholic descent in Britain: an ethnic and religious minority 150 years on." *Soc Sci Med.* 1997;45:3-14.

[27] Van Poppel, F., Schellekens, J., and Liefbroer, A.C. "Religious differentials in infant and child mortality in Holland, 1855-1912." *Popul Stud* (Camb). 2002;56:277-289.

[28] Oxman, T.E., Freeman, D.H., Jr., and Manheimer, E.D. "Lack of social participation or religious strength and comfort as risk factors for death after cardiac surgery in the elderly." *Psychosom Med.* 1995;57:5-15.

with spiritual experiences) significantly affected recovery from spinal surgery.[29] Several other studies of various cancers including colorectal, lung, and breast cancer showed no statistically significant effect of religious involvement on cancer survival.[30] A study by Blumenthal and colleagues showed no correlation between post-myocardial infarction outcomes and self-reported spirituality, frequency of church attendance, or frequency of prayer.[31]

Studies have examined whether people with high religiosity live generally healthier and less risky lifestyles than those with lower religiosity, which may account for some of the observed health benefits of religion. One hypothesis is that religion may provide structure, teaching, role models, and support to individuals so that they do not have the desire or time to engage in risky behavior. Some studies have supported this hypothesis. Regular religious attendance has been shown to correlate with increased use of preventive care, vitamins, and seatbelts; decreased bar attendance, smoking, and drinking; and walking, strenuous exercise, and sound sleep quality.[32] However, other studies have shown no relationship or even an inverse relationship between religiosity and certain risky behaviors.[33]

The impact of religion on mental health also has been widely studied. Studies have demonstrated religiosity to be positively associated with feelings of well-being in a variety of populations.[34] Hope and optimism seemed to run higher among religious individuals than non-religious individuals in some study

---

[29]   Hodges, S.D., Humphreys, S.C., and Eck, J.C. "Effect of spirituality on successful recovery from spinal surgery." *South Med J.* 2002;95:1381-1384.

[30]   Yates, J.W., Chalmer, B.J., St James, P., Follansbee, M., and McKegney, F.P. "Religion in patients with advanced cancer." *Med Pediatr Oncol.* 1981;9:121-128; Kune, G.A., Kune, S., and Watson, L.F. "The effect of family history of cancer, religion, parity and migrant status on survival in colorectal cancer." The Melbourne Colorectal Cancer Study. *Eur J Cancer.* 1992;28A:1484-1487.

[31]   Blumenthal, J.A., Babyak, M.A., Ironson, G., et al. "Spirituality, religion, and clinical outcomes in patients recovering from an acute myocardial infarction." *Psychosom Med.* 2007;69:501-508.

[32]   Hill, T.D., Burdette, A.M., Ellison, C.G., and Musick, M.A. "Religious attendance and the health behaviors of Texas adults." *Prev Med.* 2006;42:309-312.

[33]   Hasnain, M., Sinacore, J.M., Mensah, E.K., and Levy, J.A. "Influence of religiosity on HIV risk behaviors in active injection drug users." *AIDS Care.* 2005;17:892-901; Poulson, R.L., Eppler, M.A., Satterwhite, T.N., Wuensch, K.L., and Bass, L.A. "Alcohol consumption, strength of religious beliefs, and risky sexual behavior in college students." *J Am Coll Health.* 1998;46:227-232.

[34]   Markides, K.S., Levin, J.S., and Ray, L.A. "Religion, aging, and life satisfaction: an eight-year, three-wave longitudinal study." *Gerontologist* 1987;27:660-665; Coke, M.M. "Correlates of life satisfaction among elderly African Americans." *J Gerontol.* 1992;47: 316-320; Yoon, D.P. and Lee, E.K. "The impact of religiousness, spirituality, and social support on psychological well-being among older adults in rural areas." *J Gerontol Soc Work.* 2007;48:281-298.

populations.[35] A number of investigators have looked at the effects of religion on depression. Cross-sectional studies have yielded significant and non-significant associations between different indicators of religiosity and a lower prevalence of depression in various populations.[36]

Different religions may differ in how they confront suffering. While generalizations are difficult to draw since considerable variability exists within each religion, many Buddhists believe one should endure pain matter-of-factly.[37] Hindus stress understanding and detachment from pain.[38] Muslims and Jews often favor resisting or fighting pain,[39] and many Christians stress seeking atonement and redemption from pain.[40] Thus, the study of suffering offers some potentially valuable information both for the study of psychology as well as for understanding the theological aspects related to suffering. Here, neurotheology may be particularly useful in attempting to understand the biological substrate of suffering and the possible mechanisms by which suffering can be relieved.

The Negative Effects of Religion on Health

Although many studies have shown positive effects, religion and spirituality also may negatively affect health. For example, religious groups may directly oppose certain health care interventions, such as transfusions or contraception, and convince patients that their ailments are due to non-compliance with religious

---

[35] Idler, E.L. and Kasl, S.V. "Religion among disabled and nondisabled persons II: attendance at religious services as a predictor of the course of disability." *J Gerontol B Psychol Sci Soc Sci.* 1997;52:S306-316; Idler, E.L. and Kasl, S.V. "Religion among disabled and nondisabled persons I: cross-sectional patterns in health practices, social activities, and well-being." *J Gerontol B Psychol Sci Soc Sci.* 1997;52:S294-305.

[36] Koenig, H.G., Hays, J.C., George, L.K., Blazer, D.G., Larson, D.B., and Landerman, L.R. "Modeling the cross-sectional relationships between religion, physical health, social support, and depressive symptoms." *Am J Geriatr Psychiatry.* 1997;5:131-144; Musick, M.A., Koenig, H.G., Hays, J.C., and Cohen, H.J. "Religious activity and depression among community-dwelling elderly persons with cancer: the moderating effect of race." *J Gerontol B Psychol Sci Soc Sci.* 1998;53:S218-227; Bienenfeld, D., Koenig, H.G., Larson, D.B., and Sherrill, K.A. "Psychosocial predictors of mental health in a population of elderly women: test of an explanatory model." *Am J Geriatr Psychiatry.* 1997;5:43-53.

[37] Tu, W. "A religiophilosophical perspective on pain." In Koster, H.W, Kosterlitz, D., and Terenius, L.Y. (eds.), *Pain and Society.* Weinheim and Deerfield Beach, FL: Verlag Chemie, 1980:63-78.

[38] Shaffer, J.A. "Pain and suffering: philosophical perspectives." In Reich, W.T. (ed.), *Encyclopedia of Bioethics.* New York, NY: Free Press, 1978.

[39] Bowker, D. "Pain and suffering: religious perspective." In Reich, W.T. (ed.), *Encyclopedia of Bioethics.* New York, NY: Free Press, 1978:1185-1189.

[40] Amundsen, D.W. "Medicine and faith in early Christianity." *Bull Hist Med.* 1982;56:326-350.

doctrines rather than organic disease.[41] Asser and colleagues demonstrated that a large number of child fatalities could have been prevented had medical care not been withheld for religious reasons.[42] In addition, religions can stigmatize those with certain disorders such as depression or drug abuse to the point that they do not seek proper medical care.[43]

Historically, religion has widely been cited as the source of military conflicts, prejudice, violent behaviors, and other social problems. Religions may ignore, stereotype, ostracize, or abuse those who do not belong to their tradition. Those not belonging to a dominant religion may face obstacles to obtaining resources, hardships, and stress that deleteriously affect their health.[44] Religious leaders may abuse their own members physically, emotionally, or sexually.[45] Religious laws or dictums may be invoked to justify harmful, oppressive, and injurious behavior.[46]

Additionally, perceived religious transgressions can cause emotional and psychological anguish, manifesting as physical discomfort. This "religious" and "spiritual pain" can be difficult to distinguish from pure physical pain.[47] In extreme cases, spiritual abuse (convincing people that they are going to suffer eternal purgatory) and spiritual terrorism, an extreme form of spiritual abuse, can occur either overtly or insidiously.[48] When a mix of religious, spiritual, and organic sources is causing physical illness, treatment can become complicated. Health care workers must properly balance treating each source.

---

[41]   Donahue, M.J. "Intrinsic and extrinsic religiousness: review and meta-analysis." *Journal of Personality and Social Psychology*. 1985;48:400-419.

[42]   Asser, S.M. and Swan, R. "Child fatalities from religion-motivated medical neglect." *Pediatrics*. 1998;101:625-629.

[43]   Lichtenstein, B. "Stigma as a barrier to treatment of sexually transmitted infection in the American deep south: issues of race, gender and poverty." *Soc Sci Med*. 2003;57: 2435-2445; Madru, N. "Stigma and HIV: does the social response affect the natural course of the epidemic?" *J Assoc Nurses AIDS Care*. 2003;14:39-48.

[44]   Walls, P. and Williams, R. "Accounting for Irish Catholic ill health in Scotland: a qualitative exploration of some links between 'religion', class and health." *Sociol Health Illn*. 2004;26:527-556; Bywaters, P., Ali, Z., Fazil, Q., Wallace, L.M., and Singh, G. "Attitudes towards disability amongst Pakistani and Bangladeshi parents of disabled children in the UK: considerations for service providers and the disability movement." *Health Soc Care Community*. 2003;11:502-509.

[45]   Tieman, J. "Priest scandal hits hospitals. As pedophilia reports grow, church officials suspend at least six hospital chaplains in an effort to address alleged sexual abuse." *Mod Healthc*. 2002;32:6-7; Rossetti, S.J. "The impact of child sexual abuse on attitudes toward God and the Catholic Church." *Child Abuse Negl*. 1995;19:1469-1481.

[46]   Kernberg, O.F. "Sanctioned social violence: a psychoanalytic view. Part II." *Int J Psychoanal*. 2003;84:953-968.

[47]   Satterly, L. "Guilt, shame, and religious and spiritual pain." *Holist Nurs Pract*. 2001;15:30-39.

[48]   Purcell, B.C. "Spiritual abuse." *Am J Hosp Palliat Care*. 1998;15:227-231; Purcell, B.C. "Spiritual terrorism." *Am J Hosp Palliat Care*. 1998;15:167-173.

The Effects of Specific Religious and Spiritual Activities in the Context of Health

Religious and spiritual activities have become highly prevalent throughout the world and may be practiced in either religious or secular manners. Of course, practices such as meditation, when performed in a secular way, do not specifically have to do with religion or spirituality even though they are originally derived from such traditions. Thus, practicing them does not necessarily connote certain beliefs. On the other hand, evidence is suggesting that even when practices such as meditation are designed to be purely secular, there is often an increase in the spiritual or religious measures of the individual participants. Currently, many practices have been altered and combined with other activities such as aerobics to develop a multitude of hybrid techniques. As a result, some forms barely resemble the original versions. Thus, investigators must be very specific in describing the technique or activity that they are examining. Additionally, results from one form of meditation or yoga may not apply to other forms.

Neurotheology might provide an important context for understanding not only the nature of religious and spiritual practices, but how such practices have a direct impact on health and well being. Incorporating neuroscientific methods into the study of such practices can provide a mechanistic basis for the effects of these practices. Let us explore several practices that can be studied utilizing the neurotheological approach.

1. *Prayer* There is evidence that prayer may be associated with less muscle tension, improved cardiovascular and neuroimmunologic parameters, psychologic and spiritual peace, a greater sense of purpose, enhanced coping skills, less disability and better physical function in patients with knee pain,[49] and a lower incidence of coronary heart disease.[50] One interesting study showed that *petitionary* and *ritualistic prayers* were associated with lower levels of well-being and life satisfaction, while *colloquial prayers* were associated with higher levels.[51] Intercessory prayer provides a unique challenge for study in the context of health and neurotheology. While the current research has not been conclusive, should a positive result of intercessory prayer be established, it would have tremendous implications for the current materialistic scientific paradigm. A positive result (that is, intercessory prayer works) would

---

[49]   Rapp, S.R., Rejeski, W.J., and Miller, M.E. "Physical function among older adults with knee pain: the role of pain coping skills." *Arthritis Care Res.* 2000;13:270-279.

[50]   Gupta, R., Prakash, H., Gupta, V.P., and Gupta, K.D. "Prevalence and determinants of coronary heart disease in a rural population of India." *J Clin Epidemiol.* 1997;50:203-209; Gupta, R. "Lifestyle risk factors and coronary heart disease prevalence in Indian men." *J Assoc Physicians India.* 1996;44:689-693.

[51]   Poloma, M. and Pendleton, B. "The effects of prayer and prayer experience on measures of general well being." *J Psych Theol.* 1991;10:71-83.

also have significant implications for the study of the human brain and human consciousness and would of course have profound theological implications. But studies of intercessory prayer open up many other fascinating issues. For example, is one person praying for 10 hours the same as 10 people praying for one hour? How does the intensity of prayer relate to the result? Does it matter if the person praying knows the other person? Does it matter where the person praying is located? Of course, all of these questions are moot if intercessory prayer does not work. But it may require substantial study before making either a positive or negative answer. If intercessory prayer does work, there is also the more fundamental question of what actually is causing the effect. Is it really prayer to God such that God intervenes and causes the requested effect? Is it the ability of human consciousness to affect things at a distance? This has been referred to as distant intentionality. Should distant intentionality exist, this would support traditions, such as Buddhism, that consider consciousness as a universal substrate.

2. *Meditation* As previously described, meditation appears to have significant effects on the brain. While evidence is not yet definitive, preliminary studies suggest that meditation also may have a number of potential health benefits such as decreasing anxiety, depression, irritability and moodiness, and improving learning ability, memory, self-actualization, feelings of vitality and rejuvenation, and emotional stability.[52] Preliminary studies suggest that meditative practices may benefit and provide acute and chronic support for patients with hypertension, psoriasis, irritable bowel disease, anxiety, epilepsy, premenstrual symptoms, menopausal symptoms, and depression.[53] There is also evidence that meditation can improve chronic

---

[52] Bitner, R., Hillman, L., Victor, B., and Walsh, R. "Subjective effects of antidepressants: a pilot study of the varieties of antidepressant-induced experiences in meditators." *J Nerv Ment Dis.* 2003;191:660-667; Astin, J.A., Berman, B.M., Bausell, B., Lee, W.L., Hochberg, M., and Forys, K.L. "The efficacy of mindfulness meditation plus Qigong movement therapy in the treatment of fibromyalgia: a randomized controlled trial." *J Rheumatol.* 2003;30:2257-2262; Jain, S., Shapiro, S.L., Swanick, S., et al. "A randomized controlled trial of mindfulness meditation versus relaxation training: effects on distress, positive states of mind, rumination, and distraction." *Ann Behav Med.* 2007;33:11-21.

[53] Kabat-Zinn, J., Massion, A.O., Kristeller, J., et al. "Effectiveness of a meditation-based stress reduction program in the treatment of anxiety disorders." *Am J Psychiatry.* 1992;149:936-943; Kabat-Zinn, J., Wheeler, E., Light, T., et al. "Influence of a mindfulness meditation-based stress reduction intervention on rates of skin clearing in patients with moderate to severe psoriasis undergoing phototherapy (UVB) and photochemotherapy (PUVA)." *Psychosom Med.* 1998;60:625-632; Carlson, L.E., Ursuliak, Z., Goodey, E., Angen, M., and Speca, M. "The effects of a mindfulness meditation-based stress reduction program on mood and symptoms of stress in cancer outpatients: 6-month follow-up." *Support Care Cancer.* 2001;9:112-123; Reibel, D.K., Greeson, J.M., Brainard, G.C., and

pain.[54] Unfortunately, many studies do not specify or fully describe the type of meditation used. A wide variety of methods may be used, including some in which the body is immobile (for example, Zazen, Vipassana), others in which the body is let free (for example, Siddha Yoga, the Latihan, the chaotic meditation of Rajneesh), and still others in which the person participates in daily activities while meditating (for example, Mahamudra, Shikan Taza, Gurdjieff's "self-remembering"). So it is not clear which forms may be beneficial and what aspects of meditation are providing the benefits. Although physically non-invasive, meditation has the potential to be harmful in patients with psychiatric illness, potentially aggravating and precipitating psychotic episodes in delusional or strongly paranoid patients and heightening anxiety in patients with overwhelming anxiety. Moreover, it can trigger the release of repressed memories which can be disturbing or result in anxiety reactions. Therefore, all patients using meditative techniques should be monitored, especially when a patient first starts using meditation. Neurotheological analysis might help to better understand the link between meditation techniques and body and brain physiology. Such an understanding should also help better determine the positive and negative effects of meditation so that its use might be optimized.

3. *Yoga*   Yoga is also widely used, often for regular exercise. Contrary to popular misconceptions, yoga predated Hinduism by several centuries, and as The American Yoga Association emphasizes, since yoga practice does not specify particular higher powers or religious doctrines, it can be compatible with all major religions. Yoga is based on a set of theories that have not yet been scientifically proven. Yoga practitioners believe that blockages or imbalances of the body's energy, or Qi (pronounced "chee"), can cause disease or decreased resistance to disease and that yoga can restore the flow of energy to different parts of the body. Yoga uses a series of stretching, breathing, and relaxation techniques to prepare for meditation and employs stretching movements or postures (*asanas*) that aim to increase blood supply and *prana* (vital force) as well as increase the flexibility of the spine, which is thought to improve the nerve supply. Yoga also uses breathing techniques (*pranayamas*) to try to restore and rejuvenate the body's energy. The notion of energy traveling throughout the body does not currently have a Western scientific counterpart. Again, this might be a place in which neurotheological research can help to better bridge this gap and help to

Rosenzweig, S. "Mindfulness-based stress reduction and health-related quality of life in a heterogeneous patient population." *Gen Hosp Psychiatry*. 2001;23:183-192.

[54]   Kabat-Zinn, J., Lipworth, L., and Burney, R. "The clinical use of mindfulness meditation for the self-regulation of chronic pain." *J Behav Med*. 1985;8:163-190; Kabat-Zinn, J. "An outpatient program in behavioral medicine for chronic pain patients based on the practice of mindfulness meditation: theoretical considerations and preliminary results." *Gen Hosp Psychiatry*. 1982;4:33-47.

clarify if there can be a correspondence between yoga principles and the prevailing biomedical paradigm. If such a reconciliation cannot be attained, then again, neurotheology might be able to ascertain whether yoga is in fact helpful, and if so, whether a paradigm shift in Western medicine is required. The relatively few limited clinical studies on yoga have been encouraging, showing reduced serum total cholesterol, LDL cholesterol, and triglyceride levels, decreased basal metabolic rates, and improved pulmonary function tests in yoga practitioners.[55] Studies also suggest that yoga may be associated with acute and long term decreases in blood pressure[56] and acute increases in brain gamma-aminobutyric (GABA) levels.[57] Preliminary evidence indicates that yoga may benefit patients with asthma, hypertension, heart failure, mood disorders, insomnia, migraine headaches, irritable bowel syndrome, end-stage renal disease, and diabetes, and improve pregnancy outcomes.[58] However, Yoga is not completely benign since certain *asanas*

---

[55]　Schell, F.J., Allolio, B., and Schonecke, O.W. "Physiological and psychological effects of hatha-yoga exercise in healthy women." *Int J Psychosom*. 1994;41(1-4): 46-52; Stanescu, D.C., Nemery, B., Veriter, C., and Marechal, C. "Pattern of breathing and ventilatory response to CO2 in subjects practicing hatha-yoga." *J Appl Physiol*. Dec 1981;51(6):1625-1629; Udupa, K.N., Singh, R.H., and Yadav, R.A. "Certain studies on psychological and biochemical responses to the practice in hatha yoga in young normal volunteers." *Indian J Med Res*. Feb 1973;61(2):237-244; Birkel, D.A. and Edgren, L. "Hatha yoga: improved vital capacity of college students." *Altern Ther Health Med*. Nov 2000;6(6):55-63; Arambula, P., Peper, E., Kawakami, M., and Gibney, K.H. "The physiological correlates of Kundalini Yoga meditation: a study of a yoga master." *Appl Psychophysiol Biofeedback*. Jun 2001;26(2):147-153; Selvamurthy, W., Sridharan, K., Ray, U.S., et al. "A new physiological approach to control essential hypertension." *Indian J Physiol Pharmacol*. Apr 1998;42(2):205-213; Stancak, A., Jr., Kuna, M., Srinivasan, Dostalek, C., and Vishnudevananda, S. "Kapalabhati—yogic cleansing exercise. II. EEG topography analysis." *Homeost Health Dis*. Dec 1991;33(4):182-189.

[56]　Sundar, S., Agrawal, S.K., Singh, V.P., Bhattacharya, S.K., Udupa, K.N., and Vaish, S.K. "Role of yoga in management of essential hypertension." *Acta Cardiol*. 1984;39: 203-208; Murugesan, R., Govindarajulu, N., and Bera, T.K. "Effect of selected yogic practices on the management of hypertension." *Indian J Physiol Pharmacol*. 2000;44: 207-210.

[57]　Streeter, C.C., Jensen, J.E., Perlmutter, R.M., et al. "Yoga asana sessions increase brain GABA levels: a pilot study." *J Altern Complement Med*. 2007;13:419-426.

[58]　Jain, S.C., Uppal, A., Bhatnagar, S.O., and Talukdar, B. "A study of response pattern of non-insulin dependent diabetics to yoga therapy." *Diabetes Res Clin Pract*. 1993;19:69-74; John, P.J., Sharma, N., Sharma, C.M., and Kankane, A. "Effectiveness of yoga therapy in the treatment of migraine without aura: a randomized controlled trial." *Headache*. 2007;47:654-661; Kuttner, L., Chambers, C.T., Hardial, J., Israel, D.M., Jacobson, K., and Evans, K. "A randomized trial of yoga for adolescents with irritable bowel syndrome." *Pain Res Manag*. 2006;11:217-223; Narendran, S., Nagarathna, R., Narendran, V., Gunasheela, S., and Nagendra, H.R. "Efficacy of yoga on pregnancy outcome." *J Altern Complement Med*. 2005;11:237-244.

may be strenuous and cause injury. In fact, yoga practitioners believe some *asanas* actually cause disease. More studies are needed to determine the benefits (and potential dangers) of yoga. Like meditation, many forms of yoga have emerged. Some involve significant aerobic exercise. Others involve significant strength and conditioning work. Many yoga practices include changes in diet and lifestyles. It may be difficult to draw the line between yoga and other practices that have established health benefits such as exercise. Therefore, future studies should focus on specific yoga forms and movements and avoid making general conclusions about all yoga practices.

4. *Faith healing* Faith healers use prayer or other religious practices to combat disease. Surveys have found that a substantial portion of patients in rural (21 percent) and inner city (10 percent) populations have used faith healers and many physicians (23 percent) believe that faith healers can help to heal patients.[59] Despite numerous anecdotes of healing miracles, there has been no consistent and convincing scientific proof that faith healers are effective. Additionally, it has not been determined whether faith healers affect patients psychologically or physiologically, and what factors may make them effective. Conclusions cannot be drawn until further research is performed. But neurotheology might be able to help explore the phenomenological elements of faith healing and attempt to find correlates within the body and brain. Should such a connection be found, neurotheology might provide an opportunity to determine the place faith healing should have in the context of human health.

Conclusions and Future Directions

Existing evidence suggests that religious and spiritual practices may have beneficial effects on health. But the reasons behind these findings are not clearly understood. We know that religious and spiritual practices can bring social and emotional support, motivation, healthy lifestyles, and health care resources to their practitioners. However, are there other mechanisms involved? The medical world is just starting to answer this question. In general, performing clinical studies that can establish cause-and-effect relationships is difficult. This is especially true in the study of religion and health. Confounding factors abound. Religious and spiritual doctrines and practices vary significantly among and within different sects and denominations. Measuring religious and spiritual activity and monitoring and ensuring compliance among study subjects are challenging. Moreover, available resources, properly-trained investigators, and institutional support for clinical studies have been scarce. As a result, the current body of medical literature is short on well-designed clinical studies.

---

[59] McKee, D.D. and Chappel, J.N. "Spirituality and medical practice." *J Fam Pract.* 1992;35:201, 5-8.

Future studies should address a number of different issues and can be considered from a neurotheological perspective:

- What are the roles of different potential confounding factors?
- What physiologic mechanisms may be involved?
- What are the clinical implications of existing physiological studies?
- Does a person's health affect his or her ability to engage in religious activities?
- Do findings hold across different practices, sects, and denominations?
- What are the effects of varying demographic parameters such as age and gender? How do different practices affect different diseases and their biological substrate?
- How should religious issues be incorporated into the health care setting?

The findings to date already have clinical implications. Religion is clearly important to many patients. Health care providers may need to better address patients' religious concerns and be aware of how religious involvement can affect patients' symptoms, quality of life, and willingness to receive treatment. Moreover, religious and spiritual activities may serve as adjunct therapy in various disease and addiction treatment programs. The future may see the development of more specific spiritual interventions for particular medical problems, but only in the context of adequately addressing the potential advantages and disadvantages from both the biomedical and religious perspectives. This is what neurotheology might contribute.

Neuroethics

Neuroethics is an interesting blend of practical and philosophical (and sometimes theological) issues. Neurotheology might be seen as an adjunct to the study of neuroethics by encouraging an analysis of ethics from a religious or spiritual perspective as well as from a purely neuroscientific or philosophical perspective.

Principle XXXVIII: Neurotheology should contribute to neuroethics by helping ascertain the link between religion and ethics via the mechanisms of the human brain.

Neuroethics as a field has focused substantially on the ethics of doing neuroscience research, understanding the brain, and how such results might have an impact on human behavior.[60] For example, if a brain scan can demonstrate whether a criminal has now changed their ways, should such evidence be useful in determining who is paroled and who is not? But neurotheology would shift the discussion to how different brain structures and functions affect our ethical and moral decision making, particular with regard to the relationship between ethics and religion.

---

[60] Gazzaniga, M.S. *The Ethical Brain*. New York, NY: Dana Press, 2005.

This is also part of current neuroethics and provides important implications for understanding ethics more globally.

Let us look briefly at how a neurotheological approach might relate to neuroethics based upon a variety of different brain functions. For example, we might begin with a consideration of the holistic functions within the brain. Regarding ethics, there appears to be a strong influence of the notion that morality and goodness is associated with wholeness.[61] Behaviors and thoughts that contribute to a sense of wholeness either for an individual or for a group are typically considered to be advantageous and hence good. On the other hand, ideas and behaviors that cause fragmentation and a disintegration of wholeness tend to be regarded as immoral.

There is another important point to be made regarding the brain's holistic functions and a neurophysiological approach to ethical concepts especially from the theological perspective. This relates to the notion of inclusiveness and exclusiveness. It would seem that morality for many people is defined in relation to individuals included within the social or religious group. Thus, we try to act morally to those in our family, our community, or our church. But what about the desire to act morally outside of our group? There is substantial evidence that in-group/out-group bias frequently results in intergroup aggression and behaviors that might seem opposed to the morality that is applied within the group.[62] What is the physiological basis of such divergent approaches to moral behavior?

We might go one step further. It could be argued that if the holistic process functions in an absolute manner such that the entire universe is considered to be a single undifferentiated oneness, then there may be no way of separating good and bad. In an absolute unitary state, morality has no role since discrete objects and behaviors cannot exist. This may have important implications for the theological perspective of morality since the absolute unitary experience may provide no clear foundation regarding ethics. Alternatively, it might shed light on how and why morality is elaborated out of profound mystical or spiritual states.

Any attempts at reductionism of ethical concepts would suggest that moral concepts can be derived either logically or from natural law and would follow from prior notions of ethics. From the reductionist perspective, ethics becomes a kind of science with a strict methodology and analytical perspective. The reductionist perspective would tend to move away from a religious conceptualization of ethics unless considered theologically as deriving from the initial foundational doctrine of the religion which is considered irrefutable. However, depending on how reductionism is applied, even the foundational doctrine of a given religion might be critiqued when striving to determine which approach to morality is correct.

---

[61] d'Aquili, E.G. and Newberg, A.B. *The Mystical Mind: Probing the Biology of Religious Experience*. Minneapolis, MN: Fortress Press, 1999.

[62] Tajfel, H., Flament, M.C., Billig, M., and Bundy, R.P. "Social categorization and intergroup behavior." *Euro J Soc Psychol*. 1971;1:149-178; Miller, A. (ed.). *The Social Psychology of Good and Evil*. New York, NY: Guilford, 2004.

The quantitative or comparative processes of the brain also have an important relationship to ethics since it may be the basic mathematical operations that come into play when evaluating what is better than something else. That something can be "greater than" or "less than" enables a more expanded comparison of abstract concepts and ideas. The result is that some actions can be *more* ethical than others while some actions are regarded as *less* moral, or as immoral. Thus, there is value placed upon each issue that is to be evaluated from an ethical perspective and these values can then be compared. The values may not be quantitative *per se*—is it more appropriate to send someone to prison for life or give them the death penalty?—but the brain approaches this ethical dilemma by comparing and contrasting the various pros and cons of such a question. The implication is that there is a way to quantify the positive and negative components of the decision and these values can eventually be compared within the brain's processes. If the one decision outweighs the other, then at least from this perspective the ethical choice is made. The point is that quantitative assessment and the ability to compare moral value is built into the brain and helps with regard to making ethical decisions.

The brain's ability to perceive causality is similarly important to morality since moral behavior and thoughts require the presence of a causal sequence. If we cannot be held accountable for our action—that is, we did not know that what we were doing was injuring someone else—then can we be considered immoral? Theologians and philosophers alike have tangled with causality, and particularly free will, as integral to understanding ethics. The notion of free will relies heavily on causality. The issue revolves around who or what is causing things. If someone can be considered the cause of a given sequence of reality, then they can be accountable for that sequence. If the cause of a sequence of reality lies beyond that person, then that person cannot be responsible. Whether or not causality exists within a given sequence of a person's reality is what determines if they have free will. Therefore, causality within a sequence of reality allows for free will while causality that exists external to a given sequence leads to determinism.

The notion of the will itself may be derived in large part from the functioning of the prefrontal cortex which enables us to make decisions regarding actions and behaviors as well as helps to control emotional responses.[63] Free will is of particular interest to morality, but clearly is important in religious thought as well. For example, free will is a necessary part of Christianity's foundational doctrine particularly with regard to the notion of sin, and in particular original sin. Free will must be maintained in order for someone to be responsible for committing a sin. If everything is pre-determined, then a sinful act cannot be ascribed to the

---

[63]   Pardo, J.V., Fox, P.T., and Raichle, M.E. "Localization of a human system for sustained attention by positron emission tomography." *Nature*. 1991;349:61-64; Frith, C.D., Friston, K., Liddle, P.F., and Frackowiak, R.S.J. "Willed action and the prefrontal cortex in man: a study with PET." *Proc Royal Soc London*. 1991;244:241-246; Kompus, K., Hugdahl, K., Ohman, A., Marklund, P., and Nyberg, L. "Distinct control networks for cognition and emotion in the prefrontal cortex." *Neurosci Lett*. 2009;467:76-80.

person committing that act since they had no choice. If the person freely chooses to commit a sin, then they can be held accountable for that sin. In order for ethics to be viable, free will has to exist.

Eastern traditions have a different perspective in terms of causality. The Buddhist and Hindu ideologies concede ultimate causality to the realm of the absolute reality, or Brahman, which is typically regarded as a unitary state of pure awareness or pure consciousness that pervades the universe.[64] The individual ego and material reality are seen more or less as an illusion, with the unitary state being the true reality. Causality, as well as free will, only exist on the level of pure consciousness and do not apply to material reality or the human ego. However, this still presents a problem with the issue of practical ethics and the accountability of individuals. These traditions suggest that once the state of pure consciousness is attained, there is a natural flow of right behavior which derives from it and that this type of behavior is what comprises ethics. In such a system, the only way to gain a true understanding of right and wrong, free will and determinism, is by attaining the unitary state of pure consciousness.

One final aspect of brain function relevant to ethics is emotions. Any ethical decision process necessarily requires an ability to place emotional value on various elements. The value placed on each element of an ethical decision process is ultimately determined by our emotional perspective. The emotional perspective in turn is determined by our basic brain function, our past experiences, and our cultural, philosophical, and spiritual background. Individual emotional responses clearly affect moral decision making, but there can be more global effects of the emotions in terms of interpreting reality.

Perhaps neuroscientist Michael Gazzaniga expressed it best when he stated:

> I believe, therefore, that we should look not for a universal ethics comprising hard-and-fast truths, but for the universal ethics that arises from human beings, which is clearly contextual, emotion-influenced, and designed to increase our survival. That is why it is hard to arrive at absolute rules to live by that we can all agree on. But knowing that morals are contextual and social, and based on neural mechanisms, can help us determine certain ways to deal with ethical issues. This is the mandate for narrow ethics: to use our understanding that the brain reacts to things on the basis of its hard-wiring to contextualize and debate at the instincts that serve the greatest good—or the most logical solutions—given specific contexts.[65]

This is the potential contribution of neurotheology to the field of neuroethics—not only to help determine the biological underpinnings of moral behavior as it pertains to religion, but also to help associate the context within which an ethical

[64] Rambachan, A. *The Limits of Scripture: Vivekananda's Reinterpretation of the Vedas.* Honolulu, HI: University of Hawaii Press, 1994.

[65] Gazzaniga, M. *The Ethical Brain.* New York, NY: Dana Press, 2005.

system develops. A combination of a neurotheology and neuroethic approach might provide our best understanding of human ethics.

The Uncertainty Principle of Neurotheology

While neurotheology aims to evaluate many aspects of religion, theology, and spiritual experience, an important question to ponder is whether there are certain fundamental limitations that neurotheological scholarship will encounter. Such limitations would not be the result of the current state of scientific methodology, nor the state of the human mind, but would be of such a fundamental level that we should never expect to be able to overcome them. These limitations would theoretically be irresolvable. But if such limitations actually do exist, they would result in a fundamental uncertainty with regard to what we can know about the universe.

For this reason, the next two principles might be considered as part of an "uncertainty principle" of neurotheology.[66] The neurotheology uncertainty principle might be viewed somewhat similarly to the Heisenberg Uncertainty Principle which is a well known scientific statement about the inherent limitation in measuring momentum and location of a particle at the same time. The basic issue is that whenever we measure any thing, we naturally affect that thing. On the macro level of the physical world, these effects are negligible and thus practically unimportant. However, on the atomic level, these effects can be substantial.

From the perspective of the brain, there are limitations in what can be measured, particularly with regard to conscious perceptions of the world, that might constrain our ability to say anything completely definitive about the nature of the universe. This limitation is critical for understanding neurotheology and its ability to evaluate theology and the subjective experiences that arise within the brain.

Principle XXXIX: It should be realized that since the brain cannot readily escape its own functioning, there is a fundamental uncertainty in all beliefs about reality.

At the root of this principle is the notion that the brain is constantly processing everything we can perceive, think, and feel about reality. But this means that all of our beliefs are processed by the brain. The components of beliefs include our perceptions, emotions, cognitive processes, memories, and social interactions. Substantial research has demonstrated that each of these components suffers from numerous potential flaws.

Perceptions typically begin with the sensory organs for smell, taste, touch, vision, and hearing. Each of the sensory organs sends neuronal input to different

---

[66]   Newberg, A.B. and Waldman, M.R. *Why We Believe What We Believe: Uncovering Our Biological Need for Meaning, Spirituality, and Truth.* New York, NY: Free Press, 2006.

parts of the brain that process the input and begin to construct a sense of reality that we can respond to. The multiple steps towards constructing this sense of reality can result in a variety of misperceptions.[67] For example, there are many optical illusions that can convince the brain that the world appears one way when it really appears another. There are many instances in our lives where we may think that we hear something when in fact we hear something different or we misinterpret what we hear. There are also some fascinating studies that have observed the effect of distraction on our perceptions. One of the most well known experiments asks test subjects to observe a video of people throwing a basketball back and forth and to count how many times the ball is thrown.[68] In the midst of the task, a person wearing a gorilla costume walks through the video, pauses, and then walks off the screen. The large majority of people doing the task never see the gorilla even though it is in plain sight. Thus, the perceptions that we hold about reality must be brought into question whenever considering more fundamental epistemological issues.

Cognitive processes also suffer from many flaws. Numerous studies have demonstrated how we make many erroneous decisions when faced with various problems or tasks.[69] Our cognitive processes are also heavily biased by our prevailing belief system such that we tend to find logic in ideas and concepts that are consistent with our existing belief system and find those ideas and concepts counter to our beliefs to be illogical. A particularly good experiment, relevant to neurotheology as well, posed a series of syllogisms to individuals who were either religious or nonreligious.[70] Some syllogisms wore pro-religious while others were anti-religious. The results showed that religious individuals did extremely well in evaluating syllogisms that were pro-religious, but did not do as well when evaluating anti-religious syllogisms. Interestingly, nonreligious individuals did extremely well in evaluating syllogisms that were anti-religious, but did not do as well when evaluating pro-religious syllogisms. Thus, the results of this study suggest that all people make cognitive mistakes when they are dealing with situations antithetical to their own belief system. Not only does this suggest that our rational mind is far more flawed than we may appreciate, it also shows how rational thought processes are utilized to support existing belief systems rather than to construct them. This

---

[67] Newberg, A.B. and Waldman, M.R. *Why We Believe What We Believe: Uncovering Our Biological Need for Meaning, Spirituality, and Truth.* New York, NY: Free Press, 2006.

[68] Simons, D.J. and Chabris, C.F. "Gorillas in our midst: sustained inattentional blindness for dynamic events." *Perception.* 1999;28:1059-1074.

[69] Newberg, A.B. and Waldman, M.R. *Why We Believe What We Believe: Uncovering Our Biological Need for Meaning, Spirituality, and Truth.* New York, NY: Free Press, 2006.

[70] Feather, N.T. "Evaluation of religious and neutral arguments in religious and atheist student groups." *Austr J Psychol.* 1967;19:3-11.

problem may pose substantial challenges to any philosophical or theological position that argues for the exalted status of rational thinking.

Along with the problems of perceptions and cognitions, human emotions muddy the waters even further. Human beings have an extreme range of emotional responses to both external and internal stimuli. Emotions play a powerful role in our behaviors by positively reinforcing some and negatively restricting others. The social interactions we have with others are strong mediators of our emotional feelings that ultimately modify our behaviors. For example, an individual raised in a very strict, orthodox family is likely to fuel far greater experiences of guilt when questioning their faith compared to an individual raised in a more liberal environment. The pressures that one experiences would have effects not only on their emotions, but on how they decide to behave so that they maintain an optimal emotional balance. Emotions also have an impact on our perceptions as revealed by a simple experiment that showed how responses are modified depending on the emotional context of the questions. For example, one experiment showed a video of a car accident and asked individuals to evaluate the speed with which the two cars were going at the time of the accident.[71] If the question is asked, "How fast were the cars moving when they *crashed* into each other?" the speeds reported are much greater than if the question asked is, "How fast were the cars moving when they hit each other?" The word crash has much stronger emotional value and results in the perception of higher speeds.

Perhaps, more importantly, cognitive processes are modified by our emotions. Some have argued, that not only are cognitive processes modified by emotions, but that emotions are essential to appropriate cognitive functioning. Cognitive processes can only present different options to an individual whereas it is the emotional value that helps to actually appraise these different options. An excellent example might be in using cognitive processes to determine whether to eat a piece of chocolate cake versus a piece of grapefruit. Cognitions can list the pros and cons of both choices, but it is the emotions that will ultimately determine whether one really wants something sweet or whether one really wants to lose weight. Neither choice is inherently right or wrong, but one of them might be right or wrong in different contexts. The choice is based substantially on emotions rather than anything cognitive.

Emotions also arise during cognitive arguments between individuals. When two individuals do not agree, their initial approach may be to try rational thought. However, once it is clear that the other person does not agree with that rational approach, emotions become involved as an argument becomes heated. In part, this occurs because once the two individuals disagree, they have a tendency to view the other as "not rational." After all, if the other person was rational, they would be in agreement. The problem is that what is rational can vary enormously depending on the individual, the cultural background, or the religious background. But since each person believes that they make rational sense, it must be the other person

---

71   Loftus, E.F. "Make believe memories." *Amer Psychol.* 2003;58:867-873.

that is not rational. Or perhaps, worse, the other person may be knowingly stating falsehoods. Either way, as the frustration or sense of dishonesty grows, emotions will play a larger role in the argument that began in a rational manner.

Our beliefs are also heavily influenced by our social environment which begins initially with our parents and expands to our peers, colleagues, spouses, and clergy. Many studies have shown the importance of social influence on decision making and belief development.[72] Thus, while each person often assumes that their own belief system was arrived at autonomously and without undue outside influence, research suggests that we are far more malleable than we may think. On the other hand, social influence has played a major role in the adaptive ability of human beings. By communicating our ideas with others, we are able to share knowledge and advance our thoughts and technologies at a rapid pace. This is akin to Pierre Teilhard de Chardin's notion of a *noosphere* in which human thought becomes the next level of adaptation.[73] Social influence is so important to the human brain that there are specific neurons, pathways, and molecules that subserve social interaction. This social network in the brain plays a substantial role in modifying our thoughts and behaviors.

Finally, any perception, thought, or experience, must be remembered so that it can continue to play a role in our belief systems. This requires memory to be reliable so that we may maintain our belief system over time. Again, though, substantial research points to many flaws with memory processes.[74] Furthermore, emotions, social influences, and how questions regarding past memories are worded, all influence the way in which we remember past experiences and ideas. Many experiments have been conducted in which people remember things that never happened or their memories were modified by a variety of factors. Even memories that seem to the individual to be quite vivid have been demonstrated to be substantially inaccurate, with greater inaccuracies occurring over time.[75]

With the substantial problems in our perceptions, cognitive processes, emotions, social influences, and memories, Principle XXXIX above becomes all the more apparent. It seems, that there is very little that we think, feel, or experience about external reality that we can consider to be valid with any degree of certainty.

---

[72]   Asch, S.E. "Studies of independence and conformity: a minority of one against a unanimous majority." *Psychological Monographs*. 1956:70; Nemeth, C. "Dissent as driving cognition, attitudes and judgments." *Social Cognition*. 1995;13:273-291; Bloom, H. *Global Brain: The Evolution of Mass Mind from the Big Bang to the 21st Century*. New York, NY: John Wiley & Sons, 2000.

[73]   Teilhard de Chardin, P. *The Phenomenon of Man*. Translated by Bernard Wall. New York, NY: Harper Collins, 1975.

[74]   Schacter, D. and Scarry, E. *Memory, Brain, and Belief*. Boston, MA: Harvard University Press, 2000.

[75]   Newberg, A.B. and Waldman, M.R. *Why We Believe What We Believe: Uncovering Our Biological Need for Meaning, Spirituality, and Truth*. New York, NY: Free Press, 2006.

Unless we can find some way to escape these flaws, or, more appropriately, escape the processes of the human brain, we will always hold a fundamental uncertainty in our beliefs about reality.

Of course this may have critical influence on our philosophical and theological ideas about the world. If all the processes that lead up to such ideas have the potential to be substantially flawed, how are we reliably to hold any of these ideas as valid? This has led some to argue that it is ultimately a leap of faith that we believe anything about reality and thus it is not surprising that religious traditions tie into this sense of faith. Of course materialists would argue that there is an absolute reality that we have the capability to access accurately through science, but given the above flaws cited in the brain's functioning, this position must be questioned. After all, science is also perceived and conceived by the brain. But other approaches to knowledge such as religion, mathematics, or philosophy might face a similar conundrum.

Principle XL: If the brain by itself cannot definitively determine truths about the world, then a combination of approaches is necessary to evaluate epistemological and ontological claims.

It would seem that if any particular approach is limited by the human brain, perhaps the only way around this would be to utilize a constellation of approaches. Thus, combining science, theology, philosophy, and mathematics might yield a better, more complete answer regarding the nature of reality than any of those approaches individually.

These two neurotheological uncertainty principles reflect one of the most ancient problems of philosophy, religion, and science: how do we know that the external world corresponds completely, or even partially, to our mental representation of it? This neuroepistemological question is critical to theology as well since we must always ponder whether our conception of God represents a true reality or not. Certainly, the atheists would argue that any belief in God is misguided and does not represent what is real. For the religious individual in general, and theology in particular, the issue of God's existence must be addressed even if it is taken as *a priori*. The question of what is "really real" has been considered, with various answers, since the time of the pre-Socratic Greek philosophers in the West and the early Buddhist traditions in the East. Preoccupation with this question is even older in Eastern religio-philosophical traditions. The three most common criteria given for judging what is real are:[76]

1. the subjective vivid sense of reality;
2. duration through time;
3. agreement intersubjectively as to what is real.

---

[76]   d'Aquili, E.G. and Newberg, A.B. *The Mystical Mind: Probing the Biology of Religious Experience*. Minneapolis, MN: Fortress Press, 1999.

From a neurotheological perspective, all three are associated with specific brain functions and thus, it could be argued that all three of these criteria for determining what is real can be reduced to the first—the vivid sense of reality. For example, the sense of duration through time depends on the structuring of time in baseline reality. It appears that the ability to have a sense of time, or more properly duration, is structured by the brain. Alteration in function of parts of the brain, for any reason, results in a significant distortion of the perception of time in a number of ways. Most dramatically, during mystical states, there is no sense of time or duration while the person is in that state. It becomes obvious, therefore, that time and duration are not absolutes, and derive their perceived qualities from brain functions. Hence, it begs the question: how does one derive the reality of baseline reality from one of the *qualia*? In this case, the *qualia* is time, which is itself perceived by the brain. This same critique applies to any appeal for the reality of objects which depend on characteristics of baseline reality, the perception of which is known to be experienced by the brain. The third criterion for the reality of entities—that is, intersubjective validation—again arises from begging the same question. The "subjects" who agree or disagree about objects being real are themselves only images or representations within the sensori-cognitive field of the analyzing subject-theologian. Thus, it may be unfortunately true that any person analyzing his or her own experience must start out, at least, as a naive solipsist.

Neurotheological analysis suggests that the only way around this problem would be somehow to escape one's own mind. In the usual state of reality, this is a fundamental problem as stated in the principle above. This throws all beliefs into question and not just religious ones. Moral, political, social, health, and all other beliefs that we rely on each day must have at their core a fundamental uncertainty. The need for a "leap of faith" is expressed often in religious texts. However, a neurotheological approach would argue for augmenting or integrating in some manner whatever religious or spiritual beliefs one has with a scientific perspective. It might be argued that science is limited in its knowledge of reality by its perpetual need for an observer who can never fully escape the world as represented in the brain. On the other hand, spiritual and mystical experiences sometimes are described as enabling the individual to escape the self, to get beyond the objective and subjective nature of reality, and to experience ultimate reality. Mystical experiences, near death experiences, and even some drug induced experiences can fall into this category. It is interesting to note that such experiences are also perceived to be "more real" than our everyday experience of baseline reality.

If we are forced to conclude that knowledge of reality is ultimately reducible to the vivid sense of reality, then what are we to make of such states that appear to the experiencing individual as more real than baseline reality, even when they are recalled from within baseline reality? If one takes baseline reality as the point of reference, it seems that there are some states the reality of which appears to be inferior to baseline reality and some states the reality of which appears to be superior to that of baseline reality when these states are recalled in baseline reality. And this is the crucial distinction since these are not experiences that appear real only while one is experiencing them, these are experiences perceived to be more real than baseline reality *when recalled from baseline reality.*

Neurotheology should take the stance that while we may not necessarily know whether such experiences truly take the individual to ultimate reality and enable them to experience it without objective and subjective states of the brain, such experiences must be carefully considered as a mechanism by which the most profound scientific and theological questions can be approached.

Conclusions

There are many ways in which neurotheology might inform various topics in neuroscience. Neurotheology might lead to practical applications such as how religion and spirituality should be approached from the medical or clinical perspective. Neurotheology might also help to develop better cognitive neuroscience methods for evaluating complex human phenomena. Neurotheology might also help move towards a deeper understanding of the functions and processes of the human brain. And finally, some of the philosophical issues that arise out of neuroscience, such as the nature and origin of free will, subjective awareness, and consciousness, might be addressed more effectively from a neurotheological perspective. Thus, neurotheology is likely to have a substantial impact on many topics in neuroscience.

Chapter 9
Reflections on Major Topics of Theology

In this section, several of the major concepts associated with theology will be briefly considered from the neurotheological perspective in order to provide examples of how neurotheology can be more specifically applied. Of course, the details of such an inquiry will undoubtedly require significantly more arduous and rigorous scholarship than possible here. Furthermore, these theological areas of scholarship have not been as extensively investigated as some of the neuroscientific topics considered in the previous chapter. Suffice it here to provide the general approach for addressing a variety of fundamental theological questions from the neurotheological perspective. Most importantly, neurotheology should be considered a viable perspective that can bring fresh ideas to old theological questions.

Principle XLI: Neurotheology, as a field, should address any and all theological questions.

Another essential point is that it should not be assumed that neurotheology is necessarily limited in its ability to address any and all theological questions. This does not mean that it will be able to address all theological issues in the same manner. For some issues, neurotheology may only be able to provide a superficial point whereas with others, neurotheology may be able to contribute substantially. One other important point is that until neurotheology is fully employed in the evaluation of a specific theological question, one should not readily dismiss neurotheology. It may be that only after an exhaustive analysis will a neurotheological approach provide substantive information. On the other hand, it may also be found, after addressing a specific topic, that neurotheology cannot contribute substantively. Either way, this principle argues that neurotheology should at least be given its chance.

The following questions, among many others, often are at the center of much theological inquiry and hence should be considered from the neurotheological perspective:

1. Is there a God, and can the existence of God be proven?
2. What is the nature of God?
3. What is the nature of good and evil and how does this relate to sin, free will, and virtue?
4. What is the nature of spiritual revelation?
5. Is God immanent in the universe?
6. What is the nature of God's relationship to human beings?

7. Is there a soul?
8. What is the process by which salvation can be attained?

Theology attempts to make rational arguments that address these and other issues related to God and God's relationship to the world.[1] How does neurotheology examine each of these issues? We can begin by looking at these issues starting from either the neuroscientific or the theological perspective.

Brain Functions and the Origins of Theology

Before considering these topics directly, let us briefly turn our attention to the origins of theology as they may pertain to the brain. We can either start with theology and consider the brain or start with the brain and consider theology. This involution enables two different kinds of analysis and takes its approach from the hermeneutical approach considered earlier. Specifically, we can consider theological concepts from the perspective of the human brain and we can focus our analysis on experiences in which certain brain processes function in an absolute or total manner. Thus, ideas related to causal thinking, holistic thinking, and emotional responses all can have a different impact on theological development. In fact, neurotheology suggests and supports the notion that the origins of theology might relate to very different brain functions including those that are more experientially driven and those that are more rationally driven.

Principle XLII: From the neurotheological perspective, theology may proceed either from an experiential referent or from the more classical deductive process deriving from a given doctrinal foundation.

These two approaches to the origins of theology are clearly related, but also have fundamental distinctions. These distinctions arise from different physiological processes as well as different theological approaches. If theology arises via a rational deduction from a foundational doctrine rather than from a deep spiritual or mystical experience, neurotheology can offer a great deal about how this rational deduction process arises and how theological concepts, in general, might be derived. For example, if one utilizes a biblical approach by studying the contents of scripture, systematically analyzing them, and arriving at theological concepts through exegesis, we can consider the functions of the brain during each of these steps. For example, how does the brain read and interpret the Bible? We relate to different passages and phrases differently depending, in part, on our biological makeup. Why do some passages seem confusing to us while others send chills up our back? What is happening within us when we have these different experiences?

---

[1]   Migliore, D.L. *Faith Seeking Understanding: An Introduction to Christian Theology.* Grand Rapids, MI: Eerdmans, 2004.

If we study the historical aspects of theology we also utilize our brain to interpret these historical events. We can consider what happened within the brain of those scholars that preceded us? Do we interpret these historical developments differently depending on our own past experiences and memories? Systematic theology, that arranges the materials furnished by biblical and historical theology into a logical order, also requires a variety of higher cognitive and emotional processes to help with this analysis. As one considers philosophical ideas, apologetics and ethics, we can consider how brain processes associated with causality, abstract reasoning, comparative analyses, and language play a role. Does systematic theology develop along certain lines of argument because of the nature of sacred texts, the nature of God, or the nature of the human brain? How does the brain constrain and direct systematic theology and result in specific concepts? Finally, if one explores how theology has an impact on current sociopolitical issues and on personal development, then again, we can conceive of how the brain helps us in these understandings. Perhaps we need to explore how current global and social issues affect the brain. How do our emotions and cognitions respond to current moral issues related to abortion, stem cell research, or racism? How do our emotions and cognitions respond to war, ethnic cleansing, or the environment? Many of these issues have been or can be evaluated by exploring the human brain. For example, several studies have already explored how the brain perceives individuals of different racial groups. This might help to determine how our brain processes different issues related to theological questions.

Theology that arises from human experience is likely associated with very profound types of experiences associated with a sense of ultimate or divine reality. If theology concerns itself with that which is ultimate, it certainly seems appropriate that theology should involve a being, or notion of absolute reality, that is considered to be the ultimate cause of the universe (if derived from the causal functions of the brain) or the ultimate unifying force of the universe (if derived from the holistic functions of the brain). However, it could be argued from a neurotheological perspective that the driving force behind this desire to seek out ultimate things is based in large part on the brain's *striving* to understand the ultimate questions of the universe and partly on personal experiences representing this ultimate level of the universe. Such an experience may or may not actually reflect ultimate reality, but an individual can still have an experience that is perceived to represent ultimate reality.

These experiences may be associated with the total or absolute functioning of various cognitive processes on reality which we described earlier. In this way, it might be possible to consider major theological or philosophical principles from the perspective of various brain processes acting on reality. Several possible neuropsychological mechanisms might be postulated that could have a direct impact on theological conceptualization. It may be possible that the total experience of reality is "filtered" through a particular brain function. There is certainly phenomenological evidence for such experiences in which an individual perceives the entire world as will or as related to an emotion such as love or agape.[2] Physiologically what might be happening is that all sensory and cognitive processes have their neural information processed through specific higher cortical areas of the brain. And there is some evidence that such changes might occur.[3] Whether or not it is possible to physiologically filter all information through one brain process is not known, but it is certainly possible for a significant amount of that information to be filtered through one particular brain process such that the individual has the experience that everything, or almost everything, is treated in that manner.

The filtering of all information regarding reality through one brain process we have referred to as the "total" functioning of that process. In these instances, one particular brain process, and hence one approach to the experience of reality, supersedes all other functions. The person becomes convinced that the entire universe can be related to that particular process. Absolute functioning was referred to as not filtering through a particular brain process, but having that process become the fundamental "stuff" of the universe. For example, using the brain's mathematical processes, total function would use mathematics to evaluate every aspect of the universe, while absolute function would consider mathematics to be the fundamental basis of the universe. It should be mentioned that based upon phenomenological descriptions, it appears that the total and absolute functioning of different brain processes frequently occur together, but this is not necessarily the case. It also must be stressed again, that these functions in no way have a direct impact on the true nature of whatever external reality exists outside of the brain and its processes. What we are considering here is how the brain enables each of us to consider and experience reality. Thus, regardless if causality or time or matter exists in the world, we can consider how the brain perceives the attributes of what we consider to be reality. So for all of the following, we are talking about how the brain perceives the world and not whether it is accurate and not whether the world is actually built in the particular manner that we perceive it.

How such a total or absolute functioning of a cognitive process might occur can be dependent on a number of factors similar to those described for spiritual experiences. An example of how such a sequence of events might occur is the following:

The philosopher or theologian thinks very intensely in a particular way.

Perhaps, he or she is deeply thinking, almost meditating, about how things are caused.

---

2   Tillich, P. *Love, Power, and Justice: Ontological Analyses and Ethical Applications.* Oxford: Oxford University Press, 1954; Outka, G. *Agape: An Ethical Analysis.* New Haven, CT: Yale University Press, 1977; Brümmer, V. *The Model of Love: A Study in Philosophical Theology.* Cambridge: Cambridge University Press, 1993.

3   Bolte Taylor, J. *My Stroke of Insight.* New York, NY: Viking, 2009.

The intensity of this use of the causal process of the brain eventually may produce an absolute functioning of this process.

Suddenly, our thinker experiences a profound sense that all of reality is cause and effect.

This is not yet a theological or philosophical concept. In fact, it is infinitely more powerful than a concept. It is the profound sense that one has had a glimpse into the ultimate and that, in this case, it is causality itself. After this theologian's or philosopher's "flash of insight," he or she develops philosophical or theological concepts, derived from the experience. The philosopher or theologian then goes about constructing a logical system in the firm certainty that he or she has fundamentally comprehended what is "real." Such an experience can theoretically happen with any cognitive, perceptual, or emotional process, generating diverse experiences of ultimate reality, and hence, diverse philosophies and theologies.

The holistic processes of the brain most certainly are associated with the experience of deity with the subsequent conceptualization of God. Furthermore, because unitary states are associated with some of the most profound experiences described, it is incumbent upon neurotheology to explore unitary states and evaluate their epistemological, ontological, and theological claims.

Principle XLIII: Neurotheology should strive to evaluate unitary states to determine their nature and relevance to epistemological and ontological issues.

This brain process is important since it continually forces theology to account for God's omnipresence, omniscience, and ability to bind and maintain the entire universe. Thus, any serious consideration of the implications of the absolute functioning of the holistic processes necessitates, at least, considering the expansion of any foundational doctrine to apply to all of reality, including other people, other cultures, other animals, and even other planets and galaxies. In fact, as human knowledge of the extent of the universe has evolved, the notion of God has evolved to incorporate the expanding sense of the totality of the universe. The holistic processes require that whatever new reaches of the universe astronomers can find, God must be there. No matter how small and unpredictable a subatomic particle might be, God must be there, too.

The developments of science in the twentieth century, therefore, have been particularly difficult for continuing to invoke a holistic notion with regard to the concept of God. This difficulty arises not so much because of the problem in explaining how God might actually maintain a holistic nature, but because human beings are necessarily limited in their cognitive understanding of infinity. We can state that something is absolutely holistic or that it is infinite, but we cannot cognitively comprehend these constructs. The religious literature of all traditions acknowledges that God cannot be described cognitively. Only through mystical experiences, and practices designed to elicit mystical states, is it even considered to be approachable. However, the true mystic will usually maintain that it is impossible to experience this state humanly (especially since in these states, there theoretically is no discrete existence that allows for human experience). Thus, even though such a state may be attained through meditation or related practices, the experience is so ineffable as to defy any real human understanding. For the theologian, this mystical notion of God must be incorporated and maintained within the foundational doctrine if that doctrine is to be considered valid. Any rational deductions derived from this foundational doctrine must be associated with the results of the holistic processes of the brain.

That the holistic process of the brain must be taken into account when evaluating foundational doctrines is never more apparent than in the Christian concept of the Trinity. Christian thought has generated great effort to maintain the notion of the Trinity in the face of the holistic need for God to be an absolute unity. Thus, the three components of the Trinity are traditionally understood to be discrete, but also to possess the same, single, and absolutely undifferentiated divine nature.[4] Attempts at explaining this conundrum have included several approaches which have sometimes resulted in great disagreement. The *filioque*, that the Spirit "proceeds from the Father *and the son*," did not appear in the Creed confessed by the First Council at Constantinople in 381 AD. It is accepted by the Roman Catholic Church, but not the Eastern Orthodox Church. Ultimately, most theological developments typically arrive at some conception of the Trinity as the Father, Son, and Holy Spirit being unified. For example, the Athanasian Creed states: "But the Godhead of the Father, of the Son, and of the Holy Ghost, is all one, the Glory equal, the Majesty co-eternal."[5] Thus, there is always that perfectly undifferentiated divine substantiality which prevents the Trinity from deflating into tritheism. From a brain perspective, this presents substantial problems in terms of how the Trinity and the wholeness of God can be juxtaposed. This requires various brain processes that are apparently divergent from each other—namely holism vs. differentiation—to somehow exist simultaneously. Based upon the theological developments regarding the Trinity, one can observe the struggle of the brain to comprehend the Trinity and God's oneness simultaneously. But sometimes such an internal struggle can be viewed and experienced positively. Such struggles can activate the brain in such ways to invoke powerful emotions related to awe. It is, perhaps, not surprising from a brain perspective, that the "Most Holy Trinity is the central mystery of the Christian faith and of Christian life."[6] This comports with the ways in which the brain handles complex, and seemingly paradoxical, concepts.

There is one other important point to be made regarding the holistic process of the brain and the neurophysiological approach to mystical and theological

---

4   *Catechism of the Catholic Church.* New York, NY: Doubleday, 1997.

5   *Book of Common Prayer.* The Episcopal Church, 1979.

6   *Catechism of the Catholic Church.* New York, NY: Doubleday, 1997. 261.

concepts. It is interesting to note that many religions generally exclude the possibility of other religions being accurate. One may wonder why this should be the case. One might consider the holistic argument that if God is truly infinite, then God should have infinite manifestations. Why then, should any particular version of God be set completely apart and exclusive of any other version? While it may be more evident in terms of religious rituals leading to the development of group cohesiveness that excludes others not in the group, the question remains as to whether religious ideologies should be exclusive at all levels of religious experience. A state of absolute unity, in which all things are one, cannot have exclusivity because of its infinite and undifferentiated nature.

The question then is: can unitary states, other than absolute unitary states, be exclusive? A neuropsychological analysis of this question would suggest that the highest unitary states short of absolute unity can, in fact, be exclusive. In such a state, the person may feel totally absorbed into the given focus of the meditation or prayer (for example, God, Christ), but since there is still some differentiation, rather than a total unity, there might be the sense of everything being one with that particular focus. This is a state of total absorption into one particular spiritual object such as God or Christ, but it is not a state of universal unity. Thus, the entire universe is perceived to be derived from that object to the exclusion of all other things. Anything other than that object either must be a part of that object or must not exist in reality. If something were to exist in reality outside of the object of focus, this would present an irreconcilable paradox. The resolution of that paradox is that the aberrant object is really part of the object of focus even though it does not seem so. Therefore, any notion of Christ, Brahman, God, or Allah which results in a total absorption into that sacred object necessarily excludes all other interpretations.

In this way, unitary states, that are not absolutely unitary, may lead to very strong senses of one particular doctrine representing ultimate reality. This may result in the theological perspective that only one doctrine can be accurate or represent the true reality and true nature of God. In this way, the physiology and the theology present a coherent perspective of a singular religious doctrine being correct and all others incorrect, again, though, regardless of which one actually represented the true reality.

Furthermore, if the person were able to enter into a state of absolute unity, then there could be no exclusivity and all things would be considered to be inclusive. Certainly, the issue of exclusivity is prevalent throughout theologies. All religions must somehow come to terms with the existence of other religions. This neurotheological approach may help show a method by which the problem can be resolved, or at least explained. By considering the nature of the exclusivity, neurotheology may provide some direction as to how different doctrines might be considered to coexist. Further, knowledge of the neurophysiological necessity for exclusivity may help our overall understanding of the conflicted nature of religions. This might also provide information that can result, at the very least, in a deeper understanding of the differences between religions and their respective theologies.

The antithesis of the holistic process is the reductionist process. The absolute functioning of the reductionist processes of the brain on all of reality would likely lead to a primary intuition and existential sense that the whole is comprised of the sum total of the parts. When applied to a monotheistic conception of God, the result might be the notion that God is actually comprised of the totality of all of the parts of the universe. This is akin to the concept of pantheism in which God is considered to be the universe. It seems that the absolute function of the reductionist function would not lead to the notion of a transcendent God.

Certainly, the notion of divine transcendency has garnered its share of the theological literature. However, the absolute working of the reductionist processes necessarily contradicts the notions derived from the holistic processes. In fact, it seems that the absolute functioning of the holistic processes usually takes precedence over the absolute functioning of any other brain process such that all of the parts previously perceived as being discrete are now considered to be one. Thus, in its absolute functioning, the holistic function actually appears to absorb or combine both the reductionist and the holistic processes.

The quantitative processes of the brain help us turn to numbers and quantity in an attempt to organize the world. If quantitative processes are applied to the totality of objects, the result is the notion that mathematics underlies all things. Similar to reductionism, the quantitative perspective clearly both underlies and supports science and the scientific method. Science essentially is based upon a mathematical description of the universe. This is particularly true when one considers the fields of quantum mechanics and cosmology. Both of these fields attempt to discover the fundamental nature of the universe using highly complex mathematical models. Early religions certainly relied heavily on mathematical concepts in their interaction with their gods. Numbers abound in the Bible and other sacred texts and lend their significance in terms of time, people, and places. Various numerologies in the folk practices of Christianity and Islam as well as the gemetriot in Judaism all bear witness to the powerful force of the quantitative processes of the brain.

The binary process of the brain appears to have played a crucial role in the formation of various religious doctrinal and theological topics. The opposites that are set by the binary processes of the brain allow human beings to conceive of good and evil, justice and injustice, and man and God among many more. Many of these polarities are encountered throughout the sacred texts of all religions. Much of the purpose of religions and their theologies is to solve the psychological and existential problems created by these opposites. Theology, then, must evaluate the doctrinal elements and determine where the opposites are and how well the problems presented by these opposites are solved by the doctrinal structure. In particular, this concept, similar to the Hegelian triadic concept of thesis, antithesis, and synthesis, is crucial to the development of theology, because it is ultimately the foundational doctrine, and specifically the power of God, that brings together the problematic opposites.

The causal processes of the brain are crucial to theology, as we have previously considered, but let us elaborate on this process in the specific context of neurotheology. The causal function of the brain tries to find the cause for any given strip of reality. The brain has this critical ability to seek out causality in the world and to try to understand cause and effect. When applied to all of reality, this causal function forces the question of what is the ultimate cause of all things. This eventually leads to the classic notion of an uncaused first cause. For montheistic religions, the foundational doctrine posits that God is the cause of all things (that is, is the uncaused first cause). However, this very question of how something can be uncaused is a most perplexing problem for human thought. In fact, theologians and philosophers alike have tangled with causality as integral to understanding the universe and God. Aristotelian philosophy postulated four aspects of causality— efficient causality, material causality, formal causality, and final causality. These notions of causality led to the understanding of a metaphysic which would later be integrated into traditional Christian theology. The question of causality thus became applied to God to determine how, in fact, God could cause the universe.

We might ponder how human beings would be able to conceive of God if the brain did not have the ability to think causally. To some extent, the issue as to whether God caused the universe would not even be entertained. We would not be able to contemplate if God created the world or how God was able to create the world because we simply could not envision of such a concept. This would not necessarily eliminate the concept of God completely. God would have to be understood by the brain in other ways. God might be conceived of as the ultimate love of the universe. But any sense of causality could not be applied. This would not have an impact on what God actually was and whether God actually had a causal influence on the universe. Human beings would just be limited in their ability to conceive of God from a causal perspective. Similarly, this would obviate theologians from arguing God's existence on the basis of an uncaused first cause. No such argument could exist in the human brain unless it had the ability to think causally in the first place.

Even Eastern traditions would be deeply affected by an absence of a causal process in the brain. True causality for such traditions is typically attributed to ultimate reality, particularly the absolute unitary state. Any notion of the interaction between attachment and suffering or yin and yang would be drastically altered since there is a strong causal element to how these various concepts relate to each other. Thus, the causal process of the brain is critical for our understanding of a wide variety of theological and philosophical ideas.

Two of the most important concepts in religion that relate to causality are the notion of free will and ethics. Free will implies the ability of an individual to freely cause something to happen. Otherwise, we would consider a particular action to be predetermined or caused by forces outside of the individual's causal influence. Taken to the extreme, if we never had any ability to cause things to happen, the universe would be deterministic. This issue, of course, becomes critical for establishing a system of ethics. Ethics requires the ability to cause things to happen, to evaluate the responsible individual, and then determine whether or not that action was morally acceptable or not. Free will is thus the sine qua non of ethics. In order for ethics to be viable, free will has to exist. Thus, the notion of causality in relationship to free will and ethics becomes an important issue within theology.

The abstract thought processes are tied into the brain structures that underlie language and conceptual thought. The abstract processes of the brain create general concepts from a larger group of objects. Thus, oak, pine, willow, and maple are grouped into the abstract category of "tree." In some senses, these processes derive the essential characteristics of whatever types of objects they are working on. In other words, these processes present us with a sense of "thingness" or "being" since they generate the basic components of any object and reify that object as a particular thing. Going back to the example of the different trees, each of them is grouped into the category "tree" by virtue of their characteristics or things that define them as a tree, that is, they all have a trunk, roots, and leaves.

As with the other brain processes, we can consider what would happen if the abstract processes operated in an absolute manner, not just on a particular set of objects, but on the set of all objects in the universe. The basic element derived would be conceptual or abstract "thingness" as opposed to the concrete "thingness" implied by the reductionist perspective. The "conceptual thingness" of the totality of reality is akin to the Greek concept of Being either in the Platonic or Aristotelian sense. It is the formal and organizing element indwelling matter and giving matter meaning. Thus, the total functioning of the abstract processes gives a profound sense that reality is fundamentally pure being, having the same relationship to gross matter as the pure concept "tree" has to the billions of concrete trees in the world. From this profound sense soon arises philosophical/theological concepts such as Plato's "The Good," Aristotle's "Hylemorphism," Aquinas' "Essences," or Tillich's "ground of being" as a description of God. Certainly, the foundational doctrines of Western religions imply that God is not only the creator of all things in the universe, but continues to give substance and existence to all things all the time. Theology must then be forced to explain how God can be the ground substance of all being while performing other roles stipulated in the foundational doctrine. Certainly issues as to whether God constantly supports existence or simply winds up the clock and lets things work out on their own lies at the heart of important theological controversies. However, it seems that the notion of God as the ultimate being and supporting all of existence would be a natural consequence of the absolute operating of the abstractive process of the brain.

The emotional processes of the brain impart emotional values upon whatever is presented within our experience. While emotions may not represent a specific cognitive process, emotions are obviously tied to most of our thinking so that we may be able to assign value to various ideas, concepts, and experiences. If these emotions operate in an absolute manner, it applies its value upon the totality of the universe. The result might be that the entire universe is only related to an emotional response. Thus, all of existence is simply *felt* rather than *cognized*.

If there is a positive emotion operating in an absolute manner, then the result is that the entire universe appears to be an overwhelmingly beautiful, blissful, and loving place. When applied to the concepts of theology, God is the primary driver for this overwhelmingly positive emotion that pervades the universe. This being the case, God is viewed as essentially pure love and benevolence. However, this immediately presents high theological problems since the pain and suffering that exists in the world must somehow be explained in light of the overwhelming love of God. In other words, we are left with the chronic question: if God is ultimate love, then how can God allow all the suffering that occurs? This clearly has been a very difficult question for all theistic religions to address.

If the absolute working of emotions is perceived as neutral, then all is considered to be impersonal. In terms of mystical experiences (as described earlier), this neutral emotion likely is associated with Void Consciousness or nirvana in which there is an empty, impersonal consciousness that lies at the foundation of the universe. From a theological perspective, the conclusions drawn from the neutral interpretation suggest that God is impersonal or perhaps that there is no God at all and everything simply is without purpose or even meaning. This existential approach is antithetical to most theistic religions. However, theology must contend with the possibility of an existential universe.

The final possible interpretation of the absolute working of emotions is a negative one. The result is that the entire universe is viewed as intrinsically evil and horrible. There are very few examples of absolute negative emotions in the mystical literature. The absolute unitary state has rarely, if ever, been associated with a negative effect. Indeed, anecdotal reports have suggested that such a state is impossible to attain while maintaining normal life functions. Interestingly, the near-death experience is one type of experience in which there can be intensely horrifying elements, although these are not frequently unitary in their nature.[7] This suggests that a negative absolute unitary state may actually be incompatible with life. While there is no solid documentation of this bizarre notion, there are occasional rumors and anecdotal reports of mystical sects which try to achieve such a state. Whether they truly exist remains unknown. The negative interpretation applied to theology may be responsible for the notion of Hell in which all of existence becomes horrible and terrifying. In Judeo-Christian theology, though, it becomes difficult to explain how such a negative existence can be maintained alongside the generally positive image of God.

Neurotheology and God's Existence

We can now return to the specific theological topics described at the beginning of this chapter. Let us explore each one in some detail to determine if and how neurotheology might be able to contribute. The first, and perhaps most important question from a theological perspective is the question of God's existence.

---

[7]   Zaleski, C. *Otherworld Journeys: Accounts of Near-Death Experience in Medieval and Modern Times*. New York, NY: Oxford University Press, 1988.

To some extent, *proof* of the existence of God is not completely necessary from a theological perspective since the foundational elements of religion, namely that there is a God, is taken on faith. A number of "arguments" have been offered throughout the history of theological development which include the cosmological argument, that since the world exists and since the world cannot come from nowhere, there must be an original or first cause which is God; the teleological argument, which suggests that there is a purpose and intelligent design in the universe which must arise from God; the moral argument, which states that God is what must have provided human beings with their sense of morality; and the ontological argument, which generally states that that if we could conceive of a Perfect God, "that-than-which-greater-cannot-be-thought," only in the mind, then it would not be "that-than-which-greater-cannot-be-thought," and therefore this Perfect God must exist in reality. This was the argument of St. Anselm of Canterbury in his *Proslogion*.[8]

What is interesting about each of these, and the many other arguments put forth to prove, or at least support the possibility of God's existence, is that they each depend on various functions of the human brain. For example, if our brain did not perceive causality in the world, then we would not conceive of a cosmological argument; if our brain did not have abstract reasoning abilities then we could not conceive of a teleological argument; if our brain did not comprehend moral issues, then we could not conceive of a moral argument; and if we did not have an ability to consider ultimate ideas, then we could not conceive of an ontological argument. Thus, the sense or lack of sense that these arguments make to an individual are highly dependent upon the brain functions that conceive of them and reflect upon them.

Much of the historical struggle between science and religion has surrounded the primary religious tenet—that God exists. This has often been taken as a cosmological question. Did God create the universe or did the universe create itself through a process such as the Big Bang? However, we might take this argument and center it squarely on the nexus of neurotheology. After all, one can more specifically ask the question: did man create God or did God create man? The possibility that man created God is clearly a neurological issue. And the possibility that God created man is clearly a theological issue. Thus, an integrated approach such as neurotheology might be the best opportunity to take this issue to the next level.

How might this happen? Perhaps we can consider the experience of God and evaluate its phenomenological and neurophysiological characteristics. If an individual has a mystical experience of being in deep connection with God and there is no physiological change, would that not suggest a non-material component of the experience? On the other hand, if the experience is perceived as deeply real, does this have any implications for what the true nature of reality actually is?

---

[8]   Davies, B. and Evans, G.R. (eds.). *Anselm of Canterbury: The Major Works*. New York, NY: Oxford University Press, 2008.

If God does exist, then neurotheology continues to provide information about how human beings relate to God, but there is also the possibility that such studies might determine which ways of relating are "better" than others, whether for a group or individual. This is a potentially dangerous proposition since the implication is that various religious groups could utilize such information to proselytize, criticize, oppress, or attack other groups. It would seem unlikely that any neurophysiological study could provide the kind of evidence that would support which beliefs are more accurate, but results from such studies might help individuals determine what works best for them. There is probably too much variability in normal human function to clearly differentiate the effectiveness and accuracy of certain beliefs or practices. Nonetheless, neurotheology has the potential to be thrust into the middle of many different kinds of conflicts and anyone seeking to be a scholar in this field should maintain a very cautious position regarding results and interpretations of such studies.

If human beings created God, they did so with the human brain. One can make a number of arguments as to how and why the brain would construct a concept of God. One might consider the importance of the causal processes of the brain in their attempt to unravel the ultimate cause of the universe.[9] When the initial cause of the universe cannot be adequately determined, the causal processes of the brain would likely posit a First Cause Uncaused as did Aristotle over 2000 years ago. This first cause also must have some type of power to be able to cause the universe and hence the idea of a power source such as God seems reasonable to consider. Another possibility might be that put forth by Thomas Aquinas that it might be reasonable to assume that the universe is eternal, but then it would be eternally caused.

Another approach to the "brain creating God" possibility would rely on the holistic processes of the brain which might lead to the notion of a pure consciousness or an absolute oneness which is attributed to God. In fact, it might be interesting to evaluate whether the non-personal conception of absolute oneness relates more to the Buddhist perspective of nirvana while the personal conception relates more to the Judeo-Christian notion of God. The ability of an individual to arrive at such a conception during a peak mystical experience may help towards understanding a potential origin of the concept of God via the functions of the holistic processes of the brain.

Given the above arguments, neurotheology may play a prominent role in the discussion regarding the existence of God regardless of whether or not God actually exists.

---

[9]   d'Aquili, E.G. "The neurobiological bases of myth and concepts of deity." *Zygon.* 1978;13:257-275.

Principle XLIV: Neurotheology should explore the arguments regarding the existence of God, regardless of whether or not God actually exists.

The nature of the role of neurotheology in this regard needs to be more fully explored. But one important way in which neurotheology might contribute is to help explore the physiology and the phenomenology of different arguments for the existence of God. Thus, neurotheology may help understand how the brain poses such arguments and comes to accept or reject these arguments. Neurotheology must also constantly remind scholars of the limitations imposed on human beings in discerning reality by both scientific and religious approaches. For example, a brain scan that demonstrates changes in certain structures when a nun experiences being in God's presence only describes what is happening in her brain during that experience. The scan itself should not necessarily be construed as proving the existence or non-existence of God in this context. Neurotheology should continue to encourage research of brain function during religious experiences and seek to determine if a study design might be possible that could more specifically address the proof of God question. The methodological challenges of such a study are clearly very substantial, but it is important to stress the need for careful planning and interpretation of results.

The Nature and Attributes of God

It has been argued that the human understanding of God is one of the most important theological and personal issues we can face. A.W. Tozer writes,

> What comes into our minds when we think about God is probably the most important thing about us. The history of mankind will probably show that no people has ever risen above its religion and man's spiritual history will positively demonstrate that no religion has ever been greater than its idea of God. Worship is pure or base as the worshiper entertains high or low thoughts about God.[10]

Given the importance of our ability to reflect on the nature of God, neurotheology would seem an important adjunct to the more traditional theological and religious approaches. This of course treads on sacred ground. Can we ask, like Zophar the Naamathite, "Can you discover the depths of God? Can you discover the limits of the Almighty? They are high as the heavens, what can you do? Deeper than Sheol, what can you know?"[11] Neurotheology might contribute importantly in this regard by helping determine which attributes human beings can understand and which they cannot. Is it not the human brain that enables human beings to perceive the

---

[10]   Tozer, A.W. *Knowledge of the Holy*. San Francisco, CA: Harper & Row, 1961.
[11]   Job 11:7-8. *New American Standard Bible*. La Habra, CA: Lockman Foundation, 1995.

attributes of God and if so, does the brain necessarily restrict what notions of God human beings might develop?

Principle XLV: Neurotheology should play a prominent role in the discussion regarding the human understanding of the nature of God.

Theologically, God's attributes are sometimes divided into those that cannot be shared with human beings (incommunicable), and those that can be shared (communicable attributes).[12] Neurotheology might help to make a clear distinction between what the human brain can and cannot perceive. The question is: how are the brain and its functions related to the human understanding of the attributes of God? Incommunicable attributes of God usually include those related to being: omnipotent, eternal, infinite, omniscient, and omnipresent. Communicable attributes are usually related to those things that human beings can potentially perceive such as: mercy, justice, wrath, and love.

Why should incommunicable attributes be unavailable to human beings? Neurotheology would argue that the limitations the brain places on the human ability to understand the world necessarily limit our understanding of the incommunicable attributes. For example, the brain clearly has limited capabilities for interpreting the world. We are only able to perceive what enters through our senses and thus cannot directly observe much of the universe. We are therefore limited rather than infinite, restricted in our ability to control the universe rather than being omnipotent, and forced to perceive a linear progression of time rather than being eternal. Neurotheology offers an explanation though as to why we can have some notion of the concepts of being omnipotent, eternal, infinite, omniscient, and omnipresent even though we cannot actually understand them. After all, the brain does have some knowledge, some idea of time, and some control over the universe. Thus, the human brain can provide a "taste" of these attributes, or at least abstractly conceptualize them, so that we can name them and have a sense of what they are. But we clearly cannot understand or possess such attributes directly.

Of course, one potentially interesting exception to this comes in the form of mystical states. In mystical states, individuals can more directly experience some of these attributes since the individual actually feels intimately connected with God. In this connection, the individual has greater access to infiniteness, eternalness, and omnipresence. The person actually perceives that they extend beyond their limited body and brain to connect more deeply with God or ultimate reality. This may have crucial consequences with regard to incommunicable attributes. What can be made of such experiences? On one hand, neurotheology might offer a glimpse of the brain mechanisms associated with mystical states and the experience of absolute unity, eternalness, and omnipresence. For example, if the brain areas involved in temporal ordering are quieted, it might be associated with a feeling of

---

[12] Berkhof, L. *Systematic Theology*. New Combined Edition. Grand Rapids, MI: Eerdmans, 1996.

no time—eternalness. But a neurotheological perspective would also be open to the possibility that the person's experience of going beyond the self, beyond the body, and beyond the brain is actual. In such a case, it might make physiological and theological sense that a person can have access to the incommunicable attributes of God, but only in this unusual state of mystical awareness. Of course, much work is still required in order to fully determine whether the incommunicable attributes of God are, in fact, unknowable in all circumstances. It would seem that they are unknowable to the brain in general, but that there may be certain states in which such attributes can be experienced more directly. This is a question that neurotheology may help to address.

In a similar manner, neurotheology may help towards a better understanding of the communicable attributes of God. Concepts such as mercy, justice, wrath, and love are all notions that the brain tends to be able to access more easily. Many of these concepts are directly related to human emotions. Mercy, forgiveness, wrath, and love are all part of the human emotional repertoire. Furthermore, there are a growing number of research studies that have helped to show which brain structures and functions appear to be related to these emotional responses. Thus, combining neuroscience with religious concepts can lead to a better understanding of how emotional responses are associated with religion. And even though human beings are more likely to understand the nature of these feelings, the human brain still imposes limitations in terms of what we feel and how much we feel it. Thus, we can understand the human emotion of love or wrath, but we may be limited in a full understanding of what such feelings may mean for God. Neurotheology can help show how the brain's functions contribute to our understanding the communicable attributes of God.

Neurotheology, Morality, and Neuroethics

The nature of good and evil, particularly in relation to God, has great importance for theology since it helps to establish a sense of morals and also relates to sin, free will, and virtue.[13] Neurotheology may contribute directly to this question by helping explore the nature of ethics from the perspective of theology and link this relationship by appealing to a biological component as well.

Principle XLVI: Neurotheology should explore our understanding of morality and its relationship to religion while appealing to a mutual neurobiological substrate.

Of course, one of the pressing concerns most individuals have is why apparently bad things happen to apparently good people. One might question their faith if

---

[13] Cessario, R. *Introduction to Moral Theology*. Washington, DC: Catholic University of America Press, 2001.

they feel that in spite of doing everything they ought to do, bad things continue to happen to them. The individual might feel that their religious beliefs are not helping and ultimately reject them. In the Bible, of course, the story of Job plays a pivotal place in considering this issue. Theology itself strives to address such questions, but the eventual answer is that this is not always understood by the mind of human beings. Human beings can have a basic moral understanding of how to act in the world, but are limited in their ability to determine what is ultimately right and wrong. Research into the brain has also provided an interesting framework from which to consider the topics of sin and free will. Research suggests that almost any person can be driven to immoral behavior when placed within a certain environment. A well known example is the Stanford prison experiment in which everyday citizens were recruited as subjects and randomly assigned to act as prisoners or guards.[14] After only a few days, the experiment had to be halted since the subjects became increasingly violent towards each other. In other words, the human brain is easily manipulated into doing very bad things. Understanding the nature and ways in which we can be manipulated can have great importance for striving to prevent such corruption within the human person. Brain research has also explored interesting aspects related to free will as studies have attempted to determine exactly when decisions are made regarding choices and behaviors. Such research may eventually point to the mechanism by which we do have free will—or it might prove that we do not.

Research might also explore the nature of the will itself. Where and how do our thoughts and behaviors originate. An interesting neurological question which directly relates to this is to determine whether the brain begins to "think" things before they arise in our consciousness. For example, fascinating research by Rodolfo Llinas demonstrated that a millisecond prior to a person making a conscious decision, there is electrical activity in the brain which likely represents a subconscious generation of the thought.[15] While more extensive studies are required, the implication here is that we may not consciously will things to happen so much as the subconscious mind creates the things that we can do and the brain can then decide to accept or veto the idea. This has critical implications for free will because it might be that free will is not necessarily a function of consciousness. However, there is still room for morality, but it is more a question of an unconscious will with conscious decision making. This does not cause much of a problem for the behavioral component of morality since we still can choose to act out or not act out a particular behavior that the subconscious brain comes up with. It does have important implications for moral thinking. If we do not have the ability to control the unconscious thought processes that well up from inside,

---

14   Zimbardo, P. "A situationist perspective on the psychology of evil." In Miller, A. (ed.), *The Social Psychology of Good and Evil*. New York, NY: Guilford Press, 2004.

15   Llinas, R. "The intrinsic electrophysiological properties of mammalian neurons: insights into central nervous system function." *Science*. 1988;242:1654-1664; d'Aquili, E.G. and Newberg, A.B. "Consciousness and the machine." *Zygon*. 1996;31:235-252.

then we cannot be held directly accountable for immoral thoughts. One might argue that through proper training, even the subconscious mind develops certain patterns of thinking that lead to moral or immoral thinking subconsciously. This has important implications for the importance of immoral thinking in Christian belief since our conscience is necessary to help us find the appropriate path towards moral behavior. Thus, immoral thought is considered a potential problem since it can lead to immoral action. Thus, neurotheological research might help us to better understand the nature of our free will, how and when it is applied, and how much control we actually have over our thoughts and actions.

Neurotheology may also help us to address specific virtues of human behavior and thought. According to the *Catechism of the Catholic Church*, "The goal of a virtuous life is to become like God."[16] Christianity specifies three theological virtues: faith, hope, and charity. Would it not be fascinating to better understand how individuals pursue and consider these virtues. There is evidence that optimism or a faith in God can potentially be beneficial from the perspective of health and well being.[17] It would seem reasonable that there are underlying neurobiological substrates that engage when people focus on their faith or on being charitable. Could such research even help guide people to enhance their virtues? Would this be acceptable from a theological perspective? Again, neurotheology can help address such questions.

Spiritual Revelation

Spiritual revelation in the context of neurotheology is akin to the ability of the human brain to receive God and be changed by that revelation. The concept of revelation thus raises the issue of how do human beings come to have any understanding that God exists, that God wants us to do certain things, or that the path towards God leads one to salvation? In the Psalms, it states, "the heavens declare the glory of God; and the firmament sheweth his handywork,"[18] suggesting that we can find revelation in nature. But how do we experience and sense the world around us? Several scholars have stressed that revelation occurs all the time by various mechanisms: "A comprehensive doctrine of revelation, then, cannot limit itself to God's self-disclosure in biblical times; it must deal with God's active presence to the church and the world today ...."[19]

Catechism of the Catholic Church. New York, NY: Doubleday, 1997. 1803.

Matthews, D.A., McCullough, M.E., Larson, D.B., Koenig, H.G., Swyers, J.P., and Milano, M.G. "Religious commitment and health status: a review of the research and implications for family medicine." *Arch Fam Med.* 1998;7:118-124; Koenig, H.G. (ed.). *Handbook of Religion and Mental Health*. San Diego, CA: Academic Press, 1998.

Psalm 19:1. *King James Bible*.

Fiorenza, F.S. and Galvin, J. (eds.). *Systematic Theology: Roman Catholic Perspectives*, Vol. 1. Minneapolis, MN: Augsburg Fortress Press, 1991.

Of course, revelation is more religiously, rather than neurologically, oriented. However, there is much that can be considered from a neurotheological perspective.

Principle XLVII: Neurotheology should explore our understanding of revelation and provide an understanding of the human capability of receiving revelation.

For example, how are human beings limited in what can be revealed? If human beings can only have access to communicable aspects of God, then there are specific limitations that are placed on the ability to perceive and understand God. Perhaps God can only be revealed in certain ways, this is, through our senses, emotions, and cognitions. But if that is the case, then there theoretically should be a limited number of neurological avenues by which the human brain can experience revelation. It is likely the case that revelation is different for each individual. Monika Hellwig states, "What God reveals is received or seen according to our present capacity. That capacity is shaped by our individual human maturity, by the maturity of our society and its culture and language, and also by our access to testimonies of God's self-revelation."[20] The important point here is that revelation should be considered an individual experience. Another scholar states quite clearly, "The medium of revelation, therefore, is human experience. The revelation of God to man [sic] takes place in human experience."[21] How individual differences manifest in terms of the content and experience of revelation could have important implications for how to address revelation theologically. Determining the similarities and differences of revelatory experience may provide fertile ground for a deeper understanding of revelation.

Once revelation has occurred, the individual must then determine how to respond to that revelation. According to the Catholic Church, the appropriate response to revelation is faith in which "man completely submits his intellect and his will to God."[22] But how does this happen? One can consider a theological mechanism, but there must also be a biological one. If the intellect arises from the many functions of the brain, then surrendering them should entail a manner by which these functions are "shut off" or at least "reconfigured." There is evidence in several studies which show how the brain can shut down certain functions, particularly in a religious or spiritual context. Would such information be useful in providing a better means by which to respond to revelation? Furthermore, if revelation is truly an interactive process as some scholars suggest—"Within experience there is always a reciprocal flow between the subject and reality which

---

[20]   Hellwig, M.K. *Understanding Catholicism*. 2nd Edition. Mahwah, NJ: Paulist Press, 2002.

[21]   Lane, D. "The nature of revelation." *Clergy Rev.* 1981;66:93.

[22]   *Catechism of the Catholic Church*. New York, NY: Doubleday, 1997. 143.

creates a new relationship, participation, awareness and understanding in the life of the individual"[23]—then neurotheology may help in delineating how this happens.

Along similar lines, the ability of a human being to be saved is another important theological issue upon which neurotheology might provide an interesting perspective. One such perspective might be the following: salvation should pertain to both the spiritual and material nature of who we are. It might be argued that salvation involves the brain, at least to some degree, to help the individual understand what salvation requires and what thoughts, beliefs, and behaviors are associated with salvation. While salvation refers specifically to the soul, a neurotheological interpretation could be commensurate with psychiatry and neurology which continually seek out ways of improving mental life. However, a deeper understanding of the brain's ability to change and to seek religious and spiritual goals might prove highly useful in understanding the concept of salvation.

It should also be clearly stated that whatever limitations the human brain places on our ability to conceive or receive God, this has no impact on whatever is the true nature of God, or reality for that matter. If the human brain could not perceive causality in the world, then God could not be understood as the First Cause Uncaused. The inability to understand God as the first cause has no bearing on whether or not God actually is the first cause. Furthermore, one has to be very careful interpreting neurotheology as being able to comment on whether or not God does exist and whether the brain creates God or God creates the brain as mentioned above. This is an extremely complex question that often is approached with substantial biases from both believers and non-believers. The perspective that is most appropriate from a neurotheological perspective is to carefully evaluate all ways of understanding God, including an absence of God, in order to best determine what the brain can know about reality.

However, the very notion that theology pertains more to the human understanding of God is commensurate with the goals of neurotheology. Neurotheology necessarily must explore how the brain can think, feel, and perceive the concept (or the actual reality) of God. More specific theological analysis can be developed depending on the focus of a particular course of scholarship. In this regard, a historical discussion of theology from the early Christian Church, to Augustine, to Aquinas, to the Reformation, can all be elaborated upon. What is important in terms of neurotheology is to observe how the various developments in theology pertain to human perceptions, feelings, cognitions, and behaviors. Any time the focus turns to one of these aspects of theology, a neuropsychological perspective can be added that deepens the understanding of these concepts.

---

[23]   Lane, D. *The Experience of God*. New York, NY: Paulist Press, 1981.

God's Immanence

God's immanence in the world may also be an appropriate question for neurotheology in the context of how God might be immanent within the human brain. After all, the ability of God to be immanent within the human brain would seem to be crucial for understanding the relationship between God and human beings. This would be an important theological point. Given God's existence, the human brain must have some way of comprehending the nature of God, the existence of God, and how human beings are to think and behave toward God. God must be immanent in the human brain to help enable such experiences and concepts.

Principle XLVIII: Neurotheology should address how God has immanence within human beings via the effects on the brain.

There is also the further question of how much do the brain's functions for each individual contribute to, or restrict, their understanding of God and the decisions and beliefs they make regarding God and religion? Neurotheological research can ponder how the brain in general, and the brain of each individual might approach such issues based upon the genetic make-up, the overall brain function, and the environmental influences on that individual's brain function.

God's Relationship to Human Beings via the Brain

Another fundamental problem in theology is how God can have a relationship with human beings and *vice versa*. After all, how can a being that is infinite, eternal, omniscient, and all-powerful, have any kind of interaction with a being that is finite, mortal, limited in knowledge, and limited in power? From the neurotheological perspective, part of the answer to this question is that whatever the interaction, it must have something to with the human brain. One might argue that if it is the brain that reads the sacred text, hears the sacred stories, and utters the sacred prayers, then it is the brain that helps human beings interact with God.

But religious and theological texts have often remarked on the essential connection between God and human beings via the body, exploring both this interaction and the limits of this interaction. For example, we read in Luke 12:7, "Even the very hairs of your head are all numbered."[24] This implies that everything about us is known to God and that, therefore, God can communicate and interact with us through the various physical parts of ourselves. The Sufi mystic, Ibn al-'Arabi stated, "God deposited within man knowledge of all things, then prevented him from perceiving what He had deposited within him ... This is one of the

---

[24] Luke 12:7. *King James Bible*.

divine mysteries which reason denies and considers totally impossible."[25] Thus, it is interesting how human beings are given certain knowledge, but then cannot access it. Neurotheology might be able to add some important commentary in this regard since we can consider how the brain comes to know certain things and not others.

Religions also teach us how to act or behave in order to reach towards God. In the monotheistic traditions, the approach human beings must take frequently takes the form of a covenant. Judaism, Christianity, and Islam each have their respective approaches toward the covenant between God and human beings. More importantly, these approaches each rely on behaviors and thoughts that can be found to have brain correlates as well. In the Qur'an, the covenant is kept by:

1. remembering one's obligations towards others;
2. abstaining from yielding to the desires of the lower self; and
3. maintaining a constant remembrance of the Divine and seeking to reflect His attributes.

Each of these three requirements also relate to the brain—remembering, avoiding basic physiological desires, and reflecting on God. Can neurotheology explore how these processes occur and how they might relate to an individual's attempts at connecting or relating to God?

In the Christian tradition, much is made about the relationship between God and human beings. There is a great deal of discussion in the classic theological works of Aquinas, Luther, and many others regarding the manner in which human beings interact with God. Perhaps it is through faith, perhaps through good acts or charity. But it must be emphasized that if the human brain was not capable of having faith or being charitable, then we would not be able to interact with God in those specified ways.

The Eucharist is another important example of the way in which mankind is to interact with God. We must be capable of understanding the meaning of the Eucharist, not just as a metaphor, but what exactly it means to take part of the blood and body of Christ and the importance of Christ dying for our sins and our salvation. Without the memory and the emotional and cognitive elements that an individual brings to the Eucharist celebration, it cannot be understood. And if it cannot be understood, then it has no religious or theological meaning to that individual.

In Judaism as well, we see not only the various aspects of the covenant with God, but interestingly, the mystical Kabbalah teachings suggest a complex path towards God. For example, Bahya ben Joseph Ibn Paquda, an eleventh-century Kabbalist, described 10 gates or levels in the spiritual life of a human being. These gates include realizing God's oneness, worship, trust, acceptance, humility, repentance,

---

[25] *Al-Futûhât al-makkîyya*, II, 684.4, quoted in Chittick, W. *The Sufi Path of Knowledge*. Albany, NY: State University Press of New York, 1989.

and abstinence from bodily desires and pleasures.[26] Again, neurotheology might examine each of these concepts in order to understand how they affect the person, psychologically and spiritually. One can also consider whether these gates would be different if the brain was structured or functioned in a totally different way.

Each of these brief examples shows how neurotheology may begin to explore the relationship between human beings and God. Neurotheology can provide insight into the various components of that interaction, understand them on an individual and societal level, and perhaps help guide an individual toward various spiritual goals.

The Brain and the Soul

We considered the soul earlier, but here it might be helpful to review some of the basic approaches to the human soul from various philosophical or theological perspectives. Plato, drawing on the words of his teacher Socrates, considered the soul as the essence of a person. This essence was an incorporeal and eternal component of our being. For Plato, as with the Hindu and Buddhist traditions, as an individual dies, the soul is continually reborn in subsequent bodies. This, in itself, might have some fascinating neurotheological implications, especially in light of the possibility that the non-material part of the self can transcend death. The Platonic soul comprises three parts:

1. the logos (mind or reason)
2. the thymos (emotion or spiritedness)
3. the eros (appetite or desire)

In this model, logos refers to our rational being, which from the brain perspective would be related to the higher parts of the cortex. The thymos comprises our emotional responses and would be related to the functioning of the limbic system. The eros equates to the appetite and desires that drives humankind to seek out its basic bodily needs via structures such as the hypothalamus and autonomic nervous system. These three components are nicely related to the model of the triune brain which more or less comprises these three functional domains.

Aristotle similarly defined the soul as the essence of a living being. But for Aristotle, the soul was not as separable. In fact, Aristotle, in *De Anima*, refers to the soul as the activity of a particular thing. Thus, if an eye had a soul, it would be sight. But how does the brain play into this conception of the soul? If the brain can help us to think, perceive, and have emotions, do these components help establish the nature of the soul? Perhaps the soul is the sum of these different cognitive and emotional aspects of the human being. However, there is still the issue as to

---

[26] Epstein, P. *Kabbalah: The Way of the Jewish Mystic*. Boston, MA: Shambhala Publications, 1978.

whether there is something non-material that also comprises the soul. If this were the case, neurotheology would at least argue that it must interact with the brain and body in some way that might be measureable. Another view of this dual nature of the soul and body can be stated in the question whether a person *has* a soul or a person *is* a soul?[27]

Avicenna, in his "The Ten Intellects," considered the human soul as the tenth and final intellect. It is interesting that the soul would be considered an intellect, especially in light of the relationship between the brain and the intellect. The notion of the soul as an intellect also raises interesting possibilities in terms of the place or origin of the soul. Is it that the soul is related to a particular organ such as the brain or the heart or rather is it related to the entire person? Regardless of the perspective, any notion that the soul is integrated with the body also can be considered in relation to the more recent understanding of the interrelationship between the mind, brain, body, and consciousness. Neurotheology would strive to understand the various possibilities of how the soul relates to the brain in particular, and the body in general.

In his *Summa Theologica*, St. Thomas Aquinas clearly set the soul as separate from the body arguing that since the intellectual soul is capable of knowing all material things, in order to know a material thing there must be no material thing within it. Thus, he argued that the soul was definitely not corporeal and had an operation separate from the body. For this reason, the soul could also subsist without the body. It therefore could not be destroyed by any natural process. Finally, he understood the soul to be the first principle, or act, of the body. With this conception of the soul, we continue to observe the importance of trying to maintain an immaterial soul that has some ability to connect with the body and the material world.

Let us explore several other perspectives on the soul. In the *Catechism of the Catholic Church*, the soul is defined as the "the innermost aspect of humans, that which is of greatest value in them, that by which they are most especially in God's image: 'soul' signifies the *spiritual principle* in humans."[28] But the soul and the body are intimately connected with the soul considered to be the "form" of the body and that which gives life to the body. According to Jainism, the soul exists as a reality, having a separate existence from the body that houses it. One notion that sets Jainism apart is that every living being from a bacterium to a human has a soul. For the Jain, as for the Christian, the soul also can survive without the body and thus is neither created nor destroyed.

A more recent reworking of the soul by several scholars has considered the notion of "non-reductive physicalism." In this conception of the soul, "the person is a physical organism whose complex functioning, both in society and in relation to God, gives rise to 'higher' human capacities such as morality and

---

[27]   Brown, W.S., Murphy, N., and Malony, H.N. *Whatever Happened to the Soul*. Minneapolis, MN: Augsburg Fortress Press, 1998.

[28]   *Catechism of the Catholic Church*. New York, NY: Doubleday, 1997. 363.

spirituality."[29] The higher human capacities that emerge from the brain and body include language, abstract thought, empathy, future orientation, memory, and modulation of behavior. The non-reductive physicalism argument states that these processes cannot be reduced purely to biological constructs. In this way the soul is something more than just the biological, but it does not go so far as to state that there is a separate thing, material or non-material, called a soul. This notion of the soul may be quite compatible with neuroscience since we can potentially explore each of these domains of human capacities. However, neurotheology would also need to explore whether such a conception of the soul is compatible with religious and theological traditions as well.

From the brain perspective, these various notions of the soul demonstrate interesting complications by revealing the causal conflict of an immaterial thing somehow affecting or interacting with a material thing. The brain and mind struggle with such a conception. Neurotheology might help to address the complexities of understanding the soul and its relationship to the body in the first place, and how that relationship might actually occur in the second place. Thus, neurotheology may be highly useful in helping to evaluate further the nature of the soul.

Neurotheology and Salvation

Salvation is essential for human beings to understand, from the religious and theological perspective. After all, without salvation, the basis of religion is relatively devoid of meaning. But how can neurotheology contribute to the question of salvation?

Principle XLIX: Neurotheology should strive to understand the meaning of salvation by asking, from both the biological and theological perspectives, how the human person can be saved.

In this way, neurotheology can potentially be an important contributor to questions regarding the nature and mechanism of salvation. This of course does not diminish the religious and theological perspective of salvation, but again, adds a new dimension to the understanding of salvation. For example, author Ernest Valea suggested three aspects that are important to consider in assessing the meaning of salvation in a particular religion:[30]

---

[29]   Brown, W.S., Murphy, N., and Malony, H.N. *Whatever Happened to the Soul.* Minneapolis, MN: Augsburg Fortress Press, 1998.

[30]   Valea, E. "Salvation and eternal life in world religions." *Comp Religion.* June 13, 2009.

1. the resources needed for attaining salvation
2. the actual way of getting saved
3. the meaning of being saved

These aspects are quite similar to scientific approaches to a variety of mechanistic questions. After all, science recognizes the need to understand the resources, methods, and meaning of various biological and physical processes. In this way, neurotheology may provide a framework by which questions regarding salvation can be approached.

Each religion approaches salvation from different perspectives in large part based on their foundational doctrine. However, if the three components of salvation described above are universals, then neurotheology might contribute by helping understand how the brain perceives these components. For example, the Churches of Christ generally teach that the process of salvation involves the following steps:

1. one must be properly taught, and hear (Romans 10:17; Matthew 7:24);
2. one must believe or have faith (Hebrews 11:6; Mark 16:15-16);
3. one must repent, which means turning from one's former lifestyle and choosing God's ways (Acts 2:38, 17:30; Luke 13:3);
4. one must confess belief that Jesus is the son of God (Matthew 10:32-33; Acts 8:36-37);
5. one must be baptized for the remission of sins (Acts 2:38; I Peter 3:20-21; Romans 6:3-5; Mark 16:16; Acts 22:16);
6. one must remain faithful unto death (Revelations 2:10).

But each of these steps requires the brain to help comprehend and perform them. To be properly taught and to hear requires the brain to hear and comprehend the meaning of the sacred text or doctrine. To repent implies the ability to recognize one's sins and to recognize the way to move away from those sins. And belief and faith also require the brain to hold close the objects of belief and faith. Neurotheology would ask how each of these processes occur within the human brain and strive to understand how these processes relate to the theological and doctrinal basis of the religion. For example, the *Catechism of the Catholic Church* specifies that "salvation comes from God alone."[31] But it also states that we receive this salvation and must have faith in God and Jesus in order to obtain salvation. Again, we must have an abstract notion of what salvation is, why it is important, and how we are to obtain it.

Other perspectives on salvation also speak to the importance of how the human mind and brain help us to obtain salvation. For example, St. Athanasius of Alexandria wrote, "God became man so that man might become god."[32] This is not

---

[31]　*Catechism of the Catholic Church.* New York, NY: Doubleday, 1997. 169.

[32]　*Catechism of the Catholic Church.* New York, NY: Doubleday, 1997. 460.

to say that human beings literally become God, but that we can strive towards being "god-like" via the process of theosis or divinization. In this way, human thoughts, actions, and the entire self help the individual to obtain salvation. While this might be specified theologically, it remains to be seen what are the limitations that the brain places on such a process. In Eastern traditions such as Buddhism or Sikhism, salvation appears to come from ending the cycle of suffering, death, and rebirth by attaining liberation and enlightenment. This occurs through intense contemplation and meditation and by moving one's life towards a detachment from the body and physical world. Neurotheology can be of great help in understanding these different approaches toward salvation and determine which methods appear to be most conducive from an integrated physiological and theological perspective.

Conclusion

There are many ways in which neurotheology might inform various topics in theology. Neurotheology might lead to both theoretical and practical applications of theological principles and questions. Neurotheology might help us to better understand how human beings approach theological questions and attempt to resolve them. Neurotheology might also help towards a deeper understanding of the functions and processes of the human brain as they relate to spiritual and theological problems. And finally, some of the theological issues such as the nature of the soul, the nature of God, and the methods of salvation, might be addressed more effectively from an integrated neurotheological perspective.

Chapter 10
Epistemological Issues in Neurotheology

Historical Background

A fundamental problem with the use of neuroscience is what exactly it can claim about reality. Scholars from a materialist perspective might state that as neuroscience progresses, there could be enough information to understand everything that is needed in order to describe consciousness and the human perception of the external world. The implication is that by relating neurophysiological activity to various sensory and cognitive processes, a clear understanding of such processes will be developed and that consciousness and the elements within consciousness will be explained. However, the uncertainty principle described earlier prevents any absolute or ultimate understanding about the universe, at least from a scientific perspective. Is it possible that a neurotheological approach, particularly one that focuses on intense mystical states, might offer a way around the uncertainty principle?

Can neurotheology help us address the fundamental epistemological question: how can we know what is really real? Since epistemology itself is the study of the nature and scope of knowledge, it seems that the above question represents the ultimate issue that epistemology must address. While exploring such a question might be unlikely to result in any definite conclusions, if combined with an integrated scientific and experiential approach suggested by neurotheology, could it be possible to find an answer? We can see that there may be an inherent impossibility of establishing knowledge because of the neurotheological uncertainty principle. As this principle states that we can never know for certain whether the thoughts we harbor within the brain are commensurate with the actuality that exists in the external world, unless we can somehow escape the brain's functioning to look at both internal and external realities from a detached vantage point.

However, neurotheology might offer a way around this paradoxical problem by exploiting the importance of the internal experiential reality as revealed by contemplation or spiritual experience, and that of empirical reality as revealed by science. The reason this integrated perspective might be useful is that the uncertainty principle applies only as long as an observer is measuring, studying, or evaluating the external world. To understand the external world requires the brain to process information which necessarily obstructs any absolute understanding. The only possible way around the uncertainty principle would require an individual observer to eliminate all barriers between themselves and the external world. While difficult to comprehend, they would have to *become* the external world while, and at the same time, still being the observer. In other words, they would have to be simultaneously the observer and the observed. Although this sounds impossible in many respects, this is exactly the kind of experience that has been related during certain mystical states. The brain or self becomes one with the rest of the world. The brain or mind no longer intercedes and the individual experiences and fully understands the world both as the world itself and as the experiencer of that world.

To quote the famous physicist, Erwin Schrödinger:

> Inconceivable as it seems to ordinary reason, you—and all other conscious beings as such—are all in all. Hence, this life of yours you are living is not merely a piece of the entire existence, but is in a certain sense the whole ... Thus, you can throw yourself flat on the ground, stretched out upon Mother Earth with a certain conviction you are one with her and she with you. You are as firmly established, as invulnerable as she, indeed a thousand times firmer and more invulnerable.[1]

And Albert Einstein wrote:

> It is very difficult to explain this feeling to anyone who is entirely without it, especially as there is no anthropomorphic conception of God corresponding to it. The individual feels the nothingness of human desires and aims and the sublimity and marvelous order which reveal themselves both in Nature and in the world of thought. He looks upon individual existence as a sort of prison and wants to experience the universe as a single significant whole.[2]

Thus, it is conceded that such an experience in and of itself may be impossible, but if it is achievable as many mystics attest, then it might provide the mechanism by which we can address the fundamental epistemological question regarding the nature of reality and what can be known about that reality. For neurotheology to achieve its ultimate goal then, the neurotheologian must experiment within themselves to strive toward such experiences.

Principle L: The neurotheologian must pursue self exploration, as well as experiments of the outside world, in an attempt to understand completely the nature of experiences that might yield epistemological truths.

In addition to studying and evaluating the biology of these experiences, this might be the approach most likely to succeed where others have failed. But how can neurotheological investigations help toward these epistemological realizations?

---

[1]   Quoted in: Schrödinger, E. *My View of the World*. London: Cambridge University Press, 1964.

[2]   Quoted in: Hoffman, E. *The Way of the Splendor*. Boulder, CO: Shambhala Publications, 1981.

Neurotheology provides a different view from the purely materialistic perspective since it necessarily must at least consider the possibility of a spiritual or non-material element to consciousness and hence to an explanation of external reality. Thus, a neurotheological approach seeks to explore the neurocognitive components of the human experience of reality within the context of both science and spirituality. In order to accomplish this, neurotheology must necessarily include an analysis of the "everyday" experience of reality as well as the spiritual or mystical experience of reality. Both types of experiences are crucial since both provide different perspectives on the true nature of reality. This requires that the ability to "know" what reality actually is depends on certain neurocognitive and spiritual states.

Primary Epistemic States

When evaluating how we come to know the external world, we must begin with how we come to know anything. A neurotheological approach would acknowledge that the only way in which human beings come to know what is real is through the various senses and the brain's processing of that sensory input. The brain takes all of the sensory input, utilizes its cognitive and emotional resources, and puts together a "rendition" of the world with which an individual can interact. Outward actions or behaviors then have consequences in the world that are perceived in addition to whatever was already out there in the external world. The external world is what is objectively real regardless of human perceptions and cognitions. It would seem almost impossible to completely get at what is ultimately, objectively real because any information or sense that is received of this objective reality necessarily must come through the human brain.

But we must now ask another question: why does something feel real to us? In other words, when we perceive a table or listen to someone talk to us, we have the strong tendency to perceive these things as real. Is the sense that something is real based upon perceptions only, consistency of time, emotions, logic? Again, though, however we come to perceive something as real has no bearing on what is actually, absolutely real, but rather relates to our experience of whatever is real. This issue will be addressed later in this chapter since it is the neurotheological approach that would strive to link the perception of what is real to what is actually real. For now, though, let us explore how the brain does experience reality and more specifically, how it informs us what it thinks is real. At this point then, we are forced to explore only the sense of reality that is created for us by the brain. We have nothing more to go on, at least yet.

We may find ourselves contemplating the notion that what we use to assess if something is real ultimately comes down to our profound sense that it is real. This is certainly not a very satisfying conclusion. But what else can we use to assess how real something is? It seems that any criteria we might use is still reducible to our sense that it is real. Whether we cite criteria such as vividness, persistence, cross reference, logic, or any other criteria, they all seem to collapse into the sense of realness. After all, each criteria represents some aspect or *qualia* of reality that we also must sense. Thus, vividness refers to a clarity of perception. But a perception is also sensed as being real. If we perceive persistence over time, that too is a quality that requires our sense that the persistence itself is real. And if we ask for cross referencing with other individuals, their responses are sensed as being real. How do we know which of these senses of reality are actually real? We have no way of knowing other than by trying to assess the strength of the sense that something is real. Again, though, this is not necessarily comforting since it does not tell us what reality is actually like.

A substantial additional concern is that this perspective results in relativism or solipsism. After all, if everything in reality is merely a perception, then there might be no absolute. However, it must always be remembered that perceptions of reality and reality itself are not necessarily commensurate. Relativism might apply to human perceptions, but it does not necessarily apply to actual reality. Similarly, solipsism would suggest that the self is the only reality and the self is the only thing that can be known. While these notions might be true, they too are perceptions of reality and thus, even a solipsistic stance must be regarded as a perception of the brain in much the same way as any other experience of reality.

Let us now return to the statement regarding our sense of reality which leads to the next neurotheological principle:

Principle LI: From the neurotheological perspective, what constitutes something being real is the very strong experiential sense that it is real, but this does not definitively imply that it is, in fact, real.

As mentioned, although problematic, this principle should not be lightly considered since neurophysiologically, human beings may have nothing better to go on to help determine what is real. We are trapped within our brain peering out into the world and reconstructing it the best we can. We inherently experience a "second-hand" rendition of the world.

Can there be some way around this paradoxical problem in which there is a fundamental disconnect between our perceptions of reality and actual reality? Neurotheology would suggest that we begin by exploring our perceptions of reality since we have no choice but to begin here.

In the reality that we perceive on a daily basis, what might be called "everyday" or "baseline" reality, there is a very strong sense that what is perceived is, in fact, real. One might call this sense of reality a *primary epistemic state* of the brain.[3] It should be mentioned that such a state is to some extent a brain state and to some extent a mental state. It is the brain that enables that experiential state that

---

[3]   d'Aquili, E.G. "Senses of reality in science and religion." *Zygon.* 1982;17:361-384; d'Aquili, E.G. and Newberg, A.B. *The Mystical Mind: Probing the Biology of Religious Experience.* Minneapolis, MN: Fortress Press, 1999.

subsequently enables an individual to perceive that experience as real. The primary epistemic state of baseline reality, however, is only one way in which the brain can perceive reality. Thus, there may be a number of epistemic states. Further, these states might be considered "primary" because they are not derived from sense perception *per se*, but rather define the form and understanding of that perception. Theoretically, they also would not be reducible into each other.

Why are primary epistemic states important to theology and neurotheology? From the theological perspective, an understanding of such states will be crucial for helping develop a nomenclature for various religious and spiritual states, particularly mystical ones.

Principle LII: *Understanding primary epistemic states may help determine the realness of religious and spiritual experiences.*

It is in these spiritual or mystical states that individuals often recount the realness of the experience, and the divine or absolute nature of the experience. For many, such an experience lies at the heart of their religious or spiritual expression. Furthermore, an epistemological analysis of different epistemic states might be crucial for determining which view—scientific, religious, or otherwise—has the best perspective on the true nature of reality. But it must be kept in mind that distinguishing our perception of reality from reality itself is a difficult task. But we will consider this later.

What makes any primary epistemic state define reality for a particular person is the individual's sense, when they are in one of these states, that what they are experiencing is fundamentally or ultimately real. This is a crucial aspect since it would seem essential that when one is in a primary epistemic state, it is perceived as if that state represents what is actually real. Once the person leaves a state and settles into a second one, they typically perceive the original state to no longer represent actual reality. In this case, any other perception of reality is considered to be an illusion or deception. Other than baseline reality, the other epistemic state that most people are familiar with is dreams. During a dream, everything that is experienced is usually treated as real even when things do not follow logical ordering or do not appear vivid. The point here is that a dream is perceived to be real during the dream, and then recognized as "just a dream" upon awakening. Once back in baseline reality, there is the perception that the dream state, or any other for that matter, does not represent actual reality. Each of these states is associated with phenomenological elements as well as biological ones, which leads us to the next principle.

Principle LIII: *Primary epistemic states must include both a phenomenological and a biological component.*

In order to determine what is really real and the characteristics of these primary epistemic states, neurotheology can attempt to derive the nature of these states based upon both human experience and the functioning of the brain. A neurotheological approach should typically include several important elements with regard to primary epistemic states. These elements are determined primarily by how human beings sense and make sense of reality. This requires sensory elements, cognitive elements, and emotional elements. In fact, it might be helpful to break down the primary epistemic state into three parameters:

1. perceptions of objects or beings which can be manifested as either multiple discrete things (that is, more than one), or as a holistic union of all things (a unitary reality in which everything is one);
2. relationships between objects or things that are either *regular* or *irregular*; and
3. emotional responses to the objects or things that are either positive, negative, or neutral.[4]

Each of these parameters is well known to our own perceptions of the world. Human beings appear to perceive the world only as consisting of either multiple discrete objects or as a unity. We are born with the neurological capability to observe, name, and manipulate multiple objects as discrete things. The abstract and reductionist processes of the brain help in that regard. Language too is essential in labeling objects and categorizing them. Thus, we distinguish between a spruce tree, a mountain, and a dog. We have extensive nomenclature for naming flora and fauna, atoms and molecules, and ethical and religious frameworks. The areas of the brain involved in categorization and naming have been studied in the field of cognitive neuroscience and lend support to the importance of these structures and their associated functions in establishing our perceptions of reality.

If there is the perception that there are absolutely no discrete objects, the person experiences absolute unity. There may be a variety of states with an increasing sense of unification of things, but philosophically speaking, it would seem that there could only be one state in which there is a complete and absolute unity of all things. This experience includes the sense that the individual is part of the unity such that there is no self and no other. Otherwise, there would be discrete objects, namely the self and the other. There has been some evidence from brain imaging that parts of the brain that typically integrate sensory information into a sense of self and an orientation of that self with respect to the world might be affected during spiritual practices that lead to unitary states. However, it may be impossible to measure scientifically the changes associated with absolute unity primarily because of the uncertainty principle elaborated earlier. Since it is impossible for an individual to report that they are having an experience of absolute unity, it is likely that it will never be known what pattern of brain activity is associated with this experience.

---

4   d'Aquili, E.G. "Senses of reality in science and religion." *Zygon.* 1982;17:361-384.

There are also important causal and logical relationships between the objects we perceive in the world. When such relationships appear to make sense to us, we refer to them as regular. The causal processes of the brain play a critical role in the ability to evaluate relationships between objects and triggers a response in us when unexpected things occur. When causality seems disrupted, we experience an emotional response that alerts us to the disruption. When relationships are irregular, we note that they do not appear to follow established pathways based upon our prior experiences of reality. Research on infants to adults shows that we respond differently, and activate different parts of the brain, when confronted with irregular relationships whether they are grammatical, musical, logical, or any other type of relationship.

Emotional responses (or affect) in humans are far ranging in their composition. However, they appear eventually to be classified into three broad categories—positive, negative, and neutral. Positive emotions include happiness, joy, elation, love, and contentment. Negative emotions include fear, sadness, depression, anxiety, anger, and melancholy. The absence of either positive or negative emotions would be categorized as neutral. Many cognitive neuroscience studies have evaluated how the brain processes positive and negative emotions with the realization that emotions can be compared to a neutral state. The emotional responses in primary epistemic states, however, do not refer to the usual feelings of happiness, sadness, and so on, but to the overall emotional approach of the person to their reality. In other words, the entire world is viewed as positive or negative rather than feeling positive at some points and negative at others.

It is also important to mention that each of these parameters is most likely set along a continuum. Thus, one may have an experience of reality that is based primarily on having multiple discrete objects, but may also have some unitary attributes. Similarly, there may be some regular and some irregular relationships between objects. However, this notation allows for an overall perspective from which more specific elements of primary epistemic states can be elaborated. Based upon these parameters there appear to be nine possible primary epistemic states that are internally consistent, and should have neurological and phenomenological correlates. It should also be noted that an individual might enter into many different states during their lifetime. They may remain in one state briefly, for many years, or for their entire life. But they might also shift from one primary epistemic state to another, and sometimes quite frequently. The following appear to be the nine possible primary epistemic states:[5]

1.	Multiple discrete objects	—	regular relationships	—	neutral affect
2.	Multiple discrete objects	—	regular relationships	—	positive affect
3.	Multiple discrete objects	—	regular relationships	—	negative affect

---

[5]   d'Aquili, E.G. "Senses of reality in science and religion." *Zygon.* 1982;17:361-384; d'Aquili, E.G. and Newberg, A.B. *The Mystical Mind: Probing the Biology of Religious Experience.* Minneapolis, MN: Fortress Press, 1999.

4.	Multiple discrete objects	—	regular relationships	—	neutral affect
5.	Multiple discrete objects	—	regular relationships	—	positive affect
6.	Multiple discrete objects	—	regular relationships	—	negative affect
7.	Unitary reality	—		—	neutral affect
8.	Unitary reality	—		—	positive affect
9.	Unitary reality	—		—	negative affect

The first six primary epistemic states could all be considered to represent a perception of reality with multiple discrete objects. These objects can be related to other objects in terms of time, space, and causality among other possible relationships. The first three primary epistemic states refer to experiences of reality in which there are regular relationships between things. Thus, these relationships are logical and have a logical ordering. It may be said that these regular relationships are predictable and allow for a consistent understanding of reality. For example, this regularity is what allows science to work in helping to understand what is typically called "baseline reality." Science will have sizeable problems if the laws of nature are not consistent everywhere in the universe. If the relationships between objects do not remain regular everywhere, science will never be able to predict phenomena as it is designed to do.

Baseline reality refers to the primary epistemic state in which there is the perception of discrete objects with regular relationships. In our experience of baseline reality, we tend to have an overall neutral affect. Even though emotions may be positive or negative throughout our day or throughout our life, the overall average tends towards neutrality. This is the primary epistemic state that most people are in most of the time. For example, most people are quite certain of the reality of the furniture and people surrounding them. Furthermore, few if any individuals would question the fundamental reality (or the sense of that reality) of that state. This is true for virtually everyone, and particularly those who hold a materialist perspective. It is precisely because this state appears certain to represent the true objective reality while in that state that it can be called a primary epistemic state. In fact, most people would consider this state to be the true reality and that there is nothing beyond this reality. However, there are eight other primary epistemic states. Two of these are very similar to what might be called baseline reality and consist of the same discrete objects and the same relationships between these objects. The difference is in the emotional approach to this reality.

The second primary epistemic state is one in which there is the experience of discrete objects with regular relationships between those objects and carries an overwhelmingly positive affect. From a neurological perspective, it might be that such as state is mediated by the same structures described above as relating to the differentiation of objects, in addition to persistent activity in the limbic system that mediates emotions. In this case, the result is a perceptual state associated with an elated sense of being and joy in which the universe is perceived to be fundamentally good. There is a sense of purposefulness to all things and to mankind's place within the universe. This purposefulness is not derived logically, it is simply intuited because of the positive emotional state. The onset of this state may be sudden or after many years of effort. Either way, once the experience of this primary epistemic state occurs, it is often described as a conversion experience, especially in religious thought. This state has been called Cosmic Consciousness by Richard Bucke[6] and is characterized by a state of overwhelming happiness, comprehension, universal understanding, and love. Although this state may have a sudden onset, it can last for many years and even for the person's entire life. This state of Cosmic Consciousness is a primary epistemic state since the person perceives this understanding of the universe as fundamentally real (it is not an illusion) and sometimes will look with a sense of pity at those who have only the baseline perception of reality. It is important to note that people in this state are not psychotic, nor do they have any emotional or mental disorder. They perceive the objects and relationships between objects in the universe in the same way as those in baseline reality. They simply have a different emotional understanding of this perception.

The third primary epistemic state is experienced as being comprised of discrete objects with regular relationships, but is associated with a profoundly negative affect. It is a state of exquisite sadness and futility, as well as the sense of the incredible smallness of mankind within the universe and the suffering inherent in the human condition. A mild form of this state often occurs with high school or college students and other young adults when dealing with the issues of growing up and asserting one's independence in a world that often appears harsh and capricious. In the full-blown state, people often seek psychiatric help because of the extreme depression associated with this state even though they perceive this state to be fundamentally real. Essentially, they are asking to be taught to think in an "illusory" way so that they can survive and look at the world as having some meaningful framework within which they can function. They are not asking to be restored to reality. Another perception of this state is one in which the universe may be understood as one vast pointless machine without purpose or meaning. Philosophically, this might lead to an existentialist perspective. As with cosmic consciousness, this overly negative state can last many years. However, people do revert back to baseline reality especially because the negative state is in many ways incompatible with survival from a psychological perspective.

The next three states are associated with the perception of discrete objects, but contain irregular relationships between the objects in that sense of reality. Thus, the time, space, and causal relationships between various objects are distorted, bizarre, and unpredictable. Examples of this type of state include dreams, drug induced states, and schizophrenia. The dream state is perhaps the most common, and also one in which we all frequently enter and leave. In dream states, there can be many bizarre occurrences and connections between perceived objects. We have

---

[6]   Bucke, R.M. *Cosmic Consciousness: A Study in the Evolution of the Human Mind.* New York, NY: Arkana, 1991.

also all encountered dreams that feel very real and are accepted as real as long as we are dreaming. Once we awake, we reevaluate the dream state from baseline reality and typically regard the dream state as "less real." One might consider how the normal functional networks of the brain become disorganized such that the usual relationships and categories can no longer be applied appropriately. The result is the perception of relationships that do not make sense to us, although they still may feel real at the moment. Further, these primary epistemic states with irregular relationships can be associated with either, negative, positive, or neutral affect. For example, the "trip" that one has with LSD or other hallucinogenic drugs can be either incredibly elating or profoundly disturbing. Quite literally, these states can be described as either heaven or hell. Schizophrenia is similar in that the bizarre patterns of relationships between objects can be associated with negative, positive, or neutral emotion and patients can have a mood disorder with psychotic symptoms. In these cases, the patient may be extraordinarily depressed while also suffering from the delusions or hallucinations.

The important point regarding all of these states involving the perception of discrete objects, with regular or irregular relationships, is that they all are perceived as *really real* while the person is in them. Of course, once an individual enters into another primary epistemic state, they usually interpret the prior state as an illusion, delusion, or hallucination. This judgment is consistent with the nature of primary epistemic states, for once a person has moved from one state into the next, they are again in another primary epistemic state. And it is the nature of a primary epistemic state to perceive that state as actual reality, again though, regardless of whether or not it accurately reflects actual reality. A person would therefore necessarily understand what they remember from a drug experience or from a dream as an illusion or a distortion.

The final three states involve the perception of unitary reality in which everything is regarded as a singular oneness. One can see that the categories of unitary reality perceived as having either regular or irregular relationships need to be omitted. Relationships can only be considered to exist between discrete, independent objects. In unitary reality, there is no perception of discrete, independent objects that can be related to each other so there cannot be any relationships (regular or irregular). In fact, it should be emphasized that the unitary reality referred to here is meant to represent an absolute unitary state. As mentioned, there may be many other states that have a significant degree of unitary experience even though the totality of everything is not considered to be completely unified. Unitary states other than absolute unity most likely represent a number of spiritual or mystical states, but probably lie along the continuum of primary epistemic states between those that involve the perception of multiple discrete objects and those in which there is the perception of a unity without discrete objects. The absolute unitary state referred to in this discussion represents a state described in many religious and philosophical perspectives. Thus, nirvana, Absolute Reality, the Oneness of God, Absolute Unitary Being, and a number of other terms all refer to this complete and total unitary experience of the universe.

As mentioned, there is no point in referring to regular or irregular relationships regarding the experience of unitary reality since there are no discrete objects that are perceived which can be related to each other. In the primary epistemic state of unitary reality there is no sense of individual objects, there is no self–other dichotomy, and everything is perceived as an undifferentiated, unified oneness. The exact physiology of such a state is also an interesting issue since a researcher can never know when such an experience is being perceived. However, research has suggested some possible correlates. Most likely, areas that subserve the sense of self and the sense of space and time are affected. It may be that activity inherently within these areas is substantially decreased, or perhaps neuronal activity going into or coming out of those areas is blocked (that is, these areas are cut off from the rest of the brain's functions).

This raises another fascinating problem particular to the unitary state—since there is no self, there can be no perceiving self. Thus, the state is experienced without there being a perceived experiencer. There is no self, no mind, and no brain that is experienced. It is a very strange and unusual primary epistemic state. This also suggests that for the experiencer, since they have no perception of the self, they have the perception of going beyond their own ego thoughts, beyond their own brain. But these characteristics may be crucial to our neurotheological investigations since we have considered before that to try to avoid the uncertainty principle and to ascertain what is the true nature of reality, we must somehow get outside of the brain and outside of the self. This appears to be commensurate with the primary epistemic state of absolute unity. As discussed in the chapter on the physiology of mystical states, the defining characteristics of either a unifying vision, the apprehension of the One as an inner subjectivity, or a non-spatial, non-temporal, pure consciousness, all appear to suggest that this primary epistemic state is certainly experienced by individuals. That the experience of absolute unity occurs may have important relevance for evaluating epistemological issues which we will consider below. But first, let us explore further whether affect may play a role in these experiences.

It might be argued that the unitary reality state is associated with three possible emotional states which contain either positive, negative, or neutral affect, similarly to the states in which there is the experience of discrete objects. If unitary reality is associated with positive affect it is perceived as an undifferentiated oneness which is totally joyful and overwhelmingly good. It differs from the Cosmic Consciousness considered above in that when one is in the state of Cosmic Consciousness, one has a sense of the underlying unity, beauty, and goodness of the universe which contains discrete objects. However, in the unitary reality state, the person does not perceive the oneness as in Cosmic Consciousness, the person actually becomes the oneness and becomes the goodness. This might sound bizarre, but there are accounts throughout the world's philosophical and religious literature referring to this state. It appears that the sense of unitary reality associated with positive affect is most often interpreted after having the experience as "God" or the "union with God." In this manner, it is a deeply personal experience of ultimate being. Further, it is not a state that people arrive at easily and frequently. For example, people embarking on a lifelong journey of meditation can occasionally achieve this state, but only after many years of practice.

The experience of unitary reality with neutral affect is very similar to the experience of unitary reality with positive affect such that the universe is directly understood as being an undifferentiated oneness. However, with neutral affect the oneness is understood on a very impersonal level. Unitary reality is not viewed as good or bad or anything—it just is. The universe is understood on a very existential level. Everything is because it is and things happen because they happen. There is no specific purpose, no good, and no bad. However, people in this state may go even further since they understand no particular purpose, they essentially experience an undifferentiated nothingness instead of a oneness (without getting too confusing, infinite nothingness and infinite oneness theoretically are both undifferentiated and perhaps could be considered two sides of the unitary reality coin from a phenomenological perspective, but this is something that needs to be more fully evaluated, especially from a neurotheological perspective). Thus, the state of unitary reality with neutral affect would more likely be referred to as the void or infinite nothingness in religious literature. This is particularly the case in Buddhist philosophy.

It is interesting to note that, to date, there are no clear references to an experience of a unitary reality when perceived with a negative affect. It may be that such a state simply is not possible. Perhaps it cannot come about because the experience of all things as an undifferentiated oneness is so powerfully positive and integrative, that it cannot be perceived in negative terms. It may be argued that such an experience of unitary reality with negative affect is even incompatible with life, the brain, or the mind. Thus, until actual evidence can be brought forward to demonstrate the existence of this theoretical state, even if it is just anecdotal, it must be assumed that it is just that, theoretical.

An important point about the unitary epistemic states is that it could be argued that the unitary reality state should actually *include* all three possible emotional states together, since even affect should be experienced as a unity. In other words, this state cannot even be considered to have different affective components. This might also be the case since the perceiving self is not separate from the rest of the universe in the unitary epistemic state, and thus any emotion can theoretically only be felt after the person is no longer in the epistemic state. They can only reflect on the emotional response they have as the result of being in the unitary epistemic state since there is no self to have the emotion during that state. Hence, the last three states actually might collapse into one which simply is the epistemic state of unitary reality. It is not clear what the experience of positive, negative, and neutral emotions all combined into one would actually feel like. Arguably, it might be experienced as neutral since the positive and negative would cancel out. But since the positive and negative would theoretically be included in the neutral, it still might be a different experience from a state which is simply neutral. It is also not clear how such a state might correlate with neurological functions although it may be possible for structures that are associated with positive affect and those associated with negative affect to be activated at the same time. Descriptions of such unitary states do utilize a wide variety of emotions, sometimes together, ranging from fear and awe to joy and utter contentment. However, it is not clear when such emotional responses occur—either during or immediately following the state. Thus, there may be some additional value for considering the unitary epistemic state after the fact from the three possible affective perspectives, they are included here for completeness of discussion. However, unitary reality ultimately should not be differentiated, even by affect.

Given these varieties of epistemic states, one can explore a number of questions that pertain to epistemology and thus theology. One of the interesting neurotheological questions is: are different religious or mystical states truly different from each other (from a neurophysiological as well as phenomenological perspective) or are they actually very similar, if not the same, and only described differently? The answer to this question could have profound theological implications regardless of whether the experiences prove to be the same or different. If the unitary experiences are ultimately the same across traditions, it would suggest that they all derive from the same source. If the unitary experiences are ultimately different, it would suggest that each religion and its associated unitary experiences are distinct. In such a case, one might conceive of a typology and a way of relating them to each other based on neurophysiological as well as phenomenological elements. Phenomenologically, it could be argued that an absolute unitary state, in which everything is experienced to be completely undifferentiated, is by definition, the same for everyone. Everything is undifferentiated so it should not matter which tradition or belief system the experiencer started out in. The implication is that the neurophysiology would also be the same. Theoretically, this might be investigated, but there will always be the inherent uncertainty in knowing when such a state occurs so that one never knows when it should be measured. One possible approach would be to look for the neurophysiological consequences or aftermath of such an experience. This is akin to measuring the wake of a boat to determine its size and speed. It is not definitive, but it might provide some important information.

The most important aspect of the primary epistemic state of unitary reality is that unlike other primary states, when an individual "comes out of it," evidence suggests that the person does not perceive it or the memory of it as an illusion, hallucination, or delusion. Once a person has been in the state of unitary reality, they understand it to exist even though the person may not be in those states at some later time. Thus, the state of unitary reality appears to violate the rule of primary epistemic states, that they are real when in them and are perceived as not real when in another primary epistemic state. When reality is experienced as unitary, the person believes this state to be fundamentally real regardless of

---

[7]   Newberg, A.B. and Waldman, M.R. *How God Changes Your Brain*. New York, NY: Ballantine, 2009.

which other state they are in. In fact, the sense of reality is so strong during the experience of unitary reality, that when a person comes out of this experience and enters into another primary epistemic state, the new state is often perceived as a mere reflection or distortion of the unitary reality. Thus, unitary reality is perceived as real beyond all other primary states even when a person is in those other states. This property is unique to the experience of unitary reality since no other primary epistemic state is perceived of as ultimate reality once one has moved from it to another primary state.

But why do epistemic states feel real in the first place? Even if we understand the phenomenology and physiology of such states, we have not answered the more difficult question which is why they actually feel real. This leads us to the true epistemological question posed at the beginning of this chapter.

Epistemology and Unitary Reality versus Baseline Reality

In attempting to tackle the epistemological question—"How can we know what is really real?"—we can now look at the primary epistemic states and evaluate how close a neurotheological analysis might take us. We have established several ideas based upon the phenomenology and biology of primary epistemic states. Namely, we have recognized that the brain is fundamentally trapped inside of itself such that we can never know for sure, at least in baseline reality, whether we know what is actually real. This also led us to the neurotheological uncertainty principle as it pertains to any observable analysis of consciousness and the experience of primary epistemic states. We have also realized that the realness of any primary epistemic state eventually rests upon the strong perception that it is, in fact, real. We have also considered the variety of epistemic states that might be experienced. We acknowledged that the state experienced as absolute unity has several unique characteristics. It is associated with the experience of no self, no space, and no time. It is also perceived to be intensely real and carries that sense of realness with it even when the individual is no longer in that epistemic state.

It is this last aspect, the intense and persistent realness of the experience, that may become the focal point for the ultimate neurotheological investigation. If all along neurotheology requires us to accept the notion that the brain processes our experience of reality and the only way around this problem, and perhaps around the uncertainty principle as well, is to get outside of the brain, then what are we to make of an experience that claims explicitly to do just that? Not only does the experience of this epistemic state claim to break free of the self, and hence the brain, by integrating everything, including the experiencer into a unified oneness, but it claims to represent the most fundamentally real experience of reality. This seems to be a compelling target for investigation since it might be able to address several major epistemological problems together.

But what can be made of a neurotheological investigation of the unitary epistemic state? Will this investigation lead to something of value to science or religion? Theoretically, any substantial epistemological answers would indeed have significance for both science and religion. But it would also seem that in order to provide something important for both science and religion, the investigation must proceed to some degree from both perspectives. After all, the unitary state should include both materialist and non-materialist elements all integrated into the oneness. Can neurotheology combine the necessary elements from theology and neuroscience to provide a better approach to fundamental epistemological questions, especially with regard to the unitary epistemic state? Neurotheology would argue that only by combining theology and neuroscience can human beings get closer to answering some of the fundamental philosophical questions about the nature of reality and the universe. Thus arises the final principle:

Principle LIV: Any epistemological claims must be accessible to both theological and scientific analysis.

In this way, epistemology might necessitate a *neuroepistemological* approach combining neuroscientific and epistemological approaches. This does not mean to imply that one perspective should have "veto" power over the other when it comes to epistemological issues, but that any answers must be capable of satisfactorily intersecting with both viewpoints.

One might think that people who have experienced profound unitary states, in addition to day-to-day baseline reality, might have great difficulty in reconciling the two. After all, the two epistemic states are experienced to be quite different and in some ways incompatible with each other. For example, for the Mayavadi Hindu philosophers and mystics, the reality of the unitary state is so great that they deny the reality of our baseline reality. They believe that our everyday experience of reality is considered to be only a realm of illusion. Thus, all of the appearances of the external world, all of the relationships between discrete objects, all of the relationships of causality, and all of the laws of science are simply an illusion. Ultimate reality is the reality of the absolute unitary state or what the Hindu would call Brahman. One could go a step further and arrive at what certain Buddhist philosophers have postulated. Essentially, they suggest that what is going into the brain is actually *no* thing. Yet this is not "nothing" as it is understood in everyday parlance, but "no thing," simply because it cannot be conceptualized outside of the constraints of the mind.

Thus, one possibility is the relegation of baseline reality, or any of the epistemic states in which there are perceptions of multiple discrete objects, to an illusion with the experience of unitary reality reflecting the true primary reality. The other possibility is to relegate unitary experience to an illusion, a delusion, or a psychotic state. In this possibility, baseline reality reflects the true, primary reality. This is generally the position of science, and frequently atheists. The problem with both of these views is that they are both maintained while in their respective epistemic states. Thus, the scientist will provide evidence of individuals with definite neuropsychiatric disorders including schizophrenia or temporal lobe epilepsy who report unusual unitary experiences. This is cited as evidence that such experiences are "not real." However, the evidence is derived from the baseline reality epistemic state which is not considered to represent reality from the perspective of the unitary epistemic state.

Another set of possibilities might be to attempt to integrate these two epistemic states. On one hand, this begs the question as to why an attempt should be made to integrate these two specific epistemic states when others also exist and could be integrated. But, perhaps the more important question is whether any epistemic state in which there are multiple discrete objects can be integrated with the unitary state. Two approaches would involve giving priority to one state while still recognizing the importance and realness of the other. For example, one possibility is to give priority to the experience of unitary reality, but still recognize that the experience of baseline reality has substance and needs to be accepted as related to certain aspects of actual reality. The difficulty lies in developing a coherent explanation of how both of these realities can exist at the same time. In the Christian view, both baseline reality and the unitary reality are equal in terms of the certainty of their existence. On the one hand, baseline reality is definitely real, but so is the perception of the unitary state that the Christian would call God. In the Christian synthesis, the priority is given to the experience of God. For the Christian, it is as if the two realities are running parallel to each other with the unitary reality supporting the other and causing it to be. Thus, baseline reality runs parallel to the realm of God, but God is regarded as the ultimate ground, foundation, or cause of the world of everyday baseline reality.

One might also consider baseline reality to have priority, but to consider the unitary experience as still being important towards understanding the totality of the universe. Many scientists appear to have come to such a conclusion. For example, Carl Sagan frequently described the unitary nature of the universe, even though acknowledging himself as a scientist and agnostic, at least with regard to the anthropomorphic conception of God,

> Some people think God is an outsized, light-skinned male with a long white beard, sitting on a throne somewhere up there in the sky, busily tallying the fall of every sparrow. Others—for example Baruch Spinoza and Albert Einstein—considered God to be essentially the sum total of the physical laws which describe the universe.[8]

For him, the unitary state was not supernatural in the sense that it represented a scientifically unknowable realm. Rather, he considered the unitary state to be the final expression of the material universe.

Neurotheology must look at all of these possible epistemic states and attempt to help evaluate them both from the experience of baseline reality as well as from

---

8   Sagan, C. *Broca's Brain: Reflections on the Romance of Science*. New York, NY: Ballantine, 1986.

unitary reality. Thus, neurotheology might help better determine which perspective on reality provides the most accurate information. In such an exercise one can see that there is no question that the absolute unitary state takes priority as being "more real." People who have experienced an absolute unitary state, and this includes some very learned and previously materialistic scientists, regard it as being more fundamentally real than baseline reality. Even the memory of it carries the sense of greater fundamental reality than that generated by their experiences of day to day living. If we use the criterion, therefore, of the sense of certainty of the reality of any given state, the absolute unitary state would appear to be "more real" and hence representative of the "true" reality.

Therefore, we must conceive of the brain as a machine which operates upon whatever it is that fundamental reality may be and produces different versions to our consciousness. One version is what human beings refer to as baseline reality and another version is that of an absolute unitary state. Both perceptions are accompanied by a profound subjective certainty of their actual reality. Whatever is prior to the experience of absolute unity and the baseline reality of everyday life is in principle unknowable, since that which is in any way known must be translated, and in this sense transformed, by the brain.

Neurotheology might also offer one final alternative in which the different epistemic states are fully integrated. Is it possible that each epistemic state does in fact reflect some aspect of actual reality? In such a case, each epistemic state provides valuable information about the nature of actual reality, but each also leaves the experiencer with an incomplete view of reality. To some extent, one might wonder whether different epistemic states can somehow be engaged simultaneously. One of the great challenges of neurotheology will be to continue to deal with this issue of how various primary epistemic states are experienced and expressed and how differences between them can be reconciled. Such a reconciliation lies at the heart of the epistemological question regarding the fundamental nature of reality.

Epilogue: Final Conclusions

This work has expounded the principles of neurotheology as a field. The principles have ranged from the practical to the esoteric. Thus, some of the principles have pertained to methodological issues while others have set forth basic theories and perspectives that create the ideological foundations of neurotheology. We have also considered how neurotheology may begin to approach neuroscientific, health, philosophical, and theological questions. As a multidisciplinary field, neurotheology may have a unique place in academia which will enable individuals engaging in such scholarship to address topics previously unattainable by more traditional lines of thought.

It should also be mentioned that neurotheology has appeared to hit a nerve in modern thought. With the development of the cognitive neurosciences, many fields are exploring their link with the brain. Thus, neuroeconomics, neuroethics, and psychohistory have all arisen in recent times as a way of integrating current scientific knowledge with longstanding disciplines. It seems completely reasonable to do the same with religion and theology. This area, while still in its nascent stages, appears to be growing. There are more and more scholars beginning to approach neurotheology. More students are becoming interested in this area. And the general public seems quite fascinated by this field.

Many individuals see neurotheology as an approach that might help to address age-old questions in new ways. As we have considered in the preceding pages, neurotheology may help us address issues such as the nature of religion, the existence and nature of God, the basis of human consciousness, the possibility of universal consciousness, the best manner for attaining good health and well being, and how all human beings may advance to a new stage of understanding.

Given the enormity of these tasks to help understand ourselves, our relationship to God or the absolute, and the nature of reality itself, neurotheology appears poised to make a substantial attempt at addressing such issues. While other theological, philosophical, and scientific approaches have also tried to address these "big" questions, it would seem that neurotheology has a unique perspective. It is one of the only disciplines that necessarily seeks to integrate science and theology, and if defined broadly, many other relevant fields. The foundations and principles as elaborated in this Principia are designed to start neurotheology on a path of discovery that will enable a new perspective and propel scholars, and hopefully all of humanity, towards a new enlightenment.

Index